FIRST CENSUS
OF THE UNITED STATES
1790

MAINE

HEADS OF FAMILIES

AT THE FIRST CENSUS OF THE
UNITED STATES TAKEN
IN THE YEAR
1790

MAINE

GENEALOGICAL · PUBLISHING Co., Inc.

Originally published: Government Printing Office
Washington, D.C., 1908
Reprinted: Genealogical Publishing Co., Inc.
Baltimore, 1966, 1973, 1992
Library of Congress Catalogue Card Number 73-8201
International Standard Book Number 0-8063-0569-X
Made in the United States of America

HEADS OF FAMILIES AT THE FIRST CENSUS
1790

INTRODUCTION.

The First Census of the United States (1790) comprised an enumeration of the inhabitants of the present states of Connecticut, Delaware, Georgia, Kentucky, Maine, Maryland, Massachusetts, New Hampshire, New Jersey, New York, North Carolina, Pennsylvania, Rhode Island, South Carolina, Tennessee, Vermont, and Virginia.

A complete set of the schedules for each state, with a summary for the counties, and in many cases for towns, was filed in the State Department, but unfortunately they are not now complete, the returns for the states of Delaware, Georgia, Kentucky, New Jersey, Tennessee, and Virginia having been destroyed when the British burned the Capitol at Washington during the War of 1812. For several of the states for which schedules are lacking it is probable that the Director of the Census could obtain lists which would present the names of most of the heads of families at the date of the First Census. In Virginia, state enumerations were made in 1782, 1783, 1784, and 1785, but the lists on file in the State Library include the names for only 39 of the 78 counties into which the state was divided.

The schedules of 1790 form a unique inheritance for the Nation, since they represent for each of the states concerned a complete list of the heads of families in the United States at the time of the adoption of the Constitution. The framers were the statesmen and leaders of thought, but those whose names appear upon the schedules of the First Census were in general the plain citizens who by their conduct in war and peace made the Constitution possible and by their intelligence and self-restraint put it into successful operation.

The total population of the United States in 1790, exclusive of slaves, as derived from the schedules was 3,231,533. The only names appearing upon the schedules, however, were those of heads of families, and as at that period the families averaged 6 persons, the total number was approximately 540,000, or slightly more than half a million. The number of names which is now lacking because of the destruction of the schedules is approximately 140,000, thus leaving schedules containing about 400,000 names.

The information contained in the published **report** of the First Census of the United States, a small volume of 56 pages, was not uniform for the several states and territories. For New England and one or two of the other states the population was presented by counties and towns; that of New Jersey appeared **partly** by counties and towns and partly by counties only; in other cases the returns were given by counties only. Thus the complete transcript of the names of heads of families, with accompanying information, presents for the first time detailed information as to the number of inhabitants—males, females, etc.—for each minor civil division in all those states for which such information was not originally published.

In response to repeated requests from patriotic societies and persons interested in genealogy, or desirous of studying the early history of the United States, Congress added to the sundry civil appropriation bill for the fiscal year 1907 the following paragraph:

The Director of the Census is hereby authorized and directed to publish, in a permanent form, by counties and minor civil divisions, the names of the heads of families returned at the First Census of the United States in seventeen hundred and ninety; and the Director of the Census is authorized, in his discretion, to sell said publications, the proceeds thereof to be covered into the Treasury of the United States, to be deposited to the credit of miscellaneous receipts on account of "Proceeds of sales of Government property:"

Provided, That no expense shall be incurred hereunder additional to appropriations for the Census Office for printing therefor made for the fiscal year nineteen hundred and seven; and the Director of the Census is hereby directed to report to Congress at its next session the cost incurred hereunder and the price fixed for said publications and the total received therefor.

The amount of money appropriated by Congress for the Census printing for the fiscal year mentioned was unfortunately not sufficient to meet the current requirement of the Office and to publish the transcription of the First Census, and no provision was made in the sundry civil appropriation bill for 1908 for the continuance of authority to publish these important records. Resources, however, were available for printing a small section of the work, and the schedules of New Hampshire, Vermont, and Maryland accordingly were published.

The urgent deficiency bill, approved February 15, 1908, contained the following provision:

That the Director of the Census is hereby authorized and directed to expend so much of the appropriation for printing for the Department of Commerce and Labor allotted by law to the Census Office for the fiscal year ending June thirtieth, nineteen hundred and eight, as may be necessary to continue and complete the publication of the names of the heads of families returned at the First Census of the United States, as authorized by the sundry civil appropriation act approved June thirtieth, nineteen hundred and six.

In accordance with the authority given in the paragraph quoted above, the names returned at the First Census in the states of Connecticut, Maine, Massachusetts, New York, North Carolina, Pennsylvania, Rhode Island, and South Carolina have been published, thus completing the roster of the heads of families in 1790 so far as they can be shown from the records of the Census Office. As the Federal census schedules of the state of Virginia for 1790 are missing, the lists of the state enumerations made in 1782, 1783, 1784, and 1785 have been substituted and, while not complete, they will, undoubtedly, prove of great value.

THE FIRST CENSUS.

The First Census act was passed at the second session of the First Congress, and was signed by President Washington on March 1, 1790. The task of making the first enumeration of inhabitants was placed upon the President. Under this law the marshals of the several judicial districts were required to ascertain the number of inhabitants within their respective districts, omitting Indians not taxed, and distinguishing free persons (including those bound to service for a term of years) from all others; the sex and color of free persons; and the number of free males 16 years of age and over.

The object of the inquiry last mentioned was, undoubtedly, to obtain definite knowledge as to the military and industrial strength of the country. This fact possesses special interest, because the Constitution directs merely an enumeration of inhabitants. Thus the demand for increasingly extensive information, which has been so marked a characteristic of census legislation, began with the First Congress that dealt with the subject.

The method followed by the President in putting into operation the First Census law, although the object of extended investigation, is not definitely known. It is supposed that the President or the Secretary of State dispatched copies of the law, and perhaps of instructions also, to the marshals. There is, however, some ground for disputing this conclusion. At least one of the reports in the census volume of 1790 was furnished by a governor. This, together with the fact that there is no record of correspondence with the marshals on the subject of the census, but that there is a record of such correspondence with the governors, makes very strong the inference that the marshals re-

ceived their instructions through the governors of the states. This inference is strengthened by the fact that in 1790 the state of Massachusetts furnished the printed blanks, and also by the fact that the law relating to the Second Census specifically charged the Secretary of State to superintend the enumeration and to communicate directly with the marshals.

By the terms of the First Census law nine months were allowed in which to complete the enumeration. The census taking was supervised by the marshals of the several judicial districts, who employed assistant marshals to act as enumerators. There were 17 marshals. The records showing the number of assistant marshals employed in 1790, 1800, and 1810 were destroyed by fire, but the number employed in 1790 has been estimated at 650.

The schedules which these officials prepared consist of lists of names of heads of families; each name appears in a stub, or first column, which is followed by five columns, giving details of the family. These columns are headed as follows:

Free white males of 16 years and upward, including heads of families.
Free white males under 16 years.
Free white females, including heads of families.
All other free persons.
Slaves.

The assistant marshals made two copies of the returns; in accordance with the law one copy was posted in the immediate neighborhood for the information of the public, and the other was transmitted to the marshal in charge, to be forwarded to the President. The schedules were turned over by the President to the Secretary of State. Little or no tabulation was required, and the report of the First Census, as also the reports of the Second, Third, and Fourth, was produced without the employment of any clerical force, the summaries being transmitted directly to the printer. The total population as returned in 1790 was 3,929,214, and the entire cost of the census was $44,377.

A summary of the results of the First Census, not including the returns for South Carolina, was transmitted to Congress by President Washington on October 27, 1791. The legal period for enumeration, nine months, had been extended, the longest time consumed being eighteen months in South Carolina. The report of October 27 was printed in full, and published in what is now a very rare little volume; afterwards the report for South Carolina was "tipped in." To contain the results of the Twelfth Census, ten large quarto volumes, comprising in all 10,400 pages, were required. No illustration of the expansion of census inquiry can be more striking.

The original schedules of the First Census are now contained in 26 bound volumes, preserved in the Census Office. For the most part the headings of the schedules were written in by hand. Indeed, up to and

including 1820, the assistant marshals generally used for the schedules such paper as they happened to have, ruling it, writing in the headings, and binding the sheets together themselves. In some cases merchants' account paper was used, and now and then the schedules were bound in wall paper.

As a consequence of requiring marshals to supply their own blanks, the volumes containing the schedules vary in size from about 7 inches long, 3 inches wide, and ½ inch thick to 21 inches long, 14 inches wide, and 6 inches thick. Some of the sheets in these volumes are only 4 inches long, but a few are 3 feet in length, necessitating several folds. In some cases leaves burned at the edges have been covered with transparent silk to preserve them.

THE UNITED STATES IN 1790.

In March, 1790, the Union consisted of twelve states—Rhode Island, the last of the original thirteen to enter the Union, being admitted May 29 of the same year. Vermont, the first addition, was admitted in the following year, before the results of the First Census were announced. Maine was a part of Massachusetts, Kentucky was a part of Virginia, and the present states of Alabama and Mississippi were parts of Georgia. The present states of Ohio, Indiana, Illinois, Michigan, and Wisconsin, with part of Minnesota, were known as the Northwest Territory, and the present state of Tennessee, then a part of North Carolina, was soon to be organized as the Southwest Territory.

The United States was bounded on the west by the Mississippi river, beyond which stretched that vast and unexplored wilderness belonging to the Spanish King, which was afterwards ceded to the United States by France as the Louisiana Purchase, and now comprises the great and populous states of South Dakota, Iowa, Nebraska, Missouri, Kansas, Arkansas, and Oklahoma, and portions of Minnesota, North Dakota, Montana, Wyoming, Colorado, New Mexico, Texas, and Louisiana. The Louisiana Purchase was not consummated for more than a decade after the First Census was taken. On the south was another Spanish colony known as the Floridas. The greater part of Texas, then a part of the colony of Mexico, belonged to Spain; and California, Nevada, Utah, Arizona, and a portion of New Mexico, also the property of Spain, although penetrated here and there by venturesome explorers and missionaries, were, for the most part, an undiscovered wilderness.

The gross area of the United States was 827,844 square miles, but the settled area was only 239,935 square miles, or about 29 per cent of the total. Though the area covered by the enumeration in 1790 seems very small when compared with the present area of the United States, the difficulties which confronted the census taker were vastly greater than in 1900. In many localities there were no roads, and where these did exist they were poor and frequently impassable; bridges were almost unknown. Transportation was entirely by horseback, stage, or private coach. A journey as long as that from New York to Washington was a serious undertaking, requiring eight days under the most favorable conditions. Western New York was a wilderness, Elmira and Binghamton being but detached hamlets. The territory west of the Allegheny mountains, with the exception of a portion of Kentucky, was unsettled and scarcely penetrated. Detroit and Vincennes were too small and isolated to merit consideration. Philadelphia was the capital of the United States. Washington was a mere Government project, not even named, but known as the Federal City. Indeed, by the spring of 1793, only one wall of the White House had been constructed, and the site for the Capitol had been merely surveyed. New York city in 1790 possessed a population of only 33,131, although it was the largest city in the United States; Philadelphia was second, with 28,522; and Boston third, with 18,320. Mails were transported in very irregular fashion, and correspondence was expensive and uncertain.

There were, moreover, other difficulties which were of serious moment in 1790, but which long ago ceased to be problems in census taking. The inhabitants, having no experience with census taking, imagined that some scheme for increasing taxation was involved, and were inclined to be cautious lest they should reveal too much of their own affairs. There was also opposition to enumeration on religious grounds, a count of inhabitants being regarded by many as a cause for divine displeasure. The boundaries of towns and other minor divisions, and even those of counties, were in many cases unknown or not defined at all. The hitherto semi-independent states had been under the control of the Federal Government for so short a time that the different sections had not yet been welded into an harmonious nationality in which the Federal authority should be unquestioned and instructions promptly and fully obeyed.

AN ACT PROVIDING FOR THE ENUMERATION OF THE INHABITANTS OF THE UNITED STATES

APPROVED MARCH 1, 1790

SECTION 1. Be it enacted by the Senate and House of Representatives of the United States of America in Congress assembled, That the marshals of the several districts of the United States shall be, and they are hereby authorized and required to cause the number of the inhabitants within their respective districts to be taken; omitting in such enumeration Indians not taxed, and distinguishing free persons, including those bound to service for a term of years, from all others; distinguishing also the sexes and colours of free persons, and the free males of sixteen years and upwards from those under that age; for effecting which purpose the marshals shall have power to appoint as many assistants within their respective districts as to them shall appear necessary; assigning to each assistant a certain division of his district, which division shall consist of one or more counties, cities, towns, townships, hundreds or parishes, or of a territory plainly and distinctly bounded by water courses, mountains, or public roads. The marshals and their assistants shall respectively take an oath or affirmation, before some judge or justice of the peace, resident within their respective districts, previous to their entering on the discharge of the duties by this act required. The oath or affirmation of the marshal shall be, "I, A. B., Marshal of the district of ———, do solemnly swear (or affirm) that I will well and truly cause to be made a just and perfect enumeration and description of all persons resident within my district, and return the same to the President of the United States, agreeably to the directions of an act of Congress, intituled 'An act providing for the enumeration of the inhabitants of the United States,' according to the best of my ability." The oath or affirmation of an assistant shall be "I, A. B., do solemnly swear (or affirm) that I will make a just and perfect enumeration and description of all persons resident within the division assigned to me by the marshal of the district of ———, and make due return thereof to the said marshal, agreeably to the directions of an act of Congress, intituled 'An act providing for the enumeration of the inhabitants of the United States,' according to the best of my ability." The enumeration shall commence on the first Monday in August next, and shall close within nine calendar months thereafter. The several assistants shall, within the said nine months, transmit to the marshals by whom they shall be respectively appointed, accurate returns of all persons, except Indians not taxed, within their respective divisions, which returns shall be made in a schedule, distinguishing the several families by the names of their master, mistress, steward, overseer, or other principal person therein, in manner following, that is to say:

The number of persons within my division, consisting of ———, appears in a schedule hereto annexed, subscribed by me this ——— day of ———, 179-. A. B. *Assistant to the marshal of* ———.

Schedule of the whole number of persons within the division allotted to A. B.

Names of heads of families.	Free white males of 16 years and upwards, including heads of families.	Free white males under 16 years.	Free white females, including heads of families.	All other free persons.	Slaves.

SECTION 2. And be it further enacted, That every assistant failing to make return, or making a false return of the enumeration to the marshal, within the time by this act limited, shall forfeit the sum of two hundred dollars.

SECTION 3. And be it further enacted, That the marshals shall file the several returns aforesaid, with the clerks of their respective district courts, who are hereby directed to receive and carefully preserve the same: And the marshals respectively shall, on or before the first day of September, one thousand seven hundred and ninety-one, transmit to the President of the United States, the aggregate amount of each description of persons within their respective districts. And every marshal failing to file the returns of his assistants, or any of them, with the clerks of their respective district courts, or failing to return the aggregate amount of each description of persons in their respective districts, as the same shall appear from said returns, to the President of the United States within the time limited by this act, shall, for every such offense, forfeit the sum of eight hundred dollars; all which forfeitures shall be recoverable in the courts of the districts where the offenses shall be committed, or in the circuit courts to be held within the same, by action of debt, information or indictment; the one-half thereof to the use of the United States, and the other half to the informer; but where the prosecution shall be first instituted on the behalf of the United States, the whole shall accrue to their use. And for the more effectual discovery of offenses, the judges of the several district courts, at their next sessions, to be held after the expiration of the time allowed for making the returns of the enumeration hereby directed, to the President of the United States, shall give this act in charge to the grand juries, in their respective courts, and shall cause the returns of the several assistants to be laid before them for their inspection.

SECTION 4. And be it further enacted, That every assistant shall receive at the rate of one dollar for every one hundred and fifty persons by him returned, where such persons reside in the country; and where such persons reside in a city, or town, containing more than five thousand persons, such assistants shall receive at the rate of one dollar for every three hundred persons; but where, from the dispersed situation of the inhabitants in some divisions, one dollar for every one hundred and fifty persons shall be insufficient, the marshals, with the approbation of the judges of their respective districts, may make such further allowance to the assistants in such divisions as shall be deemed an adequate compensation, provided the same does not exceed one dollar for every fifty persons by them returned. The several marshals shall receive as follows: The marshal of the district of Maine, two hundred dollars; the marshal of the district of New Hampshire, two hundred dollars; the marshal of the district of Massachusetts, three hundred dollars; the marshal of the district of Connecticut, two hundred dollars; the marshal of the district of New York, three hundred dollars; the marshal of the district of New Jersey, two hundred dollars; the marshal of the district of Pennsylvania, three hundred dollars; the marshal of the district of Delaware, one hundred dollars; the marshal of the district of Maryland, three hundred dollars; the marshal of the district of Virginia, five hundred dollars; the marshal of the district of Kentucky, two hundred and fifty dollars; the marshal of the district of North Carolina, three hundred and fifty dollars; the marshal of the district of South Carolina, three hundred dollars; the marshal of the district of Georgia, two hundred and fifty dollars. And to

obviate all doubts which may arise respecting the persons to be returned, and the manner of making the returns.

SECTION 5. Be it enacted, That every person whose usual place of abode shall be in any family on the aforesaid first Monday in August next, shall be returned as of such family; the name of every person, who shall be an inhabitant of any district, but without a settled place of residence, shall be inserted in the column of the aforesaid schedule, which is allotted for the heads of families, in that division where he or she shall be on the said first Monday in August next, and every person occasionally absent at the time of the enumeration, as belonging to that place in which he usually resides in the United States.

SECTION 6. And be it further enacted, That each and every person more than 16 years of age, whether heads of families or not, belonging to any family within any division of a district made or established within the United States, shall be, and hereby is, obliged to render to such assistant of the division, a true account, if required, to the best of his or her knowledge, of all and every person belonging to such family, respectively, according to the several descriptions aforesaid, on pain of forfeiting twenty dollars, to be sued for and recovered by such assistant, the one-half for his own use, and the other half for the use of the United States.

SECTION 7. And be it further enacted, That each assistant shall, previous to making his return to the marshal, cause a correct copy, signed by himself, of the schedule containing the number of inhabitants within his division, to be set up at two of the most public places within the same, there to remain for the inspection of all concerned; for each of which copies the said assistant shall be entitled to receive two dollars, provided proof of a copy of the schedule having been so set up and suffered to remain, shall be transmitted to the marshal, with the return of the number of persons; and in case any assistant shall fail to make such proof to the marshal, he shall forfeit the compensation by this act allowed him.

Approved March 1, 1790.

FIRST CENSUS OF THE UNITED STATES.

Population of the United States as returned at the First Census, by states: 1790.

DISTRICT.	Free white males of 16 years and upward, including heads of families.	Free white males under 16 years.	Free white females, including heads of families.	All other free persons.	Slaves.	Total.
Vermont	22,435	22,328	40,505	255	[1] 16	[2] 85,539
New Hampshire	36,086	34,851	70,160	630	158	141,885
Maine	24,384	24,748	46,870	538	None.	96,540
Massachusetts	95,453	87,289	190,582	5,463	None.	378,787
Rhode Island	16,019	15,799	32,652	3,407	948	68,825
Connecticut	60,523	54,403	117,448	2,808	2,764	237,946
New York	83,700	78,122	152,320	4,654	21,324	340,120
New Jersey	45,251	41,416	83,287	2,762	11,423	184,139
Pennsylvania	110,788	106,948	206,363	6,537	3,737	434,373
Delaware	11,783	12,143	22,384	3,899	8,887	[3] 59,094
Maryland	55,915	51,339	101,395	8,043	103,036	319,728
Virginia	110,936	116,135	215,046	12,866	292,627	747,610
Kentucky	15,154	17,057	28,922	114	12,430	73,677
North Carolina	69,988	77,506	140,710	4,975	100,572	393,751
South Carolina	35,576	37,722	66,880	1,801	107,094	249,073
Georgia	13,103	14,044	25,739	398	29,264	82,548
Total number of inhabitants of the United States exclusive of S. Western and N. territory	807,094	791,850	1,541,263	59,150	694,280	3,893,635

	Free white males of 21 years and upward.	Free males under 21 years of age.	Free white females.	All other persons.	Slaves.	Total.
S. W. territory	6,271	10,277	15,365	361	3,417	35,691
N. "						

[1] The census of 1790, published in 1791, reports 16 slaves in Vermont. Subsequently, and up to 1860, the number is given as 17. An examination of the original manuscript returns shows that there never were any slaves in Vermont. The original error occurred in preparing the results for publication, when 16 persons, returned as "Free colored," were classified as "Slave."

[2] Corrected figures are 85,425, or 114 less than figures published in 1790, due to an error of addition in the returns for each of the towns of Fairfield, Milton, Shelburne, and Williston, in the county of Chittenden; Brookfield, Newbury, Randolph, and Strafford, in the county of Orange; Castleton, Clarendon, Hubbardton, Poultney, Rutland, Shrewsbury, and Wallingford, in the county of Rutland; Dummerston, Guilford, Halifax, and Westminster, in the county of Windham; and Woodstock, in the county of Windsor.

[3] Corrected figures are 59,096, or 2 more than figures published in 1790, due to error in addition.

Summary of population, by counties, towns, etc.: 1790.

CUMBERLAND COUNTY.

TOWN.	Number of families.	Free white males of 16 years and upward, including heads of families.	Free white males under 16 years.	Free white females, including heads of families.	All other free persons.	Total.	TOWN.	Number of families.	Free white males of 16 years and upward, including heads of families.	Free white males under 16 years.	Free white females, including heads of families.	All other free persons.	Total.
Bakerstown plantation	110	292	364	613	.....	1,269	Otisfield plantation	32	56	46	95	.....	197
Bridgton	60	100	81	147	1	344	Plantation No. 4	77	89	101	154	.....	344
Brunswick	197	355	328	660	14	1,357	Portland	366	564	537	1,123	16	2,240
Bucktown plantation	68	96	146	211	.....	453	Raymondtown plantation	52	81	92	170	3	346
Butterfield plantation	35	49	55	85	.....	189	Rusfield gore	20	22	30	50	.....	102
Cape Elizabeth	231	341	324	683	8	1,356	Scarborough (see Gorham and Scarborough).						
Durham	116	163	214	344	3	724	Shepardsfield plantation	83	126	140	261	1	528
Falmouth	446	648	814	1,504	28	2,994	Standish	123	183	186	346	1	716
Flintstown plantation	37	54	48	88	.....	190	Turner	57	87	104	158	.....	349
Freeport	230	322	342	654	2	1,320	Waterford plantation	36	55	32	73	.....	160
Gorham and Scarborough	786	1,108	1,134	2,186	47	4,475	Windham	152	228	265	444	1	938
Gray	290	148	139	290	.....	577							
Harpswell	217	253	268	539	11	1,071	Total	4,342	6,214	6,633	12,557	156	25,560
New Gloucester	207	320	338	694	6	1,358							
North Yarmouth	314	474	505	985	14	1,978							

HANCOCK COUNTY.

TOWN.	Number of families.	Free white males of 16 years and upward, including heads of families.	Free white males under 16 years.	Free white females, including heads of families.	All other free persons.	Total.	TOWN.	Number of families.	Free white males of 16 years and upward, including heads of families.	Free white males under 16 years.	Free white females, including heads of families.	All other free persons.	Total.
Barrettstown	53	61	44	68	.....	173	Orrington	86	114	128	234	1	477
Belfast	43	64	55	126	.....	245	Penobscot	189	249	251	542	6	1,048
Bluehill	55	69	79	125	1	274	Sedgwick	100	144	155	270	.....	569
Camden	69	93	85	153	.....	331	Small Islands not belonging to any town	18	19	17	30	.....	66
Canaan	27	34	39	59	.....	132	Sullivan	92	126	123	254	1	504
Conduskeeg plantation	103	145	170	249	3	567	Trenton (including township No. 1, east side of Union river)	54	75	92	144	1	312
Deer Isle	129	175	181	318	8	682	Township No. 1 (Bucks)	62	85	81	148	2	316
Ducktrap	53	78	82	118	.....	278	Township No. 6 (west side of Union river)	46	69	49	120	1	239
Eastern River township No. 2	54	59	63	118	.....	240	Vinalhaven	106	131	154	292	1	578
Eddy township	19	19	32	59	.....	110							
Frankfort	169	235	235	419	2	891	Total	1,796	2,436	2,531	4,544	38	9,549
Gouldsborough	45	78	64	116	9	267							
Isleborough	67	90	114	177	1	382							
Mount Desert	132	191	207	345	1	744							
Orphan Island	25	33	31	60	.....	124							

LINCOLN COUNTY.

TOWN.	Number of families.	Free white males of 16 years and upward, including heads of families.	Free white males under 16 years.	Free white females, including heads of families.	All other free persons.	Total.	TOWN.	Number of families.	Free white males of 16 years and upward, including heads of families.	Free white males under 16 years.	Free white females, including heads of families.	All other free persons.	Total.
Balltown	156	229	258	425	.....	912	Pittston	102	135	281	281	7	704
Bath	140	235	257	450	7	949	Pownalborough	330	535	535	969	4	2,043
Boothbay	164	247	248	499	3	997	Prescotts and Whitchers plantation	13	12	8	11	1	32
Bowdoin	203	237	264	468	15	984	Rockmeeko, east side of river	26	28	7	24	.....	59
Bowdoinham	73	109	127	218	1	455	Sandy river, first township	98	141	127	224	2	494
Bristol	75	115	143	257	1	516	Sandy river, from its mouth to Carrs plantation	67	77	96	160	1	334
Canaan	81	99	132	221	.....	452	Sandy river, middle township	14	17	15	33	.....	65
Carratunk	25	31	35	39	.....	105	Sandy river, upper township	10	18	17	24	.....	59
Carrs plantation, or Unity	27	32	33	62	.....	127	Seven Mile Brook	40	41	34	62	1	138
Chester plantation	15	24	19	27	.....	70	Smithtown plantation	109	142	126	240	1	509
Cushing	160	256	235	451	.....	942	Starling plantation	53	58	31	77	.....	166
Edgecomb	133	183	159	413	.....	755	Thomaston	139	207	209	379	4	799
Fairfield	98	122	114	222	.....	458	Titcomb	29	34	36	76	.....	146
Georgetown	206	345	322	655	11	1,333	Topsham	118	215	203	398	10	826
Great Pond plantation	30	43	52	69	.....	164	Twenty-five Mile Pond	30	33	27	59	.....	119
Greene	92	102	100	173	.....	375	Union	42	52	50	94	3	199
Hallowell	184	344	285	553	12	1,194	Vassalborough	197	301	317	624	11	1,253
Hancock	61	83	64	130	1	278	Waldoborough	269	429	454	821	13	1,717
Hunts Meadow	11	15	21	32	.....	68	Wales plantation	92	115	120	204	.....	439
Jones plantation	40	63	63	119	11	256	Warren	106	307	148	178	13	646
Lewistown and gore adjoining	73	127	145	260	.....	532	Washington	149	169	139	312	.....	620
Little River	13	17	15	32	.....	64	Winslow, with its adjacents	169	204	225	367	1	797
Littleborough plantation	58	71	69	127	7	274	Winthrop	252	304	329	591	2	1,226
Livermore, east side of Androscoggin river	11	15	8	21	.....	44	Woolwich	128	206	189	391	1	787
Meduncook	49	89	79	153	.....	321	Between Norridgewock and Seven Mile Brook	26	28	46	73	.....	147
New Castle	131	223	222	448	3	896							
New Sandwich	64	91	65	140	.....	296	Total	5,309	7,769	7,751	14,052	151	29,723
Nobleborough	234	312	347	544	3	1,206							
Norridgewock	83	91	89	152	1	333							
Norridgewock, settlement east of	11	11	12	20	.....	43							

WASHINGTON COUNTY.

TOWN.	Number of families.	Free white males of 16 years and upward, including heads of families.	Free white males under 16 years.	Free white females, including heads of families.	All other free persons.	Total.	TOWN.	Number of families.	Free white males of 16 years and upward, including heads of families.	Free white males under 16 years.	Free white females, including heads of families.	All other free persons.	Total.
Bucks Harbor Neck	12	14	18	29	.....	61	Plantations west of Machias—						
Machias	177	229	210	372	7	818	No. 4	40	71	59	103	.....	233
Plantations east of Machias—							No. 5	33	45	49	83	.....	177
No. 1	15	18	16	32	.....	66	No. 6	46	56	55	96	.....	207
No. 2	33	41	30	67	6	144	No. 11	16	22	24	49	.....	95
No. 4	11	16	13	25	.....	54	No. 12	3	4	1	3	.....	8
No. 5	14	24	26	34	.....	84	No. 13	43	51	61	105	6	223
No. 8	54	75	60	109	.....	244	No. 22	31	43	44	87	1	175
No. 9	7	9	7	14	.....	30							
No. 10	11	14	5	23	.....	42	Total	564	754	708	1,277	20	2,759
No. 11	7	8	10	19	.....	37							
No. 12	10	13	15	26	.....	54							
No. 13	1	1	5	1	.....	7							

Summary of population, by counties, towns, etc.: 1790—Continued.

YORK COUNTY.

TOWN.	Number of families.	Free white males of 16 years and upward, including heads of families.	Free white males under 16 years.	Free white females, including heads of families.	All other free persons.	Total.	TOWN.	Number of families.	Free white males of 16 years and upward, including heads of families.	Free white males under 16 years.	Free white females, including heads of families.	All other free persons.	Total.
Arundel	259	367	380	700	11	1,458	New Penacook	18	23	13	41	......	77
Berwick	665	983	922	1,947	42	3,894	Parsonsfield	132	174	169	311	......	654
Biddeford	169	273	235	504	6	1,018	Pepperellborough	229	342	358	650	......	1,350
Brownfield township	26	39	37	68	2	146	Porterfield	16	23	14	34	......	71
Brownfield township—in the gore adjoining	4	6	5	9	......	20	Sanford	316	450	473	876	......	1,799
Buxton	238	357	402	746	3	1,508	Shapleigh	227	310	371	630	9	1,320
Coxhall	106	165	229	371	......	765	Sudbury-Canada	60	82	89	153	......	324
Francisborough plantation	76	98	101	210	......	409	Sudbury, settlements adjoining	12	17	13	21	......	51
Fryeburgh	88	141	138	270	1	550	Suncook	16	22	25	36	......	83
Hiram	18	22	29	41	......	92	Washington plantation	58	72	51	138	......	261
Kittery	611	769	714	1,736	40	3,259	Waterborough	174	229	277	465	......	971
Lebanon	224	310	344	642	......	1,296	Waterford	31	45	35	74	......	154
Limerick	71	99	110	200	......	409	Wells	504	827	733	1,495	15	3,070
Little Falls	115	159	147	301	......	607	York	504	751	605	1,518	26	2,900
Little Ossipee	120	144	200	318	......	662	Total	5,087	7,299	7,219	14,505	155	29,178

Assistant marshals for the state: 1790.

DISTRICT.	NAME.	DISTRICT.	NAME.
Cumberland county (part of) Bridgton, Standish, and Turner towns; Bakerstown, Bucktown, Butterfield, Flintstown, No. 4, Shepardsfield, and Waterford plantations; and Rusfield gore.	None given.	Lincoln county (part of)—Continued. river, from its mouth to Carrs plantation; Sandy river, middle, Sandy river, upper, and Titcomb townships; Carrs or Unity, Chester, and Prescotts and Whitchers plantations; and settlement east of Norridgewock; and between Norridgewock and Seven Mile Brook.	
Cumberland county (part of) Brunswick, Durham, Freeport, Harpswell, and North Yarmouth towns.	Henry Dearborn.	Lincoln county (part of) Cushing, Meduncook, Thomaston, Union, and Warren towns.	Thurston Whiting.
Cumberland county (part of) Cape Elizabeth, Falmouth, Gray, and New Gloucester towns.	William Hobby.	Lincoln county (part of) Greene, Livermore (east side of Androscoggin river), New Sandwich, Rockmeeko (east side of river), Washington and Winthrop towns; and Littleborough, Smithtown, Starling, and Wales plantations.	Simon Dearborn.
Cumberland county (part of) Gorham and Scarborough towns.	Samuel Pierson.		
Cumberland county (part of) Windham town; and Otisfield and Raymond-town plantations.	David Barker.	Lincoln county (part of) Vassalborough town and Jones plantation.	Samuel Grant.
Cumberland county (part of) Portland town.	John Hobby.	Washington county Bucks Harbor Neck, and Machias towns; plantations east of Machias, Nos. 1, 2, 4, 5, 8, 9, 10, 11, 12, and 13; and plantations west of Machias, Nos. 4, 5, 6, 11, 12, 13, and 22.	Jaˢ Avery.
Hancock county Barrettstown, Belfast, Bluehill, Camden, Canaan, Deer Isle, Ducktrap, Frankfort, Gouldsborough, Isleborough, Mount Desert, Orrington, Penobscot, Sedgwick, Sullivan, Trenton (including township No. 1 east side of Union river), and Vinalhaven towns; Eastern river township No. 2, Eddy township, township No. 1 (Bucks), and township No. 6 (west side of Union river); Conduskeeg plantation; and Orphan Island, and small islands not belonging to any town.	David Howe.	York county (part of) Arundel, Biddeford, Little Falls, Little Ossipee, Wells, and York towns.	Henry Dearborn (marshal)
		York county (part of) Berwick, Lebanon, Limerick, Parsonsfield, and Shapleigh towns; and Francisborough, and Washington plantations.	Daniel Wood.
Lincoln county (part of) Balltown town and Great Pond plantation.	Stuart Hunt.	York county (part of) Hiram, New Penacook, Porterfield, Sudbury-Canada, Suncook, and Waterford towns; Brownfield township, gore adjoining Brownfield, and settlements adjoining Sudbury.	Philip Page.
Lincoln county (part of) Bath, Boothbay, Bowdoinham, Edgecomb, Georgetown, Hallowell, Hunts Meadow, New Castle, Pittston, Pownalborough, Topsham, and Woolwich towns.	Henry Dearborn (marshal).		
Lincoln county (part of) Bristol, Nobleborough, and Waldoborough towns.	John Polerezcky.	York county (part of) Buxton town.	Peter Ayer.
		York county (part of) Coxhall, Sanford, and Waterborough towns.	Abraham Annis.
Lincoln county (part of) Bowdoin, Canaan, Carratunk, Fairfield, Hancock, Lewistown and gore adjoining, Little River, Norridgewock, Seven Mile Brook, Twenty-five Mile Pond, and Winslow (with its adjacents) towns; Sandy river, first, Sandy	John Chandler.	York county (part of) Kittery town.	Jeremiah Leavitt.
		York county (part of) Pepperellborough town.	Humphrey Pike.
		York county (part of) Fryeburgh town.	None given.

CUMBERLAND COUNTY.[1]

NAME OF HEAD OF FAMILY.	Free white males of 16 years and upward, including heads of families.	Free white males under 16 years.	Free white females, including heads of families.	All other free persons.	Slaves.	NAME OF HEAD OF FAMILY.	Free white males of 16 years and upward, including heads of families.	Free white males under 16 years.	Free white females, including heads of families.	All other free persons.	Slaves.	NAME OF HEAD OF FAMILY.	Free white males of 16 years and upward, including heads of families.	Free white males under 16 years.	Free white females, including heads of families.	All other free persons.	Slaves.
BAKERSTOWN PLANTATION.						**BAKERSTOWN PLANTATION—continued.**						**BAKERSTOWN PLANTATION—continued.**					
Davis, Zebulon	1	2	2			Allen, Isaac	1	1	4			Merrill, Edmund	7	4	13		
Rollins, Stephen	1	4	6			Harlow, Ebenezer	5	3	1			Varrel, Richard, Ju[r]	1	2	2		
Nevins, John	1		6			Bradbury, Joseph	1	1	2			Varrel, Richard	2	3	3		
Bailey, Samuel	1		3			Allen, Joshua	1	2	2			Wilson, Gonen	4	2	7		
Bailey, Edmund	2	2	5			Merrill, Giles	1	2	2			Allen, Wll[m]	1	4	4		
Dunn, Josiah	2	5	2			Pecker, Nehemiah	1	1	3			Proctor, Wll[m]	1	1	4		
Strout, Nehemiah	1	1	5			Dwinell, Amos	4	1	3			Pote, Sam[l]	1		3		
Bray, Henry	1	3	4			Dwinell, Jacob	2	2	3			Pote, Tho[s]	1		4		
Wescot, Daniel	1	4	1			Chipman, Wll[m]	1	2	1			Merrill, Nathan	3	3	10		
Strout, Jacob	1	1	4			Dwinell, Aaron	1		4			Merrill, James	2	1	4		
Davis, Aaron	1	1	4			Waterman, Joseph	1	2	5			Chipman, Benj[a]	1	2	3		
Strout, Joshua	1		1			Waterman, Noah	1	2	3			Chipman, Daniel	1		2		
Davis, Wll[m]	1		3			Hawk, Edward	1	3	4			Stinchfield, Josiah	1	3	2		
Davis, Moses	1		3			Buckman, Dan[l]	1	2	3			Martin, Ezekiel	1	1	1		
Marble, Ebenezer	1		1			House, Moses	2	2	4			Hodgdon, Moses	1	2	1		
Dunn, Joshua	1	3	2			Brigham, Joseph	1	1	1			Parsons, Eleazer	1	1	3		
Camel, Alexander	1	2	2			Brigham, Willard	1		2			Varney, Ichabod	1	2	4		
Mores, William	1	2	2			Brigham, John, Jr	1	3	4			Holmes, Josiah	3	3	4		
Denning, Samuel	3		1			Brigham, John	3		2			Thurrill, Davis	1	2	3		
Downing, Sam[l]	1		2			Chandler, Reuben	1	1	3			Jordan, Sam[l]	1	2	6		
Griffin, John	1	3	2			Chandler, Ichabod	1	2	2			Ring, Eliphus	5	3	9		
Wilcot, Solomon	1	4	3			Chandler, Nath[l]	1	3	3			Holmes, Simeon	2	1	6		
Morgan, Sam[l]	1	4	4			Freeman, Joseph	1	1	2			Thurrill, Asaph	1	1	2		
Yeaton, Sam[l]	3	2	3			Freeman, Chandler	1	2	2			Briggs, Ephraim	4	2	6		
Yeaton, Stephen	1		3			Bradford, Peabody	1	1	2			Briggs, Barnabas	3	3	4		
Hagget, Moses	1	2	3			Bradford, Jonathan	1		2			Farnall, John	1	1	1		
Haskel, Wll[m]	1	1	1			Austin, George	1	1	2			Haskell, Wll[m]	1	3	5		
Hodge, John	2	2	3			Crooker, Joshua	1	2	4			Parsons, Edward	1	5	3		
Harves, Joseph	2		1			Crooker, Isaac	1	1	2			Elly, John[a]	2	1	1		
Tucker, Job	2		1			Gardiner, John	1	1	1			Worcester, John	1	1	2		
Brock, Mary			3			Benson, Caleb	1	1	7			Tripp, Richard	1		3		
Hall, Hezekiah	1	2	2			Noyes, Nicholas	1		1			Saunders, Jon[a]	1	3	3		
Hall, Job	1	1	2			Hassa, Noah	1	2	1			Shillings, Daniel	1	3	3		
Lane, Benjamin	1	3	4			Hassa, James	1	3	2								
Richardson, Benj[n]	1	3	2			Beals, Benjamin	1	2	1			**BRIDGTON TOWN.**					
Woodman, John	1	1	1			Hapa, Amos	1		2								
Woodman, True	1	1	3			Jackson, Henry	1	1	3			Kibbon, John	1	3	2		
Watson, John	1	3	3			Gurney, Tho[s]	1	4	3			Clough, Josiah	1	1	1		
Harris, Wll[m]	1	3	1			Gurney, Jon[a]	1	3	2			Yates, Timothy	1	3	4		
Waterman, John	3	3	2			Bates, Jacob	1	3	2			Sandbourn, John	1	1	1		
Waterman, Robert	1	1	1			Poole, Samuel	1	1	2			Emerson, Theodore	2	2	3		
Davis, Elias	1	5	4			Poole, Joshua	1	2	3			Jewet, Ephraim	2	2	6		
Allen, John	1	1	1			Noyes, Belia	1	3	2			Gibbs, Alpheus	1		1		
Manwell, Samuel	2		4			Davis, Allen	1		3			Farnsworth, Sam[l]	2				
Washburn, Eliab	1	1	4			Willis, James	1	1	1			Knap, Jesse	3		4		
Goff, James	1	2	2			Nash, Jon[a]	1	2	5			Church, Nathan	2	1	2		
Eaton, Ziba	1	4	3			Chandler, John, Jr	1	1	4			Stevens, Jacob	3	3	6		
King, Ichabod	1	2	1			Chandler, John	1		2			Kimball, Sam[l]	1		4		
Bray, Ebenzer	3	1	1			Lander, Edmund	1		2			Kimball, Richard	1	1	4		
Hagget, Elijah	1	3	2			Seabury, Paul	5		3			Barnam, Simeon	3		4		
Rines, Ambrose	3	4	7			Davis, Zebulon, Jr	1	3	3			Oliver, Wll[m]	3		1		
Cotton, Thomas	1	2	1			Fuller, Jesse	1	4	4			Porter, David	1	2	2		
Hammon, Bebia	1	2	1			Chubb, Jabez	2		1			Stevens, Jacob, Jr	3	3	3		
Coy, John	3	3	7			Downing, John	1	1	1			Flint, James	1	3	3		
Millet, David	1	5	6			Sottel, Nath[l]	3	1	2			Keresland, Abraham	1		1		
Clefford, Benjamin	2	3	5			Wilcom, Michael	1	3	5			Broadstreet, David	2		1		
Millet, John	1	3	6			Elwell, Wll[m]	1	2	2			Johnson, Isaac	3	1	3		
Roe, John	1	2	3			Varrell, Sam[l]	1	1	3			Perley, Enoch	3	2	3	1	
Roe, Benj[n]	1		1			Varrel, Sam[l], Ju[r]	1	3	3			Peabody, John	4	3	3		
Harris, Amos	1	2	3			Varrell, Davis	1	3	3			Howe, Moses	1	3	3		
Densmore, David	1	3	6			Varrel, Wll[m]	1	1	3			Andrews, Robert	1		1		
Bradbury, Benj[a]	1	3	5			Prince, John	1	2	2			Ingalls, Nathan	1	5	2		
Safford, Stephen	1	3	3			Hodgkins, Ebenezer	1	2	1			Hale, David	1	2	3		
Bryant, Baldwin	1		2			Hodgkins, Joseph	1	1	1			Ingalls, Asa	1		1		
Parker, James	1	2	4			Hodgkins, James	1		1			Perley, Dan[l]	1		4		
Chickering, Zechariah	1	3	7			Jumper, Edward	1	4	4			Bernard, Dan[l]	1	1	2		
Fisher, Elijah	1	1	4			Hill, James	1		2			Hale, Nath[l]	1	1	4		
Briggs, Rufus	1		4			Leach, Joseph	1		2			Ingalls, Isah	1	4	2		
Briggs, Dan[l]	1	2	1			Shaw, Isaiah	1	3	3			Ingalls, Ph[i]neas	1	3	1		
Safford, Moses	1	1	1			Shaw, Levi	1		1			Mead, George	1		2		
Castle, Simeon	1	1	3			Sottle, Henry	2					Foster, Asael	3	3	4		
Hood, David	1	1	2			Leach, John	1	2	3			Chaplin, John	1	4	1		
Holmes, Gershom	1		3			Bray, Israel	1	2	2			Simons, Tho[s]	1		3		
True, William	1		2			Herrick, John	1	4	2			Simon, Francis	2	1	1		
Dillingham, John	1		5			Hodgkins, James, Ju[r]	1	2	4			Ingalls, Francis	1	2	1		
Allen, Abel	1	3	1			Cordwell, Wll[m]	1	2	5			Burnam, Jeremiah	1	2	2		
Dillingham, Jeremiah	1		3			Jumper, Dan[l]	1	1	2			Howe, Dan[l]	1	1	1		
Pilley, John	1		2			Varrel, Joseph	1	1	1			Brockelbank, Joseph	1	1	2		
Leavit, Jacob	1	2	1			Tod, John	1		1			Kimball, Benj[n], Ju[r]	1	2	3		
Bowen, Sam[l]	1	1	2			Richardson, Elijah	1	1	2			Styles, Enoch	1	1	4		
Staples, John	1					Pettingall, Sam[l]	1	2	3			Styles, Noah	2	4	3		
Haskel, Israel	1		1			Emmory, Moses	1	3	3			Gates, Stephen	2	4	3		
Castle, Wll[m]	1	2	3			Bailey, Tho[s]	3	3	4			Brigham, Daniel	2	1	1		
Andrews, Perez	1	1	2			Emmerson, Sam[l]	2		2			Gibbs, Ezra	1	1	1		
Castle, Squire	1		1			Coombs, Benj[n]	1	4	4			Porter, David	2	2	2		
Bray, Nicholas	1	3	5			Nason, John	1	5	3			Styles, Ezra	1		2		
Perry, Dimon	2	3	3			Stevens, Jacob	1	1	3			Lowel, Tho[s]	3	1	3		
Castle, Job	1	2	2			Libby, James	1	1	3			Emerson, Wll[m]	4	1	5		
Simmons, Joel	1	1	3			Starboard, Samuel	1	3	2			Morrison, Wll[m]	2	2	5		
Sampson, Seth	1		2			Small, David	3		1			Clark, David	1		2		
Varrel, Jeremiah	1		1			Holmes, Greshom	2	2	2			Kimball, Asa	4		3		
Bradbury, Moses	2	3	3			Jackson, Dan[l]	1	3	3								

[1] No attempt has been made in this publication to correct mistakes in spelling made by the deputy marshals, but the names have been reproduced as they appear upon the census schedules.

CUMBERLAND COUNTY—Continued.

NAME OF HEAD OF FAMILY.	Free white males of 16 years and upward, including heads of families.	Free white males under 16 years.	Free white females, including heads of families.	All other free persons.	Slaves.
BRIDGTON TOWN—continued.					
Kimball, Asa, Jnr	1		1		
Davenport, Abner	1	1	1		
Davenport, John	2		1		
Beaman, Aaron	1		1		
Kimball, Benjn	2		1		
BRUNSWICK TOWN.					
Stanwood, Willm, Junr	2	3	4		
Minot, John	2	2	5		
Kennady, Patrick	2	2	4		
Scofield, Thomas	2	5	4		
Grafton, Ephraim	3	2	5	3	
Miller, Margaret	2	2	4		
Simpson, Lewis	1	2	5		
Stanwood, Willm	5	2	7		
Simpson, Josiah	3	1	3		
Clark, Nathan	1		5		
Clark, David	1	1	3		
Hugh, Saml	2	1	8		
Givens, Daniel	2	1	7		
Pennel, Thos	1	5	6		
Givens, Robert	2	2	3		
Givens, John, Junr	1		4		
Givens, John	2		2		
Moseley, Willm	1	1	5		
Scofield, Joseph	5		2		
Spear, Robert	3	1	6		
Jordan, Robert	2	2	4		
Simons, John	2		4		
Cotton, Willm	3	3	4		
Ferren, John	1		2		
Ferren, John, Junr	1	2	4		
Doughty, Willm	1		2		
Gitchel, John	1	1	4		
Pennel, John	1		5		
Marriner, Saml	1		1	3	
Woodward, Saml	2	5	4		
Ferren, Richd	1	1	1		
Danforth, Willm	1	1	1		
Gitchel, Saml	3	3	4		
Gitchel, Stephen	2	1	3		
Wallace, John	1	1	6		
Gitchel, Willm	2	1	4		
Gitchel, Stephen, Junr	2	1	1		
Gitchel, Willm, Junr	2		2		
Marriner, John	1	1	2		
Merriner, John, Jur	1	2	1		
Winslow, George	1	2	3		
Mariner, Willm	1	3	1		
Cooms, Nathan	1	1	3		
Woodward, Peter	1	2	5		
Cooms, Asa	1	2	2		
Cooms, Peter	1	1	2		
Stickney, Bailey	1	2	2		
Snow, Joseph	2		3		
Thomas, Concider	1	5	4		
Thomas, Charles	2	2	5		
Jordan, Peter	1	3	3		
Cowen, Charles	2	4	5		
Cooms, Thomas	1		5		
Cooms, Caleb	1	1	4		
Gross, Saml	2	2	2		
Lewis, Thos	1	1	1		
Snow, Isaac	4	4	6		
Cooms, Joseph	1	2	4		
Hunniford, David	1	1	3		
Godfrey, Thomas	1	2	5		
Laraba, Benja	4	3	4		
Melcher, Saml	2	2	7		
Peterson, John	25	4	5		
Hinkley, Aaron	3	1	2		
Dwinnels, John	1	3	3		
Heyden, George	2		4		
Michaels, James	2		3		
Friend, John	1	2	4	7	
Andrews, John	2	2	4	3	
Blackmore, Joseph	1		3		
Cox, Artemas	1	1	2		
Cowen, Betsy		2	3		
Cox, Ely	1	1	2		
Bates, Mercy			2		
Laraba, Nathl	3	1	2	1	
Harden, Hezekiah	2	3	4		
Cornish, John	1	1	3		
Harden, Saml	1	5	2		
Curtes, James	3	2	4		
Hinkley, Edmund	4	1	3		
Weston, Jacob	2	4	2		
Sprague, Nathl	3	2	5		
Gray, Grace	1		2		
Ham, Joseph	1	2	5		
Ham, Tobias	2	1	6		
Keith, Cornelius	1	2	1		
Crafford, James	1	4	6		
BRUNSWICK TOWN—continued.					
Bates, Hozea	2	3	6		
Thomson, Alexander	1	2	4		
Baker, Elisha	1		3		
Doughty, Daniel	2	4	3		
Thompson, Cornelius	1		1		
Thompson, Robert	2	1	5		
Lowe, Willm	2	2	4		
Latherby, Stephen	1	2	3		
Brown, Ezekiel	1	4	3		
Crowel, Thomas	1	1	2		
Ward, Nehemiah	1	2	1		
Story, John	1				
Hinkley, Ruth		3	1		
Cook, Stephen	2	1	2		
Mitchel, Willm	1	1	1		
Marten, Thomas	2	1	2		
Clark, Archibald	1	2	3		
Ross, Eliphalet	2	2	3		
Stanwood, Ebenezer	3	1	6		
Sullivan, Amos	1		2		
Weymouth, Timo	1		1		
Thomas, Lewis	1	3	2		
French, Willm	1				
Hunt, Mary			2		
Lowel, Paul	1		2		
Dunning, David	1	2	4		
Hunt, Ephraim	1	4	4		
Dunning, Robert	2	1	4		
Chase, Judah	5	1	5		
Stanwood, Robert	2	3	4	4	
Goss, Ebenezer H	2	4	6		
Starboard, Willm	1		2	5	
Dunning, Andw	5	2	7		
Woodside, Anthony	4	1	3		
Chase, James	1	2	3		
Woodside, Willm	3		4		
Dunning, Willm	1	4	5		
Swett, John	2	2	4		
Morse, Joseph	2	3	7		
Melcher, Joseph	5	2	4		
Woodside, Vincent	4		6		
Chase, Benja	3	1	4		
Ross, Willm	1	3	6		
Elliot, James	4	2	6		
Anderson, Jacob	1	2	6		
Woodside, Willm, Junr	1	1	6		
Hunt, Saml	1	1	4		
Kincaid, Peter	2	2	5		
Linscut, David	1	1	1		
Ross, Joseph	1	1	1		
Gross, Michl, Junr	1	3	2		
Toothaker, Abraham	1	3	4		
Stanwood, Saml	1	4	7		
Eaton, Daniel	2		2		
Ryan, Charles	1	1	2		
Dunning, Andrew	2	1	8	1	
Dunning, John	1	4	4		
Dunning, David	1		2		
Stanwood, Willm	4	3	6		
Stone, Benja	4	1	2		
Lunt, Amos	5	1	3	1	
Cary, James	1	2	4		
Hunt, Daniel	2	1	2		
Gorden, James	1	1	3		
Nunan, John	1		1		
Hobbs, Obed	1	1	4		
Thompson, Thomas	3		4		
Cotton, Thomas	2		3		
Dunlap, John	2	4	2		
Morse, Anthony	1	1	4		
Crips, John	3	2	5		
Dunlap, John	2	4	4		
Brooks, ——	1				
Gross, Michael	1	4	5		
Gross, Jacob	1	1	1		
Gross, George	1	1	3		
Melcher, Noah	2	1	1		
Merriman, Thomas	1	2	1		
Chase, John	1	3	3		
Morse, Paul	1	2	2		
Burrel, Humphry	1	2	2		
Philbrick, George	1	2	5		
Rogers, Josiah	2	4	1		
Pierce	1	2	5		
Spaulding, Saml	1	1	2		
Dana, Gardiner	2		1		
Jones, Edward	1	2	2		
Hacker, Jereh, Jun	1	1	4		
Hacker, Jereh	2		4	1	
Jones, Lemuel	3	1	4		
Jones, Caleb	1	4	2		
Owens, Willm	4	1	6	1	
House, Gershom	2	2	4		
Eaton, Saml	2	3	2		
Eaton, Daniel	2		1		
BRUNSWICK TOWN—continued.					
Danforth, Abner	1	2	1	8	
Willee, Edward	1	2	1		
Hogan, Michl	1		5		
Higgins, Willm	1	2	2		
Orr, Richard	1	2	2		
McMahan, Daniel	3	2	1		
Mallet, John	1	3	2		
Toothaker, Roger	1	4	4		
Toothaker, Gideon	1	4	3		
Owens, Philip	3	2	4		
Dunlap, Hugh	1	2	3		
Dunlap, Saml	1	3	6		
Flahartha, Daniel O	1		2		
Spark, David	1		2		
Eaton, Moses	1	2	2		
BUCKTOWN PLANTATION.					
Hodgdon, Jeremiah	2	1	2		
Smith, Israel	1	2	1		
Rich, Joel	1	3	4		
Gammon, Nathl	1	3	3		
Roberts, Joseph	2		3		
Irish, John, Jur	1	1	6		
Irish, John	1	1	2		
Parsons, Phillemon	1	3	3		
Lowel, Thos	1		2		
Sweet, John	1	2	1		
Thurlo, John	1	5	2		
Coburn, Jonas	1	3	4		
Matthews, Volatiah	1	1	1		
Lowel, Willm	1		3		
Mathews, John	1	4	4		
Teague, Benj	1	2	3		
Crooker, Lemuel	1	2	6		
Young, Joshua	1	4	3		
Irish, Joseph	2	1	3		
Doble, Wllm	1	4	4		
Records, Simon	2	4	4		
Records, David	1	3	2		
Irish, Thos	2	2	3		
Coburns, Thos	1	1	4		
Records, Jona	1	2	2		
Warren, David	1		3		
Spaulding, Benjn, Jr	1		1		
Lowel, Stephen	1		1		
Packer, Danl	1	2	5		
Packer, Job	1	3	1		
Taylor, Samuel	3		1		
Buck, Abijah	1	2	2		
Foster, Joel	1		2		
Tilson, Josiah	1	1	2		
Josselin, Thos	1	2	2		
Warren, John	1	3	3		
Hathway, Ichabod	1	2	3		
Mayhew, James	1	2	3		
Warren, Tristram	1	3	2		
Buck, John, Jur	1		2		
Farron, David	1	4	3		
Buck, Nathl	2	3	5		
Allen, Thos	1	3	4		
Brown, John	1		1		
Elliot, John	1		1		
Smith, Seabury	1		1		
Stevens, Moses	1	1	1		
Harlon, Andrew	1	2	3		
Davis, Joshua	1				
Damon, Jona	1				
Broch, John	1				
Clay, John	1				
Hussey, John	1				
Irish, Ebenezer	1	1	1		
Spaulding, Benjn, Senior	1	3	4		
Buck, John	1	1	6		
Berry, Willm	1	3	5		
Filbrick, Jonathan	1	3	4		
Foster, Isaac	2	2	3		
Records, Dominicus	1	2	3		
Chandler, Edmund	1	2	3		
Davis, Gershom	1	2	4		
Spaulding, Benjn, second	2	2	3		
Ricker, Abias	1	2	3		
Wescot, Joshua	1	2	3		
Forbes, Jonah	1	3	3		
Hall, Enoch	1	3	3		
Smith, Nathl	1	1	3		
Young, Cabel	1	1	3		
Shaw, Jotham	1	1	2		
Roberts, Jonathan	1	2	2		
Jordan, James	1	3	3		
Leathers, Enoch	1	3	1		
Roberts, Joseph, Jur	1	3	5		
Brown, Amos	1	4	5		

CUMBERLAND COUNTY—Continued.

NAME OF HEAD OF FAMILY.	Free white males of 16 years and upward, including heads of families.	Free white males under 16 years.	Free white females, including heads of families.	All other free persons.	Slaves.
BUCKTOWN PLANTATION—con.					
Chase, Joseph	2		3		
Chase, Nathl	1	1	2		
Tilly, Wllm	4		2		
Taylor, Saml, Jr	1	2	2		
Crocket, Danl	1	2	2		
Roberts, Joseph	1	1	3		
Whitman, Jacob	1	6	1		
BUTTERFIELD PLANTATION.					
Cummins, Oliver	1	1	2		
Ford, Joshua	1	1	3		
Fletcher, Thos	1		2		
Bisby, Moses	1		2		
Fletcher, John	1		2		
Parlin, Saml	1	1	2		
Briggs, John	1	2	3		
Sturdivant, David	1	3	1		
Sturdivant, Isaac	1	1	1		
Robinson, Increase	3		3		
Robinson, Asa	1		3		
Jennings, Eliphalet	1	1	1		
Jennings, Benjn	1		2		
Heffords, Wllm	1	1	2		
Allen, Seth	1	1	1		
Beasse, Wllm	1	1	2		
Doane, Ebenezer	1	1	1		
Bisby, Charles	5		1		
Oldham, Danl	1	5	7		
Cane, Lemuel	1		2		
Ford, Charles	1	2	2		
Bohney, Isaac	1	3	3		
Tucker, Wllm	1		3		
Bisby, Elisha	1	2	4		
Bosworth, Noah	4	2	1		
Robinson, Joseph	2		4		
Cane, Mesheck	1	1	4		
Cane, James	1	3	2		
Stetson, Hezekiah	1	5	2		
Hale, Benjn	1	1	3		
Crocke, John	5	5	3		
Hall, Enoch	1	2	2		
Buck, Moses	1	4	2		
Barret, Simeon	1	4	4		
Cane, John	1	2	3		
CAPE ELIZABETH TOWN.					
Dyer, Nathaniel	2	2	6		
Sawyer, Ebenezer	2	2	5		
Dyer, Micael	2	1	4		
Smally, Edward	1		1		
Roberts, Mary			2		
Dyer, Benjamin		1	5		
Dyer, Abigail		1	1		
Ray, William	1	1	1		
Simonton, Ebenezer	1	5	2		
Dyer, Joshua	1	3	7		
Randal, Stephen	1	1	2		
Dyer, Caleb	1	3	4		
Amory, John	2	3	4		
Sawyer, Joseph	1				
Ryon, John	1		3		
Sawyer, Jacob	1		1		
Mariner, Moses	1	1	6		
Woodberry, Israel	1	3	5		
York, Jacob	1		1		
Alden, Elisabeth	2		3		
Lovett, James	1	1	1		
Webb, Sarah	2		3		
Pilsberry, Hannah		2	1		
McCaning, Elisabeth			2		
Woodberry, Peeter	1	1	2		
Hatch, Ezekiel	1		4		
Hoole, William	2	3	3		
Simonton, Thomas	1	3	2		
Thompson, Robert	1		1		
Robinson, Samuel	1	3	2		
Simonton, Mary	2		3		
Thrasher, Benjamin	1		2		
Thrasher, Ebenezer	3	1	3		
Wallace, Jonah	1		3		
Webster, John	1	2	2		
Stout, Nathaniel	3	3	4		
Delano, Bezilla	5	1	5		
Richards, Humphrey	1		2		
Jorden, Samuel	1	4	3		
Richards, John	1		1		
Webster, James	1				
Robertson, Samuel	1	1	1		
Robertson, Joshua	2	3	4		
Miller, James	2	3	5		
Miller, Hugh	1		1		
Miller, David	1		2		
CAPE ELIZABETH TOWN—continued.					
Miller, Joshua	1	1	1		
Maxwell, James	2		2		
Marrs, John	3	3	4		
Jorden, Secomb	1	1	2		
Jorden, Noah	1		2		
Jorden, Noah	1	1	3		
Jorden, Rachel	1		2		
Jorden, Benjamin	3	3	6		
Johnston, Samuel	1	2	4		
Trundy, George	3	1	3		
Clark, Robert	2	3	2		
Davis, Simeon	1	1	3		
Abbot, James	1		2		
Atwood, Stephen	1	2	2		
Leach, James	3	1	3		
Wheeler, John	1	3	9		
Dyer, James	3	6	2		
Staples, Nathaniel	2	1	1		
McKenny, Jonathan	1	2	4		
Maxwell, James	2	1	3		
Irish, Partrick	2	1	4		
McCreat, William	1		3		
Crowley, Jeremiah	2	2	3		
Wallace, John	1	1	2		
Simonton, Thomas	1		2		
Davis, Daniel	1		2		
York, John	2		1		
Sawyer, Peeter	2	4	3		
Sawyer, Reubin	1		1		
Small, Timothy	1	2	3		
Allen, David	1	1	1		
Dyer, Paul	1	1	2		
Sawyer, Daniel	1		2		
Dyer, Ephraim	4	1	3		
Dyer, Isaac	1	2	4		
Dyer, Henry	2	3	5		
Parker, Ebenezer	1		7		
Thorndike, Ebenezer	3		2		
Jorden, Samuel	1	4	3		
Simonton, London				2	
Flint, Thomas	1	2	2		
Davis, Christopher	1		2		
Willard, Jesse	1	2	3		
Simonton, Andrew	3	2	2		
Simonton, Matthew	1	1	5		
Thorndike, Christian			3		
Clarke, Ephraim	3	1	6		
Deakes, George	1	2	6		
Welch, James	1	2	1		
Cobb, Joseph	3	1	3		
Webster, James	2	3	4		
Richards, Bezilla	1	1	4		
Armstrong, John	1	2	2		
Small, Elisha	1	3	4		
Crockett, Samuel	1		2		
Dyer, Samuel		3	6		
Stout, George	1		4		
Stout, Levi	1	1	2		
Bowa, George	1	6	2		
Stout, Eleazer	1	2	2		
Stout, Eleazer	1		5		
Cash, Nathaniel	1	2	3		
Stout, George	2		2		
Stout, Levi	2		2		
Brown, Jacob	3	2	5		
Cash, Samuel	1	2	3		
Elder, George	2	1	2		
Elder, Ellis	1		2		
Elder, John	1		4		
Elder, Joshua	1	2	1		
Babb, James	2		2		
Gent, Ephraim	1		1		
Hayes, George	2		2		
Weston, Beniah	1	2	8		
Dyer, Hannah			4	4	
Roberts, Hannah		1	2	2	
Dyer, Isaac	1	2	2		
Friket, Benjamin	3		3		
Dyer, Samuel	2	2	4		
Turner, James	2		4		
Douglis, Archbald	1		2		
Friket, John	3	3	3		
Friket, William	1	3	3		
Baley, William	3	2	5		
Leatherby, Jonathan	2	5	4		
Frikit, John	1	3	4		
Stanford, Benjamin	1	1	3		
Friket, Nathaniel	1	2	4		
Higgins, Massy	4	1	3		
Dyer, William	1		1		
Gammon, William	2		3		
Calif, Samuel	4	2	1	1	
Wuman, Valentine	1		2		
Jorden, Nathaniel	2	2	4	1	
Jorden, Ezekiel	1	4	5		
CAPE ELIZABETH TOWN—continued.					
Jorden, Trustim	2	1	3		
Bucks, Abraham	1		1		
Jorden, John	1	1	3		
Jorden, Abraham	1	1	3		
Jorden, Isaac	1	2	3		
Barnsbotom, James	1		1		
Dyer, Robert	1	2	6		
Robertson, John	1	1	3		
Woodberry, John	2	1	6		
Plummer, Robert	1		1		
Hatch, John	1	2	1		
Roberts, Ephraim	2	5	2		
York, Joseph	1	1	2		
Woodberry, Lucy		1	2		
Sawyer, Mary	2		4		
Stanford, Abigail			3		
Cushing, John	1	1	3		
Thomas, Abigail	1	2	3		
Stout, David	1		2		
Blake, John	1	1	1		
Stanford, Christopher	1		2		
Surline, John	1	1	2		
Mayew, Whitewood	2	1	2		
Sawyer, Jonathan	1	7	3		
Cushing, Abigail		1	2		
Stanford, Joseph	1		1		
Stanford, Sarah	1		5		
Stanford, John	2	3	1		
Stanford, Jeremiah	1		2		
Sawyer, Jeremiah	1		2		
Mariner, Joseph	1	4	2		
Mariner, John	1	4	4		
Bryant, Abraham	1		2		
Westcot, Josiah	1	3	3		
Millet, Elisha	2	1	2		
Plummer, Jesse	1	5	2		
Crocket, Richard	1	1	5		
Doane, Edward	4		4		
Shillings, John	1	2	3		
Shillings, Samuel	2		1	3	
Shillings, Joseph	1	4	3		
York, Samuel	1		2		
Doane, Ebenezer	1	1	1		
Shillings, Nehemiah	1		4		
Westcot, Samuel	1	1	4		
Libby, Jotham	1	2	4		
Dunn, Enoch	2	1	3		
Trickey, Zebulon	3		4		
Jackson, Thomas	1	1	2		
Bigford, Joshua	1		1		
Nason, Uriah	3	2	4		
Thombs, Benjamin	1		1		
Shillings, Samuel	5	6	7		
Shillings, Simeon	2	3	6		
Cummings, Thomas	1	1	2		
Shillings, Josiah	2		3		
Pratt, Zenas	4	3	3		
McKenny, Eleazer	1	3	3		
Fogg, John	1	2	1		
Jorden, Richard	1		1		
Jorden, Solomon	1	2	4		
Jorden, Stephen	1	3	5		
Jorden, Jonathan	3	1	5		
Jorden, Elisha	1	1	4		
Beal, Ebenezer	1	1	2		
Maxwell, Thomas	4	2	4		
Maxwell, William	1	2	6		
Maxwell, Joseph	3	3	5		
Dingly, William	1	2	2		
Jorden, Joshua	4	3	2	1	
Jorden, Dominicus	3	2	4		
Jorden, Jeremiah	2	1	2		
Cushing, Loring	1	1	4		
Jorden, Nathaniel	1		4		
Dyer, Jabes	2		4		
Mitchell, Jonathan	2	1	7		
Small, Edward	2	4	5		
Jorden, Jeremiah	2	4	2		
Clarkes, John R.	2	2	4		
Pollock, Deliverance				1	
Welch, Mary			2	5	
Jorden, Elisha	2		3		
Hunscom, Moses	3		2		
Jorden, Nathaniel	2		4		
Jorden, Timothy	1		2		
Robertson, Joshua	3	2	6		
Maxwell, Partrick	2	4	1		
Jorden, Thomas	1		1		
Jorden, Samuel	3	1	5		
Jorden, Samuel	1	3	2		
Avery, Jane	1		2		
DURHAM TOWN.					
Goodwin, Saml	3	2	1		
Adams, Andw	1	1	5		

CUMBERLAND COUNTY—Continued.

DURHAM TOWN—con.

NAME OF HEAD OF FAMILY.	Free white males of 16 years and upward, including heads of families.	Free white males under 16 years.	Free white females, including heads of families.	All other free persons.	Slaves.
Cushing, John	2	3	3		
Neal (Widow)			2		
Bavage, James	1	1	2		
Wag, John	1	2	2		
Studson, Elisha	2	1	3		
Lewis, Nathan	1	1	2		
Lincoln, John	1	4	2		
Gerrish, Charles	1		2		
Gerrish, George	1	3	2		
Pearson, Thomas	2		2		
Webb, Sam¹	1	2	1		
Warren, Pelatiah	1	3	4		
Studson, Elijah	1	1			
Jones, Ezekiel	2		2		
Duran, Matthew	2	4	3		
Roberts, Ebenezer	2	4	2		
Sanborn, Simeon	1	1	3		
Snow, Joshua	1	2	2		
Bagley, Enoch	1	2	1		
Bagley, Israel	2	1	3		
Weston, Stephen	1	3	4		
Warren, Henry	1	1	1		
Currier, Sarah		3	3		
True, Willm	3	2	4		
True, Abel	1	1	3		
Osgood, Aaron	2	3	2		
Randal, John	2	3	4		
Roberts, Willm	2	1	6		
York, Sam¹	2	2	4		
Turner, Isaac	1		2		
Roberts, Vincent	1	6	3		
Blake, Will	1	2	2		
Davis, Joseph	2		2		
Hoit, John	2	2	5		
Davis, Isaac	1	1	4		
Fifield, Edward	1	2	1		
Osgood, Nath¹	1	3	2		
Vening, Benj^a	3	1	4		
Beman, Joseph	1	2	2		
Fogginson, George	1	1	4		
Ayers, Eben^z	1	2	2		
Goodwin, George	1	2	1		
Warren, Eben^z	1	1	1		
Tarr, Henry	1		2		
Tarr, Henry, Junr	1		1		
Brown, Sam¹	1	2	4		
Pall, Joseph	1	1	1		
Bragdon, Ebenezer	1		1		
Cushing, Charles, Junr	2	4	2		
Gerrish, Nath¹	2	2	6		
York, Joseph	1	3	4		
Roak, Martin	1	1	2		
McGra, Will	2	2	2		
Nichols, Sam¹	2	4	6		
Spafford, Phinehas	1	2	3		
Stoddard, Willm	1	3	7		
Willson, James	1	2	2		
Mitchel, Rich^d	1		2		
Procter, Sam¹	1	2	3		
Stout, Joshua	2	4	6		
Plummer, Robert	1	1	2		
Jordan, Secomb	1	1	3		
Dyer, Michael	1	4	6		
Dyer, David	1	4	4		
Parker, John	3	3	4		
Merril, Roger	1	2	2		
Jones, Joshua	1	3	2		
Newal, Eben^z, Junr	1	1	1		
Duglas, John	1		1		
Newal, Ebenezer	2	3	2		
McIntosh, John	1		4		
Gerrish, Willm	3	3	4		
Bailey, Timothy	1	2	2		
Skinner, John	1	2	3		
Mitchel, Jeremiah	1	2	1		
Parker, James	1	2	2		
Farrow, John	1	3	2		
Vining, John	1	1	2		
Woodbury, Ebenezer	1	1	5		
Hibbart, James	1	2	5		
Hibbart, John	1		1		
Tracey, Christopher	1	2	4		
Bliffen, James	1	1	1		
Beal, Jon^a	2	2	3		
Night, Joseph	1	3	2		
Gitchel, Nath¹	1	1	5		
Fasset, Rich^d	1	4	5		
Tracey, Solomon	2	1	4		
Gitchel, Robert	1	4	3		
Gitchel, John	1		1		
Duglas, Elijah	2		1		
Gitchel, Joseph	1		3		
Crossman, David	1	3	7	1	
Bliffen, Job	1	3	4		
Day, Josiah	3	4	4	1	

DURHAM TOWN—con.

NAME OF HEAD OF FAMILY.	Free white males of 16 years and upward, including heads of families.	Free white males under 16 years.	Free white females, including heads of families.	All other free persons.	Slaves.
Duglas, Cornelius	1	2	3		
Jones, Noah	1	2	3		
Mitchel, Thomas	1	1	1		
Pinkham, And^w	1	3	6		
Esthers, Edward	1	1	2		
Gitchel, Hugh	1	4	3		
Dudley, Micajah	1	3	7		
Duglas, Joseph	1	2	4		
Fisher, Thomas	3		4		
Crossman, Solomon	1	2	2	1	
Welch, Patrick	3		1		
Esthers, Joseph	1		2		
Esthers, Caleb	2	5	5		
Varney, Nicholas	4	3	4		
Tuttle, Reuben	3	1	4		
Collins, Sam¹	3	1	9		
Clough, Sam¹	2	2	6		
Ring, Batcheldor	2	3	3		

FALMOUTH TOWN.

NAME OF HEAD OF FAMILY.	Free white males of 16 years and upward, including heads of families.	Free white males under 16 years.	Free white females, including heads of families.	All other free persons.	Slaves.
Merrell, Elias	1	4	1		
Merrell, James	1	1	3		
Merrell, Adam	2	2	2		
Merrell, James	1		3		
Swett, Moses	1	3	3		
Watts, Edward	1	2	3		
Knights, George	5	3	6		
Knights, Jacob	1	2	3		
Knights, Benjamin	2		2		
Sawyer, Anthony	4	5	4		
Graves, Crispus	1	1	3		
Merrell, Joseph	1		2		
Barber, John	4	1	3		
Sawyer, Thomas	1	2	3		
Sawyer, Zachariah	1	1	3		
Blake, John	4	1	4		
Waite, Benjamin	2		2		
Shaddock, Moses	1		2		
Blake, James	1	1	1		
Noyes, Peeter	5	2	2		
Noyes, Amos	1	2	2		
Lunt, Joseph	1	2	1		
Sawyer, Benjamin	1	2	6		
Knights, Amos	1	2	2		
Hilton, Emma	2		1		
Noyes, Noah	1	1	2		
Ilsley, Jonathan	1	1	2		
Blake, John	1	2	3		
Berry, Obediah	2	1	4		
Berry, Josiah	1	1	5		
Sawyer, Obediah	3	1	4		
Knights, Mark	1	2	1		
Knights, Henry	1	2	3		
Sawyer, Isaac	1	1	5		
Googin, Simon	1		1		
Reed, Jonathan	1		3		
Stevens, Joshua	2	4	8		
Adams, Jacob	4	1	7		
Night, Thomas	1	2	2		
Sawyer, Merrel	1	3	2		
Bishop, Mary			1		
Bracket, Thomas	2		2		
Bracket, Peter	1	2	3		
Bracket, William	2	2	4		
Baley, Benjamin	1		2		
Bracket, John S	1	5	4		
Whitney, Samuel	1	4	1		
Hicks, Samuel	1	2	3		
Baley, James	2	3	6		
Knights, Merrell	1	2	9		
Lord, James	1	2	3		
Winslow, Ebenezer	3	2	6		
Winslow, John	2	4	4		
Cobb, Chitman	1	4	3		
Cobb, James	1		3		
Cobb, Jonathan	1	1	2		
Pride, Isaac	1	1	3		
Minot, Thomas	1	2	4		
Procter, John	3	1	2		
Bracket, James	1	3	5		
Bracket Anthony	1	3	6		
Moody, Dorcas		2	4		
Mumford, Samuel	2	1	2		
Winslow, Nathan	4	2	6		
Howell, Silas	1	3	4		
Procter, Nathaniel	1	2	3		
Moody, Josiah	1		2		
Winslow, James	2	4	3		
Cobb, Peeter	1	3	3		
Crandall, Philip	1		1		
Baley, Daniel	1	5	5		
Baley, Josiah	1	3	3		
Thomson, David	3	1	2		
Rand, Benjamin	1	2	5		

FALMOUTH TOWN—con.

NAME OF HEAD OF FAMILY.	Free white males of 16 years and upward, including heads of families.	Free white males under 16 years.	Free white females, including heads of families.	All other free persons.	Slaves.
Rand, Lazarus	1	3	4		
Small, Zachariah	1		3		
Small, John	2	2	3		
Haskell, Thomas	1	2	3		
Swett, Israel	1	1	3		
Partridge, David	2	3	3		
Grant, James	2	2	5		
Farthingham, John	1		1		
Elder, John	1	2	3		
Cobb, Peeter	1	2	4		
Cobb, Joseph	1	5	3		
Small, Jeremiah	1	4	1		
Bracket, John	1	2	1		
Huntriss, Pearson	1	2	3		
Thombs, Benjamin	1	6	3		
Baley, Benjamin	3	4	6		
Riggs, Enoch	1	3	4		
Riggs, Joseph	1		4		
Riggs, Jeremiah	1		3		
Frost, Johanna	2	1	4		
Means, James	1		3		
Smith, John H	1	2	4		
Cox, Josiah	1	1	6		
Quimby, John	1	5	3		
Partrick, William	1	4	3		
Stevens, Trustum	4	4	5		
Low, Esther		1	2		
Brooks, Daniel	1	2	3		
Partridge, Jesse	1	1	3		
Dole, Daniel	3		5		
Titcomb, Andrew	1		3		
Tate, George	5				1
Lewis, Archelas	2	1	3		
Dyer, Josiah	1	3	6		
Pierce, Thomas	1	1	2		
Porter, Benjamin J	1				
Bartlett, Caleb	1	3	4		
Murrey, James	1	1	1		
Brooks, John	1	2	5		
McDonald, John	2	1	2		
Billings, Mary		1	5		
Thombs, Samuel	1	3	4		
Ticket, Jonathan	3	3	3		
Webb, Henry	1	3	4		
Ticket, Benjamin	4	1	3		
Waterhouse, William	1	1	3		
Waterhouse, William	2		3		
Waterhouse, John	1	1	1		
Baley, Joseph	1		3		
Slimmons, William	1	1	3		
Hagerty, Jane	1		4		
Maxwell, William	1	1	3		
Chapman, Shadrack	1	1	2		
Webb, James	1	4	4		
Herrick, Daniel	1	2	2		
Barker, Jeremiah	1	3	3		
Laten, Jedediah	5	3	4		
Staples, Joseph	1	1	4		
Merrell, James	1	1	3		
Winslow, William	2	7	5		
Hall, Jedediah	3	4	5		
Abbot, Nathaniel	1	1	3		
Allen, Isaac	2	1	2		
Steward, Peeter	1	3	5		
Baker, William	1	2	2		
Gerrish, Nathaniel	1	2	2		
Laten, Joseph	1	1	6		
Willson, Ichabod	1	1	4		
Winslow, Samuel	1	1	1		
Williams, Nathaniel	2	1	1		
Winslow, Hezekiah	2	1	2		
Laten, Peter	1	2	3		
Laten, Peitiah	1	4	4		
Woodson, Caleb	1	6	3		
Hall, Nicholis	2	3	5		
Tripp, Abner	1	3	5		
Hicks, James	1	2	4		
Fry, Benjamin	1	2	1		
Roberts, Thomas	1	3	4		
Creesy, Benjamin	1	2	2		
MGill, William	1	1	3		
Hall, Andrew	2	4	5		
Hall, Hatevil	3	2	5		
Frank, Thomas	3	1	4		
Field, Daniel	3	1	6		
Field, Zachariah	3		6		
Mumford, Edmund	3	1	2		
Mastin, Ephraim	1	2	6		
Mastin, Benjamin	1	3	6		
Stout, William	1		2		
Merrel, Edmund	6		3		
Merrel, James	3	3	5		
Lunt, Benjamin	3	4	6		
Worster, Luke H	1	4	4		
Hobbs, Jonathan	2	2	6		

CUMBERLAND COUNTY—Continued.

NAME OF HEAD OF FAMILY.	Free white males of 16 years and upward, including heads of families.	Free white males under 16 years.	Free white females, including heads of families.	All other free persons.	Slaves.	NAME OF HEAD OF FAMILY.	Free white males of 16 years and upward, including heads of families.	Free white males under 16 years.	Free white females, including heads of families.	All other free persons.	Slaves.	NAME OF HEAD OF FAMILY.	Free white males of 16 years and upward, including heads of families.	Free white males under 16 years.	Free white females, including heads of families.	All other free persons.	Slaves.
FALMOUTH TOWN—con.						FALMOUTH TOWN—con.						FALMOUTH TOWN—con.					
Hall, William	3	3	2			Latin, Hatevil	1	4	1			Davis, Roland	1	1	2		
Laten, George	3	2	2			Hayes, John	1	2	1			Merrel, Enoch	1	2	4		
Winslow, Thomas	2	2	4			Broad, Thaddeus	2	5	6			Jones, Jabes	2	3	6		
Baker, Jonah	2	1	4			Rand, James	1	2	3			Jones, Francis	1	1	3		
Hanson, Ruth		1	2			Ward, Elijah	1		3			Honeyford, Thomas	1	1	2		
Crocket, Simon	1		2			Slemmons, Thomas	2		1			Foster, Charles	1	1			
Winslow, Benjamin	1	1	3	1		Smith, William	1		3			Toppin, John	1		1		
Winslow, Olive	1	4	7			Trickey, David	2	3	5			Grant, William	1		2		
Morrel, William	1	1	2			Johnston, Robert	3		2			Pote, William	1		6		
Morrel, Stephen	2	1	6			Johnston, John	3	2	5			Pote, Samuel	1	2	1		
Winslow, Samuel	2	3	4			Porterfield, William	3	2	6			Roughf, Sarah		3			
Torrey, James	1	2	5			Slemmons, Robert	1	3	3			Pote, Greenfield	1	3	3		
Frost, Charles	1	2	4			Burns, John	1		2			Pote, Gamaliel	1	4	7		
Tripp, Nathaniel	1		7			March, Samuel	2		2			Little, Sarah			2		
Tripp, Peleg	1		2			Knights, George	2	3	5			Richardson, William	1	2	6		
Cook, John	2	1	4			Saloan, Adam	3					Allen, Hannah			3		
Night, Job	1	6	3			Parkes, Anna		4	4			York, Samuel	1		3		
Pope, Elijah	2	7	5			Knights, Nathaniel	1	1	6	1		Wormwell, Nathaniel	1	2	2		
Morrell, John	1	3	5			Andrews, Samuel	1	1	2			Pote, Jeremiah	1		2		
Night, Richard	1	3	4			Babb, Rhoda		2	1			Lowell, Mary		1	2		
Night, Peeter	1	1	5			Wright, Boston					3	Jackman, Anna		1	5		
Willson, Mark	2	5	1			Johnston, James	4	2	4			Bartlett, Thomas	1		1		
Pride, Benjamin	1		2			Tate, Robert	2	1	6			Delano, Thomas	1	5	3		
Berry, George	1	2	3			Warren, John	2		2			Dodd, Thomas	1		2		
Doubty, Thomas	4		1			Porterfield, Elisabeth			3			Dodd, Stephen	1		3		
Thurstin, Paul	1	5	4			Thompson, Jonathan	1	2	5			Williams, Ebenezer	3	4	4		
Gibbs, William	2		2			Check, Nathan	1		1			Moody, Benjamin	3	1	7		
Armstrong, Jonathan	1	2	2			Check, Peeter	1	1	1			Lock, Josiah	1	1	5		
Night, Samuel	2	1	3			Foss, Job	1		2			Sawyer, Elisha	1	1	3		
Sawyer, Unis	2	1	3			Starberd, Anthony	1		2			Lunt, Benjamin	2		1		
Merrel, Joseph	2		1			Starberd, John	1	3	5			Lunt, Daniel	1	2	1		
Moss, Anthony	4	1	3			Walker, Josiah	1	2	2			Cobb, Olive		3	4		
Willson, Nathaniel	2	3	6			Starberd, John	1	1	2			Lock, Abijah	1		4		
Night, Amos	1	2	2			Ticket, Mary	1		4			Bennet, Phineas	1	4	4		
Night, Joseph	1	4	4			Starberd, Thomas	1	4	3			Moss, Jethniel	1		3		
Night, George	1	7	7			Lincoln, Thomas	1	2	4			Merrell, Joshua	1	3	4		
Night, Jonathan	1		3			Adams, Jonathan	2		4			Merrell, Adam	5	2	5		
Cutter, Ebenezer	1		3			Babb, William	3	4	2			Merrell, Jacob	1	4	4		
Night, Stephen	1	1	3			Baley, David	3	4	4			Merrell, Humphrey	1		1		
Waite, John	1	3	5			Haskel, Solomon	5		5			Pettengill, Benjamin	1	2	6		
Toby, Page	1	2	7			Webb, Jonathan	3	2	6			Merrell, Amos	1	1	4		
Colley, John	1	1	2			Gage, Isaac	1					Doubty, James	1		4		
Colley, William	1	5	3			Chadwick, William	1					Lunt, Ephraim	1	1	5		
Carll, Nathaniel	3	1	4			March, Edmund	1		4			Noyes, Samuel	1	3	4		
Bracket, Abraham	3	1	3			Pike, Timothy	1	5	5			Merrell, Daniel	1	3	5		
Allen, Zacheus	3	3	3			Conant, William	1	2	5			Buckman, Samuel	1	6	5		
Field, Stephen	2	4	3			Bigsby, William	1	2	4			Tukesberry, John	6	3	2		
Fields, Zachariah	1	1	2			Westcot, Eliakim	1	3	3			Thrasher, Joseph	1	3	6		
Merrel, Moses	3	2	7			Jorden, Joseph	1	3	4			M¢Intire, Benjamin	1	2	6		
Allen, Isaac	4	1	4			Quimby, Joseph	1	2	5			Buxton, William	1		4		
Anderson, John	1	3	3			Quimby, Benjamin	4	3	5			Buxton, James	1	4	4		
Adams, Moses	1	5	2			Quimby, Nathan	1	2	2			Chase, William	1	3	4		
Watts, Samuel	1	3	4			Conant, Samuel	2		4			Johnston, Joseph	1	2	5		
Merrel, Silas	1	1	9			Woodberry, Hugh	1		2			Malcom, Joseph	2	1	3		
Merrel, Edmund	1	4	5			Partridge, Anna		1	3			Turner, Melzer	1	2	5		
Merrel, Humphrey	2	4	4			Webb, William	2	3	4			Buxton, William	1	3	3		
Hutchins, Joseph	1	1	1			Millikin, Benjamin	1		3			Jones, Edward	1	1	1		
Fields, Benjamin	1		1			March, Peltiah	1	2	5			Pomeroy, Joseph	3		5		
Fields, Joseph	1	2	3			Freeman, Enoch	2	1	2			Underwood, Joseph	1	1	5		
Lunt, Nathan	1	1	3			Clark, Morris	3	1	4			Underwood, David	1		4		
Cobb, Benjamin	2	3	4			Wise, Amaziah	2	1	4			York, William R	1	2	4		
Hustead, Robert	2	5	4			Johnston, George	2	1	4			Titcomb, William	1	3	2		
Sawyer, Jonathan	1	4	5			Haskel, William	1	2	4			Knight, William	1	2	2		
Small, Daniel	1	1	3			Cobby, John	1	3	6			York, Joseph	1	2	3		
Barber, Adam	1	4	6			Lamb, William	3	3	6			Lock, John	1	3	1		
Bracket, John	1	2	1			Swett, Stephen	1	1	2			Mason, John	1	3	1		
Cobb, Ephraim	1	2	4			Partridge, Jotham	1	2	3	4		Clark, Ichabod	1	1	3		
Purington, Abraham	1	2	2			Frost, Cato				4		Lock, Jonathan	2	1	2		
Purington, Elisha	1	3	2			Jorden, Cezar				2		Buckman, Jeremiah	2	4	6	1	
Hustin, Stephen	1	1	2			Riggs, Stephen	1		3			Pote, Increase	1	2	3		
Conant, Bartholomew	1	1	2			Riggs, Stephen	1	1	2			Kilpartrick, Iland	1	2	6		
Conant, Joseph	1	3	4			Riggs, James	1		4			Grover, Andrew			2		
Twamley, Daniel	1	2	2			Harper, William	2	1	6	1		Hinshaw, Sarah			2		
Woodberry, Joshua	1					Gould, John	1	2	6			Prince, Benjamin	1	3	5		
Lord, Nathan	1	2	5			Pennel, Thomas	1	3	3			Prince, Amos	1	2	1		
Abbot, George	2	3	4			Knight, Joshua	1	2	2			Buckman, Nathan	1	2	7	1	
Morrison, Robert	1	7	2			Noyes, Joseph	3	1	6			Kilpartrick, Daniel	1		2		
Bacheldor, Joseph	1	1	1			Gould, Gardner	2	3	4	1		Bangs, Joshua	1	2	2		
Knights, Moses	1	4	4			Frost, Pepperell	1	1	6	1		Wormwell, John	1	2	7		
Webb, John	1	1	7			Epes, Daniel	1		5			Blackstone, Benjamin	4	3	4		
Hale, Nathaniel	4	2	5			Frost, James	1	2	2			Noyes, Samuel	2		1		
Pride, Henry	1		4			Westcot, Richard	2	2	2			Noyes, James	1		4		
Pride, Joseph	1	1	2			Storer, Johanna		1	3			Noyes, Nathan	3	3	3		
Austin, Benjamin	1	4	9			Kimball, John	1	3	2			Noyes, Nathan	3	1	6		
Pride, William	1	5	3			Reed, Ichabod	1	3	7			Merrel, Stephen	2		4		
Walker, William	1	2	3			Whettum, Martha	1	1	4			Thompson, Nathaniel	2				
Walker, Charles	1	2	3			Brown, Thomas	3	1	4			Thompson, William	1		4		
Lunt, William	2	3	1			Sampson, Micael	2	2	7			Swett, Samuel	1	1	1		
Pride, Joseph	2	3	3			Higgins, Elisha					7	Thompson, Edward	1		2		
Grant, John	1	1	2			Thombs, Cezar				7							
Webb, Elisabeth			3			Stevens, Isaac S	2	4	5			FLINTSTOWN PLANTATION.					
Lunt, Daniel	2	4	2			Wyer, Elijah	1		2								
Ireish, John	1	1	3			Thompson, Joseph	1	1	3			Larribee, Zebulon	2	2	2		
Winslow, Job	2		8			Davis, Roland	2	1	3			Mullikin, Josiah	2	2	3		
Merrel, Jacob	2	1	4									Bandford, Wllm	1	1	2		

CUMBERLAND COUNTY—Continued.

FLINTSTOWN PLANTATION—continued.

Name of head of family.	Free white males of 16 years and upward, including heads of families.	Free white males under 16 years.	Free white females, including heads of families.	All other free persons.	Slaves.
Brown, David	2	1	2		
Whittum, Jedadiah	1	3	1		
Sweet, Benjn	1	1	2		
Fitch, Wllm	2				
Roe, Benjn	1	3	4		
Flint, Eleazer	1				
Thorn, Bartholomew	3	1	5		
Thorn, Joseph	1		3		
Sabine, Lewis	1	1	2		
Sandbourn, David	3	2	3		
Noble, Christopher, Ju	1	2	1		
Noble, Christopher	2		1		
Roe, Webber	1	1	1		
Roe, Lazarus	1		3		
Roe, Noah	1	1	3		
Sandbourn, Jona	6		5		
Philbrick, Michael	1		2		
Richardson, Joseph	1	2	2		
Burnal, John, Jr	1		1		
Burnal, John	1	2	3		
Fly, Isaac	1		3		
Fly, James	1	2	3		
Korah, Stephen	1	3	2		
Bachelor, Saml	1	1	2		
Flint, Cummins	1				
Harding, Simon	2	3	3		
Lowel, Moses	2	1	3		
Lowel, Jona	1	3	2		
Fitch, Richard	1		2		
Pierce, Josiah	1		4		
Bachelor, Ephraim	1	4	3		
Ingalls, Benjn	2	2	4		
Laiken, Joseph	2	2	3		
Howe, Jacob	1	2	3		

FREEPORT TOWN.

Name of head of family.	Free white males of 16 years and upward, including heads of families.	Free white males under 16 years.	Free white females, including heads of families.	All other free persons.	Slaves.
Jamerson, James	5	1	3		
Mann, John, Jr	2	1	4		
Dunham, John	1	2	4		
Duning, John	1	2	1		
Wentworth, Silas	3		2		
Carless, Willm	2		2		
Peckman, Bettey	1		5		
Rogers, Willm	1		2		
Kendal, Benja	1		3		
Rogers, George	2		3		
Mans, Thos	1	3	3		
Mans, John	5	1	5		
Anderson, Jacob	3		4		
Anderson, James	1	2	1		
Anderson, Joseph	2	2	6		
Anderson, James	5	1	3		
Anderson, Robert	1	3	3		
Anderson, John	1		3		
Robarts, James	1	4	1		
Pote, Green	3	1	6		
Moore, Elkins	1		2		
Adridge, Nathl	1	1	6		
Gookins, Richd	1		1		
Sole, Willm	1		2		
Cobb, Thos	4	1	4		
Bruer, Curried	1		3		
Day, Mehitable	1	1	2		
Day, Catherine	1		2		
Lake, Benja	1	1	2		
Lake, Lydia	2		2		
Anderson, John	1	1	1		
Brewer, Edward	2	1	2		
Brewer, Danl	2	3	4		
Brewer, Joseph	1	1	3		
Merrill, Jacob	1	2	1		
Leechfield, Nathl	1		2		
Leechfield, Saml	1	1	5		
Leechfield, Noah	1	3	3		
Leechfield, Willm	1		2		
Carter, Danl	2		2		
Carter, Danl, Junr	1	1	3		
Austin, Ruth		3	2		
Grant, Abram	2		2		
Curtis, Danl	3		3		
Dennison, Ame		1	3		
Cohon, John	1		3	2	
Townsend, Joseph	1		1		
Lufkin, Aaron	2	2	6		
Richardson, Benja	1	3	3		
Dennison, Abner	1	3	1		
Dennison, Gideon	1	3	1		
Curtis, Thomas	1	1	1		
Curtes, Thomas, Junr	1	4	5		
Turner, Lemuel	3		4		
Randall, Rebecca	1	3	4		
Silvester, Thos	1	1	3		
Evans, Willm	1		2		
Mitchel, Willm	2	5	3		

FREEPORT TOWN—con.

Name of head of family.	Free white males of 16 years and upward, including heads of families.	Free white males under 16 years.	Free white females, including heads of families.	All other free persons.	Slaves.
Dennison, David	2	3	5		
Silvester, Amos	1	1	4		
Silvester, John	1		2		
Frost Phinehas	2	3	6		
Townsend, John	1		1		
Silvester, Abner, Jur	1		3		
Prout, James	1	1	3		
Silvester, Abner	4		2		
Silvester, Caleb	1		4		
Silvester, Joseph	1	1	1		
Silvester, Hinhman	1		1		
Scales, Samuel	1	2	2		
Scales, Nathl	1		2		
Brown, Francis	1		1		
Lambart, Isaac	2	4	5		
Hooper, David	2	2	2		
Sole, Ichabod	2	1	3		
Sole, Robert	1		2		
Byram, David	1		1		
Byram, Melcher	1	1	4		
Lotter, Robert	1	1	4		
Rogers, Mark	2	3	4		
Dunham, Danl	1		2		
Curtes, James	3		2		
Townsend, Benja	2	1	1		
Kilby, Richd	1	3	4		
Sole, James	1	2	4		
Sole, Jedediah	1	1	4		
Bicknal, Thos	2		2		
Buzzel, Noah	1	2	2		
Prat, Noah	1	4	2		
Curtis, Obadiah	1	1	2		
Curtis, David	1	1	1		
Lane, Gideon	1	1	3		
Curtis, Benja	2	2	3		
Bennet, Job	2	1	4		
Atkinson, Moses	3	1	2		
Gardiner, ——	1	2	4		
Gurney, Eliab	1	3	3		
Townsend, Robert	1	1	1		
Grant, Richard	3	1	3		
Woodman, Jona	4	3	5		
Curtis, Joshua	1	1	3		
Tolbart, Saml	1				
Byram, Jona	1		4		
Dunham, Amaziah	1	2	1		
Tolbart, Ambros	1				
Woodworth, James	1	1	3		
Woodworth, James	1		1		
Pinkham, Elijah	2	1	4		
Pinkham, Stephen	1	1	5		
Sole, Jona	1	1	2		
Burbank, John	1	2	1		
Chapman, Mary	1		2		
Merril, Susanna	1	1	4		
Griffen, Jona	1	2	3		
Griffen, Saml	2	3	6		
Bailey, Seth	1	2	1		
White, Jacob	2	3	4		
Sawyer, Benja	2	2	6		
Dennison David, Jr	1	2	3		
Dennison, George	1	2	2		
Gorden (Widow)			2		
Dillenham, Melatiah	1	1	2		
Stockbridge, John	1	3	1		
Edes, Joseph	1	2	2		
Edes, Gideon	1	2	2		
Duglas, Job	1	4	3		
Merrill, John	1	2	2		
Silvester, Bester	1	2	2		
Rogers, James	1		2		
Johnson, Revd Alfred	1	2	2		
Townsend, Beley	1	3	2		
Dillenham, Saml	3	1	4		
Bartlett, George	1	2	6		
Porter, Seward	4	6	4		
Kimbal, Peter S.	2	3	2		
Curtis, Stephen	1	2	2		
Bartlet, John	1	4	3		
Bartlet, Willm	2	2	7		
Carvar, Reuben	1		1		
Carver, Seth	1		1		
Sole, Moses	3	1	3		
Griffen, Ephraim	1		1		
Griffen, Seth	1	1	8		
Mitchel, Abraham	1	4	2		
Weston, Nathan	1	1	3		
Mitchel, Joshua	1	2	3		
Mitchel, John	1	1	2		
Cumings, Josiah	1		1		
Millet, Thos	1	1	2		
Read, John	1	3	1		
Read, Josiah	1	1	3		
Carver, Amos	1	1	6		
Sole John	1		2		

FREEPORT TOWN—con.

Name of head of family.	Free white males of 16 years and upward, including heads of families.	Free white males under 16 years.	Free white females, including heads of families.	All other free persons.	Slaves.
Wilson, David	1		4		
Doughty, David	1	1	6		
Tory, Elisha	1	1	2		
Stockbridge, Joseph	1	1	3		
Winslow, John	1	1	1		
Porter, Benja	1		3		
Cummins, Abram	1	1	2		
Sole, John	2	5	2		
Mitchel, Abram	1	4	8		
Griffen, Ephraim	4	2	2		
Tolbart, Ambros	2	1	2		
Tolbart, Trecott	1		1		
Sherman, Margaret	1	1	4		
Parker, Benja	1	1	2		
Carver, Calvan	1	2	2		
Lowe, Willm	2		2		
Curtis, Ezra	2	1	9		
Welch, Thos	2	1	4		
Pratt, David	2	5	4		
Cromwell, Joshua	1	2	5		
Coffin, Stephen	2	6	4		
Fitts, John	2	1	2		
Welch, Molley			1		
West, Peleg	2	1	4		
Mitchel, Danl	1	1	4		
Mitchel, Joseph, Junr	4	1	2		
Holbrook Silas	1	2	4		
Brown, Willm	2	3	3		
Grant, John	2	1	2		
Crocker, James	5	1	3		
Fogg, Benja	1	3	4		
Fogg, Benaiah	2		2		
Penley, Joseph	1	1	1		
Fogg, Saml	1	1	2		
Cushing, James	2	2	2		
Staples, Joseph	3	3	3		
Stockbridge, Michael	1	3	1		
Thoil, Jeremiah	2	3	4		
Alden, Nathl	1	1	2		
Sole, Saml	1		4		
Sole, Barnabas	1	3	3		
Chandler, Edmond	1		1		
Brown, Peter	1	2	3		
Winslow, Gilbart	1	1	1		
Sole, Cornelius	3	3	4		
Harvey, David	1	4	4		
Winslow, Saml	1	4	3		
Walker, Jeremiah	2				
Godard, Robert	1	4	3		
Todd, Willm	3	3	6		
Reid, Bartholomew	2	1	2		
Bran, Ebenezer	1		2		
Reid, Abram	1	1	6		
Knight, Jeremiah	1	1	2		
Winslow, Benja	1	2	2		
Brown, Reuben	1		5		
Nason, Jeremiah	2	3	5		
Harvey, Enoch	1	2	3		
Mann, Joseph	2	1	7		
Small, Edward	1	3	4		
Lovell, Josiah	1	5	1		
Roberts, George	1	1	3		
Grant, Saml	2	3	4		
White, Elias	1	1	1		
Lawrance, Willm	2	3	4		
Barber, Robert	1	4	3		
Tuttle, Libius	1	1	1		
Reid, Stephen	1		2		
McCormal, James	1		1		
Whitney, Barnibas	1		1		
Marston, Danl	1		3		
Whitney, Elias	1	1	3		
Johnson, Jesper	1		3		
Wench, Joseph	1	2	2		
Tuttle, Libius	1	3	2		
Godard, Silas	1	5	1		
Sawyer, James	1	3	4		

GORHAM AND SCARBOROUGH TOWNS.

Name of head of family.	Free white males of 16 years and upward, including heads of families.	Free white males under 16 years.	Free white females, including heads of families.	All other free persons.	Slaves.
Alden, Austin	1				
Alden, Josiah	1	4	4		
Adams, Joshua, Jr	1				
Adams, Benjn	4	1	2		
Akers, Moses	1	1	2		
Adams, Joshua	1	4	4		
Akers, John	1	1	3		
Ashley, Abner	1				
Andrews, Jona, Jr	1	3	5		
Andrews, Amos	3	4	5		
Andrews, Jona	2		2		
Andrews, Stepha	1	5	2		
Alden, Abiather	1				
Anderson, John	1				

CUMBERLAND COUNTY—Continued.

GORHAM AND SCARBOROUGH TOWNS—con.

NAME OF HEAD OF FAMILY.	Free white males of 16 years and upward, including heads of families.	Free white males under 16 years.	Free white females, including heads of families.	All other free persons.	Slaves.	NAME OF HEAD OF FAMILY.	Free white males of 16 years and upward, including heads of families.	Free white males under 16 years.	Free white females, including heads of families.	All other free persons.	Slaves.	NAME OF HEAD OF FAMILY.	Free white males of 16 years and upward, including heads of families.	Free white males under 16 years.	Free white females, including heads of families.	All other free persons.	Slaves.
Bolton, Wm, Jr	1		3	1		Davis, Saml	1	1	4			Gilkey, Jno	1		1		
Burnel, Jno	2	2	4			Dyer, John	2	2	3			Gammon, Moses	1	2	2		
Brown, Simeon	1	4	2			Davis, prince	3		3			Gilkey, Isaac	1				
Brown, Benja	2	2	6			Dyer, Wm	1					Green, Josiah	1				
Bacon, Nathl, Junr	1	3	5			Davis, Josiah	3	2	3			Greenlaw, John	1	2	1		
Bangs, Barns	2		2			Dan, Nathl	1	4	3			Gammon, Philip	1		1		
Bremhall, Sylvs	1	1	4			Dyer, John, Jr	1		1			Green, John	1	2	1		
Bangs, Herman	2	1	5			Dun, Christopr	1	1	3			Green, Jona	1	2	3		
Blake, Ithiel	3	3	5			Davis, John	1		2			Gray, Tabitha	2		2		
Blake, Nathl	1	5	4			Darling, Jno	1	3	2			Gustin, Thos	1		1		
Bracket, James	2		8			Davis, David	1	2	1			Grace, Jno	1	2	1		
Bangs, James	1	5	4			Dorset, Jereh	1					Grace, Wm	1		2		
Blake, Benja	1		2			Davis, Ebenr	3	1	1			Grace, Wm, Jr	1				
Bangs, Barns, Junr	1	2	4			Davis, prince, Junr	1					Gilford, Jno	1		3		
Bangs, Thos	2	1	5			Davis, Sylvs	1		1			Graffam, Josiah	2	2	4		
Blanchard, Jno	1	1	1			Dyer, Levi	1	1	4			Gilford, Jno, Jr	1	1	3		
Blake, Benja, Junr	1	2	1			Duggins, Mrs			2			Hanscomb, Moses	1		3		
Bishop, Enos	2		3			Dresser, John	1	1	1			Huston, Simon	3	2	4		
Bacon, Josiah	1		2			Dresser, Mindwell	3		3			Hamblin, Danl	1	2	5		
Bacon, Timy	1	1	1			Day, James	1		1			Hamblin, Timy	2	6	4		
Butler, John	1	1	3			Dresser, Wentworth	1					Haskel, John	1	1	4		
Bangs, Ebenr	1		1			Dresser, Mark	1	1	1			Hamblin, Prince	1		5		
Beverly, Farnham	1					Downing, Dennit	1					Hamblin, Jos	2	1	2		
Brimhall, Corns	1	1	2			Dearing, Isaac	4	1	4			Hicks, Leml	1	4	3		
Blake, Jno	1	1	4			Eldridge, Danl	1		4			Hunt, Ephm	2	2	5		
Bowman, Nathl	2		2			Edwards, Richd	2	3	4			Hamblin, Gershom	1	5	4		
Bolton, Thos	2	4	2			Elder, Saml	3	4	5			Harding, Martha	2	1	2		
Barton, Wm	1		3			Elder, Reuben	2		4			Hall, Ebenr	2	3	4		
Bacon, Nathl, Senr	1		2			Elder, Isaac	2	3	2			Harding, Zepha	1	3	4		
Brown, Luthur	1		2			Elwel, Jona	3	1	2			Hanscomb, George	3	1	2		
Bragdon, Jona	1	3	4			Emory, James	1	2	2			Hanscomb, Nathan	1	6	2		
Brown, Hon. Jno Josha	2	1	3			Edwards, Joshua	1	1	4			Hamblin, Ebenr	1	3	5		
Bragdon, Gideon	1		1			Edwards, Nathl, Jr	1	3	3			Hamblin, Saml, Jr	2	4	4		
Bragdon, Jno	1	2	1			Edwards, Nathl	1	2	5			Hamblin, Jacob	1	3	5		
Beals, Isaiah	1	1	3			Emmerson, Jos	1	3	5			Hamblin, George	1	6	4		
Bragdon, Solo	2	2	4			Edgcomb, Gideon	2	1	7			Harding, Seth	3		2		
Burnam, Aaron	3	5	7			Edgcomb, Robert	2	4	2			Hanscomb, Geo., Jr	1	1	6		
Boothby, Nathl	1	5	4			Farnham, Simeon	1	2	2			Higgin, Jos	2	4	5		
Burbank, Silas	3	1	4			Frost, Nathl	2	1	4			Hunt, Ichabod	1	3	2		
Burbank, David	1	1	1			Frost, Benja	1					Haskel, Jacob	1	1	2		
Burbank, Eleazer	1	1	1			Frost, David	3	4	5			Harding, Nichl	1	1	1		
Boothby, Joseph	2		3			Frost, Peter (Widow)		1	3			Hatch, Nathl	1	1	5		
Boothby, James	1		2			Frost, Enoch	1	1	3			Hatch, Asa	1	2	2		
Burnum, Solo	1	2	5			Freeman, Jona	3	1	3			Hatch, Ebenr	1				
Burnum, Thos (Widow)	1		3			Freeman, Nathl, Jr	1					Hamblin, Nathan					
Burnum, Robt	1	2	4			File, Ebenr	1	3	3			Harris, Stepn	1	2	3	1	
Burnum, Danl	3	1	3			Fogg, Seth	1	3	2			Hall, Abm	1		2		
Boothby, Richd	1		2			Fogg, Jereh	2	2	6			Hopson, Wm	1		2		
Bragdon (Widow)	1		1			Fogg, Joseph	2	4	1			Hamblin, Seth	1				
Crocket, Saml, Jr	1	5	4			File, Wm, Jr	1	1	2			Harding, Jno, Jr	1				
Crocket, Ephm	1	1	1			File, Saml	1	1	4		2	Hines, Richd	1	2	4		
Crocket, Palatiah	1	1	1			Freeman, Benja	1	1			2	Hodgsden, Jos	1		1		
Cates, Joseph	2	1	2			File, George	1		1			Harding, David, Senr	1		2		
Cobb, Elisha	4	1	3			Frost, Abm	1	2	3			Holmes, —	1		1		
Cobb, Andrew	3		4			Freeman, Nathl	2	1	7			Hasty, Wm	2	1	4		
Carsley, Jno	2	2	4			Fogg, Moses	1		2			Hasty, Nathl	1	3	3		
Crocket, Josha, Junr	3	2	4			Fenderson, Pelatiah	1	1	2			Higgin, Edmd	1	1	1		
Cates, Benja	1	4	3			Fitz, Obadiah	2		2			Hunniwel, Richd	1	1	2		
Crocket, Jona	1	3	5			Foss, Joseph	1					Hunniwel, Sarah	1		3		
Crocket, Peter	1	3	3			Fabin, Joshua	6	2	5			Hanscomb, Elisha	1				
Cobb, Jedediah	3	2	7			Foss, Wm	1		7			Hanscomb, Ketarah	1		2		
Chadburn, Silas	1	3	6			Fenderson, Nathl	2		2			Hanscomb, Humpy	1	1	3		
Chamberlain, Benja	1					Fenderson, Nathl, Jr	3	4	4			Hicks, prout Timy	1				
Cobb, Elisha, Jr	1					Fogg, Jona	2	6	4			Hunniwel, Roger	2		2		
Creasey, Joseph	3	4	3			Fogg, Seth	3	3	5			Hunniwel, Benja	1	4	4		
Cates, Ebenr	1					Foss, Peter	1	1	3			Holmes, Ephm	1		3		
Cotton, Ebenr	2	1	2			Fabin, John	2		3			Hodgsden, John	1	4	2		
Clemons, —	1		2			Foss, Saml, Senr	1	2	2			Harman, George	3	1	5		
Cloutman, Timy	2	5	2			Foss, Zechr	1		5			Hearne, Nichs	2	1	4		
Carsley, Jno, Jr	1		1			Fitz, Simeon	1	2	3			Holmes, Jno	3	1	3		
Crocket, Joshua, Jr	1	1				Fogg, James	3	2	3			Holms, Wm	2	2	3		
Coffin, Isaac	2	2	5			Fogg, Nelson	1		1			Harman, Wm	1		1	1	
Crocket, James	1	1	1			Foss, Saml, Junr	1	2	1			Harman, Elias	1	2	2		
Cates, Andrew	1	3	1			Fitz, Saml	1	1	2			Hains, Danl	2	2	4		
Caverno, Charles	1		1			Foss, Wm, Jr	1		2			Harman, Zechr	2	1	7		
Clark, Jacob	1					Foss, Uriah	1	3	2			Harman, Benja	1	2	5		
Clemons, Jeremiah	1	3	3			Fogg, Reuben	1		2		1	Harman, Eliza	2	2	2		
Cobb, Chitman	1		2			Fogg, Reuben, Jr	2	1	4			Harman, Jno	2	1	8		
Crocket, Joshua, Senr	1		1			Fogg, Wm	1	1	2			Hodgsden (Widow)		2	4		
Chadburn, James	1	1	1			Foss, Danl	1		2			Harman, James, Jr	1	2	4		
Crocket, Saml	1		1			Fogg, Moses	3	2	6			Harman, Saml	3	5	3	1	
Cotton, John	1	3	3			Foss, Abner	1					Hasty, Robt	2	3	6		
Cutler, Timo	1		1			Fogg, Hannah (Ww)	1		2			Harman, Jona	1	2	4		
Chadwick, Benja	2		5			Fogg, Aaron	1	1	2			Harman, Moses	1	2	3		
Colebroth, George	2	3	3			Ficket, Vincent	1	2	1			Harman, Jas	2		1		
Colebroth, Jos	1	1	2			Gorham, Wm	2	1	3		2	Harford, Solo	1	3	7		
Colebroth, Saml	1	1	3			Gammon, Jos	2	2	4			Harman, Abner	1	1	4		
Carter, Benja	1					Gilkey, James	1		1			Harman, Joseph	1	2	4		
Carter, Benja, Jr	2	3	5			Gilkey, Jos	2	4	6			Hoit, George	2	1	2		
Carter, Richd	1	3	1			Green, Thos	1	1	2			Haines, Timy	2		1		
Collins, Jona	1	2	4			Gammon, Jos., Jr	1										
Carl, Saml	1	3	4			Gammon, Danl, Jr	1	3	2								
Carl, Ebenr	1	1	3			Gammon, Jona	1		3								
Colebroth, Danl	1	2	3			Gammon, Benja	1		3								
Carl, Ebenr	1	2	4														

FIRST CENSUS OF THE UNITED STATES.

CUMBERLAND COUNTY—Continued.

GORHAM AND SCARBOROUGH TOWNS—con.

NAME OF HEAD OF FAMILY.	Free white males of 16 years and upward, including heads of families.	Free white males under 16 years.	Free white females, including heads of families.	All other free persons.	Slaves.
Hunniwel, Zerubbael	1	1	5		
Higgins, Edmd	3	2	4		
Irish, James	2	1	2		
Irish, Thos	3		6		
Jones, Henry	1		2		
Irish, James, Jr	2	1	5		
Irish, Stepn	2	2	6		
Jordan, Benja	1	4	7		
Irish, Isaac	1	1	2		
Jones, Joseph	1	2	1		
Johnson, Jno	2	1	4		
Johnson, Robt	1		2		
Johnson, Matthew	1		1		
Johnson, Ephm	1				
Jenkins, Josiah	1		4		
Jenkins, Saml	2	1	4		
Jordan, Moses	1		5		
Jewett, Caleb	2	2	4		
Johnson, Stepn	1	2	5		
Jones, Saml	1	1	1		
Jones, Wm, Junr	1				
Jones, Wm	1		2		
Jones, Stepn	1				
Jones, James	1	1	2		
Jones, Js, Jr	1		1		
Jones, Wm, 3d	1	1	2		
Jordan, Benja	1	4	6		
Jose, Nathl	2	2	4		
Jose, Wm	1	3	4		
Jackson, Robt				5	
Jordan, Leml	1	3	4		
Jackson, Reuben				2	
Keniard, Thos	1				
Knights, Nathl	1		2		
Kemp, Ebenr	1	2	5		
Knights, Joseph	2	3	2		
Kirkwood, Alexr	2		2		
Killum, Ivory	1	2	2	1	
Kelly, Chrisr	2	2	3		
King, Mary			4	1	
King, Richard	1	1	1	1	
King, Willm	1				
Kelly, Peter	1	2	4		
Lewis, George	3	2	5	2	
Lombard, Richd	3	2	3		
Libby, Edwd	1		1		
Longfellow, Stepn	2	2	5		
Lombard, Solo	1	2	3		
Lombard, Calvin	2	2	4		
Libby, Simeon	1	2	3		
Libby, Joseph	2		3		
Larry, Stepn	2	1	2		
Lombard, Butler	1		3		
Lombard, Nathl	1	1	5		
Lamb, John	1	3	1		
Lombard, Jno, Jr	2	3	3		
Libby, Reuben	1	4	3		
Libby, Leml	1	2	5		
Lakeman, Wm	1		2		
Lombard, Jno	1		1		
Lakeman, Josiah	2	2			
Libby, Reuben, Jr	1		2		
Libby, Jno	1		2		
Libby, Allison	1	3	2		
Lombard, Joseph	2		3		
Libby, Wm	1	1	2		
Libby, Mark	1	1	2		
Libby, Jethro	2		2		
Lombard, Thos	1	2	1		
Libby, Edmd	1		2		
Libby, Richd	1	1	1		
Libby, Matthew	2	2	3		
Libby, Mark	1	1	4		
Libby, Jona	2	3	3		
Libby, Nathl	2	3	3		
Libby, Robt	1	1	2		
Libby, Josiah	3	2	5		
Libby, Anthy	3	1	3	1	
Libby, Simon	1	1	7		
Libby, Thos	2	3	4		
Larrabee, Benja	2	2	3		
Larrabee, Thos	1		1		
Libby, Danl	2	4	4		
Libby, Dominicus	1	3	3		
Larrabee, Nathl	2	1	6		
Libby, Seth	1	1	6		
Libby, Stepn	4	4	3		
Libby, Abner	1	1	1		
Libby, Josiah	1	4	3		
Libby, Elisha	1	1	5		
Libby, Benja	1	1	1		
Libby, Hezekiah	1		3		
Libby, Nathan	1		1		
Libby, John	1		1	1	
Libby, Jethro	2	1	4		

GORHAM AND SCARBOROUGH TOWNS—con.

NAME OF HEAD OF FAMILY.	Free white males of 16 years and upward, including heads of families.	Free white males under 16 years.	Free white females, including heads of families.	All other free persons.	Slaves.
Libby, Cps	1				
Libby, Allison	2	3	3		
Libby, Edwd	1				
Libby, Joshua	3		4		
Libby, Matthias	1		3		
Libby, Saml	1	2	2		
Libby, Ichabod	2	3	2		
Libby, James	1		1		
Libby, Hanson	1		3		
Larrabee, Stepn	2	2	1		
Larrabee, Philip	1	3	6		
Libby, Phins	1	1	3		
Libby, Ebenr	2	1	4		
Lowel, Lydia	1		3		
Libby, Amos	1				
Libby, Skilling Jno	1	1	2		
Libby, David	1		2		
Lancaster, Revd	1	2	4		
Lovet, Abm	3	2	4		
Lovet, Richd	1	1	4		
Lovet, Joseph	1	3	1		
Libby, Richd	2	3	3	1	
Libby, Roger	2	2	3		
Libby, H. Richd	1	2	5		
Libby, Eliakim	1	1	3		
Libby, Peter	1	4	3		
Larrabee, Wm	4		3		
Libby, Theos	2	2	5		
Libby, Jereh	1	2	5		
Libby, Neheh	2	2	6		
Libby, Theos, Junr	1	3	2		
Libby, R. Hubd	1	2	2	1	
Libby, Isaac	1				
Libby, Enoch	3		2		
Libby, Zebulon	1	2	4		
Larrabee, Wm, Junr	1		1		
Letherbe, Tom					7
McLellan, Thos	2	3	4	1	
McLellan, Wm	2		2	1	
Mosher, Js	2	2	4		
Murch, John	3		3		
Murch, Walter	3	1	3		
Murch, Ebenr	2	3	4		
McLellan, Js	2	2	3		
Miller, Jno	2	2	4		
McDusle, David	1		2		
McCullister, Js	4	1	7		
McDonald, Jos	1	4	1		
Murray, Anthy	1	4	5		
Morton, James	1	2	3		
Morton, Jabez	1	2	6		
Mann, Daniel	1				
Morton, Ebenr, Jr	1	2	5		
McDonald, Pelatiah	1	3	2		
McLellan, Wm, Jr	1		2	5	
Murch, Ebenr, Jr	1		2		
Murch, Saml	1		4		
Mains, Nichs	3	1	3		
Morton, David	1	3	3		
McLellan, Cary	1	3	4		
Murch, James	1	3	2		
McGuilly, Jno	1	2	2		
Moody, Joseph	2	2	4		
Murch, Matthias	1	1	3		
Morton, Thos	1	1	3		
McDonald, Abner	1	1			
Morton, Isaac	1				
Moody, Robt	1				
Mosher, Jas, Jr	1				
Murch, Jeremiah	1	1	1		
Murch, Joseph	1				
Morse, —— (Clothier)	2	2	1		
Murch, Isaac	1				
Mains, David	1				
Morton, Reuben	1				
Murray, Anthy, Jr	1	1	1		
Morton, Bryant	1		3		
Merril, Daniel	1	5	4		
Melvil, Jno	1	1	5		
McLellan (old Mrs.)			1	2	
Merril, Danl	1	5	4		
Mitchel, Job	2	1	4		
Moody (Widow)	1		4		
Mitchel, Jereh	1				
Marr, Danl	1		1		
Marr, Lydia		1	3		
Marr, James	1				
Mitchel, Wm	1	1	2		
McKenny, Moses	1	2	7		
McKenny, James	3	2	3		
Meserve, Elisha	1		4		
Meserve, Elisha, Jr	1				
Matthews, Jno	1	3	3		
Morris, Dennis	3	1	4		
Meserve, Solo	1	2	4		

GORHAM AND SCARBOROUGH TOWNS—con.

NAME OF HEAD OF FAMILY.	Free white males of 16 years and upward, including heads of families.	Free white males under 16 years.	Free white females, including heads of families.	All other free persons.	Slaves.
Meserve, Gideon	1	4	4		
March, Saml	3		4		
Myrick, Isaac	2	4	5		
Marshall, Isaac	2		1		
Marshall, Wm	1				
Moody, Mary	1	1	4		
Meserve, Danl, Senr	1		1		
Moses, Danl	1		5		
Morris, Chs	2	2	6		
Matthews, John	1	3	3		
McLellan, Jno	1		2		
McKenny, Margt			1		
McDonald, Timy, Jr	2	2	5		
McDonald, Timy, Sr	1	1	1		
McKenny, Eliza			3		
McKenny, Saml	1	4	4		
Millikan, Leml	2	2	5		
Moulton, Jona, 3d	1	1	1		
Millikan, John	3	1	5		
Millikan, Saml	1	3	1		
Millikan, Jos	2	2	7		
Millikan, Isaih	1	1	2		
Millikan, M. John	3	2	5		
Millikan, Wm	2	1	3		
Merril, Danl	2	1	4		
Merril, Levi	1	3	2		
Merril, Bradley	1	2	4		
McKenny, Robt	1	1	2		
McKenny, Robt, Jr	1	3	3		
Moulton, Danl	3		4		
Moulton, Jno	2	3	3		
Moulton, Danl, Jr	3				
Moulton, Charles	2	4	5		
Moulton, Jos	2	1	3		
Moulton, Jona, Jr	2	2	3		
Moulton, Saml	1				
Moulton, Jona	2		4		
Millikan, Edwd	2	1	3		
Millikan, Joshua	1	3	4		
Millikan, Benjn	2	2	3		
Millikan, Jona	3	3	4		
Millikan, Thos	2		4		
McLaulan, Robt	2	3	8		
Mains, Thos	1		1		
McLaulan, Wm	2	2	6		
Meserve, George	2	2	3		
Meserve, John	3	1	3		
Meserve, Wm	2		4		
Moses, George	2	1	3		
Moses, Nathl	1	1	4		
Millikan, Polly			1		
Moses, George	1		1		1
Meserve, Thos	1	1	3		
Meserve, Eliza	1	1	2		
Marston, Leml	2	5	3		
McKenny, Abner	1	1	3		
Meservy, Clement	3	4	3		
Maxwell, Willm	1	1	5		
Morris, Charles	2	3	7		
Nason, Uriah	2	3	3		
Newcomb, Enos	1	1	4		
Nason, Ephm	1	1	5		
Nason, Abm	1				
Nason, Wm	1				
Newcomb, Saml	1		1		
Newbegin, Jno	1				
Neil, John	1	3	2		
Phinny, Edmd	3		3		
Phinny, Jno	2	1	3		
Phinny, Jas	3	3	3		
Pain, Richd	1	4	3		
Pain, Wm	2	1	5		
Pain, Jno	2	2	4		
Phinny, Decker	2	3	4		
Patrick, Charles	2	5	5		
Phinny, Jos	1	5	4		
Phinny, Edmd, Junr	1	3	3		
Pain, Thos	2	2	4		
Plummer, Aaron	1	2	6		
Phinny, Jno, Jr	1	1	3		
Phinny, Ebenr	1	2	2		
Plummer, Isaac	1		1		
Parsons, Jona	1				
Phinny, Js, Jr	1				
Patrick, Benja	1				
Prentiss, Saml	5	2	6		
Plummer, Christr	1		4		
Poland, Moses	2		1		
Phinny, Stepn	1		3		
Perkins, John	1	3	3		
Peabody, Saml	2	1	2		
Perkins, John	1		3		
Parker, Hannah (Widw)		1	4		
Parker, Johns (Widow)		3	3		
Plummer, Moses	1		3		

CUMBERLAND COUNTY—Continued.

GORHAM AND SCARBOROUGH TOWNS—con.

NAME OF HEAD OF FAMILY.	Free white males of 16 years and upward, including heads of families.	Free white males under 16 years.	Free white females, including heads of families.	All other free persons.	Slaves.
Plummer, Saml	1	4	6		
Plummer, Jesse	1	6	3		
Prout, Joseph	3		2		
Prout, John	1				
Plummer, Jereh	2	4	4		
Perry, Corns	2	2	3		
Plummer, Saml, Jr	1				
Plaisted, Andrew	1		3		
Pilsberry, Jos	1	1	2		
Pilsberry, Jona	1	1	1		
Rich, Amos	2	3	5		
Ross, Alexr	1		2		
Roberts, Jos	1	2	4		
Roberts, Benja	3	2	5		
Rand, Jereh	2	1	3		
Roberts, Jos., Jr	1	2	4		
Ross, James	1		3		
Roff (Widow)		2	3		
Roberts, —	3	2	5		
Rice, James	1	1	3		
Rindse, Jotham	2	1	4		
Rand, Philemon	2		4		
Robison, Jas	1	1	3		
Rice, Matthias	1	3	2		
Runnels, Chs	1				
Richards, Saml	1	2	3		
Richards, Joseph	1	1	2		
Richards, Jos. (Dumb)	1	1	1		
Richards, Jos., Jr	1	1	3		
Rice, Mehitable		1	2		
Rice, Richd	1	2	4		
Rice, Gideon	1	3	4		
Rice, Leml	1	4	2		
Rice, Saml	2	3	4		
Skillings, Benja	2		3		
Sylly, John	1	1	2		
Stuart, Joseph	1	2	4		
Strout, George	1	1	2		
Stephens, Nathl	3	2	1		
Skilling, Jno	1	1	2		
Skilling, Thos	2	4	2		
Stephens, Joseph	1	2	2		
Snow, Thos	2	2	2		
Stevens, A. Hovey	2				
Snow, Wm	1	2	3		
Sawyer, Joel	1		6		
Strout, Elisha	1	2	5		
Sturgis, Jona	2	5	4		
Swett, Stepn	1	2	5		
Swett, Josiah	2	1	1		
Smith, Ephm	2	2	4		
Smith, Hezekiah	1	1	2		
Stone, Jona	1	3	2		
Stephens, Benjn, Jr	1	3	2		
Stimpson, Alexr	1	2	3		
Stuart, Wentworth	1				
Sawyer, Zechr	2	4	2		
Stephens, Benja	1		1		
Snow, Gideon	1	1	1		
Smith, Saml	1	1	2		
Sawyer, Stepn	1		3		
Sanborn, Mrs.			1		
Swett, Moses	1		2		
Stevens, Mary			1		
Starbord (Widow)			1		
Sawyer, Jno	1	5	2		
Skillings, Simeon	1	6	4		
Small, Saml	1		2		
Small, James	1	3	3		
Sevy, Nathl	3	2	4		
Sevy, Ebenr, Jr	1	2	1		
Steward, Jno	1		1		
Steward, Saml	1		6		
Steward, Timo	1	3	2		
Sevy, Ebenr	1		3		
Sevy, Reuben	1	3	2		
Sevy, Thos, Jr	1	2	4		
Sevy, Thos	3	3	4		
Smith, Rachel			3		
Steward, Jno, Jr	3		6		
Shute, George	1	1	3		
Steward, Joseph	3	3	6		
Shute, Js	2	1	3		
Stone, Solo	3	3	3		
Staple, Jere	2	3	6		
Sawyer, David	1		1		
Southgate, Robt	3	1	8		
Staples, Saml	2	2	6		
Staples, Saml, Jr	1				
Shute, Wm	1	2	2		
Shute, Hannah	1		1		
Smith, Josiah	1		5		
Snow, Paul	1	1	2		
Swicher, Wm	1	2	1		
Sevy, David	1	1	1		

GORHAM AND SCARBOROUGH TOWNS—con.

NAME OF HEAD OF FAMILY.	Free white males of 16 years and upward, including heads of families.	Free white males under 16 years.	Free white females, including heads of families.	All other free persons.	Slaves.
Smith, Peter		1	1	3	
Shepherd, Lewis				6	
Thatcher, Josiah	3	2	3		
Thomas, Saml	1	4	3		
Thomas, Charles		1	3		
Thomas, Turf	1	1	1		
Tyng, Wm	3	1	5	1	
Tole, Jereh	1				
Thomas, Geo	1	4	4		
Tryon (Widow)		2	2		
Thomas, Thos	1		2		
Tomson, Wm	2		2		
Tyler, Abm	2	4	2		
Tyler, Abm Jr	2		4		
Tyler, Abm, 3d	1	1	1		
Tomson, Jno & Thos	3	1	2		
Thurston, Thos	1	4	3		
Tomson, Paul	2	4	2		
Whitney, Abel	2	1	4		
Whitney, Amos	2	1	3		
Waterhouse, George	1	3	4		
Whitney, Joseph	3	3	6		
Whitney, Phinehas	2	2	4		
Whitney, Uriel	1		3		
Watson, Danl	2		2		
Whitmore, Saml	2	2	6		
Wood, Wm	2		4		
Whitney, Zebulon	2	3	5		
Watson, Ebenr	2	4	4		
Warren, Jas	1	4	3		
Whitney, Danl	1	3	3		
Watts, David	1	3	3		
Whitney, Asa	1	3	5		
Whitney, Isaac	1	6	4		
Williams, Jereh	1	2	5		
Ward, Joseph	3		1		
Warren, Saml	1	2	3		
Ward, John	2	4	4		
Whitney, Nathl	1		1		
Webb, Eli	2	2	4		
Weeks, Wm (Widw)		2	1		
Whitney, Micah	1	2	4		
Whitney, Jotham	1				
Watson, Elipht	1	1	1		
Whitney, Moses	2	3	3		
Weston, Joseph	1	1	2		
Warren, Nathl	2	1	3		
Wescot, Reuben	2	3	2		
Williams, Hart	2		2		
Webb, Edward	1	1	2		
Wood, Charles	1	1	2		
Watson, John	2	3	7		
Whitney, Jas	1	3	1		
Whitney, Priscilla			4		
Whitmore, Wm	1	2	6		
Whitmore, Danl	1	2	2		
Waterman, Malchr	1		3		
Weymouth, Cathr		2	4		
Wakefield, Jos	1	1	2		
Weeks, Wm (Widw)		2	1		
Weeks, Benjn	1		1		
Wescot, Wm	3		5		
Wescot, Zebulon	1				
Wescot, Richd	2	2	2		
Watson, Jno	1	3	2		
Wilber, Jno, Jr	1	2	4		
Warren, Walter	1		3		
Waterhouse, Jos	1		1		
Waterhouse, Nathl	1	4	6		
Waterhouse, Timy	2	4	3		
Waterhouse, Saml	2	2	2		
Waterhouse, Jno	1	2	4		
Waterhouse, Theos	1	4	1		
Warren, Benjn	3	3	6		
Wingate, Jona	1		1		
Wingate, Jona, Jr	1	1	1		
Watson, Jona	2	1	3		
Witten, Thos	1	1	1		
Wilbert, John	1	3	4		
Webster (Widow)			2		
Vickery, David	2	1	5		
Young, Joseph, Senr	1		1		
Young, Joseph, Jr	2	2	3		
Berry, Willm	1	2	3		
Burnam, Danl, Jr, (Widw)		1	2		
Berry, Benjn	2	3	5		
Berry, Jno	1	2	3		
Berry, Jona	2		5		
Berry, Solo	2	3	4		
Bryant, Jno	2	3	4		
Bryant, Eleazer	1	2	5		
Berry, Elisha, Jr	1	1	5		
Banks, Moses	3	1	2		
Banks, Bracy	1	1	1		

GORHAM AND SCARBOROUGH TOWNS—con.

NAME OF HEAD OF FAMILY.	Free white males of 16 years and upward, including heads of families.	Free white males under 16 years.	Free white females, including heads of families.	All other free persons.	Slaves.
Burnum, Jona	1		2		
Babb, Thos	2	1	3		
Beal, Simeon	2		3		
Berry, Josiah	1		2		
Berry, Ephm	1				
Berry, Enoch	1		1		
Brown, Ellison	1	1	2		
Berry, Richard	1	3	2		
Berry, Zebulon	1		3		
Berry, David	1				
Berry, Timy	1		2		
Rand, Christopher	1	3	4		
McIntosh, William	1	2	4		

GRAY TOWN.

NAME OF HEAD OF FAMILY.	Free white males of 16 years and upward, including heads of families.	Free white males under 16 years.	Free white females, including heads of families.	All other free persons.	Slaves.
Moss, Mark	1		2		
Greely, William	1	1	3		
Sprage, John	2	4	4		
Moss, John	3	2	5		
Delano, Ameziah	1	3	2		
White, Thomas	1	2	1		
Libby, Benjamin	1	1	4		
Austin, Stephen	1	3	4		
Jackson, Francis	1	3	4		
Libby, Andrew	4	1	2		
Libby, Moses	1	2	1		
Davis, William	1		5		
Dutton, Sarah		1	3		
Frank, James	1	2	3		
Fogg, Timothy	2		2		
Libby, Asa	1		1		
Libby, Arther	1	1	2		
Humphrey, Oliver	1	1	1		
Libby, Asa	1		4		
Foster, Isaac	2		2		
Moss, Nathan	2	2	2		
Jorden, David	1	4	1		
Doubty, George	1	4	7		
Stevens, Joel	1	2	3		
Stowel, Samuel	3	3	4		
Pearly, Samuel	3	2	4		
Jorden, Elijah	1	1	6		
Nights, Josiah	1	1	3		
Cummings, Isaac	1	2			
Young, Nathaniel	1		1		
Young, Abraham	1	2	2		
Lunt, John	1	3	1		
Coley, James	3	2	3		
Stevens, Jonathan	1	1	1		
Small, James	4	3	3		
Nash, John	2	1	2		
Haney, Daniel	5		4		
Merrel, Nathan	2	2	2		
Weeks, Joseph	5	2	5		
Russel, James	3	2	3		
Merrel, Joseph	1	2	4		
Swicker, Richard	1	1	5		
Fowler, John	1	2	4		
Matthews, Jabez	4	4	8		
Ford, Nathaniel	1	2	3		
Sole, Asa	1	1	3		
Webster, William	8	3	4		
Latham, George	1		1		
Soaper, Salter	3	2	4		
Latham, Eliab	2	2	2		
York, Robert	1	3	4		
Cummings, Joseph	3	3	5		
Humphreys, James	2	3	11		
Frank, Thomas	1	2	3		
Cummings, Daniel	3	1	4		
Dolley, John	3		2		
Libby, Joseph	1		1		
Doubty, Joseph	1		5		
Young, John	1	1	3		
Young, Job	1	2	6		
Libby, Daniel	3	1	8		
Libby, Joel	1	1	3		
Hayden, Jeremiah	1		1		
Nash, Samuel	1	3	4		
Twitchel, Jeremiah	1		1		
Thompson, Samuel	3	1	5		
Ramsdel, Gideon	2	4	5		
Buker, Israel H	1	3	5		
Libby, William	1	1	3		
Hunt, David	3	2	3		
Cooley, Richard	1		2		
Moss, Levi	1		3		
Merrel, John	1	1	2		
Pennel, Clemuel	1		3		
Starberd, Jethro	1	3	3		
Dyer, Jedediah	1				
Small, Isaac	1	5	6		
Moody, Daniel	1	3	2		
Barber, Lucy		1	2		

CUMBERLAND COUNTY—Continued.

GRAY TOWN—con. / HARPSWELL TOWN

NAME OF HEAD OF FAMILY.	Free white males of 16 years and upward, including heads of families.	Free white males under 16 years.	Free white females, including heads of families.	All other free persons.	Slaves.
GRAY TOWN—con.					
Cobb, Jedediah	2	1	6		
Merrel, Abel	1		4		
Berry, Pellatiah	1	2	2		
Pennel, Joseph	1	3	4		
Nason, Isaac	3	1	6		
Fletcher, Zachariah	2		3		
Nash, David	1	3	5		
Merrel, John	2		2		
Libby, Andrew	1	2	4		
HARPSWELL TOWN.					
Allen, Ephraim	3	1	4		
Clark, Josiah	2		2		
Clark, John	1	1	4		
Allen, Elisabeth			2		
Allen, Elisha	1		2		
Allexander, Hugh	1	4	3		
Allexander, Jane	1		3		
Merriman, Thomas	4		2		
Alexander, David	2	2	5		
Booker, Josiah	1	3	3		
Curtes, Ezekiel	4	2	4		
Childs, John	1	1	3		
Dunning, Andw	1	1	3		
Dunning, Benja	4		3		
Stackpole, John	1	3	5		
Doil, James	1	1	4		
Ewing, Joseph	2		3		
Ewing, Alexander	2		4		
Ewing, Joseph, Junr	1	2	3		
Ewing, James	1	2	4		
Springet, Nathl	1		1		
Snow, Isaac	3	1	4		
Snow, Willm	1		1		
Merril, Henry	1	4	4		
Snow, John	2	2	3		
Snow, Aaron	1	1	1		
Snow, Abizah	1		2		
Birthright, Peter	2	1	2		
Carr, Joseph	2	1	1		
Simscott, Joseph	1		1		
Simscott, Moses	1	2	2		
Snow, Saml	2		2		
Snow, John	2	2	3		
Dingley, Levi	1	2	3		
Small, Taylor	1	1	2		
Thompson, John	1		3		
Small, Mark	1	2	4		
Holbrook, John	2		2		
Matthews, John	1	2	2		
Purnton, Stephen	3	1	5		
Obins, Philip	2	2	4		
Easman, Nathl	2	1	3		
Hopkins, Simeon	2		3		
Ridley, Mark	1	4	3		
Jones, John Stephen	1	2	3		
Bankins, John	2		2		
Williams, Saml	1	1	2		
Otis, Saml	1	2	2		
Williams, Benja	1	1	2		
Thompson, Willm	2	1	7		
Easman, Kingsbury	3	2	5		
Ridley, James	1		2		
Snow, Isaac	1	4	3		
Totman, Joseph	1	1	1		
Cooms, Anthony	3	3	5		
Cooms, Joseph	1	2	7		
Doughty, James	1		1		
Whaling, Patrick	2		2		
Blake, Jacob	1		6		
Toothaker, Joanna	1	1	2		
Randal, Paul	2	1	4		
Thomas, James	1		3		
Stovar, Johnson	2	5	5		
Curtes, Paul	1	4	5		
Webber, David	3	3	4		
Stover, John	1		4		
Clever Harrison	1		4		
Randal, Daniel	2	3	3		
Johnson, James	1		3		
Curtes, Michl	2	6	3		
Bibber, Lemuel	2	4	3		
Haskel, Ward	1	3	2		
Haskel, Ruth			3		
Toothaker, Seth	1	1	3		
Pinkham, Ebenz	2	1	2		
Haskel, Willm	1		6		
Pinkham, Nathl	1	3	4		
Haskel, Willebe	1		2		
Johnson, Jacob	3		3		
Johnson, Jona	1	2	4		
Johnson, David	1	4	2		
Weber, Daniel	3	3	4		
Bibber, James	1	4	4		

HARPSWELL TOWN—con.

NAME OF HEAD OF FAMILY.	Free white males of 16 years and upward, including heads of families.	Free white males under 16 years.	Free white females, including heads of families.	All other free persons.	Slaves.
Bailey, Jacob	1	3	3		
Webber, Mary	1		2		
Atherton, Jona	1	5	3		
Booker, James	1		6		
Curtis, Caleb	1	2	4		
Curtes, Benja	1	1	2		
Curtes, Ambros	1	1	1		
Allen, Elijah	2	2	3		
Wheeller, David	1		1		
Buker, Daniel	1	1	3		
Duglas, Daniel	1	1	3		
Wheeler, David	1		1		
Eaton, Saml	2	1	2		
Farr, Thos	2	1	5		
Merriman, James	1	2	6		
Redock, John	2		7		
Stover, Alcot	2	5	4		
Easters, John	3	2	2		
Blake, John, Junr	1	2	5		
Duglas, Elijah	1	1	2		
Blake, John	5	3	4		
Orr, Clement	1	4	2		
Orr, John	1	3	4		
Sinnet, Michl	2		3	4	
Smith, John	1		2		2
Bishop, Luke	2		4		
Reid, John	2	2	2		
Butler, James	1	3	3		
Weare, Robert	1	4	3		
Sinnet, Stephen	1	1	3		
Gardiner, Seth	1	2	3		
Smith, Jeremiah	1	1	3		2
Alexander, Saml	2	1	6		
Wilson, Willm	1	2	8		
Allen, Elijah	1		2		
Wilson, David	1		2		
Bishop, Abner	1	1	2		
Curtes, Jacob	1	3	4		
Scofield, Clement	2	4	4		
Tinney, Seth	2		1		
Brown, John	1	3	1		
Jordan, John	1	3	1		
Martin, Matthias	1	1	2		
Booker, Joseph	2		5		
Goodridge, Jewett	1		2		
Nelson, Thos	1	1	3		
Wilson, James	2	3	4		
Alexander, Willm	2	1	2		
Doile, Elijah	1	3	2		
Merriman, Walter	3	3	6		
Silvester, Willm	3		4		2
Jordan, John	2	1	4		
Doile, Elisha	1		1		
Dyer, James	2		3		
Curtes, Nehemiah	2	1	2		1
Curtes, Mercy	1	1	3		
Merriman, Walter	1	1	2		
Merriman, Michl	1	2	2		
Gardiner, James	1		3		
Town, Willm	2	3	3		
Merriman, Hugh	2	2	4		
Merriman, Timo	1	2	1		
Scofield, Stephen	1	1	3		
Browner, John	1	2	2		
Gardiner, Luther	1	2	5		
Wilson, Alexander	1		1		
Ward, Nehemiah	2		2		
Cooms, Willm	1	1	2		
Holbrook, Jona	2	2	5		
Haynes, David	1	3	3		
Leavitt, Naphthali	1	5	3		
Anderson, Daniel	1	1	4		
Cooms, John	1	3	2		
Finney, Seth	1	1	6		
Brown, Daniel	1	2	6		
Small, Saml	1	2	4		
Totman, Josiah	1	2	3		
Dinslow, Benja	1	3	3		
Snow, Hannah			3		
Totman, Henry	1	3	2		
Ridley, Mark	1		1		
Hersey, Willm	1	1	2		
Toothaker, Ebenz	1	1	2		
Toothaker, Ebenz	1	1	4		
Toothaker, Nathl	1	1	3		
Ross, Thos	1		3		
Linscott, John	1	3	3		
Morse, Mary	1	1	2		
Purnton, Joshua	1	1	2		
Hall, Nathl	1		2		
Hall, Joseph	2	2	1		
Purnton, Joshua, Jur	1	4	3		
Hall, John	1		6		
Purnton, Robert	1	3	3		

NEW GLOUCESTER TOWN

NAME OF HEAD OF FAMILY.	Free white males of 16 years and upward, including heads of families.	Free white males under 16 years.	Free white females, including heads of families.	All other free persons.	Slaves.
Pierce, Samuel	2		3		
Baley, Robert	2		2		
Harris, John	1	4	3		
Yetton, James	1				
White, William	1	4	3		
Witham, Thomas	1	3	4		
Pierce, Joseph	1		3		
Merrell, Joshua	3	2	7		
Metguin, John	1	2	2		
Metguin, William	1				
Emmory, William	1	2	2		
Allen, Joseph	1	1	2		
Pierce, Joseph	1	1	3		
Witham, Thomas	1	3	2		
Gore, Joshua	2	5	6		
Witham, Jeremiah	3	4	5		
McIntire, David	2	2	5		
Titcomb, John	1	3	6		
Stinchfield, Ephraim	1		4		
Bennet, Isaac	1	2	2		
Stinchfield, John	3		3		
Penny, Thomas	2	4	4		
Honeyford, Robert	2	3	4		
Haskell, John	2	5	5		
Blake, James	3		3		
Bennet, Jonathan	3		8		
Bennet, Nathaniel	4	2	7		
Woodman, Joseph	1	1	5		
Tufts, John	1	1	7		
Rains, Joseph	1	4	5		
Forbush, Robert	3	1	3		
Woodman, David	3	1	1		
Nights, Phebe			2	4	
Haskel, Job	1		1		
Pierce, Joseph	2	1	4		
Irish, Willam	1	1	3		
Haskel, Jonathan L	1		2		
Smith, Josiah	4	3	4		
Harris, William	2	2	3		
Washborn, Stephen	3	3	3		
Harris, Simeon	1		3		
Parsons, William	1	1	5		
Hearsy, Elisabeth	1		3		
Stinchfield, James	1	4	3		
Stevens, Paul	1		3		
Winslow, Barnabas	2	2	7		
Foxcroft, Samuel	3		5		
Allen, Nathaniel C	3	1	4		
Arnold, Bildad	1	1	3		
Allen, James	1	2	6		
Ayers, Thomas	2	2	6		
Allen, Nehemiah	2	1	2		
Allen, Isaac	1		2		
Atwood, Solomon	1	3	4		
Bradberry, Jabes	2	3	2		
Bridgham, William	1	3	4		
Bradberry, Benjamin	2	3	4		
Baley, John	1	2	2		
Bryant, Balden	1		3		
Chandler, Peleg	5	1	6		
Collins, Ebenezer	3	1	4		
Davis, Ebenezer	3		5		
Dyer, Lemuel	1		1		
Day, Zebedee	1		3		
Bishop, James	1	1	3		
Bradford, Ephraim	1		4		
Bennet, Francis	1	5	3		
Campbell, Andrew	3		3		
Cushman, Jabes	2	1	6	1	
Bradberry, Samuel	1	3	2		
Bradberry, Moses	1		3		
Cotton, Adam	2		5		
Davis, Abel	1	2	4		
Evelith, Nathaniel	3	4	3		
Collins, Philemon	1				
Cobb, Joseph	1		4		
Chandler, Philip	1		2		
Fogg, Enoch	1	3	3		
Graffam, Mary			4		
Glass, Ezekiel	1	1	2		
Haskell, Jacob	2		5		
Grover, William	1		2		
Soames, Jonathan	1		1		
Black, Boston				5	
Philip, Eliphus	1		3		
Nevus, Samuel	1	4	1		
Haskell, Mary			5		
Ryall, Eli	1		2		
Haskell, Nathaniel	2	4	5		
Gerrish, Joseph	1	2	1		
Sergeant, Daniel	1	1	2		
Paul, David	1	1	1		
Taxbox, Samuel	1	1	4		
Woodberry, Joseph	1	1	4		
Royal, Eli	1	1	3		

CUMBERLAND COUNTY—Continued.

NEW GLOUCESTER TOWN—con.

NAME OF HEAD OF FAMILY	Free white males of 16 years and upward, including heads of families	Free white males under 16 years	Free white females, including heads of families	All other free persons	Slaves
Bradberry, William	2	3	4		
Cleaves, Ebenezer	1	1	3		
McGuire, John	1	2	3		
Stinchfield, John	2	1	3		
Haskell, John	2	4	8		
Ingersol, Nathaniel	1	2	3		
Low, Nicholis	1	4	4		
Lane, Ebenezer	1	1	4		
McQuin, Edmund	1		2		
Mastin, Robert		1	2		
Morgan, John	1	1	1		
Noyes, Simeon	2		3		
Parsons, Isaac	3	2	8		
Rearson, Luke	3	4	5		
Stevens, Paul	1		2		
Stinchfield, Mary	1	5	4		
Tufts, John	1	1	7		
Tucker, William	1	2	5		
Toal, Micael	2		4		
Witham, Benjamin	1	1	1		
Washborn, Stephen	3	1	4		
Davis, Sarah			1		
Bartlett, Josiah	1	3	5		
Bartlett, Malchi	3		1		
Emmory, Mark	1		2		
Buxton, Samuel	1	2	1		
Allen, Nehemiah	1	6	2		
Bennet, Nathaniel	1	1	1		
Welch, Joseph	1	2	2		
Cotton, Adam	2	3	5		
Cleaves, Ebenezer	1	1	1		
Cleaves, Edmund	2	2	4		
Cobb, Silvenus	1	2	4		
Evelith, Nathaniel	1	1	1		
Evelith, Isaac	1		3		
Fogg, Samuel	2	2	4		
Fogg, Edmund	1	4	4		
Mason, Ebenezer	1	5	4		
Merrel, Peeter	1	2	4		
Loring, Asa	1				
Lane, Benjamin	2	1	3		
Loring, Bezeliel	3	3	3		
Haskel, Moses	1		3		
Haskel, Benjamin	1	1	2		
Groce, Isaac	1		2		
Glover, John	2	1	3		
Forbush, John	1		4		
Honeyford, Robert B	3	3	4		
Haskell, Moses	4	1	4		
Hutcherson, William	1	1	6		
Hammon, Samuel	1		4		
Hatch, Fisher	1	3	1		
Haskell, Gideon	1	3	2		
Lane, Ebenezer	1	1	4		
Lukes, Elkany	1		6		
Lukes, Ebenezer	1		3		
Loring, Ezekiel	3		2		
Morgan, Luke	2	1	4		
Merrell, Elias	2	4	5		
Merrell, Moses	1	3	4		
Merrell, Samuel	1	1			
Haskell, Joel	2	2	2		
Haskell, Nathan	2	6	6		
Harthaway, Seth	1	3	2		
Hayes, John	1	3	1		
Merrell, John	4	2	6		
Merrell, Ezekiel	3		4		
Nellson, David	1	1	2		
Parsons, William	1	1	5		
Prince, John	3	1	3		
Row, Jonathan	2	1	4		
Webber, Micael	1	2	3		
Whorfe, Joseph	1	3	4		
Walker, James	1	2	1		
Tylor, Joseph	1	2	3		
Shaw, Benjamin	1	2	3		
Hall, William	1		2		
Ramsdel, Kimball	1		2		
Wells, Simeon	1	3	4		
White, William	1	3	2		
Parsons, Edward	3	4	3		
Penny, Thomas	2	4	4		
Pierson, Samuel	2		1		
Widgery, William	1	2	2		
Walker, Micael	3	5	3		
Robertson, Solomon	1		3		
Parsons, Moses	1		3		
Row, William	2	3	5		
Row, Zebedee	1	1	4		
Stevens, Nathaniel	4		3		
Sawyer, John	1	2	3		
Sawyer, Parker	1	1	3		
Tylor, John	3	3	7		
Tucker, Lemuel	4	1	3		
Smith, Jonah	3	2	3		

NEW GLOUCESTER TOWN—con.

NAME OF HEAD OF FAMILY	Free white males of 16 years and upward, including heads of families	Free white males under 16 years	Free white females, including heads of families	All other free persons	Slaves
Toby, Richard	3	2	8		
Toby, Page	1	2	3		
Trew, William	1	2	6		
Trew, Jabes	2	4	5		
Ryder, James	1		2		
Raymond, Lemuel	1		3		
Pierce, Abraham	1	2	3		
Forbush, Samuel	1		2		
Woodman, Joseph	2	1	6		
Webber, John	1		2		
Woodman, John	2	3	4		
Stinchfield, John	1		3		
Hearsy, Elisabeth		1	5		
Haskell, Eliphalet	2	4	5		
Herrin, Robert	1	4	3		
Haskell, William	1	4	4		
Lane, Ebenezer	1	3	4		

NORTH YARMOUTH TOWN.

NAME OF HEAD OF FAMILY	Free white males of 16 years and upward, including heads of families	Free white males under 16 years	Free white females, including heads of families	All other free persons	Slaves
Davis, Timothy	3		3		
Davis, Thomas	1		1		
Davis, John	1	3	5		
Lawrence, John	1	4	2		
Parker, Saml	1	2	6		
Chandler, Joshua	1	2	2		
Worthley, Daniel	1	1	4		
Parker, Joseph	1	2	1		
Mitchel, Horton	1	4	2		
Ross, Isaac	1	1	3		
White, Abel	1		1		
Winslow, Benja	1	2	2		
Worthley, Saml	1		1		
Seberey, Saml	3	4	4		
Moore, Joanna	1		3		
Mitchel, Saml	1	1	2		
Mitchel, Benja	1	5	3		
Sebry, Elizabeth	1	2	3		
Mitchel, Mehitable	1		3	1	
Tusk, Lemuel	2	4	3		
Elwel, Pain	2	4	4		
Elwel, Henry	1	2	4		
Elwel, Pain, Junr	1	1	1		
Russel, Hannah	1	1	4		
Cutter, Saml	4	1	4		
Mitchel, Seth	2	2	5		
Humphry, Ebenez	1	3	2		
Foster, Nathl	1		3		
Batcheldor, Peter	2	2	2		
Bysom, Oliver	2	6	1		
Prat, Sherebiah	3	3	6		
Sargeant, Willm	1		1		
Blaisdel, Jeremiah	1	2	6		
Mitchel, Willm	1	2	2		
White, Luther	1		1		
Thompson, Saml	1	1	4		
Humphrys, Joseph	1	3	2		
True, John	1	2	3		
Young, Joseph	4		7		
Perry, Ezra	1	2	2		
Ross, Peter	1				
Videto, Comfort	1	1	2		
Brown, Joseph	1	2	2	5	
Corless, Ebenezer	2	1	1		
Lowe, Solomon	1	1	4		
Johnson, David	1	1	3		
Loring, Saml	1		1		
Loring, Richmond	1				
Hix, Joseph	3	3	7		
Mitchel, Jona	3	2	2		
Marston, Levi	1	1	3		
Rider, James	2	2	2		
Johnson, Thos	1	1	1		
Marston, Simeon	1		3		
Chandler, Cona	1	3	4		
Jones, David	1	2	6		
Hatch, Abijah	3	1	3		
True, Hannah			2		
True, David	1		2		
Ludon, Joseph	2	3	7		
Brown, Jacob	1		2		
Brown, John	1	2	3		
Noyes, Nathl	1	2	3		
Weare, Elijah	1		3		
Videto (Widow)			1		
Latherby, Saml	1	1	6		
Fellows, Saml	1	1	2		
Field, James	1	3	4		
Mitchel, Solomon	4		6		
Winslow, Else			2		
Woodward, Davis	1		6		
Wortley, John	2	3	2		
Ryal, Winthrop	3		3		
Lewis, John	3		1		

NORTH YARMOUTH TOWN—con.

NAME OF HEAD OF FAMILY	Free white males of 16 years and upward, including heads of families	Free white males under 16 years	Free white females, including heads of families	All other free persons	Slaves
Mitchel, Daniel	1	4	2		
Lewis, Asa	1		2		
Brown, Moses	2		1		
True, Willm	2	3	3		
Brown, Ephraim	1	1	2		
Weare, Peter	1	1	5		
True, Jona	1		2		
Brown, Joseph	1	2	3		
Brown, Jacob, Junr	1		4		
Videto, Joseph	1	1	2		
Humphry, Benja	2	2	2		
Staple, Daniel	2		3		
Hobbs, Willm	1	3	2		
Moxy, Mercy	1	2	7		
Tuttle, Burrel	1	3	2		
Mitchel, David	1	2	3		
Mitchel, Loring	1	2	1		
Drinkwater, David	1	5	3		
Mitchel, Jona	4	1	4		
Currey, Mehitable	1	1	2		
Melcher, Ammi	4	3	2		
Loring, Ance		1	4		
Dinsmore, John	1		2		
Young, Joseph	4		7		
Sark, Polly			1		
Gilman, Revd Tristram	3	3	5		
Gorden, Nathl	2	1	3		
Sanborn, Benja	3	4	3		
Sanborn, Paul, Junr	1	2	5		
Buxton, Willm	2	1	4		
Titcomb, Edmund	5	1	3		
Titcomb, Joseph	2	1	5		
Switcher, Seth	4	1	4		
Blanchard, Bezaiah	1				
Blanchard, Nathl	4		3		
Switzer, John	3		3		
Merril, Nathan	2	1	2		
Prince, Thomas	1	2	5		5
Switzer, Benja	1	1	2		
Noyes, Moses	3	2	3		
Noyes, Zebulon	1		1		
Noyes, Willm	1		3		
Stubs, Jona	1	1	4		
Harris, Amos	3	1	3		
Merril, Sarah	1	1	2		
Thorn, Ebenezer	1	1	2		
True, Israel	2	4	6		
Drinkwater, Silvanus	2	4	5		
Stubs, Richd	1	4	3		
Stubs, Benja	1	3	4		
Stubs, Jera	1	3	5		
Spear, Joshua	1	2	2		
Allen, Ebenezer	1	2	2		
Stubs, Moses	1	1	2		
Reid, Willm	1	2	5		
Wyman, Josiah	1	2	4		
Weeks, Nathl	2	3	2		
Sawyer, Benja	5	1	3		
Clough, Amos	2	3	2		
Maxwell, Robert	1	1	1		
Drinkwater, Saml	1	2	7		
Tuttle, Elijah	1		2		
Sawyer, John	1		1		
Guerney, Lemuel	2		1		
Prince, James	2	3	7		
Blanchard, Ebenezer	1	2	3		
Lowel, Stephen	2	1	4		
Blanchard, Nathl	1	1	4		
Prince, David	1	6	2		
Shaw, Daniel	1		1		
Shaw, Joseph	1		1		
King, Eliab	1	4	2		
Hobbs, Josiah	1	1	1		
Allen, Jacob	1	1	2		
Hill, Thomas	2	1	2		
Field, Zachariah	1		2		
Harris, Amos	1		2		
Blanchard, Hozea	3	4	4		
Buxton, Benja	2	4	5		
Prat, Thomas	1	3	4		
Wyman, Willm	1	1	1		
Prince, Paul	1	3	5		
Black, John	1	1	2		
Skillens, Isaac	2		1	1	
Goodwin, John	1		3		
Bracket, Jeremiah	1	3	3		
Leighton, Andw	2	2	2		
Ridout, Willm	2	2	1		
Ridout, Nicholas	1		3		
Gurney, Lemuel, Junr	1	1	2		
Cleaver, Willm	1		2		
Reed, Zebulon	1		2		
Knight, Enoch	1	3	2		
Small, John	1	1	3		
Martin, Willm	3	3	7	1	

CUMBERLAND COUNTY—Continued.

NORTH YARMOUTH TOWN—con.

NAME OF HEAD OF FAMILY.	Free white males of 16 years and upward, including heads of families.	Free white males under 16 years.	Free white females, including heads of families.	All other free persons.	Slaves.
Dilleno, Ezekiel	3		9		
Prince, Paul	2		2		
Prince, Ammi	1		1		
Sturdivant, John	1				
Sturdivant, David	2	3	4		
Blanchard, Nath¹	5		3		
Drinkwater, Dan¹	1	4	2		
Prince, Pyan	1	1	2		
Blanchard, John	3	3	2		
Maugridge, Benjᵃ	1	1	2		
Fisher, Joseph	1		2		
Farrow, John	1		3		
Farrow, Nathan	1	1	3		
Seales, Elizabeth	2		4		
Loring, Solomon	1	2	5		
Greely, Eliphalet	3	5	3		
Prince, Cushing	1	3	5		
Fisher, Onesiphorus	1	2	4		
Blanchard, Joshua	2	2	5		
Blanchard, Seth	1	5	2		
Loring, Richmond	3	2	3		
Mason, Sam¹	2	3	4		
Moore, Edmond	1	2	3		
Kimbal, Nath¹	1	2	2		
Drinkwater, John	1	2	2		
Loring, Mary	1		2	1	
Prince, John	1	3	1		
Chase, Humphry	1	4	6		
Whitehouse, Zadock	2		8		
Chase, Willᵐ	1		1		
Parker, Benjᵃ	2	1	4		
Parker, James	2		3		
Mirach, Willᵐ	1	1	1		
Molton, Elizabeth	2		3		
Webster, John	1	2	6		
Gardner, Elisha	1	1	2		
Haze, John	3	3	4		
Buckman, Willᵐ	1	3	7		
Drinkwater, Joseph	3	1	4		
Hill, Kiah	1	4	3		
Hamilton, Roland	2	1	5		
Weeks, Willᵐ	2		1		
Shaw, Benjᵃ	1	2	2		
Carman, Francis	3	1	6		
Hill, Eleazer	1	1	3		
Greely, Stephen	1	3	3		
Hammond, Peter	2	3	5		
Eaton, Obadiah	2		3		
Trough, Solomon	4	1	3		
Haze, Amos	1	1	2		
Gray, Joseph	3	4	5		
Bates, Edsel	2	3	5		
Bennett, Nath¹	2	1	5		
Gray, Andrew	2	2	9		
Pattinger, Arthur	2	1	3		
Gray, Jabiah		1	2		
Miller, Mary			2		
Drinkwater, Perris	1	2	2		
Robin, Thaddeus	1	1	2		
Gray, John	2	2	3		
Drinkwater, John	1	2	7		
Barnwell, Edward	1	2	4		
Prince, Elizabeth	1	1	3		
Pettee, James	1	4	5		
Chandler, Elisabeth	1	2	4		
Southworth, John	1	1	7		
Gooch, John	3	2	5		
Gooch, Benjᵃ	1		2		
Gooch, Nath¹	1	3	3		
Russel, Thoˢ Chandler	2	2	9		
Lawrence, Sam¹	1	2	1		
Brown, Dan¹	1	3	1		
Mitchel, Jonathan, Jr	2	1	2		
Safford, Nathan	1	2	2		
Gipson, Thoˢ	4	3	4		
Cutler, John	1		2		
Mitchel, Jacob, Jr	1	2	1		
Storer, Matthias	2	2	5		
Stubs, Sam¹	1	3	5		
Colyer, Joshua	1		1		
Byram, Theoˢ	1		1		
Mills, Alexander	1		3		
Biles, Charles	1		3		
Merrill, Sam¹	2	1	2		
Merrill, Sam¹, Junʳ	1	1	2		
Merrill, Nath¹	1		1		
Wood, Bethuel	2		7		
Loring, John	1	2	3		
Baker, Sam¹	3		6		
Milekin, John	3		4		
Besto, Joseph	1	1	2		
Hammond, Sam¹	1		7		
Barton, Winthrop	2	3	3		
Barton, Ammy	1		2		
Ring, Eleazer	2	3	3		

NORTH YARMOUTH TOWN—con.

NAME OF HEAD OF FAMILY.	Free white males of 16 years and upward, including heads of families.	Free white males under 16 years.	Free white females, including heads of families.	All other free persons.	Slaves.
Chandler, David	1	2	4		
Wait, Daniel	1	1	3		
Chandler, Rufus	1		2		
Oaks, John	1	3	3		
Prince, Thoˢ	2	2	3		
Loring, Levi	2	6	3		
Ring, Andʷ	1	2	2		
York, Sam¹	4	1	6		
Cushman, Isaiah	1	1	5		
Switcher, Willᵐ	2	3	3		
Lowing, Thoˢ	2	3	3		
Haze, Jacob	1	2	4		
Hamilton, John	3	1	6		
Hammond, John	1		1		
Baker, Sam¹	1	2	4		
Johnson, Nathan	2	2	4		
Prince, Stephen	1	3	2		
Simpson, Thoˢ	1	4	5		
Baker, Sam¹, Junʳ	1		2		
True, Winthrop	2	1	1		
Harris, Stephen	2	3	4		
Skillens, Josiah	1	3	5		
Libbey, Reuben	1	2	2		
Porter, Nehemiah	1	1	4		
Hamilton, Willᵐ	1		4		
Lufkin, Nath¹	1	4	3		
Porter, Nehemiah	1		3		
Marston, Jesper	1	1	4		
Marston, John	3	4	6		
Marston, Joshua	2		2		
Allen, Job	1	1	3		
Chandler, David	1	2	2		
Wait, Dan¹	1	1	3		
Chandler, Rufus	1		2		
Sele, Jessa	1	3	2		
Ricker, Wintworth	1	2	4		
Webber, Jonᵃ	1	3	2		
Sawyer, Solomon	1	1	3		
Sawyer, Solomon, Jur	1	1	5		
Hamilton, John	2		1		
Hamilton, Ambros	2	4	7		
Johnson, James	1	3	3		

OTISFIELD PLANTATION.

NAME OF HEAD OF FAMILY.	Free white males of 16 years and upward, including heads of families.	Free white males under 16 years.	Free white females, including heads of families.	All other free persons.	Slaves.
Pierce, George	2		2		
Bartlett, Eleazer	3	1	3		
Gammon, William	1	3	4		
Thurston, Thomas	3		2		
Thurston, David	1		1		
Knight, Mark	4	1	2		
Knight, Jonathan	1	1	2		
Spurr, Joseph	3	1	3		
Spurr, Enoch	1		2		
Hancock, Joseph	2	1	5		
Patch, Benjamin	1	1	4		
Kneeland, David	2	3	2		
Gammon, David	1	3	3		
Pray, David	2		4		
Cobb, Daniel	1	4	3		
Moss, Joseph	2	2	3		
White, Joseph	4	1	5		
Edward, Nathaniel	1	2	4		
White, Joseph	1	2	2		
Reed, Mary	1	1	4		
Gammon, Samuel	1	3	3		
Brition, Jonathan	1		1		
Turner, Elisha	3	2	2		
Harnock, Elias	2				
Knight, Zebulon	2	1	4		
Bride, John	1	1	2		
Cates, Joseph	2	2	5		
Haskell, Catharine	2	1	3		
Green, Benjamin	1	4	3		
Mores, Jonathan	2	3	3		
Mayberry, Thomas	1	1	5		
Mayberry, David	1	1	4		

PLANTATION NO. 4.

NAME OF HEAD OF FAMILY.	Free white males of 16 years and upward, including heads of families.	Free white males under 16 years.	Free white females, including heads of families.	All other free persons.	Slaves.
Jackson, Levi	1	1	4		
Twichel, Moses	1	3	4		
Jackson, Lemuel	2		1		
Jackson, Isaac	1	2	5		
Jackson, Lemuel, Jnʳ	1	4	2		
Staples, Daniel	1	1	2		
Cushman, Caleb	1	2	3		
Jackson, Barnabas	1	2	2		
Nelson, Nathan	1	1	3		
Rawson, Ebenezer	1		1		
Whitney, Clark	1				
Barrows, Malaga	1	2	2		
Dean, Edmund	1	2	2		
Andrews, David	3	1	1		

PLANTATION NO. 4—continued.

NAME OF HEAD OF FAMILY.	Free white males of 16 years and upward, including heads of families.	Free white males under 16 years.	Free white females, including heads of families.	All other free persons.	Slaves.
Hubbard, Levi	1	2	1		
Warren, Abijah	1		2		
Gray, John	1		1		
Pratt, Luther	1		1		
Fewell, John	2	2	2		
Young, Nath¹	1	1	3		
Smith, Josiah	1		2		
Hammond, Benjᵃ, Jnʳ	1	2	3		
Chesley, David	1	2	3		
Dean, Jacob	1				
Stowel, Elias	1				
Stowel, Nath¹	1				
Fuller, Aaron	1	2	2		
Bisby, Ruben	1	1	2		
Cole, John	1				
Bray, Ezekiel	1				
Gardiner, Nath¹	1		3		
Dureld, Sam¹	1				
Billings, John	1				
Gorham, David	1				
Bessee, Thoˢ	1				
Knight, Daniel	1	3	3		
Pratt, Nath¹	1	1	1		
Wightman, Robert	1	1	3		
Sturdivant, Frances	2	3	3		
Sturdivant, Asa	1	1	2		
Dunham, Asa	1	1	3		
Bessee, John	1	2	5		
Baker, James	1	1	2		
Rerce, Nathan	1	4	2		
Perry, Joseph	1	1	2		
Ricket, John	2	2	5		
Ricket, Isaac	1	1	1		
Botster, Isaac	2	4	1		
Whitney, Dan¹	1		2		
Morse, James	1		3		
Hall, Jonᵃ	1	1	4		
Hall, Abijah	1	1	1		
Haskel, Nath¹	1	1	1		
Robinson, Stephen	1				
Stowel, Daniel	1	1	2		
Stowel, Willᵐ	1	2	2		
Dwella, Allen	1	3	3		
Briggs, Seth	1	3	3		
Cummins, Elisha	1	3	4		
Morse, Seth	1	1	1		
Buck, Peter	1	3	3		
Hubbard, Reuben	1		2		
Stevens, Thoˢ	1	2	2		
Cole, Eleazer	1	2	6		
Smith, Merodick	2				
Swift, Joseph	1	2	1		
Swan, William	1		1		
Gardiner, Sam¹	1	1	2		
Gardiner, Willᵐ	1	1	1		
Shirtliff, Jonᵃ	2				
Shirtliff, Jonᵃ, Jr	1	2	2		
Barrows, Asa	1	2	3		
Washburn, Jacob	1	3	4		
Duval, Peter	1	1	3		
Bryant, Soloman	3	2	3		
Brooks, Peter	1	1	2		
Daniels, John	2	5	4		

PORTLAND TOWN.

NAME OF HEAD OF FAMILY.	Free white males of 16 years and upward, including heads of families.	Free white males under 16 years.	Free white females, including heads of families.	All other free persons.	Slaves.
Smith, Thomas	1	2			
Dean, Samuel	4		3	1	
Stephenson, John	2	4	5		
Thorlo, John	2	5	7		
Cammet, Dudley	3	2	5		
Jorden, James	3	2	6		
Wheeler, Mary	1		2		
Crosby, Lydia	1	1	8		
Rice, Lettice			1		
Mumford, Samuel	2	2	3		
Haynes, Matthias	1	1	6		
Waite, Benjamin	1	1	3		
Weeks, Joseph	3	3	6		
Weeks, Lemuel	3	5	5		
Ramsy, John	1	2	2		
Hall, Moses	2		5		
Cobb, William	1	5	5		
Bradbury, Jacob	5	4	2		
Bradbury, Thomas	3	3	4		
Bradbury, Samuel	3	1	8		
Plummer, Moses	2		2		
Thomas, Stephen	1	2	2		
Ilsly, Enoch	2	2	4	1	
Williams, Joseph	2	1	2		
Cumings, Thomas	2		7		
Fox, John	4	3	6		
Deering, Nathaniel	2	3	6		
Sanford, Thomas	3	2	7		

CUMBERLAND COUNTY—Continued.

PORTLAND TOWN—con.

NAME OF HEAD OF FAMILY.	Free white males of 16 years and upward, including heads of families.	Free white males under 16 years.	Free white females, including heads of families.	All other free persons.	Slaves.
Harden, Stephen	1	4	3		
Cox, Lemuel	2		4		
Stout, William	1	1	4		
Starberd, Ebenezer	1	2	3		
Knights, John	1		2		
Childs, Mary		1	6		
Mailen, John	1		4		
Winslow, Samuel	1	5	4		
Beeman, Abraham	1	1	2		
Jones, John	3	1	4		
Thombs, Joseph	1		1		
Thombs, Joseph	1		3		
Boynton, Theophilus	1	1	2		
Biggs, Josiah	1		2		
Pool, Abijah	2	2	3		
Moss, Eliphalet	1	1	1		
Moss, Eliphalet	1	2	2		
Price, Elisabeth		2	3		
Noyes, David	3		5		
Hood, James	1	4	4		
Baker, John	1	1	2		
Wyley, James	1	1	1		
Berry, Jeremiah	3	2	6		
Newman, Thomas	3	1	4		
Thrasher, John	3	2	5		
Barret, James	2		3		
Brewster, William	1		1		
Gustin, Ebenezer	1	1	3		
Pennel, Matthew	1	2	4		
Moody, William	2	1	2		
Brazier, Sarah	1	1	5		
Brazier, Enoch	1	1	2		
Paine, Jonathan	2	1	7		
Cobb, Ebenezer	1		1		
Cluston, Alexander	1		1		
Pool, James	1	1	2		
Cobb, Smith	2	1	3		
Cobb, Enoch	1	3	1		
Knights, John	1	2	5		
Lowell, John	1	4	3		
Maston, Daniel	1	2	1		
Bootman, Broadstreet	1	2	3		
Sweetser, John	1		2		
Ross, David	1	5	2		
Ilsly, Joshua	1		1		
Tuckfield, Mary			2		
Waite, Thomas B	2	4	5		
Bryant, Samuel	2	1	2		
Berry, Thomas	1	6	3		
Wadsworth, Peleg	2	5	6	1	
Noyes, Moses	1	1	4		
Procter, Samuel	1		1		
Motley, William	1		3		
Nichols, Elisabeth			2		
Low, Benniah	1	1	4		
Rollins, Betheah	1	1	3		
Laroch, Thomas	1		1		
McLellan, Joseph	2	1	3		
McLellan, Hugh	4	1	5		
McLellan, Joseph	3	2	3		
McLellan, Stephen	1		2		
Tinney, Samuel	2	1	4		
Cohoon, Daniel	2		2		
Barton, Robert	4	1	5		
Preble, Ebenezer	3	2	3	1	
Preble, Mehitable	4		2	1	
Deering, James	1	1	3		
Deering, Elliot	1		4		
Mussy, Daniel	1	3	3		
Tukey, John	1	3	2		
Smith, David	6	1	4		
Ingraham, Joseph	1	3	4		
Tucker, Jonah	1	2	3		
Randall, Isaac	1				
Nichols, John	2	2	6		
Titcomb, Joseph	1	1	5		
Moody, Nathaniel	4		3		
Poland, Benjamin	2	4	4		
Toby, William	3	3	3		
Beck, Thomas	2	2	4		
Waite, Stephen	3	1	5		
Dean, Eliphalet	2	1	4		
Ingalls, Ephraim	2	1	4		
Dean, John	3	3	4		
Davis, Daniel	2	1	3		
Hardin, William	3	1			
Campbell, William	1				
Ilsly, Daniel	5	2	2		
Titcomb, Benjamin	2		4		
Stevens, Asa	1	1	5		
Woodman, Merry	4	2	2		
Hussy, Samuel	3	1	5		
Butts, Samuel	3	2	3		
Barber, Solomon	2	4	3		
Greeley, Elisabeth			2		

PORTLAND TOWN—con.

NAME OF HEAD OF FAMILY.	Free white males of 16 years and upward, including heads of families.	Free white males under 16 years.	Free white females, including heads of families.	All other free persons.	Slaves.
Robinson, Joshua	1	3	4		
Hassack, Charles	1	2	3		
Lunt, James	4	1	4		
Phillips, John	1	1	1		
Toby, Sarah	1		4		
Kenney, Thomas	2	2	2		
Shaw, Samuel	1		2		
Tukey, John	2		3		
Ingraham, William	1	2	1		
Tukey, William	1		1		
Googings, Samuel	1	1	2		
Haskel, Josiah	1	1	2		
Ilsley, Hosea	1		4		
Farrington, William	1		4		
Tukey, Hannah			1		
Cootman, Stephen	1	1	3		
Vezie, John	1	4	4		
Ayers, Jemime		3	3		
Burns, George	1	1	5		
Riggs, Joseph	1	1	3		
Freeman, Samuel	2	3	6		
Purington, William	4	2	7		
Swett, Jonathan	1	3	2		
Greenleaf, Amos	2	2	2		
Young, Abraham	2		3		
Jewett, Joseph	1	3	4		
Jewett, James	1	2	3		
Lowther, John	3	1	3		
Berry, Joshua	1	1	2		
Clap, Asa	3	1	1	1	
Atkins, Nathaniel	5	2	4		
Bryant, Jonathan	2	7	5		
Owens, James	1		5		
Pool, Thomas	1	1	3		
Bailey, Nathaniel	1	2	2		
Hore, Philip	1		1		
Stone, Benjamin	1	1	2		
Walker, Peeter	3	2	2		
Marble, Nancy	1		1		
Mussy, Daniel	1	3	3		
Motley, Alexander	1	2	3		
Starrot, David	1		1		
Emmons, John	1	1	3		
Leatherby, Benjamin	3		3		
Green, Daniel	1	3	5		
Green, William	2		2		
Drake, Robert	1		2		
Bracket, Joshua	1		2		
Lunt, Micael	1	4	3		
Vaughn, William	2		4		
Rutburgh, John	1		1	1	
Hagget, William	1	1	2		
Robinson, Thomas	7	3	8		
Smith, James	1	1	2	1	
Bracket, Joshua	2	1	2	1	
Green, Henry	1	1	1		
Molton, William	1	1	2		
Cook, John	1	1	4		
Barton, James	1	2	2		
Brackett, Thomas	1		4		
Waterhouse, Jacob	3	4	5		
Vezies, Jeremiah	3	1	3		
Knights, Benjamin	2	4	3		
Burnham, John	1	2	5		
Kent, John	1		2	2	
Scott, John	1	1	4		
Owens, Ebenezer	3	4	6		
Cushing, Apolos	1	1	2		
Rogers, Joshua	3	1	2		
Bester, Timothy	1		4		
Tukey, John	1		3		
Jenks, William	2	4	4		
Tukey, Stephen	1	2	5		
Snow, Ebenezer	1	2	4		
Bailey, James	1	3	3		
Pettengill, Daniel	1	3	4		
Goodwin, Samuel	2	3			
Brazier, Moses	1	1	4		
Barr, Alexander	2	2	5		
Stevens, Abraham	3	1	5		
Shattuck, Moses	1		2		
Warren, George	1	2	5		
Correy, James	1	1	2		
Webber, Samuel	1		3		
Bradbury, Wyman	1		2		
Storer, Woodberry	3	1	5		
Shattuck, Summers	1	2	4		
Lunt, Moses	1	2	6		
Day, George	1		2		
Waldo, Samuel	1	1	3		
Frazier, Alexander	2	1	2		
Codman, Richard	1	1	2		
Deering, Eunice	1	3	4		
Waite, John	5	4	5		
Erving, Shirley	2	1	4		

PORTLAND TOWN—con.

NAME OF HEAD OF FAMILY.	Free white males of 16 years and upward, including heads of families.	Free white males under 16 years.	Free white females, including heads of families.	All other free persons.	Slaves.
Hana, John	1		1		
Thompson, Thomas	1	1	1		
Moore, John	1				
Barber, Joseph	1	1	5		
Newell, Zachariah	1	1	1		
Knight, Robert	1	2	4		
McKensie, Mary		1	2		
Hilton, Isaac	3	1	2		
Weldridge, James	5		3		
Codman, Richard	3		5	1	
McLellan, Arthur	4	3	7		
Bradberry, Abigail			2		
Wyer, Daniel	1		2		
Riggs, Rebecca			2		
Cross, Nathaniel	2		2	1	
Thomas, Peeter	1	5	6		
Sawyer, Philip	1	1	1		
Clark, Elisabeth			1		
Clough, John	1	3	5		
Turner, Elisha	1		2		
Pervish, Adam	1		1		
Greenleaf, Joseph	1	1	2		
Childs, Rebecca	1				
Pierson, Samuel	1	4	2		
Hall, Stephen	1	4	2	1	
Higgins, Samuel	1	4	5		
Poge, Robert	1		2		
Pollard, Hezekiah	1		2		
Jones, James	1		4		
Dinsdell, Henry	3	1	4		
Cox, James	1		4		
Haite, John	1	3	2		
Goodwin, John	1	1	5		
Davis, Ebenezer	3	1	2		
Shaw, Nathaniel	1	1	4		
Sherman, Barnabas	2	2	2		
Bailey, Hudson	1	2	2		
Webb, Micael	1	1	5		
Lowell, Mary			1		
Kelley, Mary			2		
Hance, John	2	2	1		
Lunt, Job	1		3		
Majory, John	1		1		
Chamberlain, Aaron	1	4	2		
Gould, Joseph	1	4	4		
Marwick, Hugh	1	2	5		
Green, Casiah		2	3		
Coley, Noah	2		2		
Sawyer, Ezekiel	1		5		
Wiswall, Enoch	1	3	5		
Roff, Benjamin	1	3	5		
Broadstreet, Dudley	1		1		
Richardson, Edward	1		2		
Bryant, William	1	2			
Brackett, John	1		1		
Sawyer, James	1	1	2		
Sawyer, Samuel	1	1	4		
Plummer, Asa	2	1	5		
Dole, John	2	2	4		
Coffin, Nathaniel	1	3	8		
Hustin, Mary	1		2		
George, Daniel	1		1		
Moss, Nathaniel	1	3	3		
Tucker, Thomas	3	1	4		
Stover, Hannah	2	1	5		
Moss, Jonathan	2		2		
Baker, Josiah	2	3	4		
Thrasher, Sarah		1	1		
Cammet, Thomas	1	2	2		
Woodman, Sarah		1	2		
Rich, Zephaniah	1	4	2		
Oxnerd, Thomas	1	5	5		
Fosdick, Nathaniel	1	1	3		
Fosdick, Thomas	1	2	3		
Bradish, David	2	2	7		
Fernald, Peltiah	3	2	4		
Stodard, David	1		7		
Bagly, John	3		3		
Moody, Benjamin	2	1	2		
Chase, Francis	1	1	4		
Lowell, Abner	4	2	5		
Warren, Peeter	3	5	5		
Newman, Thomas	1		1		
Woodman, David	1		1		
Constable, James	1		4		
Sylvester, Joseph	3		1		
Pinkham, Daniel	1		2		
Cox, William	1	1	2		
Swan, John	1	1	3		
Cobham, Sarah			3		
Mitchell, Robert	1	2			
Pounder, William	1	1	2		
Hobby, John	2	1	4		
Hobby, William	1	3	2		
Frothingham, John	1	2	4		

CUMBERLAND COUNTY—Continued.

PORTLAND TOWN—continued.

NAME OF HEAD OF FAMILY.	Free white males of 16 years and upward, including heads of families.	Free white males under 16 years.	Free white females, including heads of families.	All other free persons.	Slaves.
Poor, Samuel	1	1	2		
Toby, Samuel	1	2	5		
Shaw, Josiah	1	2	4		
Patterson, John	1	2			
Chellis, Joseph	2	2	5		
Prior, James	1	4	1		
Brown, William	2	2	4		
Seymour, John	4	2	2		
Baker, John	1	1	3		
Fabree, Peeter	1	5	3		
Harn, Shadrick	3		4		
Bailey, Joseph	1		2		
Daily, Emour	1		3		
Motley, Thomas	5	6	6		
Stone, Hannah		2	3		
Bond, William	1	2	4	1	
Goodwin, Richard	2	2	3		
Broad, Ephraim	1		2		
Webster, Thomas	1	2	3		
Hopkins, Thomas	2	4	8		
Blasdell, Susanna	1	1	5		
Kimbal, Jeremiah	2	2	2		
Clemmons, Joseph	1	1	2		
Cross, Ralf	4	2	2		
McLellan, William	2	3	5		
Storer, Ebenezer	1	1	5		
Mussy, John	3	3	2		
Titcomb, Benjamin	2	1	3		
Leatherby, John	1	6	3		
Cole, John	1	1	1		
Cox, Sarah		1	2		
Crandall, Philip	1		2		
Aspinwall, Caleb	1	2	2		
Brazier, Daniel	1	1	2		
Wiswall, John	1	1	2		
Churchwell, Seth	1		1		
Fosdick, James	1	4	3		
Oxnerd, Edward	1	1	2		
Willson, Joseph	1	4	2		
Curtis, John	1	3	5		
Riggs, Daniel	1		1		
Bancroft, John	1				
Oneal, John	1				
Pettingal, Eliphalet	1		1		
Freman, Joshua	6	3	1	1	
Knights, Samuel	1	4	3		
Cammet, Paul	1	2	2		
Mumford, Daniel	1		2		
Trott, Benjamin	2	1	2		
Woodberry, Samuel	2	1	3		
Cushing, Ezekiel	1	3	2		
Cushing, Jeremiah	2	3	2		
Cushing, Mehitable			3		

RAYMONDTOWN PLANTATION.

NAME OF HEAD OF FAMILY.					
Dingley, Joseph	2	1	2		
West, Desper	2	1	7		
Leach, Mark	3	1	2		
Ring, Josiah	3		3		
Staples, Pertor	1	5	3		
Jackson, Henry	1	1	5		
Dingly, Samuel	2	3	2		
Jorden, James	1	1	2		
Jorden, Jonathan	1		4		
Welch, James	1	1	3		
Fowler, Moses	1		2		
Silvester, Zachariah	1	2	3		
Brackett, Daniel	1	1	5		
Whitney, Moses	2	1	4		
Gray, Lewis	1	3	3		
Mitchell, John	1	3	7		
Mann, Obediah	2	2	4		
Willbee, Thomas	1	1	2		
Tinney, Samuel	1	1	3		
Starbird, Moses	1	3	3		
Small, Daniel	1	2	1		
Small, George	3	3	4		
Small, James	1	1	1		
Jorden, Samuel	3	4	1		
Simonton, Jonathan	1	2	6		
Cash, John	2		5		
Smith, Benjamin	1	2	4		
Barton, Isaac	1	3	3		
Dyer, Ezekiel	1	2	1		
Crisp, Thomas	2	1	1		
Jorden, Roger	1	3	2		
Davis, John	3		5		
Davis, Gideon	1	2	5		
Davis, John	1	5	2		
Jordan, Hezekiah	1	2	2		
Small, Daniel	1	2	2		
Brown, Joseph	1	1	4		
Brown, Joshua	1	5	4		
Brown, Andrew	1	5	4		

RAYMONDTOWN PLANTATION—continued.

NAME OF HEAD OF FAMILY.					
Mayberry, Richard	2	1	3	2	
Jorden, Dominicus	3	2	7		
Lowell, Daney	1	2	2		
Sawyer, Jonathan	3	3	6		
Lomberde, John	1		4		
Jorden, Timothy	1		4		
Weston, James	1	1	2		
Edes, Thomas	1	1	2		
Spurr, William	1		2		
Beverly, David	3	1	1		
Rich, Ezekiel	5	3	6		
Anderson, Robert	1		1		
Greeley, John	2	2	5		

RUSFIELD GORE.

NAME OF HEAD OF FAMILY.					
Dicker, Willm	1	2	2		
Lasly, George	1	2	1		
Hobbs, Amos	1	1	3		
Stevens, Joseph	1	2	4		
Stevens, Jonas	3	2	6		
Stevens, Nathl	1	1	2		
Hobbs, Jeremiah	1	2	6		
Millet, John	1				
Witt, Benjn	1				
Lucus, Warren	1				
Perkins, Saml	1	2	1		
Ames, Saml	1		5		
Cowen, Thos	1	3	3		
Pike, John	1	1	2		
Pike, Dudley	1	3	3		
Twichel, Moses	1	2	4		
Parsons, John	1	1			
Parsons, Willm	1	2	3		
Herring, Benjn	1	2	3		
Noble, Nathan	1	2	2		

SHEPARDSFIELD PLANTATION.

NAME OF HEAD OF FAMILY.					
Western, John	2		1		
Randall, Seth	1	1	4		
Fuller, Barzilla	1		3		
Cushman, Isaac	1	1	3		
Bearce, Asa	4	1	3		
Whittemore, Isaac	1	1	4		
Greenwood, John	3	1	5		
Mireck, Bazaliel	2	2	2		
Cushman, Caleb	1	1	2		
Cushman, Sarah		1	1		
Bignal, John	4	1	3		
Churchill, Josiah	1		1		
Pratt, Thaddeus	1	2	3		
Parish, Samuel	1	1	2	1	
Churchill, Jabez	1	3	1		
Brigham, Saml	1		3		
Bearce, Gideon	2	1	3		
Keene, Joshua	3	1	6		
Keene, Snow	2		8		
Cox, Benjn	2	2	5		
Merrill, Jabesh	1	1	3		
Cobb, Pelatiah	1	3	4		
Benson, Elnathan	4	3	3		
Benson, Jepthah	1	1	3		
Roo, Zaccheus	1	3	4		
Drake, Ebenezer	1	2	2		
Drake, John	1	2	2		
Craft, Saml	1		2		
Packer, Edward	1		2		
Churchill, Willm	1	1	2		
Buckman, Danl	1	2	3		
Robinson, Elijah	6		4		
Dean, Abraham	1		3		
Dean, Zadock	1		1		
Sole, James	1	2	1		
Perkins, Joseph	1	2	3		
Thayer, Ruth		4	1		
Holmes, Job	3	1	1		
Richmond, Eliab	1	4	6		
Cordwell, John	3	1	4		
Cushman, Zebadiah	2	2	3		
Cushman, Job	2	2	7		
Fuller, Nathl	3	1	5		
Cushman, Joseph	1	1	2		
Bullings, Danl	1	1	2		
Heaton, Elijah	1	2	2		
Tucker, Lemuel	1	2	3		
Heaton, Richard	1	1	2		
Bartlet, Danl	1	1	2		
Bartlet, Asa	1		1		
Lucus, Elkanah	1	2	3		
Lucus, Elnathan	1	2	3		
Thomas, Holmes	1	3	4		
Holmes, Jona	1				
Holmes, James	1				

SHEPARDSFIELD PLANTATION—continued.

NAME OF HEAD OF FAMILY.					
Mason, Broadstreet	1	3	3		
Cushman, Gideon	1	4	4		
Packer, Reuben	2		3		
Packer, Ichabod	1	3	1		
Washburn, John	1	1	4		
Baker, Samuel	1	2	1		
LeBroke, James	1	2	2		
Barrows, Willm	2	3	5		
Barrows, Joseph	1		5		
Baker, Edmund	1				
Tobb, Jacob	1	3	3		
Glover, Robert	1	2	2		
Cary, Danl	1	2	3		
Lebarran, James	1	1	2		
Landers, Stephen	1				
Jordan, James	1		1		
Ryals, Danl	1	1	2		
Dudly, Nathan	1		4		
Pharis, James	1	3	2		
Fuller, Jesse	1	3	4		
Dunham, James	1	2	4		
Cane, Joshua, Jur	1	2	4		
Bearce, Asa, Jur	1		2		
Hill, Thos	1	1	3		
Curtis, Noah	1	3	2		
House, Moses	1	3	3		
Perkins, Ebenezer	1	1	2		
Wilborn, Robert	2	5	4		
Whitmore, Saml	1	2	2		
Bumpus, Morris	1	3	2		
Bumpus, Willm	1	3	2		
Bumpus, John	1		2		
Barrows, Ephraim	1	2	2		
Barrows, Benjn	2				
Barrows, Benjn, Jur	1		4		
Bumpus, Shubael	1	3	4		
Churchill, Joseph	1	1	2		
Curtis, Ashley	1	2	4		

STANDISH TOWN.

NAME OF HEAD OF FAMILY.					
Butterfield, Joseph	1	6	5		
Berry, Timothy	1	1	4		
Bolter, Nathl	2	1	3		
Bolter, Nathl, Jur	1		2		
Bolter, Benja	1		1		
Cram, Danl	4		2		
Cram, Danl, Jur	2	5	2		
Cummins, John	1	1	3		
Cummins, Willm	1	2	4		
Cummins, Thos	1	1	4		
Chase, Joseph	1	4	3		
Croxford, John	1	2	2		
Cookson, Reuben	2	3	7		
Camel, Phillp	4	2	5		
Dean, John	2	1	4		
Davis, James	1		6		
Dow, Jabez	1		2		
Dow, Joseph	1	3	2		
Dow, Abner	2	2	4		
Decker, John	1	2	4		
Eastman, Job	1	1	2		
Freeman, George	2	2	4		
Haskel, Benja	1	2	2		
Haskel, Jona	1				
Hasty, Danl	1	5	3		
Hasty, James	1	3	1	1	
Higgins, Ebenezer	1	2	5		
Higgins, Timothy	2	2	4		
Higgins, Robert	1		1		
Higgins, Willm	1				
Harmon, Danl	1	4	3		
Harmon, Willm	1		4		
Harmon, Elliot	1	1	1		
Hopkins, Theodore	3		2		
Hall, John	1	5	4		
Hall, Willm	1		2		
Hall, Charles	1	1	4		
How, Danl	3		2		
Jones, Ephraim	2	1	5		
Jones, Willm	2		2		
Jones, Ephraim, Jur	1	1	1		
Lowel, Danl	4	2	5		
Lowel, Jona	2	3	3		
Linnel, Enoch	2		5		
Linnel, Saml	1	1	2		
Libby, Isaac	1	3	2		
Moulton, Peter	3	2	3		
Mussey, Theodore	3		3		
Morcan, John	2	3	1		
Moody, James	2	3	5		
Moody, Joshua	1	1	1		
Mitchel, Dominicus	2	3	5		
Martin, Bryan	1	3	3		
McGill, John	2	2	2		

CUMBERLAND COUNTY—Continued.

NAME OF HEAD OF FAMILY.	Free white males of 16 years and upward, including heads of families.	Free white males under 16 years.	Free white females, including heads of families.	All other free persons.	Slaves.	NAME OF HEAD OF FAMILY.	Free white males of 16 years and upward, including heads of families.	Free white males under 16 years.	Free white females, including heads of families.	All other free persons.	Slaves.	NAME OF HEAD OF FAMILY.	Free white males of 16 years and upward, including heads of families.	Free white males under 16 years.	Free white females, including heads of families.	All other free persons.	Slaves.
STANDISH TOWN—con.						**TURNER TOWN—con.**						**WINDHAM TOWN—con.**					
Moses, Josiah	1	2	3			Briggs, Jotham	1		1			Dennis, Andrew	1		1		
Philbrick, Jonᵃ	2	1	4			Briggs, Jotham, Jnʳ	1	1	2			Mayberry, James	1	1	1		
Philbrick, Michael	2	1	3			Bradford, Ezekiel	1	2	2			Brown, Ezra	1	5	5		
Philbrick, Wᵐ	1	1	2			Bradford, Chandler	1	3	1			Millens, Robert	2		3		
Philbrick, Gideon	1					Elliot, Andrew	2	1	1			Millens, Thomas	1	1	1		
Parker, Aaron	1	1	3			Blake, Samuel	3	4	2			Stevens, Jonathan	1	3	6		
Pierce, John	1	1	2			Blake, Caleb	1					Barker, Thomas	2	1	4		
Pierce, Richard	1		2			Bradford, Jesse	2	3	1			Elder, William	4	2	2		
Paine, Joseph	3	5	5			Smith, Laban	1		1			Toler, Samuel	1	1	1		
Paine, Thoˢ	1	1	3			Smith, Josiah, Juʳ	1		1			Young, Martha	1	1	1		
Plaisted, John	1		1			Gilbert, Elijah	1	4	2			Chesley, Joseph	2	1	8		
Rockley, Chandler	2		3			Gilbert, Nathˡ	1	4	6			Little, Paul	2	3	3		
Rich, James	1	2	5			Jones, Benjamin	1	6	1			Brown, John	1	2	2		
Rich, Lemuel	4	4	3			Brown, John	1	1	2			Jelleson, John	1	3	4		
Row, Caleb	3		4			Merrill, Levi	1	4	4			Hooper, Joseph	1	2	3		
Row, Ephraim	2	2	2			Merrill, Jabesh	1	2	5			Purington, David	3	1	2		
Richardson, David	1	2	6			Phillips, Richard, Jr.	1	4	3			Merrell, Ebenezer	1		1		
Richardson, Moses	2	2	5			True, Benjⁿ	1	3	5			Mayberry, Richard	1	1	1		
Richardson, Jonᵃ	1		1			Bradford, Ezekiel, Juʳ	2		2			Hanson, Elijah	2	1	4		
Robinson, John	1	1	3			Dellingham, Jeremiah	1		1			Hutchinson, Ann			1		
Shaw, Josiah	3	1	2			Dellingham, John	1	3	1			Hutchinson, Samuel	2				
Shaw, Serjant	2	1	7			Childs, Daniel	2	3	5			Hutchinson, Joseph	1	5	3		
Shaw, Ebenezer	2	3	4			Bryant, Hezekiah	3	2	3			Starberd, Hannah			1		
Shaw, Thoˢ	2	2	2			Jones, Henry	1	3	6			Cook, Daniel	2	2	1		
Shaw, Joseph	1	3	3			Bradford, Wᵐ	2	2	1			Procter, William	3	1	3		
Sandbourn, John	3		4			Andrews, Mark	1	2	2			Ham, Benjamin	1		1		
Sandbourn, John, Juʳ	1	1	4			Andrews, Samˡ	1	1	4			Shane, Richard	1		3		
Sandbourn, David	1		2			Bonney, Ichabod	2		4			Hall, Stephen	1		1		
Sandbourn, Jeremiah	1					Bonney, John	1	1	1			Hodgdon, Israel	2	2	4		
Sandbourn, Simeon	2	3	2			Bonney, Ichabod, Juʳ	1		2			Jones, Samuel	1	3	3		
Sandbourn, Mary			2			House, Caleb	2		6			Hanson, Samuel	1		1		
Sawyer, John	2	2	5			Bradford, Martin	1		2			Hanson, William	1	2	1		
Smith, Archibald	1	2	5									Elliot, Jacob	1		3		
Sweet, Jonᵃ	1	1	4			**WATERFORD PLANTATION.**						Pettingill, Moses	1	4	2		
Sparrow, Stephen	3		3									Elliot, Jacob	2		3		
Thorn, Israel	2	2	2			Jewet, Stephen	4	1	5			Hall, Winslow	2	2	2		
Thompson, Isaa S	1	2	2			Green, Thoˢ	3	1	6			Hall, William	1	1	2		
Topping, Luther	1	1	2			Warren, Samˡ	1					Gould, Benjamin	1	4	4		
Thombs, Amos	1	4	2			Gates, Wᵐ	1	1	2			Pettingill, Daniel	1	1	4		
Waterhouse, Joseph	1	2	5			Johnson, Asa	2		3			Hanson, Jonathan	1	5	1		
Wood, John	3	1	5			Orr, Phillip	4		2			Lord, Samuel	1		1		
Whitney, David	1					Bryant, Richard	1		2			Osgood, Abraham	1	3			
Whitney, Joshua	1	1	3			Sampson, Phineas	1		2			Mayberry, John	1		2		
White, Peter	1	4	2			Whitcomb, David	1					Craige, Thomas	3	2	5		
Wiley, Wᵐ	2	1	2			Chamberlain, John	1					Elkins, William	2	3	3		
York, Isaas	1	1	2			Longley, Ely	1	1	3			Winslow, Joseph	1	1	2		
York, Jacob	1	1	3			Brown, Silas	1	2	2			Swett, Samuel	1	1	2		
York, Job	1		1			Brown, Thaddeus	1	2	2			Robinson, Stephen	1	3	2		
Yates, John	1	3	1			Chamberlain, Ephraim	1	1	2			Bolton, Rachel	3	2	5		
Chase, Isaac	1	2	2			Russ, John	2		3			Estis, Samuel	1	4	3		
Phinney, Stephen	1		1			Whitney, Phineas	1	2	3			Robinson, John	4	2	4		
Row, Robert	1	2	1			Stickney, Jonᵃ	2					Haskell, John	2	3	2		
Parker, Eliphalet	1		1			Homan, Jonas	1	2	1			Rogers, Nathaniel	1	1	1		
Higgins, Elkanah	2		2			McWane, David	1					Mugford, Nathaniel	1		1		
Lombard, Thoˢ	1	1	1			Longley, Jonᵃ	1	2	3			Punington, Sarah			3		
Lombard, Jedadiah	1	1	2			Hamblen, Africa	1	1	2			Hooper, Robert	1	1	3	1	
Woods, Joseph	1	3	2			Hamblen, America	3	1	2			Mugford, Robert	1	1	5		
Eaton, Israel	1	1	6			Jewel, Ezra	1	2	3			Lovett, Jonathan	2	6	4		
Woodman, Nathan	1	1	1			Hale, Israel	1	2	3			Cobb, Isaac	1	3	2		
Whetcomb, Silas	1	2	4			Hapgood, Oliver	1	1	3			Hooper, Abigail	1	2	3		
Wiley, David	1	1	1			Robbins, Jonᵃ	1	1	1			Mugford, John	1	2	3		
York, Ebenezer	1		1			Hale, Oliver	1	1	1			Estis, Simeon	1	3	4		
Parker, Moses	1	3	2			Gibson, Jacob	1		1			Graffam, Enoch	1	2	3		
Beaman, Noah	1	1	5			Barker, Daniel	3		2			Anderson, Edward	1	5	2		
Harmon, John	1	1	2			Holland, John	2	2	3			Dorrey, Timothy	4	1	4		
Harvey, John	3	1	2			Brown, Asaph	2	1	3			Anderson, Nancy	1		4		
Cookson, Elizabeth		2	2			Houghton, Jonᵃ	1	1	3			Mayberry, William	1	1	3		
						Jewel, John	1	1	2			Dorrey, Jonathan	1		2		
TURNER TOWN.						Saunderson, Stephen	2	2	2			Dorrey, Elijah	1	2	4		
						Chamberlain, Nathˡ	2					Tombly, Andrew	1	2	3		
Copelin, Joseph	1	1	2			Hale, Benjⁿ	1					Austin, Jonas	1	1	3		
Niles, Beniah	2		4									Lord, Simeon	1	2	4		
Smith, Jasael	1		4			**WINDHAM TOWN.**						Hanson, Ezra	1		2		
French, Daniel	1	4	1									Lord, Charles	1	1	1		
Gorham, Samuel	1	5	2			Ingersoll, John	2	1	4			Hanson, Ichabod	3	3	4		
Phillips, Mary		2	4			Craige, Eveleth	2	6				Anthine, Nicholis	1	2	1		
Heffords, Wᵐ	1	4	1			Mayberry, John	2		4			Hanson, Ichabod	1	1	3		
Bryant, Stephen	1	2	9			Graffam, Caleb	1	3	4			Crockett, Daniel	1		3		
Keene, John	2	1	5			Hawkes, Amos	3	1	5			Hawkes, Nathaniel	1	2	3		
Merrill, Danˡ	2	4	4			Hawkes, Ebenezer	3		5			Hawkes, James	2	5	3		
Leavit, Jacob	3	1	2			Honeywell, Elijah	3	3	8			Dolley, John	1	1	3		
Leavit, Joseph	1	4	3			Anderson, Ann	1		2			Dolley, Samuel	1	1	4		
Stevens, Moses	1	1	2			Anderson, Abraham	2	1	1			Jorden, Jeremiah	1	2	4		
Davis, Jacob	1	1	1			Walker, John	1		3			Rand, John	3	5	4		
Strickland, John	4	3	6			Hall, Hatevil	2	2	4			Fields, William	1	2	2		
Niles, Nathan	3	2	5			Hardy, Isaac	2	2	3			Hutchinson, Stephen	1		2		
Pratt, Jonᵃ	3		1			Campbell, Elisabeth		1	5			Elder, Joseph	2	3	2		
Young, Job	1					Knights, John	1	2	2			Kennard, Samuel	2	3	6		
Bonney, Isaiah	5		2			Gammon, Pilip	1	1	2			Legro, Elias	2	1	3		
Staples, Josiah	1	3	3			Knights, John	1	3	4			Baker, William	1	1	3		
Phillips, Abner	1	4	4			Whitehouse, Pomphrit	1	2	2			Dorrey, David	3	2	4		
Smith, Asa	1		1			Morrell, Benjamin	1		3			Clark, Gershom	1	1	1		
Phillips, Richard	2		3			Mayberry, John	1	1	2			Manchester, Stephen	2		1		
Briggs, Daniel	2	2	4			Mayberry, William	2	2	5			Manchester, Gershom	1	2	4		
Haskel, Israel	3	1	5									Allen, Joseph	1	1	4		

CUMBERLAND COUNTY—Continued.

NAME OF HEAD OF FAMILY.	Free white males of 16 years and upward, including heads of families.	Free white males under 16 years.	Free white females, including heads of families.	All other free persons.	Slaves.	NAME OF HEAD OF FAMILY.	Free white males of 16 years and upward, including heads of families.	Free white males under 16 years.	Free white females, including heads of families.	All other free persons.	Slaves.	NAME OF HEAD OF FAMILY.	Free white males of 16 years and upward, including heads of families.	Free white males under 16 years.	Free white females, including heads of families.	All other free persons.	Slaves.
WINDHAM TOWN—con.						**WINDHAM TOWN—con.**						**WINDHAM TOWN—con.**					
Morrell, Jedediah	1		1			Tobin, Matthew	3		1			Lowell, Joshua	2	1	4		
Morrell, Benjamin	1		3			Dole, Richard	1	1	3			Hawkes, Amos	2	2	5		
Morrell, Peeter	1	1	1			Windship, Ephraim	1	1	3			Allen, Pelatiah	4	2	6		
Pray, James	1	3	3			Chute, John	1	1	1			Mayberry, William	1	6	5		
Stevens, Richard	1	1	2			Chute, Josiah	1	3	2			Roberts, Jonathan	2	6	4		
Webb, Josiah	1	1	2			Swett, John	3		2			Mitchell, Benjamin	1	2	5		
Rea, Caleb	2	2	4			Willson, Jonathan	3		2			Rogers, Gershom	3	1	3		
Knights, George	3		3			Chute, Thomas	1	3	2			Stevens, Chase	1	7	2		
Waite, Enoch	1	2	2			Andrews, John	2	5	5			Jorden, Nathaniel	1	1	5		
Bodge, John	2	1	5			Smith, Peter F	4	7	1			Crockett, George	1	3	7		
Swett, Joseph	1		5			Chase, John	1	1	3			Hawkes, Amos	1	1	2		
Windship, Gershom	3	3	2			Trott, Thomas	2	1	7								
Windship, John	1		2			Barker, David	2	1	4								

HANCOCK COUNTY.

NAME OF HEAD OF FAMILY.	Free white males of 16 years and upward, including heads of families.	Free white males under 16 years.	Free white females, including heads of families.	All other free persons.	Slaves.	NAME OF HEAD OF FAMILY.	Free white males of 16 years and upward, including heads of families.	Free white males under 16 years.	Free white females, including heads of families.	All other free persons.	Slaves.	NAME OF HEAD OF FAMILY.	Free white males of 16 years and upward, including heads of families.	Free white males under 16 years.	Free white females, including heads of families.	All other free persons.	Slaves.
BARRETTSTOWN TOWN.						**BELFAST TOWN—con.**						**BLUEHILL TOWN—con.**					
Whitcomb, Abner	1					Willson, Jonathan	1		3			Candish, James	1	3	3		
Whitcomb, Ebenezer	1		1			Tufts, John	3	1	5			Hinkley, Susannah			1		
Bartlett, Isaac	1					Stephenson, Solon	2	1	3			Day, James	1	2	7		
Bartlett, Noah	1					Durham, Talford	1	3	4			Carter, Henry	1	2	2		
Bartlett, Daniel	1					Dolliff, John	1					Carter, James	2	4	5		
Sofford, Reuben	1					Durham, John	1	4	2			Carter, James, jun	1				
Mansfield, Jacob	1					Patterson, Natl	3	2	4			Carlton, Moses	1	3	2		
Kendall, Chever	1	1	3			French, Nathaniel	1	4	5			Carlton, Edward	1		3		
Barrett, Daniel	1					Patterson, William	2	2	6								
Pease, Aaron	1	1	1			Ames, Jacob	1	2	3			**CAMDEN TOWN.**					
Pease, James	3		2			Clark, Isaac	1		3			Corthall, Peletiah	2	2	4		
Symonds, Oliver	1	1	1			Clark, Abraham	1	2	2			Gibbs, Elisha	1	1	4		
Robbins, Jacob	1		3			McKean, Ephraim	2		1			Hosmer, Nathaniel	1	1	1		
Symonds, Peleg	1	1	3			McKean, Samuel	2		2			Hosmer, Nathaniel, junr	1	1	2		
Messerve, Benja	1	2	1			Dolliff, Daniel	1	4	2			Hogoman, Job	1	1	1		
Payson, Ephraim	1	2	2			Miller, James	3		2			Hosmer, Asa	1				
McClane, Fergus	1	2	2			Weeks, Lemuel	1	1	4			Harrington, David	1				
Katon, William	1	1	1			Coffran, John	1	1	2			Leavensellers, Jacob	1				
Davis, John	1	2	1			Crooks, William	2		3			Mansfield, Daniel	1				
Collamore, Isaac	1					Nesmith, Benja	3	1	4			Blodgett, David	1	1	2		
Temple, Nathaniel	1					Robinson, John	2	1	1			Derry, Lewis	1	2	4		
Pease, Prince, junr	1	2	4			Cochran, John	2	3	4			Bailey, Joseph	1	2	1		
Pease, Prince	3	1	2			Alexander, John	1		3			Wadsworth, Sedate	2	2	4		
Collamore, Joshua, junr	1	2	1			Stimpson, Richard	2		3			Thompson, John	1	1	3		
Collamore, Elisha	1											Whitney, John	1		1		
Pease, Shubael	1	1	1			**BLUEHILL TOWN.**						Cook, Paul	1	2	1		
Ripley, Abraham	1	3	3			Holt, Nickolas	1		1			McGlathry, William	3	5	2		
Thompson, John	3	1	2			Clough, Asa	1	1	1			Richards, James	3	5	4		
McMurphy, William	1					Pilsbury, Phineas	1	1	1			Metcalf, Leonard	1	2	3		
Wentworth, Shubael	1					Coggins, Samuel	1	1	2			Thorndike, Paul	2	4	3		
Wentworth, Sion	1					Coggins, Thomas	1		3			Harkness, John	1	2	3		
Messerve, Joseph	1		2			Wood, Israel	1	2	5			Ott, Peter	1	1	2		
Easinsy, Henry	1		2			Wood, Joseph	1		2	1		Ott, Peter, junr	1	2	2		
Suchfort, Andrass	1	2	2			Parker, Robert	3	4	2			Bradford, Elijah	1	4	3		
Jacobs, Andrew	1	2	1			Holt, Jedediah	1	5	1			Upham, William	2		1		
Thompson, Robert	1		1			Johnson, Obed	1	5	2			Porterfield, Wm	1	1	1		
Wentworth, Lemuel	1	3	2			Parker, Nathan	3	1	6			Nutt, David	2		5		
Martin, Samuel	2	1	3			Wood, Joseph, junr	1	3	3			Jones, Abraham	1	3	5		
Crooker, Francis	2		1			Wood, Robert H	1	3	3			Gordon, John	1	1	1		
Jones, Windsor	1	2	3			Horton, Joshua	3	2	6			Buckling, Barrack	1	4	5		
Maddocks, Ichabod	1	1	3			Parker, Joseph	1		1			Gregory, William, junr	1	2	4		
Newbet, John	2	2	4			Peters, John	3	4	6			Jeminson, Alexander	1	4	3		
Smith, Charles	1	2	2			White, John	1	3	2			Jones, James	1	2	3		
Barrett, Timothy	1					Darling, Jonathan	2	2	4			Gregory, William	4	2	3		
Ames, Jacob	1	1	3			Clough, Benja	1	1	1			Cobb, Thomas	3		2		
Hewit, William	1	2	3			Dodge, Elisha	1	2	2			Spring, Thomas	3	3	4		
Hilt, Margaret		3	2			Faulkner, Daniel	1					Reed, Frederick	1	1	5		
Hilt, John	1					Hinkley, Isaiah	1					Dunbar, Hannah			1		
Barrett, Nathan	1					Parker, Ezra	1					Gay, Ephraim	1		2		
Barrett, Simon	1					Floyd, Ebenezer	1					Gordon, John, junr	1	2	1		
Miles, Nathan	1					White, Edward	1					Conklin, Samuel	1		1		
Bartlett, Samuel	1					White, Daniel	1					Mace, Thomas	1		1		
Brooks, Silas	1					Clay, Jonathan	2	4	3			Harup, Thomas	1		2		
						Hinkley, Ebenezer	1	1	2			Nutt, John	1	3	1		
BELFAST TOWN.						Hinkley, Nehemiah	1		2			Tibbitts, Thomas	1		2		
Mudgett, John	1		7			Spofford, Daniel	1					McLaughlin, Samuel	2		1		
Gilmore, John	1		2			Robinson, Israel	1					Thorndike, Robert	3	3	4		
Smith, Winthrop	1	3	4			Osgood, Ezekiel	1	5	5			Shays, Michael	1				
Patterson, Wm	1	1	3			Osgood, Daniel	3	1	4			Simonton, James	1	3	2		
Clark, Alexander	1	1	2			Osgood, Phineas	1	3	4			Simonton, James, jun	1				
Houston, Samuel, junr	1	1	4			Holt, Nickolas, junr	1	2	1			Simonton, William	1		1		
True, Henry	1	1	2			Lecraw, Susannah			1			Gross, John	1	3	6		
Gilmore, James	1	1	2			Osgood, Christopher	1	1	2			Harrington, Isaac	1	2	4		
Houston, Samuel	3	1	3			Osgood, Nathan	1		1			Ogier, Abraham	1		1		
Houston, Robert	1	1	1			Osgood, John	1					Everton, Thomas	1		3		
Patterson, Robert	1	4	3			Dodge, Sarah	2		1			Jacobs, Samuel	2	1	1		
Brown, John	2	2	5			Parker, Peter	2	2	4			Eaton, Joseph	2	1	4		
Clark, Ichabod	1	1	2			Gra, Reuben, junr	1	2	2			Richards, Dodefer	1		1		
Clark, Elisha	1		3			Candish, John	1	1	3			Richards, Joseph	1		5		
Steel, Robert	2		1			Rounday, John	2	1	5			Richards, Jonathan	1	1	3		
McMullen, Alexander	1					Crabb, Jonathan	1	1	1			Demorse, Charles	1	2	3		
Patterson, James	1	3	4			Day, Jonathan	1		4			Young, Gideon	5		5		
Stephenson, Jerom	2	2	5			Candish, Joseph	1	2	3			Dillingham, Joshua	1	1	2		
Mitchell, Robert	1		2														

HANCOCK COUNTY—Continued.

CAMDEN TOWN—con.

NAME OF HEAD OF FAMILY.	Free white males of 16 years and upward, including heads of families.	Free white males under 16 years.	Free white females, including heads of families.	All other free persons.	Slaves.
Dillingham, Lemuel	1		1		
Palmer, Nathaniel	1		2		
Sherman, Joseph	1	2	2		
Palmer, Joshua	1				
Palmer, Benjᵃ	1				
Hewell, Henry	1				

CANAAN TOWN.

NAME OF HEAD OF FAMILY.	Free white males of 16 years and upward, including heads of families.	Free white males under 16 years.	Free white females, including heads of families.	All other free persons.	Slaves.
Thomas, Charles	1	4	1		
Raredan, David	1				
Miller, Noah	4	3	3		
Knights, Nathan	2	1	5		
Norton, John	2	2	3		
Heal, Isaac	1	4	5		
Heal, Chesley	1				
Ogier, Lewis	1	2	3		
Smith, Peleg	1	1	3		
Smith, Joseph	1	1	3		
Shelden, Ephraim	1		3		
Atkins, Cornelius	1				
McFarlin, William	1	1	2		
Dean, Joseph	1				
Lamb, Joshua	2	4	3		
Pottle, Daniel	1	1	3		
Nason, John	1	5	3		
Dunton, John	1		1		
Thomas, Joseph	2	3	6		
Whitham, Joshua	1	3	4		
Gray, Levi	1		1		
Quin, James	1	1	3		
Millikin, Abner	1	1	2		
Moody, William	1	2	1		
Fletcher, Ephraim	1				
Fletcher, Jonathan	1				
Hilton, Nathaniel	1		1		

CONDUSKEEG PLANTATION.

NAME OF HEAD OF FAMILY.	Free white males of 16 years and upward, including heads of families.	Free white males under 16 years.	Free white females, including heads of families.	All other free persons.	Slaves.
Budge, James	1	3	4		
Lovett, Francis	1	1	1		
Capers, John	1				
Tibbitts, John	3	3	5		
Noble, Seth	1	3	3		
Bussell, Jacob	2	1	1		
Howard, Thomas	2	2	5		
Hasey, William	1	1	2		
Mayo, Nathaniel	4		2		
Griffin, Jacob	1				
Smith, Elijah	1				
Bayley, Samuel	1	4	1		
Webster, Andrew	2	6	4		
Treat, James	1		6		
Harthorn, Ashbell	1		5		
Allen, Abraham	1	1	2		
Harthorn, David	1		1		
Harthorn, Silas	1	3	4		
Treat, Robert	3	4	4		
Page, Joseph	1	1	5		
Frees, Isaac	1	2	6		
Dugen, William	1		2		
McPhetres, Archibald	3	4	2		
Lovejoy, Phillip	1		2		
Tourtellott, Abraham	1	3	3		
Maddox, Ichabod	1	4	2		
Spencer, Daniel	1	4	2		
Madden, Owen	1				
Bussell, Isaac	1	1	3		
Tourtellott, Reuben	1	1	3		
Loushon, Anthony	1	2	2		
Page, James	1		2		
Page, Joseph, junr	1	1	3		
McPhetres, Archibald, junr	1	1	1		
Page, Isaac	1	2	1		
Inman, Joseph	1	5	1		
Plympton, Joseph	1	1	2		
Davis, Ezra	1	2	2		
Colburn, Jeremiah	2		2		
Colburn, William	1	1	1		
Marsh, John	1	6	1		
White, Samuel	1				
Stanley, David	1		4		
Frees, Abraham	2	3	3		
Frees, John	1	1	3		
Eayrs, Joshua	4	1	5		
Dennett, Jacob	2	1	7		
Barns, Jotham	1				
Burrill, Phillip	1				
Gross, Moses	1				
Denning, Jane		2	2		
Denning, James	1	2	2		
Campbell, Daniel	1	1	3		
Tibbitts, George	1		4		

CONDUSKEEG PLANTATION—continued.

NAME OF HEAD OF FAMILY.	Free white males of 16 years and upward, including heads of families.	Free white males under 16 years.	Free white females, including heads of families.	All other free persons.	Slaves.
Tibbetts, Abner	1	4	2		
Cook, Croell	1	1	1		
Davis, William	1		2		
Mann, Amos	1	2	4		
Tozier, Lemuel	1	6	2		
Clark, Joseph	4	2	2		
Casey, William	1		1		
Nevers, Elisha	1	1	5		
Tibbitts, William	3		4		
Mayo, James	1		1		
Boober, Benjᵃ	1	3	2		
Webber, Richard	1				
Banks, John	1		3		
Harlow, Nathaniel	2	1	2		
Smart, John	1	3	7		
Tibbitts, Daniel	3	5	3		
Hichborn, Robert, junr	1				
Plympton, William	1				
Lowe, Thomas	2	1	1		
Lowe, Charles	1				
Burges, Peter	1	1	3		
Crosby, Simon	2	1	4		
Cary, Samuel	1	3	2		
Cary, Richard	1	1	2		
Emery, John, junr	1	5	4		
Patten, William	1	3	4		
McKenzie, Kenneth	1	1	2		
Crosby, Abner	1	4	4		
Gorton, Simeon	1	2	5		
Dole, Amos	1	3	2		
Smith, Zebulon	1				
Sweat, Shebna	1	1	5		
Crosby, John	1	3	3		
Blasdell, Sanburn	1	2	2		
Emery, Nahum	1	1	4		
Emery, James	1				
Wheeler, Benjᵃ	9	2	4		
Graves, Moses	1				
Phillbrooks, James	2	3	4		
Tarr, William	2	1	2		
Patterson, Andrew	2	2	3		
Patten, John	2	4	2		
Pickard, Jonathan	1	4	1		
Hewes, Eliu	3		1		
Blagden, Charles	2		3		
Pomroy, Joseph	2	5	4		
Swan, Gustavus	1	4	5		
Pierce, Lettice			1	1	
Garrish, Jack				3	

DEER ISLE TOWN.

NAME OF HEAD OF FAMILY.	Free white males of 16 years and upward, including heads of families.	Free white males under 16 years.	Free white females, including heads of families.	All other free persons.	Slaves.
Sellers, Joseph	1	1	2		
Crockett, Josiah	2	2	2		
Torrey, William	1				
Smally, Job	3	2	2		
Smally, Thomas	2	3	5		
Smally, Thomas, junr	1				
Webster, Ebenezer	2	3	5		
Raynes, Anna			1		
Raynes, John	1	3	3		
Raynes, Martha	1		2		
Raynes, William	1	2	1		
Lunt, Michael	1		2		
Jordan, James	3	1	4		
Trundy, Samuel	3	1	7		
Emerson, Joshua	1	2	1		
Boynton, Isaac	1	3	3		
Eaton, Jonathan	2	4	5		
Sanders, James	1		3		
Sanders, Timothy	1		6		
Pressy, John, 3d	1	2	1		
Pressy, John	1	1	2		
Pressy, John, junr	1		4		
Pressy, Chace	1	4	4		
Johnson, Nathan	1	1	3		
Hooper, John	3	1	2		
Hooper, William	1				
Morey, Ezekiel	1	2	4		
Morey, Elias	1	3	1		
Haskell, Joshua	1	1	4		
Cole, Benjamin	2		1		
Cole, Benjamin, junr	1	3	3		
Powars, Peter	4		2		
Colby, Ambrose	1	2	2		
Howard, Ezra	3		2		
Fullerton, William	1				
Dunham, Elijah	1	2	1		
Haskell, Mark	4		1		4
Haskell, Thomas	1				
Haskell, Ignatius	1	3	4		
Whitelaw, James	1				
Haskell, Caleb	1	2	4		
Marshall, Ezekiel	3				
Marshall, Joshua	1	1	2		

DEER ISLE TOWN—con.

NAME OF HEAD OF FAMILY.	Free white males of 16 years and upward, including heads of families.	Free white males under 16 years.	Free white females, including heads of families.	All other free persons.	Slaves.
Marshall, Ephraim	1	5	1		
Haskell, Francis	1	1	3		
Haskell, Jonathan	1	2	3		
Carman, Levi	3	1	4		
Eaton, Theophilus	2		2		
Dow, Nathan	1	1	3		
Carlton, Jonathan	1	3	4		
Haskell, Nathan	1	1	2		
Dow, Nathan, junr	1	1	3		
Haskell, Abijah	1	2	3		
Eaton, William	1	2	4		
Eaton, Eliakim	1	3	4		
Howard, John	1	3	2		
Eaton, Jeremiah	1	2	3		
Hardy, Peter	2	2	6		
Scott, Nathaniel	3		4		
Closson, John	1	1	3		
Closson, Josiah	1	1	2		
Thomas, Richard	1	1	3		
Thompson, Thomas	1	3	5		
Staples, Joshua	1	1	3		
Sheldon, Nathaniel	1	1	1		
Willson, Samuel	1	2	2		
Linn, Robert	1		1		
Staples, Moses	1	5	4		
Torrey, Jonathan	1	6	5		
Torrey, David, junr	1				
Torrey, David	1				
Foster, William	3	2	4		
Dexter, William P.	1				
Hamblin, Nathaniel	2		1		
Campbell, John	1	5	3		
Joice, James	1	2	5		
Greenlaw, William	1	4	2		
Bray, William	1	1	3		
Bray, Nathaniel	2	4	4		
Lane, Oliver	1	1	1		
Frees, John	1		3		
Robbins, Nathaniel	1	1	2		
Babbige, Courtney	1	1	2		
Warren, Thomas	1	2	1		
Frees, George	2	1	2		
Frees, Isaac	1				
Babbige, Stephen	1	2	2		
Tyler, Joseph	2	3	2		
Tyler, George	1				
Tyler, Belcher	1	3	4		
Colby, Joseph	2	1	3		
Silvester, Edmund	1	1	2		
Webb, Hannah	1		4		
Colby, Joseph, junr	1	2	1		
Stinson, Thomas, jun	1	3	2		
Smith, David	1	2	2		
Robbins, Nathaniel	1	1	4		
Robbins, Thomas, jun.	1	1	1		
Stinson, Thomas	2		2		
Stinson, Samuel	1	1	2		
Stinson, William	1	2	1		
Babbige, William	1		2		
Hatch, Seth	1		1		
Staples, Samuel	1				
Thurston, John	3	3	3		
Lane, Hezekiah	3	2	2		
Richards, William	1	1			
Stockbridge, Benjᵃ	1		6		
Toothaker, Elijah	1				
Whitmore, Joseph	1	3	3		
Smally, Andrew	1	2	2		
Crockett, Robinson	1	3	3		
Carpenter, William	2		2		
Sellers, Charles	1	2	4		
Smith, Joseph	1	1	2		
Weed, Benjamin	3	2	5		
Gra, Christopher	1		2		
Farrell, Peggy			2		
Howard, Samuel		1	3		
Billings, Timothy	1	1	1		
Harris, Joseph	1		2		
Blastow, Noah	1	3	3		
Conry, Thomas	2	5	5		
York, Benjᵃ	2		2		
Marchant, Anthony	2	2	7		
Kimball, Solomon	2	1	4		
Moody, William	2	2	2		
Brickett, Moses	1				
Williams, Peter				4	

DUCKTRAP TOWN.

NAME OF HEAD OF FAMILY.	Free white males of 16 years and upward, including heads of families.	Free white males under 16 years.	Free white females, including heads of families.	All other free persons.	Slaves.
Burkmar, Thomas	4	3	2		
Presscott, Samuel	3	1	3		
Adams, David	2				
Miller, David	1	1	3		
Knowlton, Reuben	3	1	3		
Knowlton, William	1	1	5		

HANCOCK COUNTY—Continued.

NAME OF HEAD OF FAMILY.	Free white males of 16 years and upward, including heads of families.	Free white males under 16 years.	Free white females, including heads of families.	All other free persons.	Slaves.
DUCKTRAP TOWN—con.					
Knowlton, Thomas....	1	4	1		
Pinkham, James....	1	2	4		
Clark, Jonathan....	2	3	3		
Baty, John....	1	3	4		
Ring, Jacob....	1	1	3		
Gibson, James....	1	3	3		
Highser, Adam....	1	1	1		
Welsh, John....	1	3	1		
Welsh, Mark....	1	2	2		
Patterson, Adam....	1	4	2		
Harvey, John....	1		2		
McDermot, John....	1		1		
Lawrence, Zachariah...	2	1	3		
McIntyre, Angus....	1		1		
Carter, Edward....	2	3	2		
Richards, Joseph....	3	5	3		
Calef, Allen....	1	3	4		
Smith, John....	1	1	2		
Harding, Josiah....	1	1	1		
Pomroy, John....	1		2		
Smith, Benja....	2	3	4		
Gatchell, James....	1	3	3		
Drinkwater, Micajah...	3	4	4		
Drinkwater, Zenas....	1		1		
Thomas, Joshua....	1	4	1		
Knights, Thomas....	2	3	4		
Adams, Joshua....	1	1	1		
Wade, John....	1	2	3		
Clark, John....	1		2		
Pitcher, Lewis....	2		1		
Ulmer, George....	3		4		
Collamore, Joseph....	1				
Gammon, James....	1				
Clary, Daniel....	1				
Ulmer, Phillip....	1	2	4		
Studley, Lemuel....	1				
Studley, John....	1		1		
Dickrow, Daniel....	1	1	1		
Dickrow, Zepheniah....	2		1		
Thayer, Lemuel, junr...	1	1	6		
Thayer, Lemuel....	1		2		
Turner, Samuel....	1	2	2		
Gay, David....	3	3	4		
Brooks, Martin....	2	3	3		
Dickrow, Peleg....	1				
Harley, Ralph....	1	1	1		
Dunbar, Moses....	2	1	4		
EASTERN RIVER TOWN-SHIP NO. 2.					
Bowden, Paul, junr....	1		2		
Canfield, Ebenezer....	2		5		
Sherburne, Samuel....	1	3	2		
Boynton, William....	1	4	6		
Sherburne, Jacob....	1	2	5		
French, Dearbon....	1				
Partrige, Samuel....	1				
Gross, Joseph, junr....	1		2		
Hart, John....	1		1		
Crage, Samuel....	1	1	3		
Crage, Andrew....	1				
Crage, Moses....	1	3	3		
Gross, Joseph....	2	2	3		
Viles, Joseph....	2	1	5		
Soper, Samuel....	1		2		
Turner, Calvin....	1	4	2		
Gilman, Peter....	1	1	7		
Viles, Joseph, junr....	1	1	1		
Holt, Humphry....	1	2	5		
Hancock, John....	1	2	4		
Tower, Elizabeth....			1		
Hancock, Nathan....	1	2	3		
Smith, James....	1	2	2		
Gross, John....	1	1	1		
Gross, Zachary....	1		2		
Davis, Micah....	1				
Partrige, John....	1		1		
Hamilton, William....	1	1	1		
Partrige, Thomas....	1	1	4		
Morrill, Benja....	1	2	1		
Crage, Samuel, junr....	1	2	1		
Crage, John....	1	1	3		
Partrige, Daniel....	1	2	1		
Homes, Samuel....	1				
Treat, Samuel....	1				
Blasdell, Moses, junr....	1	2	3		
Sanders, William....	1				
Herryman, Peter....	1	1	2		
Herryman, Ezekiel....	1	3	2		
Herryman, Asa....	1	4	2		
Soper, Justus....	1	2	3		
Keyes, Samuel....	2	1	6		
Rooks, Joseph....	1	1	4		
Rooks, Benja....	1		1		

NAME OF HEAD OF FAMILY.	Free white males of 16 years and upward, including heads of families.	Free white males under 16 years.	Free white females, including heads of families.	All other free persons.	Slaves.
EASTERN RIVER TOWN-SHIP NO. 2—con.					
Gray, Mary....		2	1		
Gross, Ebenezer....			3		
Gross, Ebenezer, junr....	1				
Blasdell, James....	1	1	3		
Darling, Eliakim....	2				
Lawrence, Abel....	1	2	2		
Herryman, Joshua....	1	2	1		
Davis, Jesse....	1		1		
Herryman, Asa, junr....	1	2	2		
Evans, John....	1		3		
EDDY TOWNSHIP.					
Phillips, John....	1	3	3		
Blackman, Eleazer....	1		1		
Eddy, Elias....	1	1	3		
Eddy, Jonathan....	1	1	1		
Nickolls, James....	1	2	3		
Eddy, Ibrook....	1	3	4		
McMann, Thankful....	1		5		
Bussell, Stephen....	1	1	7		
Mahany, Patrick....	1	5	3		
Rowell, Patience....	1	2	2		
Mann, Daniel....	1	1	3		
Grant, Samuel....	1	1	3		
Grant, Alexander....	1		1		
Grant, Stephen....	1	3	3		
Oliver, Jacob....	1	2	5		
Spencer, Phillip....	1		5		
Spencer, Daniel....	1	2	2		
Spencer, Nathaniel, jun....	1		2		
Spencer, Nathaniel....	1	5	3		
FRANKFORT TOWN.					
George, William....	1	1	1		
Grant, Gooding....	1	1	4		
Grant, Andrew....	4		3		
Newcomb, Reuben....	4	1	6		
Newcomb, Jonathan....	1	1	1		
Mayo, Nathaniel....	1	1	3		
Welsh, Henry....	1		2		
Mayo, James....	1		2		
Mayo, Israel....	1		1		
Young, Zebulon....	1		2		
Whitney, Thomas....	2	1	2		
Murch, Benjamin....	1		2		
Whitney, Daniel....	1		4		
Murch, William....	1	2	2		
Doan, Amos....	1	2	1		
Billington, John....	1	2	1		
Newcomb, Simeon....	1	3	3		
Baker, Moses....	1		3		
Cobb, Ezekiel....	1	1	1		
Phillbrook, Jonathan....	1	2	3		
Hamblin, Perez....	1	2	4		
Harding, Jesse....	2	3	3		
Snow, Harding....	1	2	1		
Knowles, Freeman....	2	3	5		
Hopkins, Isaac....	1	5	4		
Hopkins, Nathan....	1	3	1		
Smith, Simon....	1	4	4		
Mayo, Ebenezer....	3		2		
Mirrick, Nathaniel....	2	3	4		
Higgins, Benja....	1	1	6		
Harding, Archibald....	2	2	4		
Ryder, Amos....	2	2	4		
Higgins, Abisha....	1	1	4		
Knowles, Mary....	1	1	2		
Snow, Thomas....	1	1	4		
Ellingwood, Richard...	2	1	1		
Holbrook, John....	2	2	5		
Cole, Pheobe....	1	2	3		
Sullivan, William....	1	4	3		
Haldershaw, John....	2		2		
Haldershaw, John, junr....	1	2	2		
Downs, Noah....	1	4	3		
Trebble, Joseph....	1	1	1		
Downs, Paul....	1	2	3		
Downs, Thomas....	1		1		
Clark, Nathaniel....	1	1	2		
Stubbs, James....	1		1		
Kempton, John....	3	5	2		
Kempton, Zacheus....	1	2			
Gibbs, Sally....			1		
Collson, James....	1	4	4		
Collson, Hateevil....	2		1		
Higgins, John....	1	1	3		
Bolen, John....	1	1	1		
Coolier, James....	1	1	1		
Whitham, Benja....	2	2	5		
Green, Thomas....	1	4	3		
Hassan, William....	1	4	4		
Johnson, Miller....	1	1	1		

NAME OF HEAD OF FAMILY.	Free white males of 16 years and upward, including heads of families.	Free white males under 16 years.	Free white females, including heads of families.	All other free persons.	Slaves.
FRANKFORT TOWN—con.					
Oaksman, Tobias....	2	1	5		
Grant, Ephraim....	2		2		
Grant, Adam....	1	3	1		
Blasdell, Ebenezer....	2	3	5		
McIntyer, John....	1		2		
Clark, Jonathan....	1	1	1		
Clark, James....	2	1	1		
Clark, Lemuel....	1	1	2		
Kingsbury, Enoch....	1				
Pratt, Seth....	1	1	3		
Kingbury, Phineas....	1	2	4		
Parker, Oliver....	2		3		
Treat, Joshua, junr....	1	4	2		
Littlefield, Moses....	1		2		
Bolton, Elisha....	5		3		
Littlefield, James....	1	1	1		
Grant, William....	1	2	3		
Carlton, John....	1		5		
Littlefield, Samuel....	1		3		
Littlefield, Stephen....	2	2	1		
Woodman, Benja....	1	2	2		
Wentworth, Grant....	1		1		
Kenny, Paul....	2	3	3		
Tyler, Andrew....	1		3		
Lane, Daniel....	1	5	3		
Danford, Phillip....	1	1	1		
Woodman, Molly....		3	3		
Treat, Joseph....	1		1		
Downs, Ephraim....	1	1	2		
Clark, Isaac....	1		1		
Downs, Asa....	1		1		
More, William....	1	1	3		
Wentworth, Wm....	1		1		
Hatch, Joseph....	1		1		
Hyde, Ezra....	3	1	4		
Tibbitts, Benja....	2		3		
Tibbitts, Solomon....	2		1		
Page, William....	1	1	1		
Grant, James....	1	6	2		
McMann, Joseph....	1		2		
Coolier, Francis....	4	2	5		
Tibbitts, Nathaniel....	2	1	1		
Carr, William....	1	2	1		
Merithue, Roger....	1	2	4		
Ames, John....	1	1	3		
Mudgett, Abraham....	1				
Bassick, George....	1		3		
Rankins, Robert....	1	1	1		
Garland, Ebenezer....	1	1	3		
McLaughlin, Wm....	1	2	1		
Sweetser, John, junr....	1		2		
Partrige, David....	1	1	2		
Boyd, Joseph....	1	1	5		
Goodale, Daniel....	2	5	2		
Partrige, Clark....	1	4	3		
Shute, Benjamin, junr....	1	2	1		
Cozens, Nathaniel....	2	2	2		
Lancaster, Daniel....	1	2	4		
Staples, John....	1	4	3		
Adam, John, junr....	1	5	1		
Adam, John....	1	2	1		
Sweetser, John....	3	2	4		
Black, Henry....	3	1	4		
French, Zetham....	3	5	4		
Pierce, John....	2	2	5		
Stowers, Samuel....	1		3		
Eustis, Jacob....	1				
Shute, Benja....	3	1	4		
Treat, Joshua....	2	4	1		
Dickey, William....	2	1	8		
Farley, William....	1		2		
Fletcher, Thomas....	2	2	3		
Cluley, Isaac....	2	1	3		
Clifford, Nathaniel....	1		1		
Clifford, Jacob....	1	2	3		
Hichborn, William....	2				
Marten, Joseph....	1		1		
Clifford, John....	1	1	1		
Dwelly, John....	1		2		
Ellis, Manoah....	1	2	2		
Ellis, Levi....	1	1	4		
Staples, Miles....	3		3		
Lanpher, Langworthy....	1	4	4		
Griffin, Samuel....	6		2		
Griffin, Nathan....	1		2		
Griffin, William....	1		4		
Young, Alexander....	1	2	1		
Staples, William....	1	2	3		
Staples, Jotham....	1	2	5		
Pendleton, William....	2				
Young, Samuel....	1				
Roff, James....	1				
Park, John....	2	3	5		
Ellis, Sarah....			1		

HANCOCK COUNTY—Continued.

NAME OF HEAD OF FAMILY.	Free white males of 16 years and upward, including heads of families.	Free white males under 16 years.	Free white females, including heads of families.	All other free persons.	Slaves.
FRANKFORT TOWN—con.					
Pendleton, Peleg	2	1	4		
Crary, Joseph	1	2	3		
Nickolls, James	4	1	7		
Nickolls, James, junr	1				
Lords, Henry	1	3	4		
Porter, Robert	1	4	2		
Stimpson, Ephraim	2	1	2		
Corsson, Ichabod	1	2	5		
Black, Henry, junr	1		2		
Ames, Josiah	2	1	3		
Ellis, Berrick	1		4		
Nickerson, Reuben	1	6	4		
Kimball, William	1				
Nickerson, Aaron	1				
Hoyt, Solomon A.				1	
Hoyt, Richard				1	
GOULDSBOROUGH TOWN.					
Smith, John	1		1		
Sargent, Benja	1				
Sargent, Diamond	1	1	3		
Bacon, Thomas	1	2	1		
Sargent, William	2	1	4		
Stephens, Abraham	1	1	1		
Sargent, Wm, junr	1				
Jones, Nathan	12	1	5		
Hill, Thomas	2	7	3		
Walker, John	1		2		
Newman, Joseph	1	3	2		
Young, Noah	2	1	2		
Gubtail, John	2	1	2		
Gubtail, Thomas	1	1	1		
Libbey, Samuel	2	1	5		
Godfrey, Benja	4	1	5		
Shaw, Hannah	4	1	2		
Allen, Tobias	2	1	2		
Noonan, Abigail		1	5		
Wright, Daniel	1	2	3		
Alline, Benja	1	1	3		
Shaw, William	4		1		
More, Joel	3	4	4		
Tracy, Asa	1	2	3		
Tracy, Jonathan	3		3		
Tracy, Samuel	1	1	4		
Gubtail, John, junr	1	2	3		
Cole, Abijah	1	1	1		
Allen, Nathaniel	1		1		
McDaniel, John	1	2	4		
Petty, Oliver	1	2	1		
Young, Samuel	1	2	1		
Perry, Jesse	1	1	2		
Simonton, William	3	2	4		
Gubtail, Abijah	1	4	2		
Pinkham, Tristam	1		2		
Spurlin, James	1	1	3		
Whitten, Phineas	1	4	6		
Joy, John	1	1	1		
Joy, Samuel	2	3	3		
Fernalld, Clement	3	2	5		
Tracy, Elizabeth	1	2	5		
Ash, Benjamin	1		4		
Ash, Robert	1	1	1		
Frazer, Thomas				9	
ISLEBOROUGH TOWN.					
Page, Simon	1	3	2		
Sprague, John	1	3	3		
Vezie, Samuel	1	4	4		
Coombs, Anthony, junr	1		3		
Coombs, Fields	1	1	3		
Woodward, Peter	1		1		
Woodward, Joseph	1	2	2		
Dodge, Noah	1	2	5		
Thomas, Benja	1	2	5		
Trim, Godfrey, junr	1	1	3		
Trim, Godfrey	3	1	5		
Marshall, Benja	2	2	2		
Marshall, Zachariah	1	1	3		
Dodge, Rathburn	1	1	1		
Lasdell, Ellison, junr	1	3	2		
Grinnall, William	1	1	4		
Coombs, Peter	1		2		
Coombs, Hosea	1	3	2		
Coombs, Anthony	3	3	1		
Williams, Samuel	1				
Williams, Shubael	3		3		
Cottrell, Silvester	2	4	3		
Hewes, Paoli	1	1	2		
Dodge, Simon, junr	1		2		
Pendleton, Samuel	3	3	6		
Dodge, Simon	1	5	3		
Bordman, Joseph	1	5	5		
Pendleton, Joshua	1	1	6		
ISLEBOROUGH TOWN—continued.					
Pendleton, Thomas, junr	1	3	4		
Pendleton, Oliver	1	4	5		
Pendleton, Thomas	1	2	4		
Pendleton, Gideon	1	1	3		
Ellwill, William	3	2	3		
Pendleton, John	2	3	3		
Carver, Benja	1				
Hill, John	1				
Pendleton, Jonathan	1	4	3		
Turner, Isaac	1				
Adams, Thomas	1				
Homes, Tilden	1				
Pendleton, Henry	2	2	3		
Pendleton, Wm	2		3		
Gatchall, Nathaniel	1	1	1	1	
Pendleton, Job	3	2	7		
Lasdell, Ellison	1	2	1		
Harthorn, Thomas	1	3	1		
Jones, Joseph	1		1		
Ames, Thomas	1	1	5		
Ames, Jabez	1		2		
Thomas, George	1		2		
Farrow, Josiah	1	2	2		
Gilkey, John	2	4	5		
McDonald, John	1				
Pendleton, Natl	1	1	10		
Thomas, David	2	2	1		
Hardy, Joseph	1	2	3		
Phillbrook, Wm, junr	1	5	1		
Holbrook, Prince	1	2	1		
Phillbrook, Joseph	1	1	4		
Phillbrook, Wm	1	1	1		
Griffin, William	2	1	3		
Hatch, Jeremiah	1	1	4		
Sherman, Valentine	3	1	3		
Coombs, Robert	1		1		
Williams, Amos	1	3	2		
Burns, William	1	1	5		
Warren, Samuel	2	5	4		
MOUNT DESERT TOWN.					
Robinson, John	2	1	3		
Tinker, David	1	2	3		
Noble, Reuben	1	3	5		
Reed, Jacob	2	1	4		
Heath, Richard	1	2	3		
Heath, William	1		2		
Appleton, Francis	1	1	2		
Wentworth, Enoch	1	4	1		
Norwood, Stephen	1	1	4		
Rich, John	4	2	5		
Barton, James	1	1	5		
Richardson, Stephen	4	1	4		
Gott, Daniel, junr	1	2	3		
Gott, Daniel	3	3	4		
Gott, Nathaniel	1		3		
Gott, Joseph	1		1		
Norwood, Joshua	2	4	4		
Richardson, Thomas	3	3	5		
Gott, Peter	1	3	4		
Richardson, Thomas, junr	1	3	1		
Ward, Benja	1	1	3		
Bowden, Samuel	1	1	1		
Mayo, Joshua	3		2		
Salisbury, Jabez	1	1	4		
Langley, Phillip	2	3	1		
Spurlin, Benja	1	4	2		
Rich, Jonathan	1	2	4		
Stanley, Sans	2	1	2		
Stanley, Thomas	1	1	3		
Bunker, Aaron	1	1	3		
Stanley, Margaret			2		
Stanley, Samuel	1		2		
Stanley, John	1	1	3		
Stanley, Peter	1		2		
Flinn, Thomas	1		1		
Peache, John	1	4	2		
More, Jeremiah	1	1	2		
Tucker, Andrew	1	4	3		
Rafanel, Augustus	1	2	4		
Emerson, Samuel	1	7	2		
Groo, Joseph, junr	1		1		
Groo, Joseph	1	1	1		
Brown, Jonathan	1		2		
Baker, William	1		1		
Whitehorn, William	1		1		
Salisbury, Reuben	1	2	5		
Bunker, John	1		2		
Bunker, Isaac	1	9	3		
Bunker, Benja	2	2	3		
Bunker, Mark	1		2		
Gilley, William	1	2	3		
MOUNT DESERT TOWN—continued.					
Scott, William	1		2		
Sommers, Thomas	1	1	1		
Tarr, Andrew	2	1	2		
Manchester, John	2	1	3		
Richardson, James, junr	1	1	1		
Manchester, John, junr	1		1		
Sargent, Stephen	2		1		
Hadlock, Samuel	1	2	3		
Richardson, James	2	1	4		
Somes, Abraham	4	3	2		
Reed, Samuel	1	3	4		
Massy, Nathaniel	1				
Richardson, George	1		3		
Gott, Stephen	1		1		
Dodge, Ezra H	1		2		
Richardson, John G	1	1	2		
Athenton, Benja	1	2	2		
Wescott, Davis	1	2	5		
Eaton, David	1	1	2		
Robinson, John, junr	1	2	2		
McKenzie, John	1	2	1		
Pray, Ephraim, junr	1	1	2		
Hodgdon, Joseph	1	4	4		
Lunt, Abner	1	4	2		
Pray, Ephraim	2	1	3		
Millikin, Samuel	1	2	4		
Freeman, Reuben	3		6		
Bartlett, Israel	1		4		
Bartlett, David	1	1	2		
Bartlett, Christopher	2	2	4		
Bartlett, Christopher, jun	1		2		
Bartlett, Elias	1				
Higgins, David	5	3	5		
Higgins, Jesse	2	4	3		
Chipar, John	1				
Mayo, Joseph	4	5	2		
Hinkley, Seth	1		2		
Higgins, Elkanah	1	2	1		
Thomas, Nickolas	1	4	3		
Thomas, John	1		3		
Thomas, John, junr	1	4	3		
Thomas, Amos	1				
Richardson, Daniel	1	2	2		
Hadley, Simeon	2	2	7		
Leland, Ezra	3	4	5		
Leland, Ebenezer	2	1	3		
Hopkins, Joseph	1	2	7		
Salisbury, Ebenezer	4	2	6		
Young, Elkanah	1	7	1		
Paine, Thomas	2		3		
Mason, William	1		1		
Doane, Seth	1	2	4		
Cozens, John	1	1	2		
Hamer, John	1	2	4		
Knowles, Henry	2	1	4		
Higgins, Levi	2	3	7		
Higgins, Jerusha	1		2		
Smellige, Timothy	1	2	7		
Smellige, Josiah	2		2		
Hamar, David	2		2		
Thompson, Peleg	1		1		
Cozens, Elisha	2	2	4		
Thompson, Cornelius	3	2	5		
Young, Ezra	2		2		
Young, Robert	1	2	2		
Stanwood, Benja	1	1	1		
Hodgkins, William	1				
Hodgkins, Joseph	1				
Day, John	1	5	2		
Wescott, Thomas	4		2		
Higgins, Solomon	2	2	2		
Higgins, Israel	2	5	2		
Rodick, Daniel	3	2	6		
Wescott, Thomas, junr	2	3	3		
Stanwood, Humphry	1		3		
Hopkins, Smith	1	1	1		
Bunker, Joseph	1	2	2		
Higgins, Stephen	1	1	1		
Gilicott, George	1	2	1	6	
Lynam, William	1		6		
Neptune, Junior				1	
ORPHAN ISLAND TOWN.					
Collins, Syrenus	2	1	4		
Hopkins, Bazilah	1	3	3		
Hearsy, Peleg	1				
Scott, James	2	2	3		
Nickerson, William	1		3		
Cunningham, James	2	2	2		
Buckley, James	1	1	1		
Mace, William	2	1	3		
Blasdell, Moses	2	1	3		
Sanders, Moses	1	1	2		

HANCOCK COUNTY—Continued.

ORPHAN ISLAND TOWN—continued.

NAME OF HEAD OF FAMILY.	Free white males of 16 years and upward, including heads of families.	Free white males under 16 years.	Free white females, including heads of families.	All other free persons.	Slaves.
Merrill, Caleb	1	2	2		
Haines, Frederick	1		1		
Webber, Isaac	1		2		
Lillie, Benja	2		1		
Walker, Eleazer	2	1	4		
Perkins, Eliphalet	1	1	1		
Abbott, James	1	3	4		
Grout, William	2	2	5		
Pomroy, William	1	2	2		
York, Joseph	1	2	2		
Crocker, John	1	3	6		
Rawlins, Benja	1	1	3		
Cummins, Thomas	1	1	1		
Blake, Jonathan	1		1		
Richards, Samuel	1	1	3		

ORRINGTON TOWN.

NAME OF HEAD OF FAMILY.	Free white males of 16 years and upward, including heads of families.	Free white males under 16 years.	Free white females, including heads of families.	All other free persons.	Slaves.
Whelden, Ebenezer	2	1	3		
Whelden, Joseph	1		2		
Smith, Thomas	2	2	2		
Wentworth, Moses	2	3	6		
Homes, Jeremiah	1	2	3		
Bartlett, Samuel	2	1	3		
Snow, Edward	3	3	5		
Freeman, Timothy	1	4	4		
Snow, Amasa, junr	1		1		
Cole, Henry	1		1		
Nickerson, Paul	1	2	3		
Nickerson, Eliphalet	1		2		
Nickerson, Eliphalet, junr	1	1	1		
Nickerson, Warren	1	2	2		
Nickerson, Daniel	1	3	2		
Dean, Thomas	1				
Dean, Thomas, junr	1		2		
Doane, Oliver	1	4	3		
Atwood, Jesse	1	5	5		
Brooks, George	1	2	6		
Fowler, Simeon	2	2	6		
Freeman, James	1		2		
Severance, Joshua	1		2		
Sweat, Shebna	1		1		
Severance, Caleb	1	3	2		
Rogers, Jesse	2	2	3		
Rogers, Moses	1	3	2		
Pierce, Nathaniel	1	3	3		
Freeman, Samuel	1	2	4		
Pepper, Mercy			1		
Snow, Benja	2	3	3		
Snow, Amasa	1		2		
Gould, Nathaniel	1	3	8		
Sweat, Solomon	2	1	2		
Baker, Joseph	3	4	5		
Ward, Nathaniel	1	1	1		
McCurdy, Robert	3		3		
Wiswall, Samuel	1		5		
Wiswall, David	1		3		
Ginn, James	3	4	6		
Brewer, John	2	2	6		
Rogers, John	1				
Brewer, Josiah	1			1	1
Tibbetts, John	1	2	4		
Kenny, Henry	1	2	3		
Hutchins, John	1	2	5		
Emery, John	1	1	1		
Fulman, George	1		3		
Skinner, Daniel	2	2	3		
Skinner, Elisha	1	4	2		
Campbell, Thomas, junr	1				
Holyoak, John	2	5	5		
Perkins, Benja	1		3		
Mayew, Andrew	1		2		
Johnson, Simeon	1	3	5		
Wall, David	1				
Ryder, John	3	4	5		
Thomas, John	2	1	4		
Campbell, Thomas	3		8		
Bradley, Levi	1	2	2		
Jeminson, Daniel	1	2	2		
Bradley, Bryant	1	2	2		
Cluley, Isaac	1	1	2		
Jones, Elijah	1	2	2		
Farrington, John	1		2		
Mann, David	1	1	2		
Blake, John	1	2	2		
Gilmore, Samuel	1	1	1		
Blake, Solomon	1	1	1		
Winchester, Silas	1	2	3		
Simpson, John	2	2	2		
Brastow, Thomas	1				
Brastow, Billings	1				
Hollbrook, Calvin	1		1		
Dupee, Elias	1				
Gilmore, William	1				

ORRINGTON TOWN—con.

NAME OF HEAD OF FAMILY.	Free white males of 16 years and upward, including heads of families.	Free white males under 16 years.	Free white females, including heads of families.	All other free persons.	Slaves.
Harthorn, Solomon	1	5	3		
Manssell, John	1		2		
Manssell, Joseph	1		2		
Orcutt, Emerson	2	4	5		
Knap, Samuel	1	3	5		
Gardiner, George	1				
Rowe, Zebulon	2	2	3		
Lancaster, William	2	2	1		
Robshaw, Peter	2		1		
Mann, Hannah	1		8		

PENOBSCOT TOWN.

NAME OF HEAD OF FAMILY.	Free white males of 16 years and upward, including heads of families.	Free white males under 16 years.	Free white females, including heads of families.	All other free persons.	Slaves.
Howe, David	1	1	1		
Crawford, James	2		2		
Halliburton, George	1				
Junin, Joseph	2		2		
Hunewell, Richard	2	1	2	3	
Lee, John	3	1	3	1	
Rogers, Samuel	2	1	3		
Higgins, Barnabas	1	1	4		
Readhead, William	1	1	4		
Mann, Oliver	1	1	6		
Orr, Debby	1	1	2		
Fields, Thomas	1		2		
Pollard, Avis			2		
Cook, Ephraim	1	1	2		
Robbins, Isaac	2	1	2		
Littlefield, Joseph	1		2		
Perkins, John	4	2	8		
Bray, John	4	1	3		
Hatch, Mark	3	3	5		
Lawrence, Rogers	1		2		
Parker, Mighill	1		1		
Perkins, Joseph	6	3	6	1	
Banks, Aaron	3	2	5		
Hayden, John	1		2		
Lowder, Jonathan	1	2	2		
Bishop, Hudson	1	1	3		
Calef, Joseph	1		1		
Cogswell, Sarah		1	3		
Hunt, Laban	1	2	2		
Douglas, James	1	2	3		
Hilton, Daniel	1		5		
Mathews, Abigail		3	4		
Maddox, Caleb	1				
Rea, Benja	1	2	7		
Perkins, Stover	1	5	4		
Willson, David	1	3	2		
Witham, Abraham	1	2	5		
More, John, junr	1	1	2		
Steel, Andrew	1	1	4		
Dolliver, William	1		1		
Willson, John	1		2		
Vezie, Moses	3		3		
Bowden, Ebenezer	1	2	4		
Dobbie, John	1	1	3		
Curtis, Joseph	1	1	4		
Bowden, William	1		4		
Bowden, Abraham	1	3	3		
Bowden, Lucy	1	1	2		
Hibbert, Joseph	2	1	3		
Devereaux, Ralph	2	1	4		
Hibbert, Joseph, junr	1	1	3		
Bowden, Thomas	1	2	2		
Bowden, Ebenezer	3	1	4		
Bridges, Henry	1		2		
Stover, Jeremiah	1	2	3		
Stover, Abraham	1	1	2		
Stover, Jotham	1	2	1		
Bridges, Edmund	1				
Heath, Eldad	1	3	5		
Bowden, Caleb	1	2	5		
Bowden, Paul	2		1		
Basteen, Joseph	1	2	3		
Bowden, Samuel	1	1	4		
Howard, Edward	1	1	6		
Hopkins, Elisha	2	1	1		
Norton, Noah	1	4	3		
More, William	1	1	1		
Blake, Andrew	1	2	1		
Darrow, George	1	2	1		
Radman, John	1	2	4		
Blake, Ephraim	2	4	4		
Radman, Israel	1		3		
Mayew, Reuben	2	3	6		
Corsson, John	1	2	6		
Radman, Benja	1				
Young, Joseph	1	1	3		
Dyer, Michael	1	3	6		
Bakeman, John, junr	1	1	2		
Bakeman, John	2	3	4		
Hollbrook, Jesse	2	2	5		
Hosmer, Abel	2	3	3		
Adams, Francis	1	1	3		

PENOBSCOT TOWN—con.

NAME OF HEAD OF FAMILY.	Free white males of 16 years and upward, including heads of families.	Free white males under 16 years.	Free white females, including heads of families.	All other free persons.	Slaves.
Costin, Daniel	1		1		
Magee, Neil	1		1		
Lowe, Daniel	1	1	3		
Howard, Benja	3	1	4		
Howard, Benja, junr	1		1		
Orcutt, Jacob	2	3	3		
Orcutt, Malachi	1	1	2		
Condon, John	3	4	2		
Wasson, John	1	2	2		
Wasson, Thomas	1		1		
Wasson, Samuel	1	2	5		
Hawes, David	1	3	4		
Henry, Archibald	1	2	2		
Perkins, Nathaniel	1	2	2		
Slack, Thomas	1	1	2		
Perkins, Abraham	1	1	5		
Lunt, Benja	1	2	6		
Wardwell, Joseph	1	1	2		
Wardwell, Jeremiah, junr	1	1	2		
Butler, James	1		4		
Lymburner, Cunningham	1	2	6		
Grindall, John	1		2		
Varnum, Mathew	1	3	3		
Jones, Jeremiah	1	2	2		
Jones, Samuel	1				
Bowden, Jacob	1		6		
Stover, William	1	2	1		
Stover, Isaac	1	1	4		
Tapley, Peletiah	1		4		
Webber, Joseph	3	2	4		
Blodgett, Seth	1	4	3		
Allen, Peter	1	2	2		
Davis, Thomas	1	2	2		
Swain, Meriam		3	2		
Curtis, Benja, junr	1	4	2		
Parker, Oliver	2	3	3		
Morgrage, Peter	1	2	4		
More, John	2		1		
More, James	1		1		
Curtis, Benja	2		3		
Curtis, Charles	1		2		
Wescott, Elizabeth	1	1	3		
Wescott, William	1	2	2		
Lowell, Eliphalet	1	4	4		
Lowell, Joseph	2	1	3		
Woodman, Joshua	1				
Herrick, Joseph	1				
Binney, Joseph	2		5		
Powars, Battry	1		1		
Webber, William	3	1	3		
More, David	1		3		
Gooding, Luxford	2	1	2		
Buckley, Daniel	1				
Burges, John, junr	1	1	4		
Blake, Moses	1		2		
Avery, Thatcher	1	2	5		
Freeman, Peletiah	3	1	5		
Stover, Nathaniel	2	2	3		
Richey, Mathew	1	2	3		
Johonnot, Gabriel	2	1	2		
Grindall, Ichabod	3	2	2		
Eaton, Thirza			1		
Atkins, Nathaniel	1		2		
Kench, Thomas	1	1	1		
Magee, Robert	2		3		
Lord, Jeremiah	1		2		
Vezie, Nathaniel	1	2	6		
Leach, Peletiah	2	4	4		
Connor, Alice		3	6		
Webster, Daniel	1	2	4		
Rhodes, Esther			2		
Hutchins, William	1	3	1		
Grindall, John, junr	1		1		
Gay, Moses	1				
Perkins, Isaac	2	4	3		
Perkins, Sparks	1	3	4		
Wardwell, Daniel	1	1	2		
Wardwell, Jeremiah	1	3	4	1	
Snowman, William	1		1		
Perkins, Mary		3	3		
Stover, William	1	2	5		
Littlefield, Elijah	3		4		
Leach, James	3		4		
Wardwell, Daniel, jun	1		2		
Herrick, Andrew	3	4	4		
Nutter, Thomas	2	1	4		
Woollins, John	1	1	3		
Vezie, Samuel	2	3	4		
Wardwell, Josiah	1	1	4		
Winslow, Elijah	1	1	6		
Snowman, John	1	2	3		
Perkins, Daniel	1	2	6		
Nutter, William	1		1		

NAME OF HEAD OF FAMILY.	Free white males of 16 years and upward, including heads of families.	Free white males under 16 years.	Free white females, including heads of families.	All other free persons.	Slaves.
PENOBSCOT TOWN—con.					
Grant, Alexander	1	4	4		
Wescott, Samuel	2	1	3		
Wescott, Andrew	1		1		
Johnson, Giles	1	2	4		
Grindall, Reuben	2		8		
Grindall, Daniel	1	4	2		
Varnum, Gershom	1	3	4		
Hill, Geofry	1				
Stevens, Thomas	1				
Larry, Michael	1				
Taylor, James	2				
Jenkins, David	1				
Mathews, Samuel	1		2		
SEDGWICK TOWN.					
Stanley, Kenny	1	2	4		
Herrick, Joshua	2		5		
Trussell, Joshua	2	4	4		
Herrick, Joseph	1				
Hale, Samuel	4	1	3		
Holly, Joanna			2		
Friend, Benjª	4	2	5		
Carlton, David	2	4	2		
Allen, Joanna	2	3	3		
Blasdell, Enoch	1	1	2		
Over, William	2	2	2		
Over, William, junʳ	1		4		
Dodge, Abner	4	3	2		
Dodge, Jonah	1	1	3		
Dodge, Amaziah	1	1	2		
Cole, Thomas	1	1	4		
Allen, Nehemiah	4	2	3		
Fly, James	1	4	4		
Dorothy, Robert	3		2		
Dorothy, David	1	1	1		
Freathy, Joseph	3		2		
Bunker, Silas	3	3	3		
Herrick, John	2	6	4		
Herrick, Samuel	3	4	3		
Herrick, Ebenezer	1	2	6		
Black, Daniel	1	1	4		
Freathey, Joseph, junʳ	1	2	4		
Reed, Abraham	1	1	4		
Black, John, junʳ	1	1	2		
Black, Samuel	1		1		
Reed, William	3		2		
Cozens, Thomas	1		3		
Mahoney, James	1				
York, Solomon	1		2		
Cozens, Samuel	2	1	1		
Cozens, Samuel, junʳ	1	2	1		
Hutchinson, Joseph	1				
Babson, Joseph	2	2	4		
Black, Moses	1		5		
Black, Sally			2		
Black, Anna			1		
Harper, William	1	1	2		
Ementon, Joseph	1	1	3		
Herrick, Shadrach	1	1	1		
Wells, Richard	1		2		
Wells, William	1		3		
Staples, John	1	1	1		
Hammond, John	1	2	2		
Bridges, Job	1	3	3		
Carter, James	1	3	4		
Gra, Joshua	1	1	3		
Cain, Samuel	1	1	2		
Harding, Josiah	1	2	5		
Carter, John	2		1		
Carter, John, junʳ	1	1	4		
Bridges, Daniel, junʳ	3	1	3		
Bridges, Daniel	2	1	2		
Bridges, Jonathan	1	2	3		
Eaton, Ebenezer	1	3	4		
Eaton, Moses	4	2	4		
Carter, Allen	1	2	2		
Norris, William	1		3		
Hooper, John	1	3	3		
Eaton, Jonathan	1		2		
Hutchinson, John	1	2	4		
Billings, Benjª	1	4	4		
Billings, Abel	1	4	1		
Byard, Robert	2	5	4		
Billings, John	2	2	3		
Billings, Solomon	1		2		
Maker, Joseph	1	2	3		
Williams, Thomas	1	2	2		
Parker, Simeon	1		2		
Lymburner, John	1	2	3		
Grindall, Joshua	3	6	2		
Bartrick, Dolly			5		
Butler, George	1	4	4		
Douglas, John	1	2	4		
Snow, Nickolas	3		5		

NAME OF HEAD OF FAMILY.	Free white males of 16 years and upward, including heads of families.	Free white males under 16 years.	Free white females, including heads of families.	All other free persons.	Slaves.
SEDGWICK TOWN—con.					
Gra, Andrew	1	3	1		
Door, John	1	2	2		
Gra, James	3	5	4		
Walker, John	1	2	3		
Watson, Shadrach	1		1		
Black, John	1	2	3		
Gra, Reuben	2	3	3		
Gra, Samuel	2	1	7		
Gra, Samuel, junʳ	1	1	1		
Stuart, Charles	1		3		
Douglas, James	2	4	1		
Snow, Joshua	1	2	2		
Door, Benjª	1		1		
Gra, Nathaniel	1	2	2		
Gra, Joshua, junʳ	1		3		
Knowles, Samuel	1		2		
Davis, Israel	1				
McCaslin, Alexander	1	1	2		
Grindall, William	1	3	6		
Dodge, Abraham	1	1	2		
Parker, Oliver, junʳ	1				
SMALL ISLANDS NOT BELONGING TO ANY TOWN.					
Blake, Daniel	1	3	1		
Webster, Andrew	1		2		
Russell, Samuel	2		1		
Corsson, Nathaniel	1	1	3		
Corsson, John	1	1	2		
Annis, Ralph	2	3	6		
Pickering, Samuel	1	2	3		
Pickering, Daniel	1		2		
Dow, John	1	4	3		
Prince, Joseph	1	1	4		
Prince, John	1				
White, Thomas	1				
Robinson, Daniel	1				
Cunningham, Thomas	1				
Orr, William	1				
Walker, Charles	1	1	1		
Woodhouse, George	1	1	1		
Green, Anna			1		
SULLIVAN TOWN.					
Buckley, John	1	1	4		
Bean, Samuel	1	2	3		
Bickford, Joshua	1		4		
Bickford, Joseph	1	3	3		
Dyer, Ephraim	1	1	2		
Johnson, John	3	1	5		
Marten, Phillip	1	4	3		
Bragden, Ebenezer	3	1	3		
Dyer, Sarah			3		
Ingalls, William	1	1	2		
Doyle, Thomas	1		2		
Simpson, Jabez	1	3	4		
Ash, Thomas	2		5		
Hammond, John	3		2		
Bean, John	2		3		
Bean, John, junʳ	1	1	1		
Sullivan, Abigail	2	1	3		
Bragden, Joseph	3	2	3		
Prebble, Nathaniel	2		3		
Bean, James	1	3	3		
Prebble, Samuel	1		4		
Urann, John	2	1	1		
Welsh, Benjamin	1	2	4		
Ingalls, Samuel	3		2		
Simpson, James	2	2	2		
Prebble, Nathaniel	1		2		
Prebble, John	1		3		
Downing, Richard	1	1	3		
York, Benjª, junʳ	2	1	3		
Simpson, John	1		3		
Salter, Francis	1		1		
Sargent, Paul Dudley	2	2	9		
Bennett, Benjª	1				
Simpson, Josiah	2		1		
Simpson, Paul	1	2	4		
Simpson, Samuel	1	1	1		
Gordon, John	1	3	2		
Miller, James	2	3	4		
Blasdell, Abner	1	5	3		
Springer, James	1				
Everett, Henry	1	1	2		
York, Bartholomew	1	1	3		
Hardison, Nathaniel	2	1	5		
Bragden, Jeremiah	2		2		
Bragden, John	1	1	2		
Bragden, Jeremiah, jun.	1		2		
Clark, Benjª	1	2	6		
Johnson, Dorcas		1	2		

NAME OF HEAD OF FAMILY.	Free white males of 16 years and upward, including heads of families.	Free white males under 16 years.	Free white females, including heads of families.	All other free persons.	Slaves.
SULLIVAN TOWN—con.					
Springer, Jacob	1	1	1		
Donnell, Abraham	1	3	4		
Card, Stephen	1		4		
Hooper, David	1	3	6		
Williams, John	1		1		
Barronock, John	1	1	2		
Scammons, Daniel	1	4	3		
Abbott, James	1		2		
Butler, Nathaniel	1	1	2		
Butler, Peter	1	2	2		
Springer, David	1	1	2		
Hardison, Stephen	2		1		
Clark, Elisha	1				
Clark, Stephen	1	2	6		
West, Judah	1	3	5		
Butler, Moses	2	1	2		
Butler, Moses, junʳ	1	3	3		
Abbott, Reuben	2	4	3		
Abbott, Reuben, junʳ	1	2	1		
Abbott, Moses	2	1	4		
Clark, Richard	1	1	3		
Grant, Francis	2	1	1		
Gatcomb, William	2	2	5		
Moon, Thomas	3	1	4		
Moon, Joseph	1		2		
Jones, Morgan	1		2		
Coates, Charles	1	1	1		
Crabtree, William	1	4	2		
Crabtree, Agreen	2	3	1		
Wooster, William	2	2	4		
Wooster, Oliver	2	3	4		
Wooster, David	1		1		
Pettingall, Edward	1	1	1		
Foss, Thomas	2		1		
Lunt, Joseph	1	2	4		
Hodgkins, Moses	1	1	2		
Hodgkins, Shemuell	2	3	4		
Hodgkins, Phillip	3	1	3		
Leland, James	1	1	2		
Young, Stephen	2	1	6		
Massy, Robert	1		1		
Cook, Betty		1	5		
Lancaster, Joseph	1	3	5		
Abram, Paddy				1	
TRENTON TOWN (INCLUDING TOWNSHIP NO. 1, EAST SIDE OF UNION RIVER).					
Wiggins, Benjª	1	1	1		
Ford, John	1	1	2		
Hodgkins, Edward	2	2	2		
Googins, Rogers	3		2		
Killpatrick, Robert	1	1	1		
Berry, Edward	1	5	4		
Killpatrick, Marten	3	1	3		
Killpatrick, Samuel	1		1		
Lord, James	1	1	4		
Harding, John	1	3	2		
Coolidge, Silas	1				
Foster, Jacob	1	2	4		
Whitaker, Elisha	1				
Black, Edmund	1		1		
Bark, Joseph	1	1	1		
Haines, Ephraim	2				
Haines, Parley	1				
Haines, Peter	1				
Hopkins, William	2	1	6		
Murch, John	2		3		
Farrell, Farrington	1		1		
Murch, John, junʳ	1		2		
Anderson, Job	2	5	3		
Sinclair, Edward	1	2	1		
Hapworth, Thomas	1	1	2		
Green, John	1	1	3		
Farnsworth, Jonas	1		1		
Dutton, Jesse	2	1	2		
Jordan, Solomon	3	4	6		
Jordan, Ebenezer	2	4	3		
Morrison, Joseph	1	1	4		
Tinker, John	1	2	4		
Beal, Joanna		1	4		
Card, Joseph	1	2	1		
Lord, Isaac	1	7	2		
Jones, Theodore	2		2		1
Hopkins, James	1	3	3		
Jealoson, Nathaniel	1	3	2		
Maddox, Henry	1	4	2		
Millikin, Robert	1	2	6		
Fletcher, William	2	2	6		
More, Joseph	2	2	4		
Smith, Nathaniel	1	7	3		
Debeck, Samuel	1		2		
Jealouson, John	1	3	3		
Jealouson, Wᵐ	1	2	5		

HANCOCK COUNTY—Continued.

NAME OF HEAD OF FAMILY.	Free white males of 16 years and upward, including heads of families.	Free white males under 16 years.	Free white females, including heads of families.	All other free persons.	Slaves.
TRENTON TOWN (INCLUDING TOWNSHIP NO. 1, EAST SIDE OF UNION RIVER)—con.					
Haslem, George	2	1	3		
Jordan, Meletiah	1	2	7		
Lord, George	1		2		
McFarlin, James	1	1	5		
McFarlin, Thomas	3	3	3		
Smith, James	3	3	5		
Springer, John	1	2	2		
Googins, Thomas	2	2	3		
TOWNSHIP NO. 1 (BUCKS).					
Herryman, Daniel	1	1	4		
Buck, Ebenezer	1	3	3		
Buck, Jonathan, junr	2	3	5		
Herryman, Benjᵃ	1				
Herryman, Ahasael	2		3		
Stanley, Nathaniel	1				
Buck, Daniel	2	1	4		
Adams, Isaac	1				
Buck, Jonathan	1		1		
Putney, Jonathan	1		1		
McDonald, Lauchlan	1	1	1		
McDonald, Roderick	2	1	2		
Herryman, John	1	1	2		
Emes, Phineas	2	1	6		
Lanpher, Stephen	1	1	3		
Lanpher, Anson	2	4	1		
Lawrence, William	1	1	5		
Murphy, Thomas	1				
Patterson, John	1		3		
Cottrell, Ezra	1	3	5		
Page, Benjᵃ	3	2	5		
Page, Moses	1	2	1		
Brown, Theophilus	1	1	4		
Cole, Joseph	1	1	2		
Atwood, Nathan	1	3	3		
Bassett, Ebenezer	1	3	2		
Higgins, Jethro	3	1	2		
Collson, Josiah	4	3	3		
Lowell, Abner	1	2	6		
Dones, Bangs	1	1	1		
Homer, William	1				
Clements, James	2	1	4		
Fowler, Levi	1	2	5		
Kenny, Stephen	1	4	4		
Snow, Reuben	1	1	1		
Carr, Silvanus	1		1		
Snow, Benjᵃ	1		5		
Coullard, Joshua	2	3	5		
Curtis, Abel	2	2	1		
Harding, Ezekiel	1	3	3		
Smith, Zoeth	1		2		
Kent, William	3		2		
Stubbs, Samuel	2	1	2		
Lowell, Benjᵃ	1	1	3		
Higgins, James	1	1	1		
Paine, Joseph	1		4		
Sears, Paul	1		1		
Eldridge, James	3	3	2		
Higgins, Josiah	1		2		
Ballard, Baze	1	2	3		
Lewis, John	1		1		
Lewis, Lathley	1	3	4		
Collson, Ebenezer	1	3	3		
Lowell, Nathaniel	1	3	1		
Miller, Robert	1	2	1		
Carr, John B	1	1	2		
Appleby, John	1				
Miller, John	1	3	3		
Buck, Benjamin	1	1	2		
Stubbs, James	5	1	2		
Black, Samuel				1	
Sturgis, Edward				1	
TOWNSHIP NO. 6 (WEST SIDE OF UNION RIVER).					
Joy, Benjamin	5	2	4		
Murch, Joseph	1		2		

NAME OF HEAD OF FAMILY.	Free white males of 16 years and upward, including heads of families.	Free white males under 16 years.	Free white females, including heads of families.	All other free persons.	Slaves.
TOWNSHIP NO. 6 (WEST SIDE OF UNION RIVER)—continued.					
Orcutt, John	1	1	6		
Maddox, Samuel	1	1	3		
More, Edward	1	3	3		
Garland, Josiah	3	3	4		
Maddox, Joshua	4		3		
Maddox, Caleb	2	2	1		
Maddox, John	1		2		
Tourtellott, Abraham, junr	1				
Smith, John	2	3	4		
Hammond, Moses	2				
Ross, Daniel	1		1	1	
Gardiner, Joshua	1				
Trueworthy, James	2	3	4		
Davis, James	2	1	2		
Steward, John	1	1	3		
Joy, Samuel	1	1	5		
Trueworthy, Daniel	1		1		
Davis, Samuel	1	2	3		
More, Wyat	1	2	6		
More, Benjᵃ	2	2	4		
Wormwood, Benjᵃ	1		1		
Wormwood, Joseph	1		4		
Lord, Jacob	1		2		
Wormwood, Eli	2	1	4		
Fly, William	1		3		
Jordan, Nathaniel	1		2		
Flood, Dominicus	1	1	2		
Means, Robert	1	2	5		
Millikin, Elias	1	1	2		
Hammond, Nathaniel	1	2	2		
Pray, James	1	2	3		
Ray, Mathew	1		1		
Patten, James	1	1	7		
Patten, Susannah			2		
Patten, John	1		1		
Flood, Andrew	2		2		
Flood, Bartholomew	1		2		
Green, Isaac	1	5	1		
Morgan, Benjᵃ	2	1	2		
Hopkins, Allen	2	1	2		
Young, Samuel	3	3	4		
Coggins, Josiah	1				
Sinclair, Edward	2		2		
Coggins, Hezekiah	2	2	3		
VINALHAVEN TOWN.					
Newberry, John	1	2	4		
Robbins, Benjamin	2	2	6		
Stewart, Charles	1				
Carver, Caleb	1	1	4		
Cooper, James	1		1		
Cooper, James, jun	1	1	1		
Cooper, Thomas	1		5		
Douglas, Robert, jun	1		2		
Douglas, Robert	1	3	2		
McMullen, Archibald	1	2	3		
Day, John	2		3		
Walton, Paul	1				
Carver, Stephen	1		1		
Kent, Susanah			1		
Winslow, Penelope	1		3		
Dyer, William	2	3	3		
Ames, Justus	2	3	4		
Norton, Samuel	1		2		
Dyer, Benjamin	1		4		
Ames, Margaret			1		
Kent, Benjamin	2	2	2		
Armstrong, Richard	1		1		
Thomas, Samuel	5	1	3		
Winslow, Joseph	1				
Waterman, Joseph	1	1	5		
Whitman, Abel	2		2		
Crabtree, Eleazer	2	4	3		
Bowen, Michael	1		2		
Carr, Benjᵃ	2	3	3		
Dunham, James	1	2	3		
Heard, James	1	4	4		
Sever, William	1				

NAME OF HEAD OF FAMILY.	Free white males of 16 years and upward, including heads of families.	Free white males under 16 years.	Free white females, including heads of families.	All other free persons.	Slaves.
VINALHAVEN TOWN—continued.					
White, George	1	3	5		
Dyer, Anthony	1	2	7		
Bramhall, Cornelius	2	2	4		
Wooster, David	1	1	3		
Wooster, Nathaniel	1	2	2		
Wooster, Joseph	1	1			
Perry, John	1	4	4		
Ames, Mark	2	3	3		
Barrick, William	2		3		
Brown, Cyrel	1		2		
Parry, William	2	2	5		
Glover, James	1	2	5		
Cox, Ebenezer	1		4		
Smith, Jonathan	1				
Whaling, James	2		3		
Cooper, William	1	2	2		
Whaling, William	1	2	1		
Beverege, Thomas	2	4	5		
Foster, Jonathan	1	3	7		
Smith, Levi	3		3		
Lindsay, James	1	1	1		
Roulstone, Benjᵃ	1				
Babrick, John	1	1	1		
Annis, Benjamin	1	2	2		
Calderwood, John	3		5		
Calderwood, Samuel	1	1	1		
Carver, Israel	3	2	3		
Norton, Pheobe			1		
Norton, Sarah			1		
Vinal, William	1	3	1	1	
Scevy, James	1	1	2		
Calderwood, James	2				
Calderwood, John, jun	1	2	5		
Morey, Ezekiel	1		2		
Norton, Uriah	1		3		
Luce, Bethuel	3	1	2		
Daggett, Benjᵃ, jun	1	2	8		
Daggett, Benjᵃ	1		1		
Young, Samuel	1	1	2		
Phillbrook, Jeremiah	1	3	5		
Leadbetter, Increase	1		2		
Leadbetter, John	1		2		
Leadbetter, Luther	1				
Crockett, Isaac	2	5	2		
Burges, John	1	1	2		
Brown, Thomas	1	6	5		
Ginn, Thomas	1	1	3		
Green, Joseph	1	5	5		
Stinson, James	1		2		
Lane, Benjᵃ	1		2		
Fernalld, Nathaniel	1				
Carver, Thadeus	1	1	7		
Arey, Isaac	1	5	4		
Leadbetter, Increase, jun	1	7	4		
Jewell, James	1	3	7		
Lane, Joseph	1		2		
Arey, Ebenezer	1		1		
Jewell, James, junr	1				
Cain, John	1	1	3		
Phillbrook, Job	1	2	4		
Smith, John	1	4	4		
Phillbrook, Joel	1	3	4		
Coombs, Anthony	1	5	4		
Lane, Isachar	1		3		
Hall, Ebenezer	2	4	6		
Young, Abraham	1	4	5		
Young, Joseph	1				
Cree, John	1	1	1		
McDaniel, James	1	3	1		
Tolman, Isaiah	1	2	2		
Nickolls, Alexander	1	2	2		
Andrews, Amos	1		4		
Young, Benjᵃ	1		5		
Allen, Jonathan	1	2	4		

LINCOLN COUNTY.

NAME OF HEAD OF FAMILY.	Free white males of 16 years and upward, including heads of families.	Free white males under 16 years.	Free white females, including heads of families.	All other free persons.	Slaves.
BALLTOWN TOWN.					
Bond, David	1	3	3		
Whiten, Joseph	1	1	2		
Clark, James	1	1	3		
Rice, John	1		1		
Rice, John, Junier	1	1	1		
Trask, Thomas	2	2	3		
BALLTOWN TOWN—con.					
Trask, Thomas, Juner	1	2	3		
Hopkins, William	3		3		
Hopkins, William, Juner	1	3	3		
Hopkins, Solomen	1	4	1		
McCollistor, Archable	3		1		
McCollistor, Richard	1	1	3		
BALLTOWN TOWN—con.					
Henry, Robert	2	4	3		
Cunningham, James	2	2	3		
Cambol, James	1	1	3		
Jones, John	1	2	3		
fish, Jonathan	1	1	2		
Jackson, Joseph	2	3	3		

LINCOLN COUNTY—Continued.

NAME OF HEAD OF FAMILY.	Free white males of 16 years and upward, including heads of families.	Free white males under 16 years.	Free white females, including heads of families.	All other free persons.	Slaves.
BALLTOWN TOWN—con.					
Jackson, Samuel	2	3	3		
Dow, Peter, Juner	1	1	2		
fanders, Enoch	4	4	3		
Kanadey, Thomas	3	3	3		
Rollins, John	1	1	6		
Avrill, Samuel	1		7		
Perham, Rias	1	2	1		
Crumell, Thomas	1	1	3		
farnan, Daniel	1	2	1		
Noys, Jonathan	2	6	4		
withouse, Samuel	2		2		
Whithous, Samuel, Ju	1	5	2		
Whithouse, Jacob	1	1	3		
Hatch, Zach	1	1	5		
Jones, Joseph	3	3	6		
Linsuit, John	2	2	6		
Linsuit, Joshua	3		3		
Clark, William	4	3	2		
Clark, Elisha	1		2		
Gliden, Adndrew	1	3	4		
Palmer, Simon	1	3	1		
Kain, John	1	1	3		
Heath, Abraham	1	1	2		
Cunengham, Isacc	1		1		
Starns, Ebennesor	2		2		
Dow, Peter	1	2	2		
murphy, James	1	7	3		
Carr, Josiah	1	2	2		
ford, Abner	1		3		
ford, Abner, Juner	1	3	1		
Ripley, Josiah	1	1	2		
Trask, Jonathan	1	2	2		
Casten, Thomas	1		1		
Cuningham, Samuel	1		3		
Cuningham, David	1	1	1		
Howard, Andrew	3		2		
Wire, John	1		1		
Hilton, Isaac	1		3		
Hilton, John	3		3		
Boynton, John	1	1	1		
Boynton, John, Juner	2	2	3		
Cuningham, William	1		3		
Cuningham, John	1	1	2		
Glidon, Charles	1	4	3		
Weaks, Winteig	1				
Balley, Joseph	1		2		
Balley, Nathan	1		2		
Potte, John	1	6	4		
Woodman, John	3	2	2		
Little, Joshua	5		2		
Toby, William	1	2	4		
Heath, Asa	1	4	5		
Pesley, Olover	1	1	5		
Pesley, Ezekiel	1	3	3		
Peasley, Nathan	1	2	5		
Gilman, Samuel	1		3		
Bartlet, Caleb	1	3	3		
Heath, Isaac	1				
King, Benjæmen	3	4	2		
Ware, Nathan	1	1	4		
Noris, Benjamen	3	2	3		
Choat, Aaron, Juner	1	1	2		
Carlow, Martin	1	2	3		
Cresey, Abel	1		2		
Turner, Thomas	3		2		
Turner, Nichlass	1	2	2		
Tarry, David	3		5		
durley, John	3		2		
Plumer, Daniel	1				
Wire, Obed	1	2	1		
Kinkade, Samuel, Juⁿ	1	2	3		
Winslow, Benjamin	1		6		
Prible, Jedediah	1	3	3		
Cartton, Samuel	1	3	5		
Trask, Joseph	2	2	4		
Choat, Abraham	1	1	2		
Grover, Ebenezor	1		5		
Milikin, John	1		2		
Peasley, Jonathan	1	1	1		
Poor, Richard	3		4		
Heath, Jonathan	1	1	4		
Longfelow, Nathan	3		2		
Kinkad, Samuel, Juner	1		2		
Choat, frances	1		1		
Philbrooks, Ebenezor	1	1	5		
Bartlet, Jonathan	1		2		
Bartlet, Joseph	1	3	3		
Peasley, Daniel	1	5	3		
Erykins, George	1		2		
Tarr, Abraham	1	2	1		
fowls, William	1		2		
fowls, Samuel	1	1	2		
Philbrooks, Ebenezor	1		1		
Philbrooks, John	2	3	7		
Potter, Solomon	1	3	4		
Vining, Jonah	2	4	4		
BALLTOWN TOWN—con.					
Plumer, Joseph	2	3	3		
Speed, Joseph	2	1	5		
Gliden, Charles	1	4	3		
Hutchens, Elisha	1	2	2		
Richardson, Abather	1		3		
Chenneston, Benjamen	1	1	1		
Hall, John	1	4	2		
Hall, Isac	1	2	2		
Hall, James	1	4	2		
Thomas, Henry	1	1	7		
Horks, Joseph	1	1	2		
Johnson, John	2	2	2		
Weaks, John, Juner	1	1	3		
Weaks, Joseph	1	2	6		
Weaks, Thomas	1	2	2		
Weaks, Mark	1	1	2		
Weaks, John	3		2		
Rollins, Nathaniel	1	2	1		
Rollins, Eliphlot	1	1	1		
Parker, Joseph	2		2		
Ames, Jonathan	1				
Eams, Phinas	1	5	1		
Shepard, James	3	2	3		
Day, Thomas	2	6	4		
Separd, Samuel, Juner	1		3		
Shepard, William	1	1	2		
Brand, Isac	2				
Johnson, Samuel	2	2	2		
Plumer, Timothy	1	3	3		
Stickney, Benjamen	1	3	5		
mcClary, Robert	1	2	3		
Decker, John	2		5		
Waters, Samuel	2	4	5		
mcCurdey, Samuel	1	1	2		
Plumer, Benjemen	1		1		
Reaves, James	2	3	4		
Rowall, Jacob	3	3	4		
Choat, Abraham	4	1	4		
Trask, Joseph, Juner	1		3		
ferrin, Timothy	1		1		
Rogers, Joseph	1	3	4		
Rogers, Prince	1	3	2		
BATH TOWN.					
Cooms, George	2	5	4		
Eaton, Abel	2		2		
Williams, John	1	4	3		
Williams, George	2		5		
Higgins, Reuben	1	4	3		
Holbrook, Abizah	3	2	3		
Higgins, Philip	2	4	4		
Pain, Joshua	3	3	3		
Bailey, Christopher	1	6	2		
Cooms, Stephen	4	2	5		
Higgins, Benjª	3	4	6		
Higgins, Simeon	1	2	3		
Mariner, Jonª N	2	2	5		
Brown, Benjª	1		1		
Smith, Joseph	2	1	3		
Andrews, John	2	1	2		
Ham, Benjª	3	2	3		
Ham, John	2	3	5		
Grace, Patrick	1		1		
Purington, Joshua	1		1		
Lemont, Thomas	1	1	5		
Howland, Arthur	1		3		
Foot, Thoˢ, Jnr	1	2	2		
Labree, James	1		2		
Williams, John	1	2	1		
Whitney, Samˡ	3	2	2		
Whitney, Ebenᶻ	1	3	1		
Welch, Edward	4	1	2		7
Crafford, Mary			3		
Grace, Jane	1		2		
Crafford, Thoˢ	1	3	3		
Crafford, John	1	4	1		
Gran, Willᵐ	1	1	3		
Clark, John	1	4	8		
Ranes, Joshua	2	1	2		
Loring, Jeromy	3	3	2		
Hodgkins, Francis	2	1	2		
Cushing, Christopher	1		2		
Marsh, Caleb	1	1	1		
Foster, Mary	1	2	3		
Philbrick, Joshua	3		4		
Sewall, Dummer	3	1	3		
Sewall, Stephen	1	1	3		
Kimball, Richard	2	1	6		
Sewall, Henry	2	2	5		
Lambert, Joseph	3	2	9		
Lambert, Luke	2	1	4		
Moody, Samˡ	3	4	6		
Turner, Simeon	3	3	7		
Tod, Samˡ	1	3	5		
Capon, Theoˢ	1	1	3		
BATH TOWN—con.					
Ewers, John	1	1	2		
Thorn, Susanna		4	1		
McFarlen, John	3	2	4		
McHonnen, James	1		2		
Bracket, James	2				
Bean, Samˡ	1		1		
Colson, David	1	3	3		
Welsh, Samˡ	1	5	3		
Lincoln, Zadoc	1	2	6		
Marshal, Willᵐ	1	1	3		
Robertson, John	1	2	6		
Robertson, Alexander	1	3	5		
Pettingale, Edward	2		2		
Trufaut, David	5	3	6		
Whitmore, John	1	3	3		
Cook, Isaiah	1	2	2		
Worster, Francis	1	2	3		
Davis, Jonª	4		3		
Page, Edward H	2	3	4		
Swanton, Willᵐ	3	5	3		
Summer, David	1	1	4		
Swanton, Willᵐ	1	1	5		
Ross, Willᵐ	1	3	3		
Cook, Elisabeth	6	1	4		
Fitts, Ephraim	1	3	6		
Bradford, Isaac	2	1	2		
Sampson, Caleb	1	1	3		
Pettingale, Summon	1	6	2		
White, Joseph	2	1	3		
Cooker, Isaiah	4	4	3		
Webb, Willᵐ	1	5	5		
Wood, John	1	1			
Turner, Consider	1		5		
McDaniels, Betsy			2		
Emerson, Samˡ	2		4		
Berry, James	1	5	2		
Osgood, Jonª	2		2		
Berry, Samˡ	3	4	4		
Ring, David	1	3	4		
Mitchel, Jonª	5	2	6		
Brown, James	1				
Brady, John	1	4	4		
Mitchel, James M	1	4	2		
Lumber, Thoˢ	1	1	3		
Clifford, David	1	2	3		
Williams, John	1	3	4		
Bridges, Isaac	1	5	2		
Clemmons, Ruth	1		2		
Lumber, Samuel	2	1	4		
Lowel, Martha	1	1	4		
Clefford, Benjª	4	1	5		
Williams, Thoˢ	4		4		
Campbel, John	1				
Standish, Lemuel	1				
Hodgkins, Willᵐ	2	2	4		
Weeks, Silvanus	1	2	2		
Low, Jacob	2	2	2		
Soward, Theodore	1	4	5		
Lowel, John	1	1	1		
Lemont, Adam	1		2		
Foot, Thoˢ	1		1		
Foot, John	1	3	2		
Russey, David	3		4		
Runnel, Nathˡ	1	6	1		
Lemont, James	3	3	5		
Stanford, John	1	1	2		
Morse, Stephen	1	3	6		
White, Joseph	2	1	2		
Lemont, David	1	3	2		
Lemont, Samuel	1		2		
Purnton, Humphry	1	2	3		
Sargeant, Jonª	1	1	2		
Gould, Joseph	4	1	6		
Cooms, Joshua	1	2	4		
Durnton, John	1	3	3		
Brown, Willᵐ	1	3	3		
Sargeant, Joseph	1				
Sargeant, Jonª	1	1	2		
Higgam, Philip	1	5	2		
Higgam, Simeon	2	2	4		
Cooms, Stephen	3	2	6		
Morrison, Nathˡ L	2	1	1		
Lemont, John	1	3	3		
Woodward, Willᵐ	1	3	3		
Pray, Ebenezer	2	1	2		
Shaw, David	1				
Shaw, Joshua	1	3	2		
Berry, John	2	1	5		
Brown, Benjª	2	3	6		
BOOTHBAY TOWN.					
Brown, John	2		3		
Burnham, Solomon	3	3	2		
Brown, Margaret	1	1	3		
Burnham, Ephraim	1	1	1		

LINCOLN COUNTY—Continued.

NAME OF HEAD OF FAMILY.	Free white males of 16 years and upward, including heads of families.	Free white males under 16 years.	Free white females, including heads of families.	All other free persons.	Slaves.
BOOTHBAY TOWN—con.					
Burnham, Solomon	1				
Carlisle, Joseph	1	2	1		
Trask, Obadiah	1	1	2		
McPharlen, Benjᵃ	1	2	3		
Bryer, Elihu	1	2	2		
Perkins, Joseph	3	3	5		
Burnham, Solomon	4		6		
Bowland, John	3	3	4		
McCobb, Samˡ, Jur	1	2	2		
Kennady, James	3	2	6		
Kelley, Benjᵃ	3		1		
Kennady, Willᵐ	2		3		
Brier, Samˡ	5	3	4		
Boyd, Thomas	2	2	2		
Boyd, Thomas, Junʳ	2	3	6		
Boyd, George	3	1	6		
Booker, Joseph	1	2	3		
Adams, Samˡ, Junʳ	1	1	3		
Booker, John, Junʳ	1	1	2		
All, James	1	4	7		
Wall, Andʷ	1	2	6		
Beath, Jerᵉ	2		2		
Holton, John	1	2	4		
Dawes, John	1	1	2		
McCobb, Willᵐ	2	2	4		
Reid, Joseph	2	5	4		
Booker, John	1		1		
Montgomery, Lydia	2	5	3		
Montgomery, Samˡ	3		4		
Race, George	1	1	1		
Farnham, Joseph	4	1	3		
Farnham, Ansel	1		1		
Farnham, Chapen	1	1	2		
Farnham, Jonᵃ	1	1	3		
Linnecon, Benjᵃ	3		3		
Alley, Samˡ	1	4	6		
Ratclif, John	1		2		
Wallace, David	1	2	2		
Cooper, Philip	1	2	2		
Reid, Paul	2	1	6		
Lishman, John	3		1		
Creamer, Edward	2	1	4		
McCobb, Samˡ	1		3		
McCobb, David	1		3		
Seargeant, Benjᵃ	3	2	2		
McPharlen, Elizabeth	2	1	6		
McPharlen, Andʷ	1				
Fullerton, Ebenezer	1	1	4		
Beath, John	1		1		
Beath, Joseph	1		4		
McCobb, John	1	6	3		
Wilee, Robert	1		2		
Wilee, Martha	1		2		
Kenny, Abijah	1		2		
Reid, David	5	1	4		
Reid, David, Junʳ	1	2	3		
Reid, David, 3rd	1		5		
Poor, Willᵐ	1	2	4		
Sawyer, Benjᵃ	2				
Sawyer, Jonᵃ	2		5		
Sawyer, Aaron	2	4	2		
Sawyer, Jacob	1	1	2		
Reid, Andʷ	1	1	2		
Reid, Andʷ, Junʳ	1	2	3		
Greenough, Jonᵃ	1		5		
Reid, Andʷ, 3rd	1		6		
Reid, Willᵐ	1		2		
Murray, John	1		2		
Hern, Patrick	1		3		
Hern, Daniel	4	4	3		
Adams, Samˡ	3	3	3		
Reid, Mary	3	1	2		
Reid, James	1	1	1		
Willee, Robert	1	2	5		
Willee, John	1	1	1		
Decker, David	1	1	1		
Decker, Thomas	1	3	3		
Brewer, John	2	3	5		
McCown, Margara	1	1	3		
Thomson, Samˡ	2	2	4		
Thomson, Joseph	3		1		
Harris, Samˡ	1	5	3		
Emery, David	1	2	2		
Horn, Thoˢ	1		2		
Horn (Widow)	1		2		
Pierce, Silvester	2	2	4		
Pierce, Joseph	1	3	4		
Hamilton, John	1	2	4		
Decker, Willᵐ	2	3	3		
Bird, Edward	2		2		
Nelson, David	1		1		
Clambo, Willᵐ	1	1	1		
Pierce, Ezekiel	1	2	3		
Barter, Samˡ, Jur	1	1	5		
Pierce, Samˡ	2	3	8		
BOOTHBAY TOWN—con.					
Tibbits, Ichabod	1	5	3		
Preble, Ebenezer	1	1	2		
Abbot, Henry	1	3	3		
Abbot, John	1		1		
Horn; Cornelius	1	4	6		
Poor, John	1	4	6		
Langdon, Joseph	1	3	2		
Decker, Abraham	1	3	2		
Ball, Samˡ	1	3	2		
Ball, Levi	1		2		
Reid, Robert	1	1	3		
Rand, John	2	2	5		
Knight, Daniel	5	2	6		
Knight, Pettishal	1	2	4		
Cross, Joshua	1	1	2		
Cunningham, Ruggles	1	1	2		
Tibbits, James	1		2		
Kenny, Benjᵃ	1	1	1		
Lamson, Samˡ	2	1	2		
Lewis, Joseph	1	2	1		
Lewis, John	1	1	1		
Dawes, Jonᵃ	2	1	8		
Matthews, John	1	3	3		
Southard, John	1		2		
Lamson, James	1	2	4		
Lewis, Stephen	2	3	3		
Lewis, Willᵐ	1	5	1		
Carlton, Stephen	1	2	2		
Sawyer, Ebenezer	1	2	3		
Stover, John	1	1	1		
Webb, James	1	2			
Skidmore, Elias	1		2		
Reid, John	1	2	1		
Kenny, Samˡ	1	2	4		
Barter, Samˡ	1		1		
Barter, Joseph	2		3		
Day, James	2		1		
Barter, John	1	3	4		
Pinkham, Calvin	1	2	3		
Kent, Benjᵃ	1	2	6		
Alby, Obadah	1	1	2		
Tibits, Giles	1	1	2		
Lewis, Joseph, Junʳ	1	2	4		
Emerson, John	1	1	4		
Pinkham, Ichabod	6	1	7	1	2
Cromett, John	1		2		2
Cromett, Jereʰ	1		6		
Rollins, Stephen	1		2		
Pinkham, Nathˡ	2	3	2		
Perkins, Samˡ	1	4	4		1
Alley, John	1	1	2		
Alley, John, Jnʳ	2		5		
Sherman, Eleazer	2	6	6		
Willey, Alexander	1	3	3		
Giles, Joseph, Junʳ	1		2		
Kenny, Thoˢ	1	2	1		
Kenny, Henry	1		3		
Train, Jonᵃ	1	3	3		
Giddings, Joseph	1		4		
Giles, Joseph	2	1	4		
Pinkham, Solomon	2	1	5		
Tibbits, Nathˡ	1	1	2		
Stover, Joseph	1		6		
Webber, Gersham	1	2	4		
Alley, Joshua	1	2	4		
BOWDOIN TOWN.					
Hewey, John	2	2	3		
Hewey, John, Jur	1				
Hewey, James	1				
Waymouth, Jonathan	1	4	5		
Whitney, Jonathan	1				
Spokin, Joseph	1		2		
Wood, Joseph	1	1	2		
Waymouth, Edmond	3	1	5		
Ross, Robert	1	2	1		
Merril, Samuel	1	3	3		
Sanborn, Jethrow	1	1	4		
Macmanners, John	1	2	2		
Heath, William	1		1		
Gray, Alexander	1	4	4		
Hewey, Robert	1	4	2		
Freeman, Samson				5	
Gilpatrick, Nathaniel	1	3	1		
Higings, Timothy	3	5	4		
Handerson, Benjamin	1	2	2		
Wilson, Samuel	1				
Wheeler, Joseph	1		1		
Smith, Nathaniel	1		1		
Smith, John	1				
Temple, Ichabod	1	1	3		
Temple, Ebenezer	1	4	3		
Emery, Joseph	1	1	2		
BOWDOIN TOWN—con.					
Chace, Isaac	1	2	3		
Rideout, Benjamin	1	2	1		
Wheeler, Hannah	1	1	4		
Wheeler, Joseph	1	1	5		
Starbord, Samuel	1	1	4		
Grover, Andrew	1	3	2		
Grover, James	1				
Richardson, John	3	2	3		
Wheeler, Joseph	1		1		
Booby, Joseph	2		1		
Booby, William	1		3		
Barrat, Benjamin	1	2	3		
Sparks, Nicholas	2		2		
Booker, David	1	2	3		
Luis, George	1		3		
Whiting, William	1	1	3		
Wheeler, John	1	1	2		
Temple, Levi	1	3	3		
Tibbits, Benjamin	1		1		
Flag, John	1	1	2		
Marston, Nathaniel	1	1	2		
Allen, Daniel	1	2	2		
Jeleson, Nathaniel	1	1	2		
Allexander, Robart	1		1		
Combs, Leonard	1				
Alexander, William	1	1	1		
Alexander, John	1	1	2		
Richardson, John	2	2	2		
Richardson, Joseph	1				
Galloway, Job	2		1		
Baker, Judah	1	2	3		
Baker, Smith	1	2	4		
Baker, Barnard	1	5	1		
Jones, Isaac	1				
Booby, Christopher	1				
Alexander, James	1	1	2		
Shephard, John	1				
Sheen, Jonathan	1				
Temple, John	1	1	3		
Smith, Joseph	1				
Booker, Zacheus	1		1		
Pain, Timothy	1				
Myreen, John	1				
Hodgman, John	1	1	1		
Bramijon, Thomas	1	2	1		
Morey, Phillip	1	1	2		
Jiluce, Joseph	2	1	2		
Duncan, Robart	1		4		
Hogings, William	1		2		
Rideout, Stephen	1	2	4		
Hall, Lemuel	1	2	5		
Varnum, John	1	1	4		
Varnum, John, Jur	1				
Varnum, Wanton Jnr	1				
Truant, Job	2	3	7		
Potter, James	1	2	2		
Wire, John	1	4	2		
Bishop, William	1		3		
Poores, Richard	1	5	4		
Potter, Alexander	2		2		
Potter, David	1	3	4		
Kinnicum, Daniel	1	2	4		
Kinnicum, Edward	1				
Potter, James	4		4		
Rose, Prince	1	1	4		
Hinkly, Aaron	1	1	3		
Rose, George Potter	1				
Whitney, Isaac	1	2	5		
Mallet, John	1	2	7		
Alexander, James	2		3		
Thompson, Amos	2	2	7		
Brown, Jonathan	1	1	3		
Alexander, John	1	3	3		
Alexander, William	1				
Wilson, David	1	4	4		
Barnes, Benjamin	2	4	2		
Gowel, William	2	3	4		
Hall, Luther	1	3	3		
Polley, Samuel	3	1	4		
Jaquish, Richard	2		3		
Williams, William	1	2	3		
Combs, John	2	4	3		
Thompson, John	1		2		
Potter, Alexander	1				
Campbel, William	2	1	6		
Truant, Stephen	1				
Campbel, John	1	2	2		
Buker, Job	1				
Stinson, Robert	1				
Robertson, William	1	1	5		
Perry, David	1		3		
Townes, Noah	1	1	2		
Townes, Isreal	1				
Jaquish, Benjamin	1	1	2		
Purrinton, Humphry	1	4	4		

LINCOLN COUNTY—Continued.

BOWDOIN TOWN—con.

NAME OF HEAD OF FAMILY.	Free white males of 16 years and upward, including heads of families.	Free white males under 16 years.	Free white females, including heads of families.	All other free persons.	Slaves.
Adams, John	2	3	5		
Purrinton, Nath¹	2		4		
Tarr, Joseph	1	1	5		
Raymon, Samuel	1	2	3		
Small, Ephrom	1	3	3		
Dinslow, Joseph	1	2	3		
Hopkins, Elisha	1	1			
Randal, Joseph	1	1	2	1	
Thompson, Joseph	2	4	4		
Toothacher, Mary		1	3		
Ridly, James	1	2	4		
Buker, Joseph	1	1	5		
Adams, Samuel	1	1	3		
Buker, Dimmick	1	1	4		
Ridly, Daniel	1	2	3		
Boah, Alexander	1		3		
Ridly, George	1	2	2		
Williams, Jonathan	1	3	2		
Huff, Moses	1	1	1		
Williams, George	1	2	2		
Sparkes, James	1	1	3		
Cornish, Sipperon	1	1	1		
Smalley, David	2	3	3		
Rogers, James	2	3	2		
Small, Joseph	2	2	4		
Small, Taylor	2	2	6		
Townes, Joseph	1	1	3		
White, Hugh	1	1	4		
Stinson, William	1	1	3		
Jack, Andrew	3	2	4		
Jack, Joseph	1				
Brieryhurst, Thomas	1	2	6		
Forbus, John	1		3		
Rideout, John	1	1	2		
Varnum, John	1		3		
Jaquish, Isaac	1		1		
Raymond, Samuel	1	2	3		
White, James	1				
Woodard, David	1				
Campbel, David	1	1	2		
Hibbard, Jonathan	1	3	3		
Weekes, James	1		3		
Nutting, Abel	1	1	4		
Davis, Jesse	1	1	4		
Davis, Thomas	1				
Cushing, John	1	2	5		
Gould, Jacob	1				
Seals, William	1				
Higings, Seth	1	1	3		
Simons, Samuel	1	2	3		
Jones, Phinehas	1	1	2		
Jordon, Ephrom	1				
Jordon, Abner	1	1	1		
Sinkler, Adoniram	3	5	1		
Tibbits, Timothy	2		2		
Freeman, Cesor					8
Hinkly, Isaac	1	3	3		
Hinkly, Reliance			1		
Whitrage, Jacob	1				
Whittimore, Stephen	1				
Smullin, John	1	1	1		
Combs, Hezekiah	1	2	2		
Donnehue, Joseph	1	2	3		
Mitcalf, Hugh	1	3	3		
Tibbits, Samuel	1	3	3		
Tibbits, Isaac	1		1		
Hinkly, Samuel	1				
Hinkly, Samuel	1		2		
Ham, Thomas	1	2		1	
White, Hugh	1				
Cowing, Calvin	1	3	3		
Mulloy, Hugh	1	3	3		
Spoldin, Nath¹	1				
Berry, Josiah	1	2	4		
White, John	2	1	2		
Tibbits, Thomas	1	5	3		
Staples, Stephen	1		5		
Woodard, John	1	5	5		
White, James	1				
Tibbits, Esther			1		

BOWDOINHAM TOWN.

NAME OF HEAD OF FAMILY.	Free white males of 16 years and upward, including heads of families.	Free white males under 16 years.	Free white females, including heads of families.	All other free persons.	Slaves.
Preble, Zebulon	1	4	3		
Blanchard, Theoˢ	2	2	3		
Smith, Herman	1	4	5		
Blanchard, Solomon	1		3		
Gobart, Nicholas	1	1	8		
Pottle, David	2	1	3		
Perry, James	1	1	3		
Southard, John	2	2	2		
Parks, John	1	5	6		
Chesham, John	1	4	2		
Porter, Frederick	1	3	2		
Weston, Caleb	2	5	3		
Burk, Willᵐ	1	3	3		

BOWDOINHAM TOWN—continued.

NAME OF HEAD OF FAMILY.	Free white males of 16 years and upward, including heads of families.	Free white males under 16 years.	Free white females, including heads of families.	All other free persons.	Slaves.
Purnton, Hezekiah	1	1	4		
Hatch, Jethro	1	4	4		
Gitchel, Elihu	1	1	1	1	
Purnton, James	1	3	3		
Whitmore, Stephen	4	1	4		
Whitmore, Francis	1	1	1		
Hatch, Ephraim	2		3		
Maxwell, George	2	2	6		
Harwood, Thomas	2	4	6		
McLallen, Nath¹	2	2	8		
Gardiner, Charles	2		1		
Coffin (Widow)	1	3	5		
Thomas, George	2	1	5		
Takins, Thomas	1	1	2		
Hatch, Clark	1	3	3		
Dinsmore, Thoˢ	1	3	3		
Dinsmore, Thoˢ, Junʳ	1	2	2		
Preble, Zebulon	1	1	2		
Preble, David	1		2		
Beel, Zachariah	2				
Beel, Josiah	1			1	
Beel, Joshua	2	1	4		
Hatch, Jethro	3		5		
Adams, John	1	3	4		
Adams, Jere	1		1		
Booker, James	2	1	4		
Sedgley, Joseph	2	1	4		
Maxwell, James	2	3	5		
Gardiner, Benjᵃ	2		3		
Preble, Sam¹	1	2	1		
Preble, Abraham	2	1	3		
Wiggins, Phinehas	1	1	2		
Jellitson, Job	1	3	2		
Sedgley, Robert	2	1	3		
Meloon, Abraham	1	2	1		
Raman, Elaphan	3	2	5		
Preble, Jonᵃ	3		3		
Prat, Elisha	1	2	2		
Whitmore, Abraham	2	1	3		
Springer, Taoˢ	2	1	3		
Prat, John	1	1	2		
Springer, Jᶜhn	1	2	1		
Dunham, Willᵐ	2		2		
Macumber, Ebenezer	1		2		
Jack, Robert	1	4	2		
Macumoer, Seth	2	2	2		
Headon, John	1	1	3		
Mallee, James	2	5	1		
Ross, Joseph	3	2	2		
Macumber, Job	1	3	6		
Adams, Nathan	1	2	3		
Preble, Abraham, Junʳ	2	2	5		
Cobb, Abiah	1	2	3		
Cooms, Sam¹ C	1	1	3		
Stuart, Isaac	2	2	2		
Ross, Paul	1	1	1		
Staboard, John	1	3	3		
Booker, Willᵐ	1	1	1		
Dinslow, ⎯⎯	1		3		
Dinslow, Willᵐ	1		1		

BRISTOL TOWN.

NAME OF HEAD OF FAMILY.	Free white males of 16 years and upward, including heads of families.	Free white males under 16 years.	Free white females, including heads of families.	All other free persons.	Slaves.
Rollings, John	1	2	4		
moody, Richard	1	1	1		
moody, John	1	1	3		
moody, Cernes	1	4	4		
Grant, Moses	1		3		
winslow, David	1	1	5		
umbehind, Charles	1		2		
Hussey, Abner	1	3	2		
Smith, Joshua	1	1	2		
Smith, Steven	1	3	2		
Dunbar, Elizer	1	1	3		
Merril, thomas	2	6	3		
hall, James	1	3	5		
hall, Seth	2	3	7		
hussey, Joseph	3		3		
hussey, Joseph, Jᵘⁿ	1	1	3		
hussey, Samuel	1	2	2		
winslow, John	1	3	6		
Zentner, philliss	1	4	3		
wolts, Andrew	1	3	4		
Sidelinger, George	1	3	3		
kenssil, fredrich	2	2	4		
Sidlinger, peter	1	3	4		
awstin, Ichabod	4	4	2		
clerk, John	1	1	6		
oliver, Jonathan	1	4	3		
Chapman, Jonathan	1	2	5		
knowlton, andrew	1	1	4		
Mᶜfadien, Thomas	1	1	5		
turney, Edmond	1		3		
becker, Silas	1			3	
hatch, fridrik	1	3	4		
hall, levy	1	2	2		

BRISTOL TOWN—con.

NAME OF HEAD OF FAMILY.	Free white males of 16 years and upward, including heads of families.	Free white males under 16 years.	Free white females, including heads of families.	All other free persons.	Slaves.
hogekins, David	1	4	5		
winslow, Ez¹	1	3	4		
hall, william	1	3	2		
temesson, Joseph	1	1	1		
barslow, John	1		2		
linscutt, John	1				
hopkins, bill	1				
Ross, benjamin	3	3	3		
Juwet, nathan	1	2	4		
Rollings, John	2	2	5		
Plummer, Benj	3	2	8		
Dennis, David	2	1	5		
Gilbert, Daniel	1		2		
tigue, Daniel	3	1	2		
knowlton, Jeremiak	2	3	5		
flint, Thomas	3	2	6		
hisscock, John	3		3		
Rust, Joseph	2	2	6		
flint, Jas	2	5	1		
hogeden, Stephen	4	1	3		
hogeden, benjamin	1	1	1		
kawanagh, James	1		1		
chapman, John	1	3	2		
chapman, Isral	1		3		
holland, John	2		1		
Grotten (widow)	3		4		
Palmer, Elnathan	2	3	7		
Rollings, Samuel	3	4	4		
chapman, Nathaniel	1	4	4		
chapman, thomas	1	5	5		
chapman, Joseph	2	3	6		
Gentner, David	1	3	3		
Perkins, James	1	1	3		
chapman, benjamin	1	1	2		
chapman, nathan	1	2	4		
knowlton, nathaniel	1	2	4		
Noble, arthur	5	3	5	1	
linscott, David	1	3	4		
heckelton (widow)	1		1		
clarck, john	1		6		
wethren, arnold	2		2		
Eten, philip	3	2	6		

CANAAN TOWN.

NAME OF HEAD OF FAMILY.	Free white males of 16 years and upward, including heads of families.	Free white males under 16 years.	Free white females, including heads of families.	All other free persons.	Slaves.
Wood, Robert	2		5		
Steward, William	1	1	3		
Kindal, Biethy	1	3	4		
Castle, Ephrom	1				
Powers, Levi	2	4	4		
Burril, Nathaniel	3	1	3		
Steward, Phinihas	1	1	2		
Steward, Samuel	1	1	5		
Wyman, Seth	1	6	3		
Pratt, Elam	1	2	2		
Hunt, John	1		1		
Stewart, William	3	3	3		
Jewet, Maxie	2	3	3		
Ireland, Abraham	1	3	5		
Brown, Rebekah		2	1		
Okes, Solomon	2		3		
Okes, Levi	2		3		
Fowler, John	1	2	5		
Turner, James	1		2		
Smith, Isaac	1	6	4		
Russ, Luther	1				
Miriek, Andrew	1	2	2		
Okes, John	1	1	3		
Steward, Phinihas	2		3		
Steward, Abraham	1	2	4		
White, Solomon	1	3	4		
Wesson, Samuel	1	1	4		
Howard, Peter, Jᵘ	1	1	1		
Macblin, Brice	1	1	1		
Dartman, Noah	1		2		
Clerk, Noah	1		4		
Stewart, Solomon, Jr	2	1	5		
Fletcher, William	1	1	2		
Webb, James	1	1	1		
Hornestead, Daniel	1				
Carson, Adam	1		4		
Russel, Isaac	1	6	3		
Snow, Daniel	1				
Howard, Peter	1		1		
Whitten, Toboias	1	3	2		
Pratt, Michal	1		3		
Savage, Joseph	1	5	3		
Varnum, Samuel	1		3		
Castle, William	2	3	4		
Lambart, Daniel	1	6	2		
Kincade, David	1	4	2		
Lewis, George	1	3	5		
Lambart, Sherebiah	1		1		
Lambart, Sherebiah, Jr	1	2	1		
Kindal, Barzeliel	1	3	5		
Maulbone, James	1	5	5		

LINCOLN COUNTY—Continued.

CANAAN TOWN—con.

NAME OF HEAD OF FAMILY.	Free white males of 16 years and upward, including heads of families.	Free white males under 16 years.	Free white females, including heads of families.	All other free persons.	Slaves.
Ireland, Abraham	1	1	1		
Pishen, Charles	1		1		
Emery, John, Jur	1	1	2		
Robins, Jonathan	1	3	5		
Emery, Levi	1		1		
Lankister, Joseph	1	2	3		
Davis, Jonathan	2		4		
Emery, John	1				
Emery, Samuel	1	2	4		
Ireland, John	1	1	2		
Ireland, John, Ju	1	1	1		
Kindal, David	1				
White, John	1		1		
Wesson, Joseph	1	1	4		
Wesson, Ely	1	2	3		
Piper, Edward	1		2		
Clerk, Solomon	2		4		
Whitiker, Nathaniel	4		3		
Whiteman, Samuel	1	2	3		
Rogers, Darly	1	1	3		
Stewart, Solomon	1		1		
Bigelow, James	2	2	2		
Bigelow, George	1				
Pratt, Micah	1	2	6		
Smith, Daniel	1	5	4		
Webb, Christopher	2	3	4		
Hartwell, Edward	1	7	1		
Wesson, John	1	2	2		
Piper, John	1				
White, John	1		2		

CARRATUNK TOWN.

NAME OF HEAD OF FAMILY.					
Williams, Jacob	1	4	2		
Ball, John	1	1	3		
Foster, Daniel	1		1		
Hale, Ephrom	3				
Wear, Abel	1		2		
Russel, Joseph					
Chace, Rogers	2	2	4		
Chace, Ezekiel	1	2	2		
Gutridg, Joshua	2	3	4		
Wood, Ephrom	1				
Russel, Solomon	1	1	1		
Bosworth, Jonathan	1	3	2		
Chamberlain, Moses	1				
Wilson, John	1	2	2		
Cleavland, Joseph	1	1	1		
Cleavland, Timothy	1				
Trumbul, William	1				
Fletcher, Amos	1	1	1		
Baker, Joseph	2	3	4		
Churchhill, John	1				
Fletcher, William	3	1	4		
Parlin, Silas	1	3	2		
Pattin, Thomas	1	3	2		
Churchhill, Joseph	1	5	2		
Whipple, Elezer	1				

CARES PLANTATION, OR UNITY.

NAME OF HEAD OF FAMILY.					
Baker, Prince	2	5	5		
Rollings, Benjamin	3	1	4		
Lankister, Ezekiel	1		2		
Meloon, Elizabeth			1		
Rollings, Joseph	1	2	4		
Tibbits, Nathaniel	1	2	5		
Blackston, William	1	3	3		
Welts, Nathaniel	1	1	1		
House, James	1	1	1		
Blackston, William	1		2		
Webber, John	1	1	2		
Russ, Jonathan	1	2	3		
Chambers, Benjamin	1	2	2		
Davis, Simon	1	2	1		
Stover, Timothy	1				
Dutton, Rial	1				
Yongill, Enoch	1	2	4		
Alley, Ephrom	1	1	2		
Rollings, Benjamin, Jr	1	1	1		
Boubey, Gideon	3	1	3		
Welts, John	1	2	4		
Fellows, Joseph	1		2		
Stover, Dependence	2	1	3		
Pilsbury, Edmond	1		2		
Hollis, Stephen	1	2	1		
Whitcum, Stephen	1	1	2		
Porter, Gideon	1		2		

CHESTER PLANTATION.

NAME OF HEAD OF FAMILY.					
Perry, Samuel	1	1	1		
Judkins, Samuel	4	5	2		
Wyman, Abraham	4	1	2		
Sewall, Dummer	1		2		

CHESTER PLANTATION—continued.

NAME OF HEAD OF FAMILY.	Free white males of 16 years and upward, including heads of families.	Free white males under 16 years.	Free white females, including heads of families.	All other free persons.	Slaves.
Bradbury, William	1		2		
Bradbury, John	1		3		
Devinport, Thomas	1				
Lock, Edward	3	3	4		
Bragdon, Jeremiah	1	1	1		
Wyman, Daniel	1	4	4		
Dunning, William	1		2		
Kinscott, Samuel	1	3	2		
Mitchel, John	1		1		
Sewall, Jonathom	2	1	1		
Devenport, Abraham	1				

CUSHING TOWN.

NAME OF HEAD OF FAMILY.					
Smith, John	1	2	1		
Packard, Micah	1		2		
Packard, Marlborough	2		1		
Vose, Seth	2	5	3		
Vose, Elijah	1		2		
Young, Richard	2		1		
Young, Sarah			3		
Tissaker, John	2		1		
Nutting, Jonathan	2	3	2		
McCarter, John	3	1	5		
Hiler, Simeon	2	1	7		
Hiler, Jacob	3		2		
Hiler, Cornelius	1	2	1		
Thomson, Mary	2	3	2		
Malcom, Andrew	2		3		
Malcom, James	1	1	5		
Robinson, Haunce	5	1	5		
Robinson, Haunce, Junr	1		2		
Annis, Samuel	1	1	1		
Robinson, Joseph	3	2	3		
Brison, John	2		1		
Burton, William	1	2	3		
Hutting, Jonathan	3	1	2		
Benton, Benjamin	1	3	3		
Nehnenhawsen, Henry Frederick	1	3	2		
Lewis, Daniel	2	1	5		
McIntyer, Robert	2	3	5		
Kelleran, Edward	2	4	5		
Parsons, Lawrence	2	1	3		
Parsons, William	2	2	1		
Melony, Walter	3	1	2		
Carnay, Thomas	1		1		
Carney, James	1	3	4		
Wiley, William	4	2	2		
Rivers, Moses	1	2	3		
Robinson, Moses	3		3		
Rivers, Archibald	2	1	4		
Harthorn, Samuel	2	3	4		
Robinson, Archibald	4	1	6		
McLallen, Simon	1	1	1		
Sweetland, Sampson	1	1	5		
Sweetland, James	2		2		
Barton, John	1	1	5		
Sweetland, Stephen	2	1	1		
Starling, Josiah	1	2	3		
Higman, Edward	1	1	2		
Graffam, Jacob	1	1	6		
Graffam, Joseph	1		2		
Adams, Richard	2	1	2		
Brazier, John	3	2	3		
Brazier, Bathsheba					
Carby, James	3	2	1		
Young, George	2	1	2		
Young, William	3	1	2		
Harthorn, Alexander	2	1	2		
Harthorn, John	1		2		
Henderson, Robert	2	3	2		
Henderson, Dunbar	3		3		
Canary, Dennis	1	1	1		
Young, Henry	1	1	2		
Gay, Elezer	2	2	4		
Robinson, Sarah	5		3		
Kelloch, Moses	1		1		
Kelloch, Matthew	1	2	6		
Kelloch, John	4	2	2		
Nichols, John	1	1	2		
Hendley, John	2	3	5		
McKellar, John	2	3	3		
Robinson, John	1	1	2		
Robinson, Moses, Junr	1		6		
Robinson, Joseph, Junr	1	2	5		
Robinson, Andrew	1	3	2		
Watt, Samuel	2	5	5		
Gilchrist, Samuel	1	5	1		
Gilchrist, George	2	1	3		
Rivers, Thomas	3		6		
Fogerty, Dennis	3	2	5		
Long, Alexander	1	2	3		
Long, Michael	1	2	5		
York, John	1	3	4		
Henderson, Thomas	1	3	2		

CUSHING TOWN—con.

NAME OF HEAD OF FAMILY.	Free white males of 16 years and upward, including heads of families.	Free white males under 16 years.	Free white females, including heads of families.	All other free persons.	Slaves.
Henderson, Jabez	1	2	2		
Harthorn, Alexander, Junr	1	1	5		
Starling, Richard	2		5		
Rawley, Michael	1	1	1		
Murphy, Jeremiah	1	4	2		
Glover, Thomas	1	2	2		
Jameson, Ebenezer	1	2	1		
Howard, Daniel	1	1	4		
Hillwell, Thomas	1	1	4		
Daly, Ellis	3	1	3		
Kiff, Thomas	3	3	4		
Hart, Avery	1	2	4		
Hart, John	1	3	3		
Hart, Jesse	1	1	1		
Maddon, John	1		4		
Norwood, Isaac	2	3	4		
Butler, Abraham	1		3		
Ripley, Enoch	2				
Wall, Patrick	2	3	6		
Linniken, Clark	2	1	1		
page, William	1	1	2		
Martin, Richard	1	3	4		
Melzar, John	1		2		
Teel, Adam	2	1	6		
Barter, Pelatiah	2	4	5		
Barter, John	2	5	3		
Allen, Gideon	3		1		
Murray, John	3	1	1		
Covy, David	1	1	2		
Levey, Joseph	1	5	2		
Thorndike, Robert	1	1	1		
Graffam, Pierce	2	2	3		
Rawley, Edward	1	1	1		
Norwood, Solomon	1	3	4		
Simmonds, Aaron	1	2	5		
Simmonds, Nathaniel	1		4		
Wells, John	1		3		
Vickery, Stephen	4	1	3		
Davis, John	1	2	5		
Jameson, Martin	1	2	6		
Rogers, Howland	2	2	2		
McCobb, James	1	4	5		
Wiley, Isaac	1	2	5		
Pickard, Nathan	1	2	3		
Thorndike, Joshua	1	1	3		
Ellwell, Andrew	1	4	3		
Roundy, Azor	1	1	2		
Mathews, James	2		3		
Hawes, Robert	1	1	5		
Rackleff, William	1	1	5		
Gardener, Daniel	1		1		
Wheeler, William	1	3	5		
Linniken, David	2		2		
Willis, Thomas	1	1	3		
Lea, James	1	1	2		
Davis, Mary		1	3		
Linnekon, Daniel	1				
Mathews, Daniel	1	1	3		
Smalley, Joshua	3		5		
Hall, Isaac	2				
Hall, Isaac, Junr	1	3	3		
Hall, Elijah	1		1		
Curtis, John	1		1		
Hall, Caleb	2	5	1		
Hall, Peter	1		2		
Hall, Ephraim	1	1	1		
Hall, Ephraim, Junr	1		1		
Pearson, William	3	3	2		
Dyer, Anthony	1	3	1		
Amory, George	1	1	3		
Crocker, Paul	1	2	2		
Crocker, Timothy	1		1		
McCarty, Thomas	1				
Coombes, Joshua	1	2	5		
Clark, William	1		1		
Foster, Ebenezer	2	3	4		
Marshal, Samuel	2	1	3		
Marshal, Samuel, Junr	1	2	2		
Stone, John	1				

EDGECOMB TOWN.

NAME OF HEAD OF FAMILY.					
Clefford, William	2	6	4		
Trask, David	3	5	3		
Davis, Moses	2	2	3		
Patterson, Willm	2	2	5		
Cunningham, John	1	3	2		
Burk, David	1		1		
Patterson, James	1	2	2		
Dodge, Moses	1	1	2		
Trask, Moses	1	4	2		
Trask, Joseph	1		5		
Trask, Saml	2	1	1		
Gove, Enoch	1	1	2		
Hough, Joseph	1	1	2		

LINCOLN COUNTY—Continued.

NAME OF HEAD OF FAMILY.	Free white males of 16 years and upward, including heads of families.	Free white males under 16 years.	Free white females, including heads of families.	All other free persons.	Slaves.
EDGECOMB TOWN—con.					
Young, Theodore	1		3		
Rigs, Goen	1	3	4		
Trask, Willm	1	1	2		
Hough, Daniel	1		5		
Gove, Asa	2	1	6		
Riant, John	1	4	2		
Chase, John	1	3	4		
Baker, Amos	1	1	1		
Moore, Nathl	1	1	4		
Moore, Ebenezer	1	1	2		
Allen, Rachael			1		
Seers, Barnabas	1	1	2		
Gove, David, Junr	1	1	2		
Chase, James	2	1	2		
Horn, Jacob	1	1	2		
Trask, David	1	1	3		
Cunningham, Willm	2	7	4		
Hutchins, Jon^a	2	1	2		
Hutchins, Benj^a	1	2	4		
Merril, Stephen	2	2	5		
Hough, Moses	1	2	1		
Cunningham, John, Junr	1	3	2		
Sullivan, John	1	1	1		
Moore, James	1	3	3		
Moore, Isaac	1	1	3		
Cunningham, John	2		2		
Gove, Nathan	1	2	3		
Gove, Solomon	3	3	5		
Trask, Solomon	2	2	3		
Clefford, Isaac	1	5	4		
Gove, Ebenezer, Junr	1	1	4		
Gove, Ebenezer	2	2	2		
Leman, Nathl	1	1	2		
Leman, Willm	1	3	3		
Hodge, Willm	1	1	1		
Hodge, Mary		1	1		
Leman, Danl	1	2	4		
Berny, Thomas	2	3	6		
Fly, Willm	1	3	4		
Ratclif, Benj^a	1	5	3		
Tilton, Abraham	3	5	3		
Merrow, Saml	1		4		
Merrow, Joseph	2	1	5		
Webster, Daniel	2	3	4		
Winslow, Nathl	1	2	4		
Stephens, Hubbard	4	1	3		
Brown, Joseph	2	5	2		
Dodge, Sarah		3	5		
Webster, David	1	3	5		
Dodge, Winthrop	1	3	4		
Dodge, Malachi	1	4	2		
Dodge, Porter	1	3	2		
Hagget, Benj^a	2	3	4		
Dodge, Daniel	1	1	2		
Williams, Henry	2	4	4		
Richards, Jesse	1	3	3		
Duntan, Willm	1	1	3		
Emerson, Edward	2	4	2		
Peters, John	1		2		
Cunningham, Tim^o	1	1	2		
Lamson, Willm	1	3	3		
Deering, John	2	3	3		
Cunningham, Willm	1	2	3		
Pinkham, Joseph	1		2		
Gove, Nathan	1		2		
Baker, Solomon	3	1	5		
White, Nathl	2		3		
Knight, John	2	2	5		
Stone, Gabriel	1	1	4		
Colbey, James	1	2	2		
Colbey, Saml	1		3		
Parsons, Joseph	2	4	6		
Fowle, Joshua	1	1	1		
Knight, Westbrook	1	2	6		
Greenleaf, Stephen	1	4	5		
Norton, Lemuel	1		1		
Elby, Benj^a	2	2	5		
Elby, Willm	1	3	2		
Colby, Silvester	1	1	3		
Mutchmore, Jacob	1	2	3		
Young, Benaiah	1	2	2		
Greenleaf, Saml	1	1	2		
Greenleaf, Enoch	1	1	5		
Cromwel, Joseph	1	2	5		
Rymes, Joseph	3	3	3		
Tyler, Joseph	1	1	2		
Harrington, Elisha	1	4	3		
Dorril, Thos	1		2		
Colbey, Henry	2	2	5		
Decker, Spencer	1	1	5		
Nutter, Volentine	1		2		
Colbey, Nehemiah	1		1		
Keene, Abel	1	1	3		
Brooks, Charles S	3		3		
Jewett, James	2	1	5		
EDGECOMB TOWN—con.					
Bowland, John	1	3	2		
Gardiner, John	1		3		
Whitten, Joseph	1	2	3		
Newell, Zebulen	1	2	3		
Neal, David	1	2	4		
Wallace, John	1	1	1		
Hodgdon, Benj^a	1	6	2		
Hodgdon, Thomas, Junr	2	2	1		
Hodgdon, Thomas	2		4		
Damerin, Zabiah	1	3	3		
Webber, Saml	2	4			
Harrington, Benj^a	1	5	1		
McCartha, Florence	1	1	1		
Hibbard, Daniel	1	1	5		
Duntan, Saml	4	3	7		
Duntan, Daniel	1	1	3		
Duntan, Joseph	2	1	7		
Duntan, John	2	4	5		
Duntan, Tim^o	1	3	4		
Chadwick, Levi	2		2		
Knight, Nathl	2	6	1		
Thomas, James	1		1		
Thomas, James, Junr	1	1	3		
Tarbox, Conelius	2		2		
Hall, Saml	1	2	4		
FAIRFIELD TOWN.					
Pushan, Peter, Ju	1				
Ausburn, Jonathan	1		1		
Hutson, Timothy	1	1	3		
Hustings, James	1	2	3		
Pushan, Abraham	2	2	2		
Kindal, William	1	3	4		
Rose, Jeremiah	1				
Wyman, Daniel	2	1	6		
Hill, James	1				
Emery, Jonathan	2		2		
Spensor, Solomon	1		4		
Kimbal, Jacob	1	1	2		
Jewit, Pickard	1				
Kitridge, Benj^a	1		3		
Persons, David	1	1	4		
Emery, James	1				
Goodwin, Daniel	1	1	1		
Jackings, James	1				
Gullison, John	2	5	4		
White, Joshua	1		2		
Sperring, John	1	1	3		
Emery, Edward	2	2	2		
Emery, David	1	3	2		
Noble, Benjamin	1	1	1		
Mackkee, George	1	1	2		
Darling, Joseph	1	3	3		
Sibley, John	1	1	4		
Wheeler, Daniel	1				
Hoxie, Ludwick	1	2	2		
Blackwell, Joshua	1	1	1		
Blackwell, Jabez	1	1			
Burquis, David	1		1		
Blackwell, Thomas	1	2	3		
Jones, Appollo	1		1		
Hoxie, David	1	2	1		
Bowman, Harper	1		1		
Bowman, Samuel	1				
Allen, Ebenezer, J^r	1	2	2		
Shephard, John	1	1	1		
Wing, Phillip	1	1	5		
Blackwell, Isreal	1	2	5		
Mendal, John	1	1	4		
Holloway, Ludwick	1	3	2		
Allen, Caleb	1	3	5		
Jones, Simon	1	1	3		
Hoxie, Gidion	1		4		
Allen, Ebenezer	2	1	2		
Hoxie, Barnis	1				
Holloway, Barnibus	1	1	1		
Copland, Abraham	1				
Holoway, Gideon	1	1	3		
Cannon, John	1		1		
Nigh Bartlett	1	3	2		
Doe, Joseph	1		1		
Davis, Benjamin	1	3	5		
Darling, James	1				
Noble, John	2	3	5		
Bodfish, Nimfis	1	3	4		
Chace, Mathew	2	3	4		
Townes, Joseph	2		1		
Wyman, Reuben, Jr	1		3		
Wheeles, Enos	2	1	3		
Sturdifent, Lot	1		1		
Mackfarling, Solomon	1		2		
Bates, Samuel	1	2	4		
Bates, Seth	1		2		
Shorehead, Daniel	1		2		
FAIRFIELD TOWN—con.					
Bowman, Joseph	1	2	1		
Bowman, Zacheus	1	1	1		
Bowman, Benjamin	1				
Bowman, Allihu	1	3	2		
Davis, John	1				
Davis, Eber	1				
Atwood, Nathl	1				
Fuller, Alden	1	1	3		
Burquis, Josiah	2	2	5		
Lawrence, James	1	3	2		
Toby, Samuel	2	6	3		
Toby, Samuel	1	2	3		
Blossom, Benjamin	1	1	3		
Lovewell, Zelottus	1	2	6		
Jones, John	1	3	3		
Jones, Ephrom	7	2	5		
fuller, Seth	1	2	5		
Landers, Thomas	3	1	5		
Nigh, Samuel	1				
Lawrrance, John	1				
Holloway, Prince	1				
Nigh, Elisha	1	2	5		
Tosier, John	1		2		
Tosier, Benjamin	1				
Pong, Harnis	1	1	6		
Tosier, Jeremiah	2	1	3		
Pushan, Peter	2	1	1		
Tosier, Amos	1				
fish, Eliab	2	1	3		
Tosier, John, J^ur	1	1	2		
Tosier, Jonathan	1	4	2		
GEORGETOWN TOWN.					
Oliver, Thomas	1	1	2		
Oliver, Jacob	1		2		
Oliver, Parker	2	2	4		
Oliver, Willm	1	3	4		
Oliver, Benj^a	1	1	2		
Oliver, John	3		3		
Oliver, John, Jn^r	1	4	1		
McFadan, James	1	3	3		
Clary, Jane			1		
Campbel, John	1	5	5		
Flitner, Willm	1		2		
Trafton, Thos	1	4	3		
Spinney, Jer^s	2	1	3		
Grover, Thos	1	1	4		
Tarr, Benj^a	1	1	5		
Gahan, John	1	1	2		
Hinkley, Matthew	1	2	3		
Stephens, Thos	4		3		
Brewer, Nathl	2	2	4		
Powers, Jon^a	1	1	5		
Oliver, Eben^z	3	4	3		
Rowe, Ebenezer	4	3	2		
Grover, And^w	1	4	3		
Mallee, Daniel	1		3		
McMahan, Daniel	1	1	5		
McMahan, Tim^o	2		3		
Wyman, Willm	1	1	5		
Kelley, John	1	3	4		
Gahan, James	1	1	2		
Duley, Mich^l	1	2	3		
Coffee, Edward	3	2	2		
Whalen, John	3		3		
Whalen, Thomas	1				
Drummon, Elijah	2	1	1		
Bubler, Thos	1	4	2		
Welch, James					
Booker, Joseph	1	3	6		
McCob, Mary	3	2	2		2
Colyard, Charles	3	2	5		1
Sewal, Sarah			3		
Parker, Jordan	3	1	9		
Parker, John	4		5		2
Day, Abram	1		3		
Silvester, Nathl	1	1	4		
Sylvester, Nathl, Junr	1		1		
Sprague, William	1		2		
McIntire, Joseph	1		1		
Wallace, John	1	1	1		
Gitchel, Benj^a	1		1		
Morse, David	1		3		
Day, Jacob	3	4	4		
Manes, James	1	4	1		
Morse, John	1	4	1		
Griffen, Ichabod	1	4	1		
Manes, John	1	2	1		
Rogers, Hugh	1	1	3		
Fisher, John	1		2		
Lee, Willm	3	2	4		
Rogers, John	2	1	3		
Lee, Willm, Jn^r	2	1	4		
Burnham, Francis	1		3		

LINCOLN COUNTY—Continued.

NAME OF HEAD OF FAMILY.	Free white males of 16 years and upward, including heads of families.	Free white males under 16 years.	Free white females, including heads of families.	All other free persons.	Slaves.
GEORGETOWN TOWN—continued.					
Turner, Forbs	1		3		
Parsons, John	1	1	2		
Pane, Edward	1	1	3		
Malcom, Willm	2		7		
Malcom, John	2	2	2		
Lithgow, Willm	6	1	7	1	
Rogers, Thos	2	3	5		
Morse, Danl	1	4	4		
Persy, Thos	3	1	4		
Piercy (Widow)	1	1	2		
Stinson, John	4		1		
Stinson, Willm	1	2	5		
Coolyard, Mary	1	2	3	2	
Hogan, Thomas	4	5	6		
Swanton, Robert	1		2		
Conway, Francis	2		2		
Wallace, Willm	3	1	1		
Green, Willm	1	1	4		
Gushing, Ezekiel	1	2	5		
Rogers, George	5	1	3		
Butlar, Willm, Jnr	1	1	3		
Butlar, Willm	4	1	4		
Dosey, Jereh	1	1	2		
Pettey, Benja	3	1	5		
McCobb, Saml	3	2	6	3	
Fisher, John	3	1	6		
Brown, Daniel	1		1		
White, John	1	3	6		
Fisher, Henry	1	1	1		
Swett, Benja	2	4	3		
Sullivan, Danl	1	2	1		
Pettey, Saml	1	2	5		
Pettey, Benja, Jnr	1	1	1		
Pettey, Jane		2	2		
Sewal, James	1	1	6		
McFadan, John	1	1	4		
Potter, Willm	1	1	4		
Sewall, John	1				
Sewall, John, Jnr	2	1	2		
Sewall, Theodore	2	1	4		
Potter, John	2	1	4		
Stinson, Willm	2	2	4		
Emerson, Revd Ezekiel	4		4		
Drummon, James	3	3	3		
McFadan, Abigail	2	1	3		
McFredericks, James	3	2	7		
Drummon, Alexander	6	2	5		
McFadan, Danl	4	2	6		
Stinson, James	2	1	2		
Snipe, John	4	1	4		
Preble, Joseph	2	1	3		
Higan, James	1	1	3		
Stinson, John	3	2	4		
McKenny, Robert	1		2		
Preble, Jona	1		2		
Shay, Michl	1	4	4		
Carter, Saml	1	1	3		
Hall, John	2	5	6		
Reardon, John	1	1	4		
Quin, John	2	1	3		
Welch, Mark	1		1		
Rigs, Benja	1	1	6		
Reardon, Timothy	2	1	3		
McKenny, George	2	2	3		
Tarr, Joseph	1	2	5		
Tarr, Sarah	1	5	3		
Tarr, Seth	2		6		
Mars, Willm	1	1	1		
Heal, John	2	2	6		
Heal, Gilbart	1		3		
McKenny, Brook	3	2	8		
McFadan, Andw	2		1		
Williams, James	1	1	2		
Hunt, David	2	3	3		
Michaels, George	1	4	3		
Harford, William	2	1	3		
McKenny, Matthew	2	5	1		
Clary, Allen	1	3	2		
Mahony, James	2	4	6		
Poor, Robert	4		7		
Heal, John	1	2	3		
McCarty, Timo	1	4	2		
Higgans, Thomas	2	2	3		
Linnen, Bryant	3	1	5		
McKenny, Thomas	1	1	2		
Trafton, Joseph	2	2	3		
Trafton, Thomas	1		1		
Hinkley, Josiah	2	2	2		
Beal, John	1	2	3		
Oliver, David, 4th	1	1	4		
Oliver, David	3	1	3		
Oliver, David, 3rd	2	1	5		
Linnen, Thomas	1		4		
Lary (Widow)			3		
Grover, James	1	5	5		
GEORGETOWN TOWN—continued.					
Oliver, David, Junr	2	2	6		
Beal, Saml	1	2	3		
Rackley, Saml	1	1	2		
Rackley, Saml, Jnr	1	3	1		
Hunt, Willm	1	2	5		
Hinkley, Edmund	2	2	5		
Green, Richd	1	1	2		
Perkins, Nathl	4	2	4		
Mars, John	1	6	1		
Spinny, Hannah	1		3		
Spinney, John	1	4	4		
Spinney, Jere	1	1	2		
Oliver, James	1		2		
Neal, John	1	1	1		
Oliver, Ephraim, Jnr	1	3	4		
Oliver, Henry	1	2	3		
Oliver, John	1	1	1		
Morrison, Saml	2	2	5		
Ingerson, George	2		2		
Oliver, Ephraim	1	3	4		
Oliver, Nicholas	1	2	4		
Perry, Ely	1	2	2		
Warry, John	1	1	1		
Bachelder, Theos	3	1	4		
Snow, Joseph	1	1	2		
Batcheldor, Tima	1	2	3		
Spalding, Ezekiel	4	1	4		
Batcheldor, Elijah	1		1		
Morrison, Moses	1	2	3		
Batcheldor, Josiah	1	1	1		
Marum, John	3	1	1		
Hall, Joseph	3	1	2		
Booker, Joseph	1	2	1		
Walten, John	3	1	1		
Blasdel, Christopher	1	1	3		
Blasdel, Daniel	2	1	2		
Rogers, Robert	1	4	5		
Bisby, Charles	1	1	5		
Lowell, John	1		1		
Lowell, Stephen	1	2	4		
Day, Stephen	1	1	7		
Wallace, Saml	1	2	4		
Totman, Henry	2		3		
Wallace, Willm	1	5	2		
Campbel, Danl	2	1	4		
Wyman, Francis	2	2	3		
Wyman, Martha	1	3	6		
Sprague, Willm	1	2	2		
Whalen, Joseph	1	1	1		
Hinkley, Hannah	2	1	4		
GREAT POND PLANTATION.					
Davis, James	3		2		
Davis, Charles	1	2	2		
Davis, Joshua	1	2	2		
Davis, William	2	1	2		
Weeks, Shubial	3		3		
Mugridge, Simon	1	1	1		
Waters, Samuel	1		3		
Clay, Daniel	1	2	1		
Silvestor, Ebenesor	2	4	4		
foy, Robert	1	3	4		
Greley, Jacob	1	1	1		
Cresey, Abel	2	2	3		
Sanford, Daniel	1	3	1		
Bolin, William	1	1	1		
Belden, Stephen	3	1	5		
Heselton, Samuel	1	2	2		
Longfelow, Samuel	1	2	4		
Longfellow, Stephen	1	2	3		
Broadstret, John	1	5	4		
Grealey, Jonathan	1				
Huckens, Holis	3	4	3		
Turner, David	1		2		
Erskins, Christopher	1	2	1		
Turner, Benjamen	1	4	5		
Bartlet, Jonathon	2	1	3		
Calley, Aaron	1	3	3		
Bron, Jeremiah	1				
Gilpatrick, Thomas	2	1	2		
Gilpatrick, Charles	1		1		
Parkers, Nathan	1	3			
GREENE TOWN.					
Bales, Jabas R	1		2		
Robins, Luther	1	4	2		
Sprags, Jamas	1	3	2		
Sprages, William	1		1		
Tompson, Elick	1		1		
Shaw, Elisha	1				
Shaw, Zebulon	1				
Astons, Stephen	1		3		
GREENE TOWN—con.					
Sprage, William, Ju	1	2	5		
Lanes, Edman	1	3	5		
Call, Benjn	1		1		
harris, Silas	1				
Wilmy, Daniel	1		1		
harris, John	1	2	3		
Cobin, William	3	2	3		
Cobin, Jesse	1		2		
Bings, Elijah	1	1	2		
Sargant, David	1		1		
Cobin, Reuben	1				
herick, Joseph	1	6	2		
Stodard, Phinhas	2		2		
Marill, Benjn	2	2	2		
Marill, John	1	1	1		
Daggett, John	1	4	3		
Ames, Jacob	1	1	3		
Coming, Samuel	3	1	5		
Judkins, Philip	1	2	5		
parham, William	1	1	1		
heredin, William	1	1	7		
Butler, John	1				
Cole, Samuel	1	3	1		
Stevens, Jacob	1		4		
Cole, Benjn	1	1	2		
Barker, Uriah	1				
Evens, hannah		1	2		
Barrey, George	1		2		
Smith, thomas	1				
Stephens, Thomas	1	2	4		
Marrill, Benja	1	4	2		
Marrill, Benja, Ju	1	1	2		
larrabb, Stephen	1	3	5		
larrabb, John	1	3	6		
Night, Edman	1		1		
Brown, abner	1	5	2		
Rackley, Benjn	1	3	4		
Astins, Jacob	1	2	7		
Barker, William	1	5	2		
Waterman, Primes	1				
Reed, amesiah	1	2	2		
Bates, Levi	1	1	2		
Bates, Solomon	1	1	1		
Richman, Biethur	1		3		
Allan, John	1	3	4		
Jones, Cuandy	1	1	1		
Rose, Simeon	3		1		
Keen, Elisha	1				
Jones, Nolon	1				
Philips, Gray	2	1	4		
turner, Oliver	1	1	1		
Brigs, abiether	1	1	1		
Rose, asha	3	1	4		
Rose, Zebulon	1				
Rose, Seth	1				
Chamblen, William	1	1	4		
Philip, Ichabod	1		1		
Coshman, Jonm	1	3	3		
hiland, abner	1				
Oldon, Benjn	1	2	3		
Sampson, Joseph	1	2	4		
Linsday, thomas	1	2	2		
Saford, andrew	1				
Dean, Seres	1		1		
Mower, Jonm	1	1	3		
Mower, John	1	2	3		
Silvester, Elisha	1				
Bates, Douly	1	1	1		
Bates, Samuel	1				
Brown, Benja	1	1	2		
Brown, Moses	1				
Man, andrew	1				
herrick, Ely	1		2		
herrick, Samuel	1		2		
lander, Robenson	1				
Mower, William	1	1	2		
Keen, Elezer	1				
Saford, hay	1		1		
petergill, Ephram	1				
quimbey, Benj	1	1	2		
Bates, Lamuel	1				
Bates, Joseph	1				
Drew, Clemant	1	1	1		
HALLOWELL TOWN.					
Perkins, Eliab	1	2	3		
Clark, Uriah	3	1	4		
Clark, Charles	1		4		
Cobb, David	1	2	5		
Smith, Moses	2	1	2		
Bolton, Daniel	1	2	3		
Doin, Saml	1	1	3		
Bisby, Elisha	2		3		
Springer, James	2	1	6		

LINCOLN COUNTY—Continued.

HALLOWELL TOWN—con.

NAME OF HEAD OF FAMILY.	Free white males of 16 years and upward, including heads of families.	Free white males under 16 years.	Free white females, including heads of families.	All other free persons.	Slaves.
Dane, Simeon	2	4	2		
Badcock, Henry	1	1	5		
Springer, Edward	1	4	5		
Sprague, William	1	4	3		
Wells, David	2	3	5		
Blackborn, Josiah	1	1	2		
Cowen, Abisha	1	1	5		
Cowen, Jabez	2	2	2		
Ingraham, Beziah	2	2	3		
Woodward, Noah	4	1	3		
Williams, Asa	1	1	4		
Reid, George	1	1	2		
Shaw, John	1	1	2		
Williams, Seth	5	4	4		
Stow, Willm	1	1	2		
Shaw, John	2	1	4		
Savage, Isaac	1	1	1		
Savage, James	1	1	2		
Brown, Benj^a	1	3	3		
Anderson, John	1				
Bolton, Savage	1		3	2	
Shaw, Eliab	1	2	4		
Chamberlin, Saml	4	1	3		
Andrews, George	1	4	4		
Sewal, Henry	1	1	3		
Nowland, John	4		2		
Savage, Edward	2	2	6		
Usher, Willm	1				
Pettingale, Benj^a	2		2		
Allen, Phinehas	1	3	4		
Thomas, David	2	1	3	1	
Clark, Isaac	2	3	5		
Carr, James	2				
Foster, Joseph	1	2	1		
Savage, Danl	3	2	4		
Hallowel, Willm	1	4	4		
McKnight, David	1		2		
Cole, Saml	1		1		
Pettingale, Benj^a, Jn^r	1	2	3		
Norcross, Saml, Ju^r	2	3	4		
Couch, John	1	3	3		
Dana, Edmund	1	2	1		
White, Benj^a	1	1	3		
Chase, Ezekiel	3	1	1		
Winkley, Thomas	2	3	4		
Norcross, Saml	4		2		
Norcross, Philip	1	1	4		
Beeman, John	3		4		
Clark, Peter	2	1	2		
Fletcher, David	1	2	1		
Ingraham, Jere^h	3	2	3		
Fletcher, Robert	1		5		
Pierce, Saml	1	3	3		
Pierce, Eliphalet	2	2	4		
Fletcher, Briant	2	1	5		
Gill, John	3	4	6		
Fletcher, Briant	2	1	4		
Badcock, Jer^h	1	1	2		
Huen, Willm	1	1	1		
Badcock, Saml	1	3	4		
Badcock, Saml	1		1		
Badcock, John	1	3	2		
Tolman, Saml	1	3	3		
Dennison, Robert	2	1	2		
Church, Saml	1	2	2		
Stackpole, Joseph	1	5	3		
Cowen, James	2		3		
Clark, Isaac	4	3	4		
Harden, Isaac	1	1	2		
Harden, Isaac, Jn^r	1	2	2		
Page, Enoch	2	1	6	1	
Cass, Moses	1		4		
Hovey, John	1	1	3		
Hewen, Eben^r	1		3		
Dutten, Saml	6	2	5	1	
Page, James	6	1	4		
Moore, James	1	1	4		
Cottle, Isaac	1	4	5		
Taylor, Nathl	1	3	5		
Follet, Benj^a	1		1		
Follet, Jesse	1	2	2		
Freeman, John	1	1	2		
Coy, Daniel	1		2		
Gould, Jabez	1		1		
Stevans, Daniel	3	1	9		
Dudley, Saml	1		1		
Floyd, Nathl	1	2	3		
Hall, Oliver	1	3	1		
Benson, Jacob	2	1	3		
Shaw, Nathl	3		4		
Snell, Thaddeus	1		2		
Bullen, Saml	3		5		
Jones, Peter	1				
Hatch, David	1	1	1		

HALLOWELL TOWN—con.

NAME OF HEAD OF FAMILY.	Free white males of 16 years and upward, including heads of families.	Free white males under 16 years.	Free white females, including heads of families.	All other free persons.	Slaves.
Goodwin, Andrew	1	4	4		
Cox, James	5	1	3		
Huzzy, Mary	2	2	5	1	
Caldwell, Ganham	1				3
White, Moses	1	5	4		
White, Benj^a	2	1	4		
Jackson, David	5	1	5		
Ward, Benj^a	1		3		
Colburn, Margaret	3		6		
Davenport, Jan^a	2	2	3		
Page, Ezekiel	2	1	5		
Page, Abraham	1	2	5		
Coney, Saml	1		3		
Cumming, Solomon	1		1		
Coney, Danl	2		5		
Patrige, Amos	1				
McMaster, Willm	3	2	3		
Vose, Jesse	1		2		
Church, John	1	2	4	1	
Belcher, Supply	1	4	4		
Brooks, Willm	4	2	4		
Hersey, Nathl	1	4	3		
Howard, Willm	9		6		
Colman, Saml	5		3		
Parker, Peter	1	2	2	1	
Greely, Enoch	2	3	5		
Burges, Ephraim	2		2		
Gilman, Eliphalet	3	3	5		
Walker, Benj^a	1		3		
Dummer, Nathl	3	1	4		
Sewall, Moses	4	2	3		
Palmer, Willm	2	3	2		
Sherborn, Abiel	1		1		
Swett, Saml	2	4	4		
Perkins, Ebenezer	1		2	1	
Metcalf, Joseph	5		2		
Daws, Willm	1	4	1		
Fillebrown, Thos	1				
Dutten (Widow)	2	1	2		
Goodwin, Lazarus	3	2	3		
Nye, Elisha	3	2	6		
Prescott, Benj^a	1	2	1		
Prescott, Joseph	1	1	3		
Davis, John	1	2	1		
Nye, Elvel	1	1	1		
Hinkley, James	2	5	4		
Smith, Daniel	3	1	4	1	
Switland, Nathl	1	3	3		
Brown, Joseph	1	3	5		
Davis, Benj^a	3	1	6		
Church, Ebenezer	3	5	6		
Harris, Obadiah	1	2	4		
Haynes, John	2	3	5		
Cumming, Saml	2	2	3		
Cumming, Asa	1		1		
Cumming, Saml	2		1		
Curtex, Willm	1				
Brown, John	1	3	2		
Field, Elias	1		2		
Ballad, Ephraim	3	1	4		
Savage, Isaac, Ju^r	1	4	5		
Pollard, Amos	4	1	5		
Black, James	2		3		
Twing, Nathl	1				
Craige, Elias	3		1	1	
Welch, Saml	1	1	3		
North, Joseph	4	1	6		
Childs, James	2	1	2		
Burten, James	1		1		
Hamlin, Theophilus	1		2		
Burges, Joshua	1	2	3		
Wesson, Nathan	3	3	2		
Brigs, Willm	1	2	3		
Taylor, Ebenezer	1		4		
Hodges, Ezra	1	2	4		
Dinsmore, Thomas	1	3	7		
Canada, Robert	1	3	2		
Edson, Elisabeth		2	3		
True, Zebulon	1	1	1		
Livermore, Jason	2	2	5		
Hinkley, Shubal	1	2	5		

HANCOCK TOWN.

NAME OF HEAD OF FAMILY.	Free white males of 16 years and upward, including heads of families.	Free white males under 16 years.	Free white females, including heads of families.	All other free persons.	Slaves.
Prat, Asa	3		3		
Prat, James	1		2		
Chace, Varnum	1	3	2		
More, Mordica	1	1	4		
Wyman, Dean	1	3	3		
Burril, John, Jur	1	3	4		
Wyman, Reuben	1		1		
Burril, John	1		1		
Burril, Zibe	1	1	4		
Kimbal, David	1		2		

HANCOCK TOWN—con.

NAME OF HEAD OF FAMILY.	Free white males of 16 years and upward, including heads of families.	Free white males under 16 years.	Free white females, including heads of families.	All other free persons.	Slaves.
Brown, Ezekiel, Jur	1	3	4		
Brown, Ezekiel	1		1		
Hale, Ebenezer	2	2	4		
Spensor, David	2	2	4		
Richardson, Andrew	1	4	3		
Read, Samuel	2		4		
Burrows, Garrat	1	1	1		
Burton, Nathan	3	1	4		
Leman, John	1				
Gray, John	2	2	5		
Roundly, Job	1	1	1		
Roundly, Micah	1				
Sandes, Joseph	1	1	1		
Philbrook, Jonathan	4		2		
Goodwin, Stephen	3	2	2		
Spern, Benjamin	1				
Jackings, Fredrick	1	2	3		
Pollard, Barton	1		2		
Flag, Gershom	2	2	2		
Spensor, Isaac	2	1	3		
Read, Samuel, Jur	1	1	2		
fuller, Bartholomew	2	1	2		
Costigen, Lawrance	2		2		
Brown, James	1	1	3		
Barnes, Silas	1				
Roundly, Lacet	1		1		
Roundly, Ebenezer	1	1	1		
Burton, Nathan	1	1	2		
Grave, Paul	1	2	2		
Brown, Charles	3	1	4		
Fitsgerald, George	1	4	4		
Kimbal, David	1		2		
Hartford, John	1				
Cone, Samuel	1	3	2		
Sherring, John	2	1	2	1	
Burril, Belial	1	3	4		
Crosby, Robert	1		2		
Bigsby, Solomon	1		2		
Davis, Samuel	1				
Bigelow, James	1				
Lovejoy, Francis	2	1	2		
fowler, Samuel	1				
Glitton, Reuben	1				
Burgoin, John	1		1		
Mecaheny, Michal	1		3		
Crosby, Jonah, Ju^r	2	3	2		
Shelden, Henry	1	5	1		
Simpson, Simeon	1		3		
Haywood, Nathan	1		2		
Fowler, Thomas	1		2		
Hines, Aushur	1		2		

HUNTS MEADOW TOWN.

NAME OF HEAD OF FAMILY.	Free white males of 16 years and upward, including heads of families.	Free white males under 16 years.	Free white females, including heads of families.	All other free persons.	Slaves.
Pearson, Mark	1				
Longfellow, Sewall	1	2	6		
Mason, George	1	2	3		
Tinkham, John	1	2			
Davis, James J.	1	5	3		
Lambart, Danl	1	5	2		
Greenleaf, Ebenezer	3		9		
Preble, James	1	4	3		
Prat, Seth	1	1	3		
Cooper, Moses	3		3		
Hunt, Silas	1				

JONES PLANTATION.

NAME OF HEAD OF FAMILY.	Free white males of 16 years and upward, including heads of families.	Free white males under 16 years.	Free white females, including heads of families.	All other free persons.	Slaves.
Morton, Michael	3	4	4		
Bragg, Nathl	3	7	3		
Getchell, Elihu	1		2		
Burrel, Abr^m	3	3	5		
Ward, Josiah	2	2	8		
McGlothlin, Geo	2	4	2		
——, ——*	1	(*)	(*)		
Fairfeld, Edwd	1	1	2		
Evins, Joseph	2	3	4		
Robinson, Geo	1	3	3		
Rose, Seth	1				
Gliddon, Gidion	1	4	2		
Godfry, Prince	1	2	3		
Ward, Mijah	3	2	2		
Langcaster, James	4	1	6		
Brown, Enock	1		3		
McGlothling, Geo., jr	1		2		
Dickey, Elezer Boyad	1		3		
Evens, Nathl	1		7		
Lewis, Jabez	1	3	5		
Ward, Th^s	1	2	2		
Wiggins, Nathl	1	5	3		
Williams, Joshua	2	2	5		
Clerk, Jonathan	2	2	6		
Clerk, Edmond	2	1	5		
Fish, George	3		1		

* Illegible.

LINCOLN COUNTY—Continued.

NAME OF HEAD OF FAMILY.	Free white males of 16 years and upward, including heads of families.	Free white males under 16 years.	Free white females, including heads of families.	All other free persons.	Slaves.
JONES PLANTATION—continued.					
Marithew, William	1	3	2		
Webber, Joseph	1	1	5		
Webber, Lewis	2	2	4		
Clerk, Eph^rm	2		4		
Goodspeed, Nathl	3		3		
Weeks, Abner	1	1	1		
Weeks, Solomon	1				
Weeks, Solomon, J^r	1		2		
Chadwick, Job	1	2	2		
Chadwick, Ich^d	1		2		
Chadwick, James	1	2	5		
Chadwick, Lot	1				
Chadwick, Judah	1		1		
LEWISTOWN TOWN AND THE GORE ADJOINING.					
Hinkley, Gidion	1	1	3		
Merril, Emly	2		2		
Coal, Samuel	1	3	1		
Pettingill, Sarah		2	4		
Pettingill, Ebenezer	1	2	4		
Coal, Job	2	1	3		
Hacket, Ezekiel	1	1	6		
Right, Timothy	1	3	4		
Thorn, Samuel	3	1	2		
Right, Jesse	1	3	5		
Hacket, Jude	1				
Taylor, Thomas	2	3	2		
Pettingil, Abraham	1	3	3		
Herrick, John	2	2	5		
Barker, Jacob	2		3		
Cutter, Nathan	1	2	4		
Blasdel, William	1	3	5		
Marshal, John	1	2	2		
Winslow, Kernelm	1	4	4		
Right, Joel	1	7	2		
Rose, unis			2		
Mars, John	1				
Hildrick, Paul	2	2	5		
Herris, Abner	2	1	5		
Grafton, John	2	2	5		
Lamps, Peter	1	4	5		
Pinkhum, Elisha	1				
Morril, Jedediah	1	1	3		
Davis, Daniel	1	2	6		
Thompson, Joel	1	2	4		
Ham, Tobias	1	3	6		
Lake, Elisha	1		1		
Davis, Aaron	1		1		
Wilkins, David	2	2	4		
Golder, William	1	3	2		
Pettingill, David	1		2		
Pinkham, Ebenezer	1		2		
Hacket, Ezekiel, Jur	1	1	1		
Hatch, Samuel	1		5		
Hatch, Ellihu	1	1	1		
Landers, Freeman	3		4		
Lake, Joshua	1	2	2		
Randal, Isreal	1	2	1		
Barker, Caleb	1		2		
Barker, Jacob	1		1		
Firck, Samuel	1	3	2		
Davis, Amos	3	2	3		
Far, Seth	1		2		
Herris, Lydia			1		
Blake, John	1	2	4		
Hodgkins, Jonathan	3	1	2		
Carver, Henry	1	2	3		
Ham, Sarah	2		2		
Joslin, James, Jur	1		5		
Joslin, Peter	1	1	2		
Dire, Elhanah	1		2		
Millbank, Phillip	1		4		
Joslin, James	2	1	4		
Joslin, William	1	2	3		
Joslin, Daniel	1		1		
Proctor, Joseph	1				
Bliffin, John, Jur	1				
Kimbal, Simeon	1	2	2		
Dean, William	1	1	2		
Mores, Nathan	1	2	4		
Green, Daniel	1	2	1		
Mitchel, Josiah	2	4	6		
Merril, Moses	1	3	3		
Purrunton, Ezra	1				
fields, Samuel	1	2	4		
Mitchal, Thomas	3	1	4		
fish, John	1	1	1		
Booby, Andrew	1				
Ran, Thomas	1				
Jaeson, James	3		2		
Thompson, Joseph	1	2	2		
Dill, John	2	3	2		
Anderson, Robert	1	3	3		

NAME OF HEAD OF FAMILY.	Free white males of 16 years and upward, including heads of families.	Free white males under 16 years.	Free white females, including heads of families.	All other free persons.	Slaves.
LEWISTOWN TOWN AND THE GORE ADJOINING—continued.					
Hart, Stephen	2		3		
Davis, Joseph	3	1	3		
Read, Dan	1		2		
Adkins, Williams	1		1		
Davis, Joseph, Jur	1	2	1		
Ray, Benjamin	1				
Ray, Hannah	1	1	2		
Dill, Josiah	1	2	3		
Green, William	1	1	4		
Bliffin, John	2	6	4		
Bliffin, James	1	1	1		
Dean, John	1		1		
Dean, John, Jur	2	3	3		
Sawyer, John	1	1	2		
Fields, Joseph	1	4	4		
Jones, Josiah	1		1		
Carvel, William	1				
Meeder, Tobias	1				
Robertson, Samuel	1	3	3		
Ames, Winslow	1	2	1		
Ames, James	1		6		
Higings, Jesse	1		2		
LITTLE RIVER TOWN.					
Fellows, Ebenezer	2		3		
Foster, Stephen	1	1	2		
Tilton, Samuel	1		1		
Right, Ozias	1		1		
Whitney, Abraham	1	3	3		
Moulton, John	1	3	5		
Wilson, Samuel	2	1	3		
Wilson, John	1		1		
Purnton, Allihue	1	1			
Whitney, Benjamin	3	1	6		
Whitney, Jacob	1	1	1		
Southeslin, Alex^d	1	3	4		
Crabtree, William	1	1	2		
LITTLEBOROUGH PLANTATION.					
Gilbert, William	1	1	3		
Bither, Samul	1				
Crocker, Joseph	2	1	4		
Dudson, Jabas	1				
whiting, John	1		2		
Bates, Jacob	1		1		
house, nathaniel	1	2	4		
Samson, michal	1				
Gilbert, henry	1	2	6		
Gilbert, Samuel	1		2		
whitney, John	3	1	6		
Duncat, Prine					3
wood, Simeon					4
Barry, amos	3		1		
Choshman, andrew	1	1	1		
Gincing, John	1	2	1		
Gincing, Samuel	1	1	2		
Treeman, Joseph	2	2	4		
Collard, Isaac	1	2	2		
Shaw, Elisha	1	2	2		
addition, thomas	1		2		
Jones, Edward	1		2		
Samson, Bryen	3		2		
Samson, James	1		3		
Shaw, Elisha, jur	1				
Dunnam, Joseph	1				
Oties, Oliver	1				
Turner, Gorge	1	1	3		
Turner, Joseph	1	4	3		
andris, Ephram	1	2	5		
Drake, Oliver	2	6	2		
Millet, Solomon	1	3	6		
Bruster, Morgin	1	1	2		
Curtice, Gasham	1	3	1		
Foster, Stephen	1	2	1		
Tarbble, David	1	2	3		
Lane, Daniel	2	2	3		
Dunnam, Jon^n	1				
otis, thomas	1				
Lane, Daniel, Ju	1				
lane, James	1	1	3		
lane, Giddeon	1		2		
Riols, Adam	1		2		
Smith, Zebulon	1	2	3		
francis, thomas	1	3	1		
Nap, Joseph	2		2		
linsday, William	2	2	6		
Gorge, Franices	1	1	2		
Paul, Narshfield	1	1	1		
West (widow)		1	2		
whitcker, Nanse	1				
Fish, Jicah	2	3	3		
Robins, Daniel	1		2		

NAME OF HEAD OF FAMILY.	Free white males of 16 years and upward, including heads of families.	Free white males under 16 years.	Free white females, including heads of families.	All other free persons.	Slaves.
LITTLEBOROUGH PLANTATION—continued.					
hicks, Zefeniah	1		2		
Stinchfield, Roger	1	4	4		
larnard, hains	1	3	4		
Norcross, Nathaniel	1				
Stinchfield, thomas	2	3	3		
LIVERMORE TOWN, EAST SIDE ANDROSCOGGIN RIVER.					
Dayley, Daniel	2		4		
Dilenow, Jabish	1	1	3		
Wing, Reuben	3	4	3		
Bargish, Seth	1		3		
linsy, William	2	3	4		
George, Francies	1		3		
Learned, Henry	1				
Browner, William (bachlor)	1				
Greay, James	1		1		
Stevens, William	1				
Cobb, Josiah	1				
MEDUNCOOK TOWN.					
Bradford, Carpenter	2		3		
Gay, Jonah	1	1	2		
Gay, Wellington	1	3	6		
Davis, William	3	1	3		
Davis, Ebenezer	2	3	4		
Bickmore, John	4	1	3		
Bickmore, John, Junr	1	2	3		
Morton, Ebenezer	1		1		
Morton, James	1	3	4		
Morton, Joshua	1	2	7		
Morton, Ebenezer, Junr	4	1	5		
Collamore, Joshua	2	3	4		
Bartlet, Nathaniel	1	1	1		
Jameson, Robert	2	2	4		
Jameson, Paul	5		3		
Bradford, Joshua	1	4	4		
Morton, Cornelius	1		1		
Peckard, Samuel	1	3	3		
Demorse, John	2	1	4		
Cook, Elijah	2	2	7		
Cook, James	1	1	5		
Cook, Hannah		1	3		
Bradford, Joshua, Junr	2	3	5		
Thomas, Asa	2	2	4		
Thomas, Jesse	4		1		
Jameson, Alexander	1	1	2		
Laury, Samuel	6		3		
Motte, William	1	2	4		
Conden, Samuel	3		2		
Conden, George	1	1	1		
Wutton, Benjamin	3	5	3		
Geyer, Martin	1	3	3		
Delano, Alpheus	2	2	5		
Trask, Joseph	1		1		
Newhouse, Christopher	1		1		
Davis, Robert	2	1	5		
Davis, Samuel	5	1	4		
Demorse, John, Junr	1	6	2		
Conner, Charles	1				
Parker, Simon	1		2		
Wingumpaugh, John	1	3	1		
Miller, William	1	4	4		
Wolpgrover, John	1	1	4		
Sage, William	1		2		
Chaples, Richard	1	5	4		
Davis, Jacob	1	1			
Davis, Zechary	1				
Davis, Samuel, Jun		2	4		
Thompson, James	1	3	4		
NEW CASTLE TOWN.					
Tayler, Joseph	2		4		
Trumbal, John	1	1	5		
Brown, James	1	3	5		
Leavitt, Israel	1	2	4		
Hopkins, Christopher	1	1	1		
Hopkins, Willm	1	2	1		
Bester, George	1	4	6		
Winslow, Mary	1		2		
Farley, John	3	1	9		
Kennady, Willm	2		8		
Kennady, Henry	1				
Kennady, Saml	1	1	5		
Cook, Orchard	4	1	5		
Morrison, Jon^a	1				
Carlton, David	1	3	3		
Heath, Moses	1	1	1		
Clough, Daniel	1		6		
Jewett, Moses	1	4	6		

LINCOLN COUNTY—Continued.

NAME OF HEAD OF FAMILY.	Free white males of 16 years and upward, including heads of families.	Free white males under 16 years.	Free white females, including heads of families.	All other free persons.	Slaves.	NAME OF HEAD OF FAMILY.	Free white males of 16 years and upward, including heads of families.	Free white males under 16 years.	Free white females, including heads of families.	All other free persons.	Slaves.	NAME OF HEAD OF FAMILY.	Free white males of 16 years and upward, including heads of families.	Free white males under 16 years.	Free white females, including heads of families.	All other free persons.	Slaves.
NEW CASTLE TOWN— continued.						**NEW CASTLE TOWN—** continued.						**NOBLEBOROUGH TOWN—** continued.					
Jewett, James	1		1			Hall, Isaac	1	3	3			werner, John, jun	1		4		
Nelson, John	1	3	3			Jones, Jonᵃ	3	1	7			werner, John	2		1		
Herriman, Simon	2					Jones, John	2	3	2			werner, andrew	1				
Sawyer, Willᵐ	1		5			Hall, Ebenezer	3	1	4			oberlach, John henry	1	2	2		
Turner, Nehemiah	2	1	4			Clark, James	3	2	6			hofses, mathias	3		5		
Cook, Mehitable			2			Rollins, Nathˡ	5		3			ludwig, Jacob	2	1	4		
Carlton, Moses	2	1	3			Jones, Jonᵃ, Jnʳ	1	2	3			Stall, henry	2	2	2		
Glidden, Benjᵃ	3	4	5			Clark, Ebenᵃ	2	4	5			bornheimer, godfried	2		4		
Gilman, Peter	2	3	6			Lincoln, Benjᵃ	1	1	1			bornheimer, Jacob	1		4		
Labree, Peter	1		3			Ridlon, Robert	2	3	4			weber, george	1	2	3		
Hilton, Samˡ	7	1	3			Rice, John	1	2	3			wolfgruber, Stofel	1		1		
Simpson, Samˡ	1	1	4			Prudent, Willᵐ	1	2	3			oberlach, charles	1	2	3		
McQuig, Danˡ	2		4			Whitten, John	1	2	1			keler, Jacob	2	1	1		
Harley, John	2		2			Whitten, Ebenezer	1		2			miler, peter	2		1		
Cooper, Jesse	1	4	3			Jones, Benjᵃ	2	4	6			winkenbach, Jacob	1	5	6		
Leighton, Ezekiel	2	4	2			Bester, Isaac	1	2	2			oberlach, frank	1	1	2		
Cooper, James	1	1	3			Huzzy, John	3	1	7			waliser, John	1		2		
Harley, John, Jnʳ	1	2	4			Glidden, Joseph	4	1	5			gros, peter	3	2	5		
Greely, Jacob	1	1	4			Holmes, John	1	1				gros, John	1		1		
Leighton, Richard	2	1	1									gros (widow)	1		1		
Leighton, Rebecca	1		3			**NEW SANDWICH TOWN.**						huier, conrad	1	2	3		
Waters, Daniel	2	1	2									miller, frank	3		1		
Woodbrige, Thoᵐ	1	1	4			Wing, Simeon	2		1			miller, frank, jun	1	1	1		
Woodbridge, Benjᵃ, Jnr.	1	3	7			Wing, Alan	1		1			Sterer, christian	1	2	7		
Simpson, James	1	4	5			Wing, Aron	1					Sarius, Isaac	1	2	2		
Kennady, Thoˢ	1	4	6			Wing, Simeon, Jr	1		2			woltz, andrew	4	1	1		
Murray, David	3	3	5			Besse, Ebenezer	1		5			Gentner, andrew	1	2	2		
Campbel, James	5		2			Adkins, Nathaniel	2	2	4			hilt (widow)			4	4	
Hopkins, Solomon	1	1	7			Lovjoy, Moses	1	2	4			lincoln, Joshua	2	4	5		
Chase, Charles	2	5	5			Blak, Thomas	1		2			brown, benjamin	1	1	3		
Woodbridge, Christopher.	1		2			Norris, Nathan	1	2	2			beckler, daniel	1	2	3		
Perkins, Elias	1	2	2			Judkins, Jesse	1		2			wilman, benjamin	1	2	4		
Turner, Briggs	3	1	6			Norris, Ephrim	1	1	4			benner, mathias	1	2	5		
Kennady, Molly			2			Norris, Samˡ	1		2			Gentner, Jacob	1	3	1		
Averal, Ezekiel	2	2	3			Norris, Woodin	1	1	1			wickly, bernhard	4	3	5		
Holmes, Hugh	1	1	1			Norris, Josiah	1					hoch, george	1	1	5		
McAnen, John	1	3	2			Sawell, thomas	1		1			chwartz, Jacob	1		3		
Woodbridge, Benjᵃ	1		3			Mason, Ebenezer	1	4	2			Reed, michel	2	2	8		
Glidden, Joseph, Jʳ	1	3	6			Besse, Jabe	1	2	1			keen (widow)	2		2		
Tugal, Elkanah	3	4	3			Parrey, David	1	2	2			keen, philip	1	1	2		
Cargill, Abanathar	1	1	1			Bilenton, Isaac	1	2	4			keen, niclas	1	3	4		
Cunningham, Thoˢ	2		2			Curtice, David	1		3			miller, francis	1	3	1		
Kennady (Widow)	3	1	2			Sturdevent, Gamaah	1	1	1			hofses, anton	1				
Cunningham, Sarah	2	1	2			Smith, John	1	3	1			hilt (widow)	2	2	6		
Cunningham, John	2	1	7			Tompson, David	1		1			Eichorn, Jacob	1		3		
Cargill, James	3	2	2			Handey, Ebenezer	4	1	4			orf, fridrich	1				
Givens, John	1	2	5	1		Rament, William	1	2	5			wilman, Samuel	1	1	1		
Nichols, Samˡ	6	4	4	1		Besse, Jabas, Ju	2	3	4			hoch, michel	1		2		
Hitchcock, Daniel	2	1	1			Gower, laras	1		3			boseman, Godlieb	1	2	3		
Davidson, Alexander	2	2	3			Perry, Zechriah	2		3			welt, pleosus	1	2	3		
Robinson, Robert	1	2	3			frost, Samˡ	4	2	3			Cramer, peter	2		1		
Nichols, Alexander	1	1	1			Stevens, Christepher	1					cramer, cristoph	1		2		
Webb, Nathˡ	1	3	4			Dexter, Isaac	4	4	3			oberloch, John	1	4	4		
Clap, Enos	3		3			Besse, Reuben	3	1	1			keller, william	2	6	5		
Gledden, Nathˡ	1	5	8			Bilenton, Nathaniel	1	1	1			feiler, Stofel	1		5		
Catland, John	2	2	8			Bilenton, Ichabod	3		4			Schwartz, peter	1	3	2		
Speed, Benjᵃ	2		4			washburn, hosea	1		6			martin, John	2	1	3		
Bester, Benjᵃ	1	3	3			Maseam, Nathan	3	4	3			Shmit, christian	2		3		
Robertson, Archibald	2	4	3			Wing, Moses	1	2	2			horn, frederick	1	4	5		
Glidden, Tobias	2	2	3			Bumpas, Zefeniah	1	1	2			Shuman, philip	1	2	2		
Perkins, Lemuel	2	1	3			Bumpas, Zefeniah, Ju	1	1	1			abraham, Susman	1				
Perkins, Abizah	3	1	3			Reneff, Charly	1		1			levenzeler, adam	3	2	2		
Tufts, Moses	1	2	4			How, Jonᵃ	1					wewer, John	3	3	1		
Nichols, John	1	1	1			Doutey, John	1		2			Shuman, John	3		3		
Campbel, Thoˢ	1	1	1			Bartlet, Jonⁿ	1					hoch, martin	1		2		
Somer, David	3	2	5			fuller, Job	1	1	3			orf, nicolas	1	1	2		
Cargill, David	1	3	4			Lawrance, James	3	1	2			orf, Stophel	2	1	2		
Trask, John	3	3	10			Parry, Judah	1					Sidenspire (widow)	1	1	4		
Cochran, Robert	1	4	5			handy, Richard	1	4	2			Sidenspire, charles	1		1		
Patterson, Peter	1	3	3			Wing, Ebenezer	1	1	2			keller, Jacob, Jun	1	2	2		
Malcom, Allen	2		2			Jennis, John	2		1			Remly, mathias	1	2	1		
Groves, Samˡ	1	3	3			Watlon, Abiah	1	1	4			lear, peter	1	2	3		
Cochran, John	1	1	2			Walton, William	3	3	3			hossies, christian	1	1	3		
Cochran, Adam	1	3	3			Judkins, Jacob	1		3			mink, philip	2	3	6		
Tufts, Moses	1	2	4			ford, Nathaniel	1		4			keiser, francis	1	2	4		
Dodge, Paul	3	1	2			ford, James	1					Stall, philip	1	2	4		
Dodge, David	1	3	1			Cornell, John	1	2	3			miller, henry	1	4	4		
Little, James	2	4	6			Southword, Constant	2	1	3			walk, henry	1		2		
Little, Henry	2	3	5			Southword, thomas	2		2			kalor, charles	2	2	5		
Day, Tobb	1	2	3			ford, Isaac	3	1	3			farnswort, william, Jun	1	2	6		
Perkins, Ebenezer	2		2			Petengall, Mathew	1	2	2			farnswort, william	1		2		
Dodge, John	2	2	4			Sampson, Jonⁿ	2	1	2			farnswort, Robert	1	1	2		
Dodge, Zachariah	2	3	4			Gliten, Jeremiah	1	2	2			farnswort, Isaac	2	1	5		
Dodge, Daniel	1	1	1			handey, Benjᵃ	1					morgin, James			4		
Dodge, Moses	1	1	2			ford, henry	1					pitcher (widow)	3	4	7		
Campbel, Thoˢ	1		1			Wiket, Abraham	1	2	2			howard, Joshua	1	4	5		
Givens, James	4	2	5									burghart, henry	1	4	4		
Dunbar, Solomon	2		4			**NOBLEBOROUGH TOWN.**						ewell, henry	1		4		
Mirach, Josiah	1		2	1								houpe, Joseph	1	1	2		
Barker, Hannah		1	2	1		hines, Conelis	1	2	4			heat, John	1	1	3		
Bryant, Nathˡ	2		1			heabner, george	1		2			Studley, John	1	1	2		
Jones, Kinsley	4	4	3			burghart, John	1	5	2			wihal, francis	1	2	3		
Morgan, Joseph	1		5			welch, Charles	1	1	4			Jones, luke	1	2	5		
Jones, John, Jnʳ	1	3	2			welch, John, jun	1	3	2			hevener, mathias	1	1	3		
						welch, christopher	1	2	2			cumerer, Joseph	1	1	5		

LINCOLN COUNTY—Continued.

NOBLEBOROUGH TOWN—continued.

NAME OF HEAD OF FAMILY.	Free white males of 16 years and upward, including heads of families.	Free white males under 16 years.	Free white females, including heads of families.	All other free persons.	Slaves.
hossies, godfried	1	1	3		
Mink, valantin	1	1	2		
Payson, John	1	1	2		
warner, george	1	3	3		
oldham, peleg	2		2		
loring, judah	1		3		
pitcher, nath¹	2	2	3		
brow, Joseph	1		3		
turner, alexander	1		3		
drawbridge, John	1	3	1		
From Port Royal				2	
Simons (widow)			1		
haupt, John	1		1		
heisler, martin	1	1	3		
feiler, jaspar	1		1		
fitchgearald, John	1	3	5		
Sider, cornelius	2	3	6		
cramer, John	1	1	1		
Sidlinger, martin	1		1		
Sidlinger, charles	1	1	2		
Sidlinger, daniel	1	2	1		
kintzel, John	1	1	5		
Sprague, nathan	4		3		
Sprague, michel	1	2	2		
Rota (widow)	1	1	3		
walter, peter	1	2	2		
hunt, John	2	1	3		
fielhauer, daniel	1	1	2		
bradex, John	2		1		
Simons, Stephen	1	2	4		
Mᶜgayer, thomas	2	3	2		
cramer, Jacob	1	1	4		
cramer, charles	1	1	2		
cramer, fridrich	1		1		
turner, cornelius	3	4	4		
leicht, george	1		1		
leicht, peter	2	3	4		
kohn, paul	2	2	2		
winal, david	1	3	6		
keen, abner	2		1		
keller, charles	1	3	3		
Claus, george	1	2	2		
leicht (widow)	1	4	3		
bracht, peter	2	1	1		
bracht, John	1		2		
wagner, william	1		1		
wagner, andrew	1	1	2		
freeman, barnabas	1	2	1		
Eichorn, george	1	1	2		
benner, John	1	1	1		
benner, martin	2	1	4		
Snaudel, william	3	1	3		
werner, george	2		1		
Eichorn, daniel	1	1	4		
Eichorn, John	1	4	2		
hedwic, Joseph	2	3	6		
lach, asmus	1	3	4		
talheim, george	1	1	4		
Eichorn, michel	1	1	4		
Reed, Jacob	1		2		
brodman, Charles	1	2	2		
feller, Charles	1	1	3		
benner, John, Jun	1	1	2		
Snouteigle, John	1		3		
benner, charles	1	2	4		
benner, Jacob	1	2	5		
benner (widow)			1		
ulmer, John	4	3	5		
Razor, charles	1	3	2		
koon, george, jun	1	5	3		
werner, John	1		1		
werner, charles	1				
Schwartz (widow)			3		
Schwartz, friderich	1		5		
demut, george	2	5	5		
demut, henry	1				
lish, paul	1		6		
leisner, george	1		2		
chapman (widow)	1	2			
chapman, abraham	1				
howard, caleb	3	3	7		
cole, Jabish	1	1	1		
Cole, Isaack	1	2	3		
Isley, michel	1	1	1		
kaastner, ludwig	2	5	3		
nash, Church	2	2	4		
andres, Sthephen	1		2	1	
Sides, loring	3	2	4		
newbert, Stophal	2		2		
newbert, John	1	2	2		
filor, John	1	2	2		
thomas, Joshua	1		1		
walk, peter	3	5	6		
heavener, charles	1		3		

NOBLEBOROUGH TOWN—continued.

NAME OF HEAD OF FAMILY.	Free white males of 16 years and upward, including heads of families.	Free white males under 16 years.	Free white females, including heads of families.	All other free persons.	Slaves.
burns, cornelius	1		3		
warner, John, Jun	1		3		
pilcher, abner	1		3		
winchafsaw, henry	1		4		
wade, jacob	2	5	5		
Simons, barnabas	1	2	4		
winal, ezechial	1	1	4		
Swatland, Samuel	2	3	4		
coles, ables	1	4	2		
Russell, Lewis	1	3	3		
prior, John	1	5	4		
fitch, william	3	2	3		
fogler, John	3	3	3		
Sidenspire, John	1	1	2		
andrew, michel	1			1	
mink, pacel	1	5	2		
Simons, Zebede	1	2	2		
Simons, Joseph	1	2	2		
lasse, John	1	1	4		
Shenck, Andrew	3		4		
kesler, John	1	1	2		
Shanemar, christian	1				
Shenk (widow)	1	3	3		
Starow, mathias	3	3	6		
Starow, andrew	2	3	3		
Samson, charles	1		1		
Samson, charles, Jun	2	3	5		
Simons, Eckiel (Hungh Island)	1	4	3		
Simons, Joab (Hungh Island)	1				
Simons, Isaac (Hungh Island)	1				
Sidenspire, george	1				
thomas, waterman	5	3	9		
payson, Samuel	1				
Sole (widow)			1		
cole, Josephus	1				
morphi (widow)			3		
hofses, george	1	2	3		
maning, Edward	1	2	5		
winchapaw, John	1	4	2		

NORRIDGEWOCK TOWN.

NAME OF HEAD OF FAMILY.					
Stewart, Daniel	1	3	2		
More, Benjamin	1	2	4		
More, John	2	1	2		
More, Miriham			1		
Parlin, Joseph	1	3	2		
Parlin, Alford	1				
More, Goff	1	2	3		
Richard, Robert	1		3		
Spolden, Elezer, Jur	1		3		
Spolden, Elezer	2		2		
Spolden, Seth	1		2		
Wesson, William	1	2	1		
Lankister, David	1	3	4		
Smith, James	1				
Howard, oliver	2		3		
Linsy, Ephrom	1		1		
EsVuire, John	1		2		
Richard, Samuel	1		2		
Fernsworth, Peter	1	3	3		
Gilman, Zebulon	1		3		
Gilman, Robart	1	1	1		
Hale, Josiah	1	5	1		
Hale, Elizabeth			2		
Varnum, William	1				
Withey, Luke	1	4	1		
Parker, Edmond	1	2	1		
Adams, Amos	2	2	5		
Nutting, Josiah	3	4	2		
Adams, Amos, Ju	1				
Tarble, Joseph	1	1	3		
Withey, Uziel	1				
Layton, Jane		1	3		
Spolden, William	1				
Adams, James	1		2		
Wear, Ephrom	1				
Wood, Silas	1	1	2		
Amerson, Ezekiel	1				
Hines, Benjamin	1		1		
Amerson, Calvin	1				
Parlin, Jonathan	1				
Samson, John	1		1		
Martain, Moses	1	1	2		
Brown, George	1	5	3		
Bickford, Moses	1	1	2		
Laplain, James	1		3		
Devinport, John	1	1	3		
Gould, Meriah	1	1	3		
Thompson, Benjamin	1		1		
Hale, Josiah	1	5	1		
Brown, Ephron	1		3		

NORRIDGEWOCK TOWN—continued.

NAME OF HEAD OF FAMILY.	Free white males of 16 years and upward, including heads of families.	Free white males under 16 years.	Free white females, including heads of families.	All other free persons.	Slaves.
Layton, oliver	1				
Spolden, Thomas	1				
Layton, John	1	1	2		
Spolden, William, Ju	1	1	4		
Spolden, Josiah	1		1		
Withey, William	1				
Withey, Nathaniel	1				
Richard, Benjamin	1				
Clerk, John	1	6	5		
Withers, Longly	1				
Withers, Obediah	2	1	3		
Tarble, Joseph	1	1	3		
Longly, Zachry	2	2	3		
Hale, Thomas	1	1	3		
Ward, Ephrom	1	4	3		
Adams, Abraham	1				
Wood, Oliver	1	1	2		
Silvester, William	1				
Hale, John	1	5	4		
Parlin, Nathan	1	2	3		
Parlin, John	1	1	1		
Samson, Levi	1				
Keth, Zepheniah	1		3		
Sawyer, Silvinius	2	2	3		
Longly, Zacheriah	1	2	3		
Cook, Anna			2		
Brown, John	1	1	2		
Whitcum, Thomas	1		3		
Keth, Unite	1	1	3		
Pierce, David	1	1	1		
Peirce, Simon	3		1		
Keth, Alford	1				
Cook, John	2	1	2		

NORRIDGEWOCK TOWN, SETTLEMENT EAST OF.

NAME OF HEAD OF FAMILY.					
Macfassen, Dagle	1	1	3		
More, Joseph	1		1		
Whitcum, Robart	1				
Russel, Jonathan	1		2		
Russel, Jason	1	1	1		
Nutting, Samuel	1	3	2		
Becker, Magnus	1	2	6		
Russel, Josiah	1				
Warrin, Josiah	1	5	3		
Shade, Amos	1		2		
Shade, William	1				

PITTSTON TOWN.

NAME OF HEAD OF FAMILY.					
Springer, Thomas	1	3	2		
Andrews, Ely	2	1	2		
Soper, Seth	1		1		
Owens, Thomas	1	2	3		
Lapham, Roger	1	2	4		
Colburn, Benjamin	2	4	6		
Jackson, Thomas	1	2	1		
Smith, Henry	7		6		
Law, John	1	1	2	1	
Philbrook, David	1	1	2		
Winslow, Carpenter	1	1	1		
Winslow, Jonᵃ	1		1		
Tarbox, Eleazer	1	4	1		
Currier, James	1				
Barker, John	1	1	1		
Whidden, Mark	1		3		
Mason, Saml	1	3	6		
Young, David	2	4	4		
Dudley, James	2	1	3		
Clark, Isaac	1	2	4		
Clark, Burnham	1	1	1		
Dudley, Jeremiah	1	2	3		
Burnes, Joseph	1		1		
Dudley, Samuel	2	3	2		
Blodget, Joseph	2		1		
Hatch, Isaac	1		2		
Hunt, Benoni	1		3		
Hunt, Benoni, Jur	2		1		
Clark, Timothy	1	1	4		
Prat, Ebenezer	1		3		
Moody, Scribner	1		4		
Moody, Jeremiah	1	1	3		
Pickard, James	1	2	4		
Little, Daniel	1		1		
Pickard, Thomas	1	2	1		
Palmer, Anna	3	1	2		
Cooper, Leonard	1	2	3		
Bailey, John	1	2	6		
Blin, David	1		2		
Glidden, Arnold	1	1	4		
Pulcifer, Joseph	3		3		
Grant, Saml	4	1	3	1	
Leasunesse, John	2	4	2		
Lang, Saml	2	3	2		

LINCOLN COUNTY—Continued.

NAME OF HEAD OF FAMILY.	Free white males of 16 years and upward, including heads of families.	Free white males under 16 years.	Free white females, including heads of families.	All other free persons.	Slaves.
PITTSTON TOWN—con.					
Piper, Jona	1		1		
Doar, James	1		3		
Broadstreet, Andw	3		5		
Towns, Thomas	1		7		
Moore, Reuben	4	3	3		
Goodwin, Simeon	1	3	5		
Wakefield, Dominicus	1	1	1		
McCaslin, Robert	1	2	1		
Berry, Nathl	1	2	3		
Kimbal, Nathl	4	2	2		
Doar, Henry	1	1	2		
Shaw, Benja	2	3	5		
Pollard, Ezekiel	1	2	1		
Byram, Ebenezer	4		5		
Gay, Seth	2	1	5		
Barker, Willm	2		3		
Jewett, Zedadiah	2	3	5		
Oldham, Jona	1			4	
Gardiner, Gideon	1	1	3		
McCasslin, Henry, Ju	2	2	2		
McCasslin, Henry	2	1	3		
Nason, Robert E	1	3	2		
Doar, Benaiah	2	1	3		
Warren, Petten	1	2	4		
Pollard, Elijah	1	1	4		
Doar, Allen	1		2		
Berny, Thos	1	3	1		
Wakefield, Jereh	1	1	2		
Evans, James	1	1	2		
Jewett, Stephen	4		1		
Fitts, Brown Farm	2	1	1		
Lawrence, David	4	2	2		
Eastman, Saml, Jur	1				
Quincy, Henry	2				
Haley (Widow)	4	1	3		5
Moore, David	1	4	3		
Mason, Abner	5	3	5		
Mason, Abner, Jur	1		1		
Bailey, Nathel	2	4	5		
Dunham, David	1	4	4		
Fuller, Edward	1	3	4		
Bailey (Widow)	1		1		
Davis, Ezra	4		4		
Agry, Thomas	2	1	4		
Agrey (Widow)	4		2		
Colburn, Reuben	7	1	8		
Oakman, Saml	2	1	5		
Springer, Willm	3	1	5		
Blanchard, Jona	3	1	6		
Easman, Saml	2		4	1	
Shepherd, Levi	1		1		
Robinson, ——	1		2		
Pitts, Abel	1				
Flitner, Willm	2	2	3		
Taggot, James	1	2	2		
Walker, Richard	1		1		
Jakens, Christopher	2	3	2		
Dearborn, Henry	3	2	5		
POWNALBOROUGH TOWN.					
Hodge, Henry	6	1	3	2	
Lee, Silas	1	1	3		
Wood, Abiel	31	4	7		
Price, Thomas	3	3	6		
Thaxter, William	1	1	2		
Whittier, Ebenezer	2	1	3		
Cook, Francis	1	3	5		
Payson, David	2		2		
Payson, David, Jnr	2		4		
Bryson, Peter	3		2		
Hughes, John	4	1	3		
Tinkham, Seth	1	2	3		
Crooker, Elijah	2		1		
Arvel, John	2	2	3		
Colby, Betty	1	1	2		
Carter, Samuel	1	1	2		
Craft, Foster	1				
Robey, Henry	1				
Sanborn, Bradbury	1				
Cowley, John	2	1	2		
Foster, William	2	1	2		
Seavey, Michael	1		2		
Stacey, Nimphar	2	3	4		
Place, Annas	1		3		
Place, Samuel	1	1	2		
Ranlet, Charles	1	3	2		
Stephens, Joseph	2	4	2		
Dalton, Jeremiah	3		2		
Blight, Mehitable		1	1		
Clough, Stephen	1	1	3		
Collins, Lemuel	1	2	4		
Stutson, Zealous	1	3	3		
Haynes, Patty		1	2		
Holmes, John	2		1		

NAME OF HEAD OF FAMILY.	Free white males of 16 years and upward, including heads of families.	Free white males under 16 years.	Free white females, including heads of families.	All other free persons.	Slaves.
POWNALBOROUGH TOWN—con.					
Light, Robert	6	3	5		
Clark, Nathan	2	1	3		
McAnere, Joseph	1		3		
Parsons, Timothy	9	3	10		
Elbes, Betty		1	4		
Woodman, Thomas	2				
Clark, James	1	2	3		
Langdon, John	3	3	3		
Barker, William	1	1	4		
Bradbury, Anna	1	1	2		
Nute, Paul	1	2	6		
Huntoon, Jonathan	1	3	1		
Blagdon, Rollins	2		2		
Acorn, Jacob	4	1	3		
Young, Reuben	1		1		
Harridon, Ignatious	1	1	1		
Foy, Robert	2		2		
Foy, John	1		3		
Colby, Susanna	4		4		
Holbrook, Joseph	1	1	3		
Moore, Thomas	1	1	4		
Wilson, John	1	1	2		
Kincaid, Reuben	1		6		
Ranlet, Henry	2	1	5		
Grandee, Charles	1		2		
Jones, Willm	1	1	3		
Holbrook, Richard	1		4		
Canady, Dennis	1		2		
Moffat, James	3	1	2		
Cunningham, Isaac	1		1		
Harrington, Joseph	1	1	3		
Bridge, John	1		4		
Seavey, John	3	1	3		
Appleton, John	1	2	2		
Flanders, Samuel	1		2		
Silvester, David	2	2	2		
Silvester, Mary	1		1		
Askins, Alexander	4	3	3		
Decker, Joseph	3	3	3	1	
Langdon, Timothy	1	2	5		
Hammon, Frederick	1		2		
Noyes, Thomas	1	1	4		
Lion, Ezekiel	1	1	4		
Waldo, Benjamin	1	1	1		
Evelet, James	1	2	3		
Hammon, Seth	1		1		
Frizzel, Benja	4	1	2		
Bennet, Spencer	1	2	1		
Christopher, Joseph	1	2	6		
Woodman, Jacob	1	1	1		
Oaks, Joshua	1	1	1		
Adams, John	1		3		
Merrow, Patrick	1	1	4		
Decker, John	1	1	2		
Seavey, William	2	1	3		
Pottle, Hezekiah	2	2	5		
Holbrook, John	2	1	3		
Young, Isaac	4	2	3		
Silvester, Samuel	1	4	4		
Handy, Jonathan	1	2	2		
Sterrey, David	2	2	2		
Williamson, Jonathan	1		3		
Blaire, William	1	1	2		
Duncan, John	1	2	4		
Williamson, Sarah			6		
Kanady, James	1	1	2		
Capen, James	2	2	6		
Quinham, James	2	2	1		
Scott, Daniel	1	1	4		
Smith, Manassa	1	4	5		
Smith, Silas	1		2		
Averel, Samuel	1	6	4		
Averel, Job	2		3		
Fairservice, John	1				
Fairservice, Thomas	2	1	2		
Cheney, Ralph	1	5	3		
Smith, Rogers	2	2	5		
Kincaid, Abigail		2	1		
Forestel, James	1	1	3		
Tucker, John	1	1	3		
Frissel, John	1	3	3		
Clark, William	1	3	3		
Kean, John	1	2	2		
Baker, John	1	5	4		
Dickerson, Abijah	2	4	3		
Dickerson, Samuel	1		1		
Hilton, John	1		3		
Sloman, William	2	2	2		
Honnowel, John	2	2	4		
Dole, Nathan	1	1	1		
Kenny, Benjamin	1		3		
Gitchel, John	1		2		
Hilton, William	1		3		
Hilton, Samuel	1	1	2		
Honnowel, Israel	1	1	4		

NAME OF HEAD OF FAMILY.	Free white males of 16 years and upward, including heads of families.	Free white males under 16 years.	Free white females, including heads of families.	All other free persons.	Slaves.
POWNALBOROUGH TOWN—con.					
Hilton, Joshua	2	1	4		
Dilano, Amasa	1		1		
Chapman, John	2	2	5		
Boynton, Hannah	3	2	4		
Taylor, Joseph	2		3		
Gray, Alexander	1	1	1		
Boynton, William	1		1		
Chovey, John	1		3		
Briggs, John	1	2	1		
Boynton, Joshua	1	1	1		
Blackledge, Jonathan	1	2	3		
Chapman, John, Jr	2		1		
Colman. Jonathan	1	1	2		
Pierce, John	1		1		
Nutter, Anthony	1	2	5		
Young, Joshua	6		5		
White, Jesse	2	3	5		
Nason, Abraham	2	1	5		
McKenney, David	2	3	2		
Boynton, Joshua, Jnr	1	1	1		
Hilton, Joseph	1	3	3		
Hilton, Morril	1	1	5		
Savage, John	1	1	2		
Hilton, Moses	2	2	3		
Hamden, Gabriel	1	3	6		
Mansfield, James	1		2		
Baker, Willm C	2	3	2		
McKenney, John	3	4	6		
McKenney, Danl	1		1		
Muncey, David	1	1	3		
Kincaid, John	1		3		
Muncy, Napthali	1	4	5		
Jackson, James	1	1	1		
Blagdon, Paul	1				
Coffin, Benja	1	2	3		
Coffin, Benja, Jnr	1	1	3		
Decker, William	1	2	5		
Pressey, Will	1	1	3		
Jackson, Samuel	1		1		
Jackson, Benja	1	4	6		
Hersey, Solomon	1	5	3		
Hodge, James	3	1	5		
Prince, Isaac	1				
Mannis, Nathan	1	1	2		
Frost, Ichabod	3	2	5		
Brookin, Hannah			1		
Webber, Nicholas	1	5	2		
Boynton, Oliver	2	4	4		
Fletcher, Samuel	1		3		
Boynton, John	1	3	3		
Bayley, Thaddeus	1	2	3		
Bailey, Richard	4		2		
Plummer, David	2	3	6		
Mason, Stephen	1	2	5		
Allen, Amos	1		1		
Monro, Samuel	1	2	3		
Gardiner, Willm	3		1		
Brackley, Willm	1	2	1		
McGown, John	3		4		
Dunlap, Archibald	1	3	2		
Goodwin, Jeremiah	3	1	2		
Call, James	1	1	2		
Clancey, David	1				
Bickford, Henry	3	1	3		
Bridge, Edmund	3	4	7		
Bickford, Paul	1	4	1		
Barker, Carr	1	3	2		
Barker, Caleb	1	2	6		
Allen, Peter	1	4	7		
Obrien, William	1	5	5		
Page, John	2	3	4		
Call, Obadiah	2	5	6		
McPharlen, Joseph	2	1	1		
Patterson, William	1	2	3		
Pushaw, George	2	4	2		
King, Moses	1		1		
Stiflen, George	2	5	2		
Kendal, Abiathar	2	1	3		
Goud, James	2	2	3		
Parish, John	1	2	3		
Parish, George	1		2		
Southward, Abram	1	2	2		
Holland, Lemuel	1	2	2		
Carlow, Jacob	1		1		
Hoodlet, Lewis	1	5	4		
Miers, Philip	1	6	6		
Rittle, Francis	1	1	1		
Hunt, Steward	5	2	3		
Andrews, Asa	2	1	5		
Ely, Samuel	1		2		
Averel, Mary	2	3	3		
Averel, Samuel	1	1	1		
Clark, William	2	3	6		
Lord, Abraham	2	1	3		

LINCOLN COUNTY—Continued.

NAME OF HEAD OF FAMILY.	Free white males of 16 years and upward, including heads of families.	Free white males under 16 years.	Free white females, including heads of families.	All other free persons.	Slaves.
POWNALBOROUGH TOWN—con.					
Smith, Cheney	4	3	4		
Averal, John	1	3	5		
Gray, Moses	2	1	3		
Hilton, Joseph	2	1	4		
Hoit, Thomas	1		2		
Tobey, Barnabas	1	2	4		
Averel, Willm	2	5	2		
Boynton, Pelatiah	1	3	2		
Meirs, George	1	6	6		
Reid, Jonathan	3	3	2		
Gould, George	1	3	3		
Fisher, Peter	1	2	2		
Kidder, Richard	3	2	3		
Goodwin, Saml	1	1	1		
Goodwin, Saml, Ju	4	4	4		
Johnson, John	1	5	3		
Fwicross, Lydia	1	2	1		
Hatch, Paul	1	1	5		
Ramsdale, George	2	2	4		
Patten, Willm	1	2	2		
Woodward, Saml	3	3	4		
Tupper, James	1	4	2		
Taylor, Ezra	1		4		
Dinsmore, Asa	1	2	4		
Stilfan, Michl	2	2	1		
Brown, Jacob	2	3	5		
Theobald, Philip	1	1	5		
Atkins, James	2		1		
Corteloe, John	1	3	3		
White, Saml	1		4		
Spring, Daniel	2	3	5		
Lamercier, Peter	1	1	5		
DePollereski, John	1	1	4		
Rittle, Francis	2	1	5		
Rittle, John	1	2	1		
Pushaw, Peter	2		6		
Lewis, William	1	2	2		
Segar, John	1	1	1		
Call, Stephen	2	4	1		
Hatch, Nathan	1	1	2		
Call, Deliverance	1	2	3		
Call, Philip	1	2	1		
Patterson, Margaret	3		3	1	
Calahan, Rebecca	1		2		
Hatch, Simeon	1	3	2		
White, John	1	2	4		
Reid, Amos	1	2	2		
Libbey, George	4	3	3		
Hathorn, Nathl	1	3	3		
Gray, Samuel	1	3	2		
Hathorn, James	1	1	3		
Currice, Ephraim	2	1	6		
Doe, Mary	1	3	3		
Nelson, Jacob	2	1	4		
Smith, Asa	3	3	3		
Askins, George	1	3	3		
Ayers, James	2	2	6		
Nelson, Mary	2	1	4		
Carlton, Joseph	2	4	3		
Carlton, Moses	4	1	9		
Adle, Cornelius	1	1	4		
Askins, Christopher	1	1	4		
Plummer, John	1	5	5		
Rollins, Moses	1	1	2		
Perkins, John	1	1	2		
Seavey, Stephen	2		2		
Seavey, Solomon	1	5	3		
Young, Benja	1	1	6		
Pressey, Benja	1	2	2		
Lowel, Joseph	2	1	4		
Chatman, Saml	1	1	1		
Burr, Joseph	1		2		
Dwinnel, Moses	1	1	3		
Leman, Henry	1		1		
Lambert, James	1		4		
Pressey, Sarah			2		
Groves, William	1	1	3		
Greenleaf, Benja	1	3	2		
Arnold, Willm	1	1	2		
Foy, Willm	1	4	3		
Stinson, Willm	1		2		
Thompson, Joseph	2	3	4		
Ranlet, Nathl	3	4	2		
Kingsbury, John	2	5	5		
Pressey, Jacob	4		2		
Churchill, Susanna		2	4		
Pressey, Jacob, Jur	1	1	2		
Booker, Nicholas	2		1		
Averal, Israel	1	3	4		
Gurrel, John	1	2	2		
Clark, Joseph	1		1		
Clark, James, Jur	1	2	1		
Clark, John	1	1	3		
Boynton, David	1	3	4		
Booker, Benja	1		1		

NAME OF HEAD OF FAMILY.	Free white males of 16 years and upward, including heads of families.	Free white males under 16 years.	Free white females, including heads of families.	All other free persons.	Slaves.
POWNALBOROUGH TOWN—con.					
Hamlen, Levi	1	2	2		
Lowel, Jacob	1	3	3		
Sole, Amasa	1	1	2		
Whittier, Joseph	1	2	3		
Farr, Joseph	2		1		
Walker, Abraham	1	4	5		
Gray, Moses, Jnr	1	3	6		
Bean, Jona	1	2	1		
Rowe, John	1		3		
Muncy, Jonathan	3	1	3		
Flanders, Saml	1		2		
PRESCOTTS AND WHITCHERS PLANTATION.					
Thompson, John	1				
Withern, Arnold	1				
Ladd, Josiah	1		3		
Lambart, Abraham	1				1
Howland, Elijah	1	2	3		
Gordon, David	1				
Mattock, Richard	1				
Allen, William	1	1	1		
Killsroth, Patrick	1	2	2		
Allen, John	1	1	1		
Whiteher, Moses	1				
Whiteher, Clerk	1	2	1		
Gordon, Jonathan	1				
ROCKMEEKO TOWN, EAST SIDE OF RIVER.					
Addams, John	1		1		
Weston, abraham	3	2	6		
Jackson, Nathaniel	1		4		
fullar, thomas	1	1	1		
fuller, Nathaniel	1	1	2		
Discomb, Thomas	1	2	2		
Mills, Josiah	1		2		
Rogars, John	1		2		
Winter, John	1		1		
Cocah, David	1	1	3		
leucrmore, William	1				
black, Garsham	1				
Wright, Oliver	1				
Wiman, thomas	1				
Craft, Moses	1				
fuller, Oliver	1				
fuller, Salham	1				
Craft, henry	1				
Craft, Moses, jr	1				
West, Isaac	1				
west, Obediah	1				
Uslis, William	1				
Bartlet, Solomon	1				
Bartlet, Peter	1				
Massey, Benjn	1				
fuller, Nathan	1				
SANDY RIVER, FIRST TOWNSHIP.					
Sewall, Samuel	1	3	2		
Brainard, Ely	1	2	1		
Knowlton, Samuel	1	2	1		
Wood, John	1	3	5		
Chandler, Samuel	1	3	2		
Gould, Silas	1	3	3		
Butterfield, Ephrom	1				
Nutting, Thomas	1				
Green, Josiah	1				
Hiscock, Thomas	1	1	4		
Gould, Jesse	1				
Gould, William	1		4		
Weathern, Benjamin	1	1	2		
Chandler, Moses	1	3	2		
Kinney, Thomas	1		2		
Mores, Thomas	1		2		
Page, Timothy	1		4		
Butterfield, Samuel	3	3	4		
Turner, Reuben	1		5		
Worit, Josiah	1	1	3		
Powers, Isaac	1		2		
Starling, Moses	3	2	1		
Eaton, Jacob	1		3		
Maccardy, James	1				
Surtain, John	1	2	4		
Page, Isaac	1	3	2		
Butler, Benjamin	1	3	4		
Bradford, Joseph	2	1	6		
Handy, Benjamin	1	2	3		
Potter, Ezekiel	1	2	3		
Battle, Joseph	1	1	3		
Rions, Joseph	1		5		
Smith, Jotham	1	2	2		

NAME OF HEAD OF FAMILY.	Free white males of 16 years and upward, including heads of families.	Free white males under 16 years.	Free white females, including heads of families.	All other free persons.	Slaves.
SANDY RIVER, FIRST TOWNSHIP—con.					
Gay, Peter	4	2	7	1	
Pickit, Jonathan	1		2		
Cox, Hugh	1				
Brigs, Samuel	2		2		
How, Lemuel	1	4	3		
Parker, Josiah	2	2	2		
Winslow, James	3		3	1	
Cowing, Ephrom	2	1	2		
Brigs, Adin	1		2		
Cowing, David Baley	1	1	1		
Adams, Moses	2		2		
Russ, Simeon	1	5	3		
Jones, Robart	2	2	1		
Clayton, John	1	2	1		
Hustings, John	2	5	2		
Brown, Joseph	3		2		
Swift, Turner	1	1	1		
Rise, John	1				
Butterfield, Reuben	1				
Tibbits, Edward	1		4		
Cregg, Enoch	1	1	2		
Cannaday, William	1	1	1		
Silvester, Joseph	4	4	3		
Greeley, Seth	3	4	6		
Keen, Samuel	1		3		
Bullin, Joshua	1				
Brainard, Church	1	2	2		
Blackston, Lydia		2	3		
Gore, Robart	2	3	7		
Tufts, Francis	3	3	3		
Blunt, Lydia	1		1		
Lowell, Reuben	2	2	2		
Knowlton, Jonathan	2	4	5		
Norton, Elijah	2				
Clough, Benjamin	1				
Whiteher, Benjamin	3	1	4		
Baly, Oliver	1	2	2		
Baley, Eliphalet	1	2	2		
Ralph, Joseph	1				
Howland, Joseph	1		2		
Perham, Lemuel	4		2		
Greely, Joseph	3	1	2		
Sweet, Ebenezer	2		1		
Blake, Josiah	1	2	1		
Davis, Nathaniel	1		1		
Page, Amos	2	2	3		
Butterfield, Samuel, Jur	1		1		
Page, Ezekiel	1		1		
Hartwell, Oliver	1				
Ames, Samuel	1	2	1		
White, William	3	3	1		
Bullin, Samuel	1		1		
Smith, Abraham	2	1	3		
Adams, Solomon	2	1	3		
Corbet, Peter	2	2	2		
Jiteum, Stephen	1	3	5		
Blodget, Nehemiah	1	1	1		
Withers, Zoe	1		2		
Webber, Ezekiel	1	2	4		
Gore, William	1		3		
Lowell, Joshua Bartlet	1				
Butterfield, Jesse	1	2	3		
Luice, Daniel	1	3	4		
Butterfield, Jonas	2	1	3		
Blunt, Ebenezer	1				
SANDY RIVER, FROM ITS MOUTH TO CARRS PLANTATION.					
Mackinney, Daniel	1	2	1		
Boldin, Nahum	1	1	2		
Davis, John	1	1	1		
Grover, John	1	2	2		
porter, Peter	1				
Bickford, Henry	1	1	2		
Bickford, James	1		1		
Leman, Jacob	1	1	5		
Leman, David	1	1	2		
Wilson, oliver	1	4	5		
Hitton, Benjamin	2	3	4		
Nichols, George	2	2	5		
Houghton, Thomas, Jr	1		2		
Whitcum, Thomas	1				
Sawyer, George	1		2		
Dutton, Elijah	1		2		
Dutton, John	2		2		
Waugh, Thomas	1	3	3		
Waugh, James	2	3	3		
Sawyer, Luke	1	1	3		
Wood, Nathan	1	2	3		
Crosby, Jonathan	1		2		
Greenlief, Joseph	1	1	2		
Skillin, Lewis	1	1	5		
Sheaf, Samson	1	1	2		

NAME OF HEAD OF FAMILY.	Free white males of 16 years and upward, including heads of families.	Free white males under 16 years.	Free white females, including heads of families.	All other free persons.	Slaves.
SANDY RIVER, FROM ITS MOUTH TO CARRS PLANTATION—con.					
Whittum, Caleb	1	2	6		
Fish, Nathan	1	6	2		
Williamson, Samuel	2	3	3		
Green, Joseph	1		2		
Crosby, Asa	1		1		
Greenlief, William	1				
Greenlief, Joshua	1				
Gray, Amos	1		2		
Yongue, Joshua	1	1	2		
Williamson, Jonathan	2	2	2		
Whittum, Daniel	2	1	1	1	
Pattin, Nathaniel	1				
Gray, Ebenezer	1				
Crosby, Robert	2	3	3		
Whittum, Benjamin	1	2	3		
Whittum, Benjamin, Ju	1				
Yongue, William	1	3	4		
Parker, James	1		2		
Pumroy, John	3	3	6		
How, John	1	1	2		
Taylor, Robert	1	1	2		
Gray, Reuben	1	3	4		
Hinkly, Samuel	1	1	1		
Kimbal, Nicholas	1		3		
Whittum, Ebenezer	1	1	1		
Sanders, Rufus	1		3		
Arnold, Benjamin	1	3	3		
Greenlief, John	1	2	3		
Greenlief, Ebenezer	1	2	4		
Brawn, Jeremiah	1	1	2		
Cook, Joseph	1	2	3		
Brown, Ephrom	1	3	3		
Williamson, Stephen	1	2	1		
Emery, Nathaniel	1	6	1		
Taylor, Joseph	2	1	5		
Taylor, Joseph, Ju	1				
Taylor, Nathaniel, Ju	1	1	4		
Holbrook, Peter	1	4	1		
Taylor, Nathaniel	1	1	3		
Whittum, Benjamin, Ju	1	1	2		
Pattin, Benjamin	1	1	1		
Landers, Alvin	1				
SANDY RIVER, MIDDLE TOWNSHIP.					
Withern, Michal	1	2	1		
Read, William	1	2	5		
Eaton, Eliab	1		1		
Hiscock, William	2	1	2		
Bates, Thomas	2	2	3		
Sawyes, Jacob	2				
Dodge, Benjamin	1	1	3		
Humphries, David	1	1	2		
Flint, Edward	1		3		
McClary, Robert	1				
Day, John	1	3	2		
Humphries, Joseph	1	1	2		
Colbey, Abel	1	1	4		
Morrow, Timothy	1	1	2		
SANDY RIVER, UPPER TOWNSHIP.					
Humphries, Thomas	1		1		
Dudley, Moses	1	5	3		
Thompson, Ebenezer	2	5	3		
Allen, Pirkins	2	2	7		
Church, Charles	2		1		
Ingham, Daniel	3		2		
Dudley, Eliphalet	2	1	2		
Spreague, Samuel	1	2	1		
Soul, Joshua	3	2	4		
Thompson, Isaac	1		1		
SEVEN MILE BROOK TOWN.					
Taylor, John	1				
Taylor, Amos	1				
Hines, Nimrod	1				
Hilton, Ellihu	1				
Drummon, Rutherford	1				
Parker, Josiah	1		2		
Richardson, Ebenezer	1		2		
Huchings, David	2	4	3		
Churchwell, John	1				
Huchings, Olive		2	4		
Craging, Simon	1		2		
Cleavland, Jonathan	1				
Cleavland, Joseph	1	3	3		
Pain, Isabillah		2	4		
Perry, Reuben	1	1	2		
Alby, Jonathan	1	2	2		

NAME OF HEAD OF FAMILY.	Free white males of 16 years and upward, including heads of families.	Free white males under 16 years.	Free white females, including heads of families.	All other free persons.	Slaves.
SEVEN MILE BROOK TOWN—con.					
Gray, George	1	1	1		
Alby, Isaac	1		1		
Fling, Morris	1		4		
Yongue, David	2	2	5		
Macdanniels, James	1	2	5		
Forbus, John	1				
More, John	1		2	1	
Gitchel, John	1		1		
Midcalf, John	2		1		
Mackinney, James	1				
Pain, David	1				
Pain, Joseph	1				
Drummon, Reatherford	1				
Wade, Charles	1	3	1		
Alby, Samuel	1				
Pain, Thomas	1				
Pain, William	1	2	1		
Williams, Samuel	1	4	4		
Hunniwell, Thomas	1	2	3		
Danforth, David	1	2	6		
Fling, Samuel	1				
Savage, Jacob	1	2	4		
Mores, Abraham	1				
Drummon, Rutherford	1				
SMITHTOWN PLANTATION.					
Kinmah, James	1	1	3		
Caheel, Thomas	1		2		
Springer, David	1		1	2	
Tayler, James	1	1	2		
Johnson, John	1				
Salley, William	1				
Hall, Timothy	1	3	3		
Parker, Elisha	3		4		
Springer, David, ju	3		4		
Springer, Andrew	1	1	3		
Jewell, Enoch	1	1	5		
Morgin, John	2	1	2		
Johnson, James	1	3	3		
West, Samuel	2	1	3		
Priscott, James	1		2		
Loont, Johnson	1		2		
True, Daniel	1		2		
True, John	1				
True, aron	1				
True, abner	1		3		
Ores, William	1				
Palmer, Mulbry	1				
Shaw, Isaac	1		1		
bab, Joshua	1	4	2		
bab, Bot (widow)			4		
Bab, Jonthan, Ju	1		1		
bab, Jonthan					
Richiston, Irah	1	2	1		
Hall, Calvin	1	3	3		
Johnson, Adam	1		1		
Richison, Joshua	1	2	1		
Hunttington, John	2				
huntington, Benjn	1	2	2		
Jewell, Henry	1	4	4		
Huchinson, Samuel	2	6	3		
Borman, Jonas	1	2	1		
Potter, John	1	1	2		
Potter, William	1	4	3		
Watson, Daniel	1	1	5		
Watson, Daniel, ju	1		3		
Neall, —*	1	1	3		
Smith, Eliphelat	3		2		
Sawyer, Joseph	1				
Sawyer, John	1				
Potter, hugh	1	2	1		
Potter, Andrew	1		2		
Colbee, thomas	1	1	1		
huntington, Timothy	1	1	4		
tuckes, abraham	1	2	1		
Peace, James	1	1	1		
Heal, John, jur	1	1	1		
hevemon, Levi	1	1	1		
Loud, James	2	1	3		
Daniel, John	1	2	4		
Smith, Thomas	1	2	4		
Brocks, James	1				
Neal, Joseph	1				
neal, George	1				
noton, Jacob	1				
noton, Joab	1		4	1	
Jackson, Benjn	1	2	5		
Ring, Daniel	1	4	4		
Barry, Nathanel	2	1	3		
MacCaslin, James	1	2	3		
MacCaslin, andrew	1	2	5		
Piper, John	2		3		

NAME OF HEAD OF FAMILY.	Free white males of 16 years and upward, including heads of families.	Free white males under 16 years.	Free white females, including heads of families.	All other free persons.	Slaves.
SMITHTOWN PLANTATION—continued.					
Bary, Jonn	2		3		
McGunrey, John	2	1	2		
Weber, Stephen	2	1	2		
Webber, Joseph	1		2		
Dudley, andrew	3	2	3		
Baker, Jonn	1	3	1		
Baker, Elkrer	1	2	2		
hinkley, Benjn	1	3	4		
Richardson, abijah	1	4	4		
Dunlap, James	1	4	2		
Potter, Saml	1	5	2		
Robinson, Jabez	1	6	5		
Potter, Joseph	1		1		
Dunlap, Ebereser	1	3	4		
Dunlap, Robert	1	2	7		
Goocer, Edward	1	1	1		
Baker, Barraws	4	1	4		
Smith, Thomas	3		7		
Smith, Benjn	3	3	6		
Dunlap, William	1				
Shirtlef, James	1	3	1		
Cook, Saul	1	1	4		
Jackson, Joseph	3	2	5		
Brown, John	1	2	1		
michel, Danbr	1				
Brown, William	1				
Robinson, David	3		3		
Smith, Samuel	1		3		
mograge, Thomas	1	2	3		
mograge, Charly	1				
Smith, thomas, Jr	1	2	4		
Johnson, Adam	1	4	6		
marston, Nathaniel	1	2	1		
Baker, abner	4		4		
Baker, Smith	1	2	3		
Baker, Judah	1	2	3		
haggat, Isaac	1				
huchinson, Nemiah	1				
Starrde, Edward	1				
huchinson, Isaac	1				
Bunker, James	1				
hatch, hapcie				1	
Buterfeld, aron	1				
Galowell, Job	2		2		
STARLING PLANTATION.					
Manter, David	1		3		
wing, Benjn	1	1	3		
wing, Isral	1		3		
hubard, franices	1		3		
Marston, Joseph	1		2		
Morse, Isaac	1		2		
Morse, Philip	1	2	6		
knowly, David	1	3	2		
Judkins, Joel	1		2		
Judkins, Joseph	1				
Judkins, Daniel	1				
lane, Nathan	1				
Barry, John	1				
Goodin, Elezer	1	1	2		
wiggens, Asa	1		2		
Judkins, Benjn	1	2	3		
Page, John	1	1	2		
Rowell, Daniel	1				
Rusel, Abal	2	3	3		
Wolton, Joshua	3	2	3		
anderson, Joseph	1	1	2		
Walton, Moses	1	2	6		
Batchelor, Daniel	1		1		
Batchelor, Moses	1				
French, Moses	1				
Cliford, Benjn	1				
Brown, Isaac	1				
Brown, Ephelat	1				
Palmer, Benjn	1				
Tuck, Samuel	1				
Tuck, John M	1				
Basse, Jabas	1				
Basse, Solomon	1				
Sturdevant, andrew	1	1	3		
Sturdevent, abisha	1		2		
tilton, David	3				
lane, Ephram	3	1	3		
lane, Ebenezer	1				
Davies, James	1				
Davies, Philp	1		1		
hilkon, William	1	2	2		
Richard, Jeremiah	1		3		
Barnfard, James	1				
Billings, Oliver	1		1		
Pitts, Shubal	1				
Wough, Robert	1				
Emrson Brown	2		2		

* Illegible.

LINCOLN COUNTY—Continued.

NAME OF HEAD OF FAMILY.	Free white males of 16 years and upward, including heads of families.	Free white males under 16 years.	Free white females, including heads of families.	All other free persons.	Slaves.
STARLING PLANTATION—continued.					
Emrson, ——					
Elhings, Chase	1	3	2		
knowly, John	1	2	3		
Thomas, Richard	1				
Brocks, Gorge	1	3	3		
Ingham, David	1	1	2		
THOMASTON TOWN.					
Dillaway, John	3	2	4		
Dodge, Ezekiel Goddard	1	1	2		
Fales, Nathaniel	2	1	6		
Fales, Nathaniel, Junr	1	1	4		
Fales, James, Junr	1	1	2		
Fales, John	2	1	3		
Fales, David	5	5	6		
Jenks, David	2	2	4		
Porterfield, Patrick	2		4		
Shibles, Robert	2		1		
Vose, Thomas	4		5		
Vose, Spencer	2	1	2		
Wheaton, Mason	2		1		
Smith, Oliver	1	3	2		
Smith, Abiathar	1	4	3		
Woodcock, Nathaniel	2	2	2		
Stevens, Thomas	2	1	3		
Babbidge, Benjamin	1				
Stevens, Nehemiah	1		1		
Lamson, Jonathan	1	1	6		
McIntosh, William	1	1	1		
Tings, John	1	2	2		
Brown, Samuel	2	1	6		
Brown, James	1	3	3		
Green, William	3	2	6		
Kelloch, Findly	1	3	3		
Loveit, Israel	3	3	3		
Lackay, William	1	1	2		
McLallen, Thomas	2	2	2		
Robbins, Oliver	2	1	3		
Robbins, Otis	1	2	2		
Stackpole, James	2	3	4		
Simonton, John	2	3	5		
Case, Isaac	2	1	3		
Sayward, George	1	4	4		
Weed, James	1	3	5		
Foster, Charles	1		1		
Batchelder, Hezekiah	2		10		
Bridges, John	1	3	6		
Dean, Jonah	1	1	1		
Snow, Ephraim	2	2	3	1	
Rowell, William	2	1	3		
Coombes, Joseph	1	3	5		
Crouch, David	1	3	1		
Covell, Micajah	1		1	1	
Jordan, Israel	3	4	3		
Jordan, Robert	1	3	3		
Kating, Richard	1	4	4		
Webb, William	1		1		
Mathews, Anthony	1	2	2		
Mathews, Joseph	1		2		
Orbeton, James	1	1	5		
Orbeton, Jonathan	1	2	6		
Snow, Elisha	3	1	3		
Snow, Ambrose	1	1	2		
Sweetland, David	1		1		
Amory, George	1	1	2		
Crockit, Nathaniel	1		1		
Crockit, Nathaniel, Junr	2	4	7		
Heard, William	3	4	4		
Haskell, Francis	2	1	4		
Killsa, Hugh	1		4		
Killsa, George	1	3	2		
Packard, Benjamin	1	3	3		
Pilsbury, Joseph	1	4	4		
Pilsbury, Nathan	2	1	1		
Post, Stephen	1	3	4		
Spaulding, Timothy	1		3	1	
Witham, William	1	1	2		
Drought, Richard	1		1		
Stetson, William	2	4	2		
Spaulding, Jedidiah	1	1	3		
Gray, Eliphalet	2	3	2		
Brown, John	1				
Brown, Gideon	1				
West, John	2	3	3		
Bartlett, Samuel	1	4	5		
Butler, Phinehas	1	2	3		
Chapman, William	1	3	4		
Godden, John	1	2	4		
Hix, Thomas	1	3	3		
Ingraham, Job	1	6	2		
Ingraham, Joseph	1	2	2		
Ingraham, Josiah	1	1	1		
Lindsey, John	4	2	7		
Lowell, Rosamus	1	2	1		

NAME OF HEAD OF FAMILY.	Free white males of 16 years and upward, including heads of families.	Free white males under 16 years.	Free white females, including heads of families.	All other free persons.	Slaves.
THOMASTON TOWN—con.					
Perry, Joseph	1	2	1		
Perry, William	2		3		
Rendell, James	1	1	3		
Rendell, Thomas	2		4		
Sherman, Nathan	1	1	3		
Tolman, Jeremiah	1	1	2		
White, John	1	1	1		
Barrows, Ichabod	3		1		
Barrows, Comfort	1	1	3		
Barrows, Benajah	1	1	1		
Brewster, Zadok	2	1	5		
Crockit, Jonathan	2	3	3		
Crockit, John	1		2	1	
Fales, James	1	1	6		
Jameson, Robert	3		1		
Keen, John	1				
Renkins, Constant	2	4	3		
Spear, Jonathan	3	2	4		
Walsh, William	1		1		
Spear, William	1	2	1		
Spear, Jonathan, Junr	1		2		
Smith, Jonathan	1	2	1		
Tolman, Isaiah	1	4	4		
Ulmer, George	1	3	5		
Ulmer, John	1	1	1		
Watson, David	1	3	6		
Tolman, Samuel	2	2	2		
Tolman, Curtis	2	2	2		
Thomson, William	1	2	5		
Barnard, Isaac	1		3		
Bennett, David Mill	1				
Waterman, Nathaniel	1				
Hewitt, Waterman	1				
Cook, John	1				
Blackington, Benjamin	2	1	4		
Bly, Ebenezer	1		4		
Creighton, David	2	3	4		
Killsa, James	2	1	3		
Lewis, William	1		3		
Morse, Daniel	2	2	4		
Palmer, Daniel	2	3	6		
Robbins, Oliver, Junr	1	3	3		
Stevens, Thomas, Jun	1		3		
Thomson, Ebenezer	2		3		
Bentley, John	4				
Emerson, Thomas	1	1	1		
Stevens, Daniel	1				
Kelly, William	1				
Farrow, Peter	1				
Kingman, Loring	1				
Bacon, Michael	1				
Coll, John	1				
McIntyer, James	1				
TITCOMB TOWN.					
Hilton, Ebenezer	1	1	4		
Hilton, John	1	2	3		
Hustings, William	1	2	3		
Hambly, William	1	1	3		
Gray, John	2	1	7		
Mackfaying, James	1	4	7		
Chamberlain, John	1		1		
Chamberlain, Jeremiah	2		3		
Chamberlain, Stephen	1				
Hunniwell, William	1	3	3		
Hilton, William	1	3	4		
Thompson, Benjamin	2	3	3		
Calliborn, John	2	2	5		
Thompson, Aaron	1	3	5		
Green, Moses	1	2	3		
Thompson, John	1	1	3		
Martain, Nathl	1		5		
Stephens, Jonathan	1		3		
Thompson, Moses	1	2	1		
Airs, Moses	2	2	4		
Pelton, Joel	1				
Colbey, Benjamin	2	4	3		
Dor, Ruel	1				
Pain, Rachal			2		
Hancock, John	1		1		
Campbel, Wm	1				
Pierce, David	1				
Pierce, Calvin	1				
Pierce, Luther	1		1		
TOPSHAM TOWN.					
Graves, Johnson	2		2		
Graves, John	3	1	3		
Graves, Joseph	2	1	3		
Graves, Saml	2	4	4		
Henry, James	1	4	4		
Small, John	1	4	5		
Sanford, John	1	4	4		

NAME OF HEAD OF FAMILY.	Free white males of 16 years and upward, including heads of families.	Free white males under 16 years.	Free white females, including heads of families.	All other free persons.	Slaves.
TOPSHAM TOWN—con.					
Winchel, John	3	4	5		
Staples, Saml	1	2	6		
Foster, Josiah	1	3	6		
Owens, Gideon	2	5	5		
Rogers, John	3	2	3		
Patten, Thos	1	2	2		
Burk, Willm	1	6	4		
Berry, Joseph	2	4	2		
Rogers, Alexander	4	2	5		
Purrington, James	2	3	3		
Thompson, Saml	6	3	7		
Duglas (Widow)	1		3		
Whitney, Jona	2	2	3		
Patten, John	3	2	4		
Jennison, Saml	3		9		
Sprague, Joseph	1	3	2		
Patten, Robert	2	4	4		
Sampson, James	2	4	5		
Sampson, Enoch	2		3		
Reid, David	2	4	4		
Fulton, John	4		5		
Stockman, Thos	3	2	5		
Stockman, Jacob	1	2	5		
Allen, Saml	1	1	2		
Patten, Joseph	1		3		
Perkins, John	1		1		
Knowles, Richard	3		4		
Roy, Francis	1	1	4		
Gorden, Robert	1	1	1		
Winchel, Anna			2	1	
Putnam, Caleb	1	1	3		
Perry, Jona	3	1	2		
Merril, John	2	2	2	1	
Patten, Actor	3	2	4		
Haley, Pelatiah	2	2	5		
Dunlap, James	3	1	2		
Haley, Joseph, Jnr	2	3	7		
Wilson, Hugh	2	1	4		
Thompson, Alexander	1		2		
Whidden, John	3	2	4		
Alexander, Robert	5	1	3		
Ferren, Ebenezer	1	2	2		
Orr, Robert	1	1	6		
Whidden, John	1		2		
Wilson, Willm	2	5	4		
Mellet, Willm	1	2	3		
Seers, Willard	1		1		
Hinkley, Theos	1	1	3		
Pennel, Stephen	1	2	3		
Hinkley, Elnathan	1	3	3		
Dugan, Thos	2		3		
Lunt, Jobb	1	2	5		
Orr, John	2		4		
Allen, Pelatiah	1	2	5		
Wilson, James	2	5	3		
Blanchard, John	1	1	2		
Walker, Gideon	2	1	3		
Thompson, Benja	5	2	4		
Purington, James	1				
Hodgkins, Moses	2		2		
Owens, Moses	1	2	4		
Doughty, Stephen	1	2	5		
White, Elijah	1		2		
Jack, Joseph	1	3	4		
Wiman, Nathan	3		3		
Gray, Daniel	1	1	2		
Gray, Alexander	1	1	2		
Thompson, Alexander	1	1	3		
Wilson, Saml	1	1	2		
Wood, Isaac	1	1	2		
Ford, Daniel	2		3		
Walker, Jesse	1	1	3		
Rident, Mark	1		2		
Hewey, James	1	1	4		
Hewey, John	2	1	2		
Dunlap, John, Jnr	1	1	2		
Haley, Joseph	2	4	3		
Eaton, Benja	2	3	3		
Foster, Steel	1	4	7		
Cleaves, Robert	3	1	2	1	
Dow, Henry	1	5	3		
Hunter, James, Jnr	2	2	2		
Mustard, James	3		3		
Hunter, Arthur	1	5	4		
Hunter, Robert	3	3	2	1	
Hunter, James	3		4		
Work, Ebenz	3	2	7		
Hunter, Willm	1	2	3		
Malcom, Willm	1	2	2		
Randal, Ezra	2	1	3		
Randal, Willm	4	2	3		
Jones, John	1		5		
Reid, John	2	2	4		
Reid, Willm	4	1	3		
Reid, John, Junr	2	1	6		

LINCOLN COUNTY—Continued.

NAME OF HEAD OF FAMILY.	Free white males of 16 years and upward, including heads of families.	Free white males under 16 years.	Free white females, including heads of families.	All other free persons.	Slaves.
TOPSHAM TOWN—con.					
Smith, Thomas	1		1		
Hoit, Elizabeth	1	2	3		
Wilson, John	1	1	4		
Hunter, Willm	1	1	1		
Stockman, Saml	1	1	3		
Gowel, Charles	1	1	5		
Head, Moses	1		2		
Waid, Calvan	2	2	2		
Howland, Abraham	1		3		
Graves, John, Jur	1		3		
Duglas, Francis	1	4	5	6	
Staples, Stephen	3	3	3		
Fulton, James	3	1	3		
Rollins, Saml	1	3	1		
Tufts, Barnabas	2		4		
Thompson, Ezekiel	5	2	4		
TWENTY-FIVE MILE POND TOWN.					
Fowler, Matthew	1		2		
Chace, Stephen	1	2	6		
Runnels, Ephrom	1	3	6		
Brions, Baruch	1				
Dodge, Caleb	1	3	5		
Douglas, William	1	3	4		
Mirick, John	2	2	3		
Bennit, Peter	1		2		
Chace, John	1				
Fly, James	1		2		
Chace, Job	1				
Dody, Nicholas	1	1	1		
Runnels, Robert	1		2		
Bliffin, Increas	1		4		
Wesson, Edmond	1	2	3		
Mitchel, John	4	3	3		
Sewall, Thomas	1	3	3		
Smart, John	1				
Bartlett, Lamuel	1	2	2		
Mitchel, Joseph	1	1	4		
Hinkly, Miller	1	2	2		
Battle, Benjamin	1				
Burton, John	1				
Burton, Jabiz	1				
Brainard, Rachal			1		
Pishen, Charles	1		1		
Foot, John	1				
Whitten, George	1		2		
Whitny, Benjamin	1		1		
Carter, Padius	1				
UNION TOWN.					
Woodcock, David	3	1	5		
Nill, Samuel	1	2	2		
Maxey, Joseph	2		2		
Guild, Joseph	1	2	2		
Hawes, Abijah	1		2		
Robbins, Philip	1		4	2	
Robbins, Josiah	2	1	1		
Robbins, David	2	5	3	1	
Robbins, Ebenezer	1		1		
Mero, Amariah	1	1	4		
Hawes, Moses	1	1	4		
Hawes, Matthias	1	1	3		
Adams, Joel	3	3	4		
Robbins, Jesse	1		1		
Cummings, Richard	1	3	4		
Gilmore, Rufus	1	1	2		
Irish, Ichabod	1	3	5		
Butler, John	1	4	2		
Butler, Phinehas	2		4		
Butler, Christopher	1	2	6		
McLintock, Robert	2		3		
Daggett, Thomas	3		1		
Daggett, Samuel	1	4	2		
Daggett, Thomas, Jun	1	1	4		
Jennison, Ebenezer	1				
Luce, Seth	1	4	3		
Morse, Levi	1				
Robbins, Bela	1	1	3		
Ware, Jason	1	1	4		
Newhall, Jonathan	1	1	1		
Walcott, Spencer	1				
Hart, William	1				
Steward, Timothy	1				
Bowen, Ezra	1	2	4		
Dunnam, Samuel	1	2	2		
Grinnell, Royal	1		4		
Grinnell, Bailey	1	3	1		
Robbins, Philip, Junr	1		1		
Wight, John Morse	1				

NAME OF HEAD OF FAMILY.	Free white males of 16 years and upward, including heads of families.	Free white males under 16 years.	Free white females, including heads of families.	All other free persons.	Slaves.
UNION TOWN—con.					
Coffin, Uriah	1				
Reed, Josiah	1				
Bennett, Asa	1				
VASSALBOROUGH TOWN.					
Fairwell, Ebenr	4	1	3	2	
Fairwell, Isaac	2		5	4	
Pirkins, Solomon	2	2	1		
Moore, Ebenr	1	5	5		
Horner, Capt	4	1	4		
Haws, Thomas	3	2	3		
Haws, Thomas, junr	1	3	2		
Merchant, John	1	1	3		
Gardiner, Gothro	2	2	5		
Cowin, William	1	1	5		
Bassett, Saml	1	3	5		
Fought, Jacob	1	2	5		
Brawn, Joseph	1	3	6		
Green, Richard	1	2	2		
Newcomb, David	1		5		
Webber, —*	1	6	5		
—, —*	(*)	(*)	(*)	5	
Raglin, —*	2	2	5		
Cowin, George	2	5	3		
Mathews, James	1	2	3		
Bacon, James	2	3	2		
Robinson, Winthropt	1	1	3		
Webber, Joseph	4		3	1	
Ballard (Widow)	3		4		
Wing, Gidion	1	1	3		
Bragg, Shuball	1	1	1		
Freeman, Benjamin	1	3	4		
Getchell, Samuel	3	6	3		
Wyman, Francis	1	5	2		
Freeman, Reuben	1	4	2		
Weeks, Phinias	1	1	2		
Fairwell, Bunker	3		4		
Hatch, Sylvanus	1	3	2		
Crowell, Joseph	2		2		
Warren, Richard	2	2	4		
Clark, Jonathan	1	2	4		
Cross, Willm	4	2	3		
Cross, Benj	2	3	5		
Cross, James	1				
Tarbell, —*	1	2	3		
Robins, Herman	2	1	3		
Robins, David	2	1	5		
Wing, Willm	1		2		
Wing, Willm, Junr	2	1	2		
McGlothlin, Gibbins	1		1		
Tilton, John	2		5		
Burges, Jonathan	1	1	4		
Burges, Avery	1				
Jackson, David	1		2		
Cross, Cabot	1		7		
Linkley, Saml	1	2	2		
Fairfield, Jeremiah	2	2	3		
Seaward, Giles	1		4		
Robinson, Levi	3	2	2		
Getchell, Neheh	3	6	2		
Redington, Asa	3	1	1		
Getchell, Majr	3	1	3		
Childs, Amos	1	1	2		
Low, Jonathan	1	2	4		
Hobbey, Remington	1	4	7	1	
Hussey, Palithl	1	1	2		
Taber, Jacob	3		1		
Jackson, Charles			2	5	
Jackson, John	1				
Doe, Nathl	2	5	3		
Pilsbury, Thomas	2	2	5		
McFaden, Daniel	1	2	4		
Doe, James	2		5		
Taylor, John	2	2	4		
Pettee, Elenr	1	1	11		
Pettee, John	2		10		
Pinkham, Reuben	1	2	2		
Mathews, Edmond	1		3		
Fought, Anthony	1	1	6		
Mathews, Elisher	1	2	5		
Fought, Fredrick	1	3	4		
Runels, Esqr	3		2		
Runels, Nathl	1	2	3		
Runels, David	1				
Runels, Jonathan	1	1	7		
Dyer, Benjamin	1	5	4		
Brach, Benjamin	1	3	3		
Branch, Samuel	1		4		
Sherwin, Mr	2	1	2		
Tiffany, Saml	1		3		
Fowler, John	1		1		

NAME OF HEAD OF FAMILY.	Free white males of 16 years and upward, including heads of families.	Free white males under 16 years.	Free white females, including heads of families.	All other free persons.	Slaves.
VASSALBOROUGH TOWN—continued.					
Thomas, Ichabod	2		2		
Thomas, Joseph	2		4		
Cromit, John	1	2	1		
Dudley, Daniel	1	1	1		
Chase, Ebenr	1	2	1		
Tiffany, Daniel	1				
Sawtel, David	1		3		
Sawtel, Moses	3	2	3		
Sawtel, Nathl	1	1	4		
Sawtel, Reuben	1		2		
Swift, John	1	1	3		
Longley, Nehh	1	2	7		
Sawtel, Jonas	1		1		
Trask, John	1	2	3		
Trask, Ebenr	1	2	1		
Cowin, Isaac	1	1	3		
Jackson, John	2		1		
Jackson, Lemul	1	2	3		
Jackson, Samel	1	1	4		
Jackson, John, Jur	1		1		
Hutcherson, James	1	4	1		
Branch, Benj	1		4		
Jackson, Joseph	1		1		
Townsen, Daniel	1	2	3		
Lovejoy, Capt	2	3	5	3	
Lovejoy, Abiel, Jr	1	1	1		
Hastings, Moses	2	3	6		
Marsh, John	1		1		
Hasting, Marthew	1		2		
Towsend, Dodifer	2	2	5		
Clerk, Joseph	1	1	3		
Doe, Dudley	1	3	6		
Smiley, David	1	1	4		
Balintine, Samel	1		4		
Fish, David	1	1	1		
Moor, Levi	2	3	3		
Roberts, Willm	1	1	7		
Smiley, Thomas	1	1	5		
Smiley, Hugh	1		2		
Smiley, Alexr	1	2	2		
Smiley, Willm	1	2	3		
Moor, Collins	1	3	4		
Bragg, John	1	3	5		
Hoxkey, Hezh	4		3		
Barton, Flint	2	5	3		
Robinson, Timothy	2	3	2		
Bacon, Ebenr	4		2		
Davis, Joshua	2	3	5		
Brown, Solomon	2	1	4		
Deleno, Peleg	2	1	3		
Deleno, Benj	1		1		
Brooks, Willm	1	2	2		
Butterfield, Ephrim	3	1	7		
Stedman, James	1	3	5		
Bowman, Thomas	1	2	3		
Butterfield, Samuel	1	1	2		
Dinsmore, Samuel	1		1		
Lincoln, Marthew	2	1	1		
Ward, John	2	1	3		
Wilman, Asa	1		4		
Ward, Samuel	1		2		
Cross, Moses	1	1	3		
Page, Calob	1	4	4		
Butler, John	1	3	4		
Pullin, Oliver	1	2	2		
Hamblin, Timothy	2	2	2		
Hamblin, Timothy, jr	1	2	1		
Dow, Jonathan	1	1	1		
Bisby, Stephen	1	3	2		
Butler, Phinius	1	3	3		
Weeks, Benj	3	4	8		
Butler, Jeremh	1	1	2		
Butler, Obadiah	1		2		
Robinson, Goreh	4	2	4		
Hammond, Ephrim	1	1	4		
Bolton, James	1		2		
Bolton, George	1	2	3		
Butterfield, Mathew	1	2	3		
Taber, John	4	3	8		
Fry, Joshua	1	1	1		
Sleeper, Moses	1	1	2		
Taber, Jacob	3	2	3		
Balcome, Elijah	1	1	2		
Taber, Bathw	1		2		
Getchell, John	3	3	3		
Cushing, Willm	1	1	3		
Dow, Benj	1	4	2		
Spratt, George	2	2	5		
Priest, Jonas	1		4		
Priest, Joseph	1		4		
Burges, Benj	3		2		
Gould, Nehemiah	1	5	4		

* Illegible.

LINCOLN COUNTY—Continued.

NAME OF HEAD OF FAMILY.	Free white males of 16 years and upward, including heads of families.	Free white males under 16 years.	Free white females, including heads of families.	All other free persons.	Slaves.
VASSALBOROUGH TOWN—continued.					
Spalding, John	1	1	1		
Dickey, David	2	2	4		
Baxter, John	1	1	3		
Haskell, Willm	1		3		
Ewer, Jonathan	2		1		
Haws, Jacob	1	2	1		
Doe, Samson	1	3	4		
Dow, Benj., Junr	1	3	1		
Getchell, Dominicus	1	3	5		
Getchell, Edmond	1		2		
Blish, Stacy	1	3	6		
Bragg, Marthew	2	2	3		
Blish, John	1		1		
Brackett, James	1		3		
Farfield, Reuben	3	1	10		
Pitts, Ichabod	1	1	1		
Emerson, Phillip	1	1	4		
Fairfield, Jonathan	1	2	2		
Robinson, John	2	4	4		
WALDOBOROUGH TOWN.					
day, benjamin	2	3	5		
chapman, nathaniel	1	5	1		
church, nathaniel	1	3	4		
hatch, Elizer	3	3	7		
hatch, Jonathan	1		1		
Cortis, Seth	1				
hiscock, Richard	2	1	4		
miller, nickles	2	3	3		
jones, william	3	1	4		
huston, james	5	1	5		
woodard, Sam	4	4	4		
harmond, John	3	1	3		
huston, John	2	2	5		
huston, Robert, jun	3	2	5		
huston, Robert	3		4		
Story (widow)	2		1		
paul, Robert	4	1	5		
patterson, John	2	2	6		
tompson, Robert	2	3	5		
hunter, henry	4	3	3		
Mccluer, thomas	1	1	2		
wille, James	1	1	2		
askins (widow)		1	4		
page, william	2	1	2		
hutchons, david	1	1	1		
hutchons, thomas	1	2	2		
askins, ninain	3	1	4		
hersey, Eben	1	2	3		
Mcmical, dowgal	3		7		
fitch, Jonas	1		5		
fitch, tim	1	1	2		
fitch, John	1		1		
howlen, Zeblen	2	4	4		
culbrath, lithen	2	1	3		
kelka (widow)	1		2		
wintworth (widow)	1	3	3		
little, John	1	3	3		
little, hugh	1	2	1		
fliming, James	1				
wintworth, juke	1	2	4		
Clark, Elisha, jun	1	5	1		
Sproul, robert, jun	1	3	2		
jones, Richard	3	2	4		
jones, mical	1		2		
jones, richard, jun	1	2	2		
huston, robert	1	2	3		
kellce, James	1		1		
paul, John	1				
paul, mathew	1	1	1		
askins, John	1	1	2		
askins, alexdre	1	3	3		
askins, george	1		2		
Hanley, Rodger	1	2	4		
hanley, pertrik	1	3	3		
crucker, Elijah	4	2	4		
hous, joshua	1	1	2		
askins, william	1	4	3		
Sunders, Sam	1		3		
tompson, natel	1	3	3		
elsworth, Joseph	4	3	3		
nolton, Joseph	1	2	4		
Reed, John	3	3	4		
killse, John	1				
bowly, Epherm	1	4	4		
fitch, John	1		1		
askins, david	1				
Stewart, Steven	1				
page, george	1		2		
clark, Eliza	2		4		
miller, Robert	1	1	4		
Gowday, Emez	1	2	8		
Mcgoyer, pertrick	2	1	3		
bowli, oliver	1	1	3		
WALDOBOROUGH TOWN—continued.					
Sprouls, william	1	3	2		
Clark, Sam	1	3	8		
cacklin (widow)	1		1		
clark, joseph	1	5	4		
Sprouls, Robert	2	2	5		
young, Edward	3		4	1	
plumer, bedfil	4		4		
faster, wilm	1	5	6		
Roberson, alexdr	1	2	4		
connely, John	1		1		
tompson, george	1	4	4		
tompson, thomas	1	3	2		
Stuard, thomas	1	5	4		
fullonton, archibal	1		1		
fullonton, Robert	1		2		
dodge, thomas	1	2	4		
gametch, Joshua	2	3	3		
persons, andrew	1	2	1		
Cattlen, daniel	1	4	3		
Story, Sam	1	4	3		
oats, Samuel	2	2	3		
tompson, mils	1	6	2		
Cums, Syl	1	2	2		
oats, Eben	1		3		
faster, nathen	1	1	2		
martin, thomas	1		2		
Mccurdy, dan	2	3	4		
farren, Ezechiel	1	5	2		
bates, calab	1	3	2		
omfry, Eben	1	2	4		
pardridge, John	3	2	2		
tarrow, John, jun	2	1	4		
Rods, John	1		1		
terral, isaac, jun	1	1	4		
terral, isaac	2		1		
stotson, Joseph	2	3	5		
weston, arona	1	2	6		
farow, timt	2	7	2		
farrow, Joseph	1	1	4		
colimer, peter	2	1	2		
keen, Ezak	1				
keen, Robt	2		3		
brow, John	1	4	4		
keen, prince	3		2		
keen, dan (hoge Island)	1	3	3		
osyer, Joseph	1	1	9		
burns, Joseph	1	5	8		
palmer, nat	3		2		
paine, John	1	1	1		
heads, john & joshua	2		1		
hilten, James	4		4		
Rohds, cornelus	1	1	4		
palmer, bazl	1	1	2		
Mcclain, John	1		1		
hilten, Willlam	1	2	2		
martin, John	1		2		
misherver, nath	4	1	5		
palmer, benjm	2		2		
lincoln, Isaac	1	2	7		
cushman, paulus (long Island)	2	4	5		
Studle, sichl (long Island)	1	2	3		
faster, nat, jun	2	4	3		
faster, John	1	2	4		
faster, Sebert	1		2		
tabet, Steven	1	2	3		
tabet, henry	1		2		
Mcfarling, John	5	2	4		
Mcfarling, John, jun	1	1	3		
molton, James	3	3	4		
portefield, Robert	2	2	4		
drumens, James	2	2	4		
Sprouls, william	4		3		
winslow, nicklas	1	2	5		
hatch, philip	1	3	8		
Sproul, James	3	2	2		
nickles, alexander	2		5	1	
nickles, william	1	3	2		
McIntire, william	1	4	4		
nickles, James	2	2	5		
Rodger, patrick	1				
Rodger, willm	2	1	2		
Rodger, george	2	2	6		
Mcglathery, alexdr	2	2	9		
Robertson, alexdr	2		1		
Mcfarland, andrew	1		2		
Mcfarland, Robert	1				
curtice, daniel	1	3	8		
martin, John	2	3	3		
randal, Robert	1				
cox, Israil	3	1	1	1	
gwin, James	1	1	4		
Sproul, James, jun	1		3		
greely, jonathan	1	2	7		
WALDOBOROUGH TOWN—continued.					
miller, thomas	3				
Russel, william	2	2	6		
tibbets, Jacob	2	1	2		
Greenlew, alexdr	1	1	1		
fossat, alexdr, jun	1	3	3		
child, thomas	2	4	4	1	
doliver, Joseph	1	2	4		
miller, John	2	3	3		
upham, Jabiz	2	4	5		
geven, Robert	3		3	5	
fassat, william, jun	1	1	2		
fassat, henry	2	4	7		
fossat, alexdr	2	1	2		
fossat, william	2		3		
Mckown (weidow)	2		5	1	
Mckown, John	3	3	3	1	
Sproul, william	2	2	6		
boyd, Sam	2	3	7		
boyd, william	2	6	5		
boyd, John	2	3	4		
dwo, lem	2	3	2		
leighton, James	1	2	5		
calderwood, thomas	1	2	3		
Stuard, James	2		2		
fountain, Jacob	1	1	4		
hercy, Eben	1	1	3		
fassat, henry, jun	1	3	6		
blunt, Ebenr	3	2	4		
kent (widow)	2		2		
polline, Ezra	1		4		
lalor, patrik	1	3	3		
bracket (widow)	1		3	1	
Mclen, alexdr	2	3	5		
gates, George	1	4	4		
Richards, Erastus	1	3	6		
baily, Zery	1	1	1		
poland, thomas	1	2	4		
poland, nohemiak	1	1	3		
Smilidge, nathan	2		2		
Elliot, Simon, jun	1	1	2		
fuller, Zenos	1	4	4		
Greenlaw, william	1	1	4		
hanley, malachi	1		1	1	
Elliot, Simon	6		6		
briant, david	2	1	2		
Gates, Samuel	1	4	2		
briant, lemuel	3	6	4		
Richard, william	1				
Richard, william, jun	4	2	4		
Richard, william, 3rd	1	3	1		
Richard, benjamin	2	1	2		
hetcher, thomas	1	3	1		
morton, John	1	1	1		
berms, william	1	5	6		
poland, Stuawrd (mach Island)	1	5	1		
lawd, william (mescongus Island)	1		1		
Salomon, william (mescongus Island)	1	4	5		
Mcmorfey, peter (mescongus Island)	1	1	4		
fountain, barnabas, jun. (mescongus Island)	1	1	2		
fountain, barnabas (mescongus Island)	2	1	4		
fowler, andrew (mescongus Island)	1	2	2		
carter, ephram (mescongus Island)	2	1	5		
morfey, John (mescongus Island)	1				
morfey, peter (mescongus Island)	1	1	1		
Shmit, joseph (mescongus Island)	2		1		
lidge, Sinas (mescongus Island)	1		2		
warren, james	1				
le balister, charles	2	1	3		
hurland, prince	1	3	4		
morton, John	1	4	1		
arnold, thomas	1	3	3		
keen, william	1	1	4		
woodbery, ephram	1	2	3		
tarrow, John	1	1	2		
colimer, Isaac	1	2	3		
Sier, John	1	2	3		
Studley, dan	3				
martin (widow)	1	1	3		
Mcclain, william	2	2	2		
misherve, clemt	1	1	4		
dilinham, leml	3		2		
macher, Richard	1	3	4		
Stevens, alexander	2	1	4		

LINCOLN COUNTY—Continued.

NAME OF HEAD OF FAMILY.	Free white males of 16 years and upward, including heads of families.	Free white males under 16 years.	Free white females, including heads of families.	All other free persons.	Slaves.
WALDOBOROUGH TOWN—continued.					
bennet, becheldor	2		6		
dockendorf, Jacob	3	7	6		
mackendorsh, John	1		1		
nash, oliver	1	1	1		
johnson, thom	3	1	3		
poor, james	2	1	2		
Rohds, george	1	2	2		
mats (widow)			2		
mirrit, Jonathan	3	2	2		
Rohds, thomas	1		1		
Mcclain, Sam	1		2		
wilman, ben	1				
wilman, Joseph	1	1	5		
wilman, Sam	1	1	3		
little, henry	1	1	4		
crucker, trenter	3		2		
turner, calab	2		3		
turner, Robt	2	2	3		
tinkam, elen	1	5	1		
calomer, sickl (long Island.)	1				
WALES PLANTATION.					
ham, Reuben	1	3	6		
Backer, Young	1		3		
Backer, Eliphelat	1	1	2		
Jacking, David	1	2	2		
niles, Robert	1				
ham, Samuel	1	1	2		
niles, Calab	3	1	2		
ham, Saml	1				
ham, Reuben	1				
ham, John	1	1	2		
Arno, John	2	3	3		
Gray, James	1	3	2		
Ramake, William	1	1	1		
Janking, Philip	4	2	8		
Allen, Joseph	2	1	8		
tompson, Richard	1	2	3		
Andres, John	1	2	4		
labree, James	1	1	4		
labree, Richard	1	2	1		
Astery, Benoney	2	1	4		
Gray, Stephen	1	1	2		
Ramaks, Joseph	1		2		
Cannon, Partrick	1		2		
Cannon, James	1	1	2		
Wamoth, Benjn	1	3	4		
Wamoth, Joseph	1				
Wamoth, Samuel	1	5	1		
tompson, Jonathan	1	3	6		
Gray, Thomas	1	2	3		
Gray, Thomas, ju	1		2		
Kimble, Benjn	1	1	4		
Brown, Josiah	1	2	1		
Deadem, Benjn	1	1	4		
Day, Joseph	1	1	1		
Wite, Timothy	3	4	4		
Gilman, Daniel	2	4	5		
MacCslin, Gardner	1	1	3		
Norris, James	3	3	2		
Norris, Nathl	1				
Titas, Saml	1		6		
titas, William	1	3	5		
Allen, Edman	1	2	2		
Allen, Woodard	1		3		
Allen, Daniel	1		4		
Blake, Phinhas	2	1	3		
Blake, Dearborn	1		2		
Dearborn, Levi	3	2	4		
Baker, Ichabod	2		2		
Wetch, John	1	3	5		
Allen, William	1	3	3		
Chandler, John	1	1	3		
Blake, Ashel	1	4	3		
Blosom, Mathias	1	2	1		
Blosom, James	1	1	2		
Priscott, Suwel	1				
Fogg, Caleb	1	4	1		
Dearborn, Simon. ju	1	2	2		
Sargant, John	1				
Smith, Nathan	1	3	3		
Dearborn, Simon	1		1		
Smart, Robert	2	2	4		
Smart, Eliphelat	1				
Smart, James	1				
Smith, Daniel	1		1		
Blake, John	1	1	1		
Clough, Benjn	1				
Morril, Abraham	1				
Norris, James, ju	1	1	2		
Tompson, Mary		1	4		
tompson, William	1				
Stocking, Thomas	1		3		
WALES PLANTATION—continued.					
Branard, Nathn	1		1		
Bishop, Zadock	2	4	3		
Witherton, Robert	2	3	1		
Moodey, Gilman	1	5	3		
hopkins, Peter, Ju	1	2	3		
hopkins, Peter	2	1	3		
hopkins, William	1				
Thursten, Jonn	1				
Thurston, Peter	1				
Lyon, Peter	1	3	2		
Judkins, Robert	3		1		
Judkins, James	1				
Streter, John	2		1		
Wilson, James	1				
bayweatt, William	1	2	3		
Goadon, Thial	1	1	2		
falls, Joshua	1	1	1		
Parker, Joseph	1	2	5		
Wile, Timothy, Ju	1				
Kimble, thomas	1				
Druce, Climan	1	1	1		
WARREN TOWN.					
Crawford, John	3		1		
Kirkpatrick, Anne	4	1	3		
Robinson, Thomas	1	2	2		
Boggs, Mary	3	1	4		
Boggs, Samuel	1	1	4		
Boggs, John	2		2		
Boggs, William	3	2	5		
Cobb, Miles	2		1		
Bird, Alexander	1	3	3		
Copeland, Nathaniel	2	2	2		
Crane, Rufus	3	3	3		
Weston, Samuel	1	1	5		
Head, James Walter	2		4		
Morrison, Thomas	1	1	2		
Whiting, Thurston	4	1	2		
Anderson, Archibald	2	3	4		
Anderson, James	2	2	5		
Anderson, Samuel	1	1	3		
Dickey, William	1	3	4		
Dickey, John	2		2		
Alford, Lore	1		2		
Davis, Aaron	1	1	1		
Davis, Jacob	1		1		
Matthews, Robert	1				
Matthews, James	1		2		
Counce, Lemuel	1	3	2		
Fisher, James	1		3		
Crawford, Archibald	1	1	3		
Crawford, James	1				
Copeland, Joseph	2	2	3		
Watt, John	4	1	5		
McCallum, John	2	3	3		
Crawford, John, Junr	2	4	3		
Standish, James	1	2	2		
Paseal, John	1	2	3		
Libbey, John	1	3	2		
Libby, Nathan	1	1	3		
Libbey, Eliakim	1	1	4		
Bosworth, Eli	1	2	4		
Jameson, Joseph	2		3		
Young, Francis	1	2	5		
Fairbanks, Joel	2	1	2		
Kirkpatrick, William	1	1	2		
Crane, Samuel	1	1	1		
Starret, Thomas	5	1	7		
Starret, Thomas, Junr	1	1	1		
O'Bryan, John	2	1	4		
James, Sarah	2		3		
Wiley, John	2	3	5		
Lermond, William	3	4	5		
Cox, James	1	1	6		
Lawrence, Amos	1	3	1		
McIntyer, William	1		3		
Spear, John	5	5	5		
Spear, Robert	2		1		
Robinson, William	2	3	2		
Pebples, Patrick	1	2	2		
McIntyer, John	1	1	2	1	
McIntyer, John, Junr	1		2		
Tolman, Reuben	2	1	2		
Sumner, Ezra	1		4		
Hall, Reuben	3	2	5		
Libbey, Hatevil	2	3	4		
Buckland, Nathan	3	3	5		
Creighton, Lucretia	2		2		
Eastman, Sarah			2		
Sumner, Hopestill	1	1	7		
Counce, Samuel	2	1	2		
Copeland, Moses	3	2	4		
Copeland, Rufus	1	3	1		
WARREN TOWN—con.					
Watson, William	3	2	5		
Crane, Calvin	2		6		
Scheffer, John Martin	3		5		
Secrist, Philip	1	1	3		
Roker, Daniel	2	1	5		
Skinner, Joseph	1	7	4		
Lermond, John	2	2	5		
Farrington, Abner	1	3	4		
Peabody, Stephen	3	1	4		
Peabody, Daniel	2	1	2		
Peabody, Andrew	1		1		
Peabody, Josiah, & Saml Peabody	2				
Andrews, John	3	5	8		
Caravan, James	1	1	2		
Montgomery, Robert	2	2	5		
Kelloch, Alexander	3	3	3		
Kelloch, David	2	2	4		
Cooper, Boice	1				
Keith, James	1	2	2		
Dunbar, Daniel	3	1	6	1	
Lermond, Alexander	2	2	5		
Payson, Samuel	2	1	2		
Sprague, Nathan	1	2	3		
Hooffes, George	1	2	2		
Isley, Martin	1	1	4		
Rogers, Jesse	1	1	2		
Snell, David	1	2	2		
Fairbanks, John	1	1	1		
Watson, James	1	2	4		
Mink, Peter	1				
Mink, John	1				
Fuller, Isaac	1	1	1		
Otis, William	1				
Leach, Apollos	1				
Prince, Sylvester				5	
peters, Amos				6	
WASHINGTON TOWN.					
Moors, Timothy	1	1	1		
Tayler, Wilebey	1	1	2		
French, Levi	1		1		
Blake, Robert	1	2	6		
Thomas, Nathan	1	2	4		
French, David	1	2	2		
Tayler, Phinhas	1				
higins, Seth	1		2		
latin, Ephraim	1		2		
Stevens, John	1	1	3		
latin, Moses	1		2		
Roggers, John	1	1	2		
Colbath, lamuel	1		2		
Kilbath, Partrick	1	2	2		
huchings, John	1		3		
Smith, James	1		1		
Paul, Simeon	1		5		
Paul, Silas	1		2		
Blake, Paul	1	1	2		
Ingham, David	1	1	2		
Boocks, Gorge	1	3	3		
Bishop, Esquire	1	1	2		
Laten, Solomon	1	4	3		
Laton, andrew	1				
Latan, David	1				
latan, John	1				
latan, Benjn	4	1	5		
latan, Ephram	1		2		
Bean, John	1		2		
Bean, Neele	1				
Bean, Josiah	1		2		
Bean, Edward	2		3		
Brown, Nathan	1	1	4		
Keerls, Enoch	2		6		
Weels, Joshua	1				
Weels, James	1	1	2		
Wiggins, Nichelos	1		2		
Robinson, John	1				
Dollor, Richard	2	1	3		
Philbrock, Benjn	1	3	2		
Allan, Nathaniel	1				
Philbrock, Joseph	1	1	3		
Daniles, Reuben	1				
Kane, Reuben	1	1	1		
Killey, William	1		1		
latan, James	1	1	1		
Brown, Samuel	1		2		
Philbrock, Stephen	1	1	1		
Scribner, Stephen	1		3		
Eslman, Benjn	1	1	4		
ladd, John	1	2	6		
Rands, Daniel	1				
Ladd, Nathaniel	3	2	7		
Caols, John	2		6		

LINCOLN COUNTY—Continued.

WASHINGTON TOWN—continued.

NAME OF HEAD OF FAMILY.	Free white males of 16 years and upward, including heads of families.	Free white males under 16 years.	Free white females, including heads of families.	All other free persons.	Slaves.
Kidden, Richard	1				
Emerson, Samuel	1	1	2		
Row, Stephen	1				
Philbrock, Nathaniel	1	1	2		
Philbrock, Calab	1				
Gordon, Daniel	2	1	4		
Gordon, Saml	1				
Lyon, Mary			1		
folsom, Trustom	1	3	1		
folsom, John	1	2	3		
Bean, Joab	1	1	1		
Gilman, Nathaniel	1	2	3		
Gilman, Nathaniel, Ju	1				
Cram, Saml	1				
Cram, Saml, ju	1	1	2		
Smith, Liddah			2		
Cram, Timothy	1		2		
Dudley, Nathaniel	1	1	3		
folsom, Nathaniel	1	1	3		
philbrok, Nathaniel	1		6		
folsom, Benja	1		1		
folsom, Peter	1	2	1		
Stair, John	1	1	6		
folsom, Nathaniel, Ju	1	1	3		
Philbrock, Tites	1	3	5		
Philbrock, John	1				
Stevens, Ebnezer	3	1	2		
Dudley, John	2	3	1		
Dudley, Daniel	1	3	4		
Batchelor, William	1		1		
Hills, John	1	1	2		
Rade, Joshua	1				
Rade, Amos	1				
Hills, Joseph	1				
marston, Theoder	1		3		
Ladd, Josses	1	1	3		
Priscott, Jona	1	2	1		
Eaton, Jesse	1		3		
Rade, Joshua	1				
Morse, andrew	1				
Smith, Wolden	1				
Smith, Moses	1				
Hills, Robert	1				
Bartlet, Timothy	1	3	5		
Gilman, Samuel	2	4	4		
Hall, Josiah	1		2		
Hall, nathan	1		2		
Hall, allen	1		3		
Page, James, jur	1				
Smith, Samuel	1	1	2		
Page, Chase	1	2	2		
Page, abraham	1	2	3		
Williams, Obediah	1	5	3		
Bisbee, Benja	1	2	3		
Mosher, Elisha	1	1	2		
Lambord, James	1	1	2		
Sawtell, hezekiah	1		2		
Towle, Francies	2	2	3		
Page, John	1				
Else, Robert	1				
Varnam, Stevan	1				
Snow, Philip	1	5	5		
Clark, Sherebah	1				
lincell, Lamuel	1				
Towsanden, Robert			3		
lincell, Joseph	1	3	3		
Right, Asa	1				
Tilden, Elisha	1				
Rowe, Stephen	1				
Crowell, Ezekiel	1	1	2		
Wiman, Jona	1	2	3		
Wiman, Simon	3	3	2		
Cane, ——	1				
Tilton, Cornelias	1				
Springer, Job	1	3	4		
Page, Jesse	1	2	3		
Kimball, Andrew	1	1	2		
Wiman, James	1		4		
Lenel, Joseph	1	3	4		
Townsand, Robart	1	1	4		
Lenel, Saml	2		3		
Snow, Philip	1	5	5		
Sartwell, Hezekiah	1		2		
Lombart, James	1	1	2		
Mosier, Elisha	1	1	2		
Hall, Saml	2	1	1		
Hall, Aaron	1		4		
Ellis, John	2	4	2		
Blake, Nathl	1	1	2		
Hamelton, John	1		2		
White, John	1	2	2		
Howland, Wilm	1	2	4		
Rankens, John	1	2	2		
Brandt, Daniel	1	1	2		

WINSLOW TOWN, WITH ITS ADJACENTS.

NAME OF HEAD OF FAMILY.	Free white males of 16 years and upward, including heads of families.	Free white males under 16 years.	Free white females, including heads of families.	All other free persons.	Slaves.
Fairwell, Josiah	1	2	1		
Bradford, William	1	2	6		
Printice, Voluntine	1	4	3		
Richardson, Joseph	1	3	2		
Smith, Manuel	1	3	4		
Parker, Phinihas	1				
Hammon, Fredrick	1	2	3		
Leonard, Abigail			1		
Dudley, Francis	3	2	3	1	
Lithgow, Aurthur	1				
Bounsan, Samuel	1				
Harriss, Winslow	1		1		
Runnils, Benjamin	4	2	5		
Turner, Ebenezer	1				
Brooks, John	1				
Carter, Joseph	1	2	5		
Wear, David	1	3	1		
Wood, Bennit	1	6	2		
Parker, Solomon	2		5		
Brawn, Charles	2	1	2		
Carter, Nathaniel	1		1		
Wood, Jean			1		
Haden, Josiah	3	1	5		
Haden, Charles	1	1	1		
Lanson, Suttil	1				
Jones, Amos	1	1	2		
Pettis, Ezekiel	4	4	4		
Phillips, Asa	1	2	4		
Dingly, Barker	1	2	2		
Allen, Francis	1				
Warrin, George	1				
Whitten, George	1	1	1		
Stagpole, James	1	2	4		
Philbrook, John	1				
Stagpole, James, Jr	1				
Stagpole, Samuel	1	2	2		
Townes, Ephrom	1	1	5		
Barton, Betty		1	1		
Stratton, Hezekiah	1	3	4		
Collier, James	1	1	4		
Collier, John	1				
Richardson, William	1	2	5		
Macfarling, James	1				
Fuller, Enoch	1				
Craging, Joseph	1				
Shores, Samuel	1		3		
Combs, Jonathan	1		2		
Hallet, Solomon	1		3		
Hallet, Elisha	1	1	3		
Pierce, John	1	1	1		
Lewis, William, Ju	1	1	2		
Chace, James	1	3	2		
Cook, Thomas	1		2		
Amerson, Daniel	1				
Leman, John	1	6	3		
Macathany, Thomas	1	1	2		
Goodwin, Caleb	1				
Ausburn, Jonathan	1		1		
Simpson, Benjamin	1	1	6		
Copeland, Abraham	1		2		
Landers, Joseph	1		8		
Copeland, Abraham, Jur	1		1		
Rose, Benjamin	1	1	2		
Lankister, John	1	1	3		
Mackim, James	1	4	1		
Cool, John	1	1	1		
Amerson, John	1		5		
Priest, Jonathan	1	1	2		
Taylor, Timothy	1				
Taylor, Jonas	1				
Crosbey, Jonah	2	1	5		
Wilson, Ephrom	1	1	4		
Crosbey, Ezra	1	1	3		
Chalmor, William	1	4	3		
Hale, Timothy	2	3	6		
Haywood, Zimri	4	1	4		
Hartford, Benjamin	1		2		
Dexter, Nathan	4	2	5		
Fuller, Jonathan	1	1	2		
Thomas, Richard	1		2		
Chace, Benjamin	1		5		
Soul, Asa	1	3	1		
Coal, John	1		1		
Wyman, James	1	1	1		
Ausburn, Isaac	1	1	1		
Wyman, Moses	2	1	2		
Spoldin, John	1	3	4		
Spoldin, Willard	3	3	5		
Ausburn, Ephrom	2	3	2		
Spoldin, John	1	3	4		
Simpson, John	1	1	4		
Temple, Jacob	1	3	2		
Gullifin, Thomas	1	4	4		
Simpson, Reuben	1		2		

WINSLOW TOWN, WITH ITS ADJACENTS—con.

NAME OF HEAD OF FAMILY.	Free white males of 16 years and upward, including heads of families.	Free white males under 16 years.	Free white females, including heads of families.	All other free persons.	Slaves.
Simpson, John	1	1	2		
Sturdifent, Lot	1		1		
Bates, Thomas	1	3	2		
Alles, Micah	1	1	2		
Landers, Abraham	1	4	2		
Tupper, Peleg	2	2	4		
Rose, John	1		4	2	
Fowler, John	1		1	1	
Tosier, Simeon	1	1	2		
Mackackeny, Mary	1				
Mackackeny, Thomas	1	1	4		
Lewis, John	1				
Serles, John	1		2		
Temple, Isaac	1	3	2		
Leman, Thomas	1	6	4		
Pettis, David	1	4	2		
Pettis, Daniel	1				
Macfarlin, Samuel	1	3	2		
Lewis, Thomas	1				
Dile, Ralph	1		1		
Low, Nathaniel	2	3	2		
Crammet, James	1	3	4		
Crowell, Levi	1	3	4		
Larree, John	1				
Green, Timothy	1	2	2		
Killey, Joseph	1				
Wyman, Simon	3	2	1		
Springer, Job	1	2	3		
Titton, Cornelius	1	3	3		
Springer, Stutely	1	2	3		
Springer, Edward	2		1		
Keen, Shibottaish	1	1	1		
Humes, John	2	1	1		
Humes, John, Jur	1				
Amerson, Daniel	1		2		
Soul, Jonathan	1	3	3		
Shannon, William	3	2	7		
Wade, David	2	2	6		
Smith, Eliab	1	4	4		
Toner, Elias	1	4	1		
Blanchard, Edward	1	4	3		
Low, Jonathan	1				
Brawn, John	1		1		
Crowell, Manoah	1				
Wade, Samuel	3	1	2		
Megraw, John	3		2		
Crowell, Samuel	2		6		
Crowell, David	1	3	3		
Richardson, Joel	1	3	3		
Page, Caleb	1	3	3		
Dullen, oliver	1	2	2		
Crowell, Joseph	2		1		
Taylor, Samuel	1		2		
Mosier, Elisha	1		2		
Howland, William	1	3	4		
Blake, Nathaniel	1		1		
Mosier, Daniel, Jur	2	4	4		
Settle, Hezekiah	1		2		
Mosier, Daniel, Jur	1	1	2		
Rankins, John	1	2	2		
Whitehouse, Robart	1		1		
Whitehouse, John, Jur	1	2	2		
Whitehouse, John	1	2	2		
Hamblin, John	1	1	2		
Crowell, ——*rdock	1	2	4		
Mills, John	2	1	8		
Branch, Daniel	1	1	2		
Fall, Aaron	1		3		
Richards, Joseph	1	1	3		
Crowell, Ezekiel	1				
Mills, Robart	1				
Hall, Samuel	1		2		
Fall, Samuel, Jur	1				

WINTHROP TOWN.

NAME OF HEAD OF FAMILY.	Free white males of 16 years and upward, including heads of families.	Free white males under 16 years.	Free white females, including heads of families.	All other free persons.	Slaves.
Filer, Ebnezer	1		1		
Tayler, Elias	1	1	4		
Knowls, Elisha	1		2		
Knowls, Simon	1	2	2		
lyon, Squier	1		2		
lyon, Nathan	1	2	4		
Priscott, Elisha	1	1	6		
Willman, Abraham	1	2	3		
Cottle, Isaac	1	1	6		
Knowls, Jonathan	1	1	4		
lyon, Eliab	2	3	3		
Jewet, John	1		2		
Shad, John	1		2		
Gilman, David	2	3	5		
fuller, Francies	1	5	4		
Tayler, Wilebe	1				
hinkley, David	1	1	1		

* Illegible.

LINCOLN COUNTY—Continued.

WINTHROP TOWN—con.

NAME OF HEAD OF FAMILY.	Free white males of 16 years and upward, including heads of families.	Free white males under 16 years.	Free white females, including heads of families.	All other free persons.	Slaves.
Reed, Benjn	1	2	1		
Sweet, Arnol	2		1		
Standly, Jacob	4		1		
Standly, Solomon	3	2	5		
Bakon, Josiah	1				
Standley, Reah	1	1	3		
furenton, Timothy	1	1	4		
Smith, Daniel	1		1		
Smith, Mrs Eliphelat	2	3	4		
Smith, Comford	1	1	2		
Streter, John, ju	1	1	2		
Richman, Nathan	1	2	2		
Smith, Benjn	1	4	1		
Smith, Jacob	1	1	3		
King, Ebnezer	1	1	1		
King, Samuel	1	2	2		
fairbanks, Joseph, Jur	1	4	8		
Allen, Benjn	1	2	1		
fuller, John	3	3	6		
Allen, Philip	1	4	3		
Tayler, Thomas	2	5	4		
Sweet, Elias	1				
Turnner, John	1	2	4		
Atkinson, James	2	3	5		
whrorter, Roling	1				
Atkinson, thomas	1				
Perley, amos	1	3	5		
Devenport, Ebenezer	2		4		
Devenport, Isaac	1	1	1		
harris, Charls	1	2	3		
Stevens, William	1	1	6		
Brown, unite	2	1	3		
Brown, Jeremiah	1				
Brown, John	1				
Stevens, Joseph	1		2		
Stevens, Jonas	1	3	2		
Wheler, Moris	1	1	1		
Atkins, David	1	1	2		
Works, James	1	4	3		
Puling, John	1		4		
hurlane, Peter	2	4	4		
Gray, John	1	4	4		
Brown, Steven	1	3	2		
Macfason, Paul	1	1	2		
harkerson, John	1		2		
Stephens, Samuel	1	4	6		
Sampson, Noah	2		2		
Carwill, John	1	1	3		
hankerson, William	1	2	3		
hankerson, thomas	1		1		
Dutten, Joshua	3	3	4		
Burden, Primes					2
Walton, Moses	1				
Stephens, Amos	2	6	5		
Secars, Paul	1	4	3		
Boney, hannah (Widow)		2	2		
turner, Christopher	2	5	6		
Hains, Dudley	1	1	1		
lane, James	1	2	3		
Wittiny, Joseph	1		6		
Smith, mathias	3	2	2		
Smith, mathias, Jur	1	2	1		
Mayhew, Samuel	1		2		
Norris, Josiah	1	1	3		
Kint, Charles	1		5		
Kint, Warrant	1	1	2		
thomas, Nathaieh	1	1	2		
Packad, Joshua	1		2		
Packad, Ralf	1		2		
Packad, Calab	1		1		
ford, Nathaniel	2	1	4		
Crigg, James	1		1		
Crigg, Thomas	1		3		
Crigg, James, Ju	1	1	1		
Crigg, William	1	1			
michals, Josiah	1	3	4		
Packad, Joshua Jr	1				
Packad, libary	1		1		
Norton, Stephen	1		2		
Norton, Peter	1				
Norton, Constant	1		3		
wing, Paul	1	3	1		
Pitts, Seth	2		4		
Savage, Benjn	1		3		
Wing, Daniel	1		4		
peterson, abraham	2	3	6		
peterson, abraham, Ju	1				
peterson, Carnalas	1		2		
Bean, Joshua	2	6	5		
Bean, Joel	1	1	1		
Bean, Elijah	1	1	2		
Johnson, Joseph	2		5		
Johnson, Joseph, Ju	2		2		
Johnson, Joshua	1		1		

WINTHROP TOWN—con.

NAME OF HEAD OF FAMILY.	Free white males of 16 years and upward, including heads of families.	Free white males under 16 years.	Free white females, including heads of families.	All other free persons.	Slaves.
Morrill, Levi	2	2	1		
Norton, Daniel	1	1	2		
Page, Robert	1	4	6		
Wing, Ichabod	1				
huccosen, henry	1				
Wiman, henry	1		4		
Waugh, Robert	3	1	2		
Simonons, Ichabod	1	1	3		
Whicher, Moses	1	2	3		
Whicher, Moses, Ju	1	3	2		
Wing, Daniel, Ju	1		3		
Wing, Reuben	1				
luce, Uriah	1		3		
luce, Shuble	1	3	2		
luce, freeman	1				
Smith, Cyril	1				
Shurborn, Job	1	4	3		
Shurborn, Richard	1		2		
Steper, John	1		1		
Dudley, Stephen	1		2		
Dudley, Eliphelat	1	3	3		
Hoitt, Petralea	2	3	5		
Clough, Jabes	1	3	5		
Greeley, Joseph	1		1		
Greeley, Noah	1	3	2		
Greeley, Joseph, Ju	1	2	2		
flacher, Gideon	1				
Clough, John	1	1	3		
Gordon, thiah	2	1	5		
Gordon, Jona	1	2	1		
Gordon, Josiah	1	3	1		
Parram, Samuel	1	2	2		
hutchison, Joseph	1	2	2		
hutchison, theophas	1		1		
Whicher, Thomas	1	3	4		
Whicher, Nathaniel	2	4	6		
Whicher, William	2	2	5		
Judkins, Samuel	1	2	2		
Stevens, John	1				
Evens, Jonn	1	1	1		
Evens, Daniel	1				
hubard, John	1		5		
Carr, Benjn	1	5	4		
French, Moses	1		1		
Mark, Abijah	1		3		
French, John	1	2	4		
French, John, Jur	1	2	1		
Gage, John	1	2	3		
hovey, John	1	1	3		
Smith, Jesse	1	1	2		
Boyd, Samuel	1		1		
Boyd, Calorn	1				
Cater, lamuel	1	1	1		
freeman, John	1		2		
Talbot, William	1	3	3		
farthaton, Ithamer	1	4	2		
Whiting, Jonathan	1		2		
Whiting, Jonathan, Jur	2	1	7		
Branard, Timothy	1		3		
Matheys, Joseph	1				
White, Joab	1	3	1		
Estes, Solomon	1	3	7		
Robins, Daniel	1	2	1		
Richard, William	2	1	3		
Cran, Abijah	1	1	2		
Wadworth, John	2	1	1		
Branard, Ruth (Widow)		2	3		
Branard, Reuben	1		3		
Comings, John	3	4	3		
Standley, Nathaniel	2	1	2		
french, Josiah	1	1	6		
Porter, Benjn	1	3	3		
Pond, William	1		1		
Keefer, John	1		3		
Washbane, Edward	1	1	1		
Wardworth, Samuel	1		1		
Stevens, Ephraim	1	4	3		
foster, Sabel (Widow)			1		
Rice, Joseph	2		2		
foster, Stuard	2	2	2		
foster, David	2	2	4		
foster, Saml	3	4	3		
foster, Ebnezer	1				
foster, Richard	1				
Wood, Moses	1		1		
Gay, Moses	1	1	1		
fairbanks, Joseph	1		1		
fairbanks, Benjn	2	2	6		
foster, Timothy	2	1	4		
Dileno, Zebulon	2		1		
Dileno, Seth	1	1	4		
Cushman, Josiah	1	4	3		
Marrow, Daniel	1	2	5		
Marrow, Daniel, Ju	1	3	3		
Morrow, Ebnezer	1				

WINTHROP TOWN—con.

NAME OF HEAD OF FAMILY.	Free white males of 16 years and upward, including heads of families.	Free white males under 16 years.	Free white females, including heads of families.	All other free persons.	Slaves.
fairbanks, Elijah	2	2	3		
Robins, Daniel	2		2		
Robins, Asa	1	1	1		
Blunt,.John	1	1	2		
Priscott, Samuel	1	2	3		
white, Benjn	1	2	3		
Priscott, Jediah	1		1		
Priscott, Elijah	1				
Priscott, Jesse	1		4		
Priscott, Odlin	1	1	3		
Priscott, Benjn	1				
Longfelow, Jonn	1				
Standley, Adain	1	2	1		
Page, Simon	3	3	7		
Blunt, Andrew	1		3		
Priscott, Jedeah, Jun	2	3	6		
Mathew, Daniel	1				
Bishop, Squire	1		1		
Bishop, Nathaniel	1		1		
Pooling, Stephen	2	3	6		
fairbanks, Nathaniel	1	3	2		
midcufs, Joseph	1	1	1		
Wood, Samuel	1	1	1		
Wood, Elijah	1		1		
Morton, levy	1	1	1		
Morton, Ebnezer	1	1			
Cilley, William	1				
Pooling, William	1	2	4		
Woodcock, David	1	4	5		
Chandler, John, jur	1	5	2		
herkley, James	1				
How, Stephan	1				
Coal, John	1		2		
Boldon, Jiras	1	1	2		
How, Ichabod	2		6		
Chandler, John	1	1	2		
Daxter, Constant	1				
Chandler, Joab	1	3	3		
Chandler, Joseph	1				
Chandler, Moses	1		1		
Chandler, Jacob	1	1	2		
lambord, Gideon	1	1	4		
lambord, Paul	1		1		
lambord, Silas	1				
lyford, William	1				
Curne, James	1				
WOOLWICH TOWN.					
Stephenson, Nathl	1	1	3		
Tibbits, Nathl	3	2	4		
Mitchel, Jonas	1	1	7		
Burford, Robert	1		1		
Bailey, John	3	1	2		
Farnham, Saml	1	2	5		
Card, John	1		2		
Farnham, Jere	1		2		
Savage, James	2	2	5		
Sloman, Simon	1	2	6		
Pelson, Joel	1	2	2		
Honowell, Rich	2	1	2		
Abbot, Aaron	1		4		
Foster, Nathl	2	2	6		
McMurphy, Archibald	1	3	2		
Shilden, Ephraim	2		5		
Lummis, Saml	1	2	2		
Skinner, Henry	2	3	5		
Hamlen, Richard	2	2	2		
Wade, Abner	2	2	3		
Sole, John	1	1	4		
Snell, Thos	3	1	2		
Smith, Israel	3		4		
Savage, Edward	1		1		
Booker, Josiah	2	6	5		
Snell, James	1	1	1		
Booker, Josiah, Junr	1	1	1		
Booker, Ebenr, Junr	2		2		
Booker, Ebenr	1	2	4		
Blin, James	2	1	3		
Dilleno, Ebenr	1	3	1		
Bailey, Joshua	1	1	2		
Blin, Charles	1		2		
Bailey, Josiah	1		3		
Leman, Samuel	1		4		
Leman, Saml, Junr	1	2	1		
Leman, Abigail			2		
Twing, Nathl	2		3		
Hathorn, Willm	1	1	4		
Eames, Jacob	1	3	2		
Reid, Jona	2		2		
Reid, Saml	2	2	1		
Reid, Robert	3	3	3		
Reid, Joel	1	2	6		
Frost, Lemuel	2	6	4		
Frost, John	3		2		

LINCOLN COUNTY—Continued.

WOOLWICH TOWN—con.

NAME OF HEAD OF FAMILY.	Free white males of 16 years and upward, including heads of families.	Free white males under 16 years.	Free white females, including heads of families.	All other free persons.	Slaves.
Blair, John	1	2	2		
Baley, Thos	1	3	4		
Stinson, Thos	1	2	3		
Blair, Robert	1	2	4		
Blair, James	2	1	5		
Blair, James, Junr	1	3	1		
Dillano, Jona	1	2	4		
Manes, Saml	2	3	2		
Ford, Francis	3	1	1		
Grace, Willm	1	1	3		
Manes, Betsy	1	1	4		
Harnden, Willm	1	1	3		
White, Robert	4	1	4		
Motheswill, Thos	2	1	4		
Day, Nathl	2	1	5		
Smith, Zebulon	1	2	3		
Preble, Saml	1	4	3		
Witherby, Jona	1	3	3	1	
Harndon, Saml	3	1	4		
Preble, Jona	4		7		
Ryan, Michl	1	2	3		
Curtes, Charles	2	1	5		
Stinson, James	1	2	2		
Curtes, John	2	5	5		
Card, Thos	1	1	2		
Card, Danl	1	4	2		
Paine, Moses	1	1	1		
Preble, Martha		1	2		
Winshop, Josiah	2	1	3		
Stinson, James	3	1	3		
Hathorn, John	2	2	3		
Hathorn, John, Junr	1		3		
Perkins, Robert	1	2	3		
Smith, Mary		1	1		
Curtes, Joseph	1		1		
Grover, Benja	1		1		
Fuller, Joshua	1	1	1		
Stinson, Robert	1	2	4		

WOOLWICH TOWN—con.

NAME OF HEAD OF FAMILY.	Free white males of 16 years and upward, including heads of families.	Free white males under 16 years.	Free white females, including heads of families.	All other free persons.	Slaves.
Otis, Galen	1	1	2		
Dilleno, Hopestill	4	1	4		
Ballard, Thomas	1		3		
Stinson, Saml	5	2	4		
Whitten, Asa	1	2	2		
Farnham, Joshua	3	1	2		
Trott, Joanna			2		
Weymouth, Moses	3		3		
Gilmore, Willm	5	1	7		
Gilmore, David	1	2	4		
Lancaster, Joseph	3	2	4		
Smith, Ebenezer	1	2	1		
Webb (Widow)	1	1	1		
Blanchard, James	4	3	5		
Carlton, Jane	1	2	3		
Farnham, Zebedee	1	1	1		
Dilleno, Ephraim	1	2	3		
Trott, Benja	4	4	4		
Wright, John	1	1	1		
Wright, Joseph	1	1	1		
Wright, Joseph, Junr	1	1	5		
Blackman, Eliphalet	1	4	6		
Bailey, John, Junr	1		2		
Cross, John	3	1	2		
Bowen, Jabez	1	1	2		
Gray, John	1	4	3		
Shaw, John	1	1	3		
Sheldon, Willm	1	1	3		
Shaw, Mary		3	4		
Fullerton, James	2	2	4		
Bailey, Benja	1	2	3		
Gould, Saml	3	2	5		
Walker, Joseph	1	1	2		
Grant, Elijah	2	1	3		
Walker, Andw	3	1	7		
Walker, Solomon	2	5	3		
Williams, Nathl	2		5		
Williams, Timo	1	3	3		

WOOLWICH TOWN—con.

NAME OF HEAD OF FAMILY.	Free white males of 16 years and upward, including heads of families.	Free white males under 16 years.	Free white females, including heads of families.	All other free persons.	Slaves.
Cushman, Robert	3	3	5		
Savage, Ebenz	1	3	4		
Blin, James	1	2	2		
Hathorn, Seth	1	1	4		
Gould, John	3	1	6		
Savage, Abraham					
BETWEEN NORRIDGEWOCK AND SEVEN MILE BROOK.					
Allis, Benjamin	1		2		
Dor, Ambrius	1	1	3		
Houghton, Thomas	2		1		
Johnson, John	1	2	4		
Piper, John	1	2	2		
Gray, Sarah	1	2	4		
Savage, James	1	4	4		
Savage, Charles	1	1	5		
Mores, Joseph	1	1	3		
Fairbroth, Lovewell	1	4	4		
Lovejoy, Thomas	1	2	1		
Crosby, James	1	1	3		
Forgerson, John	1	3	5		
Chapman, Nathaniel	1	2	1		
Wesson, Benjamin	1	1	2		
Walker, Stephen	1	4	4		
Rogers, Robert	1	2	3		
Putnam, John	1	2	4		
Walker, John	1		3		
Littlefield, Ebenezer	1	2	4		
Barnes, James	2	4	3		
Lovewell, Thomas	1				
Jones, James	1	3	2		
Ames, Jonathan	1	3	5		
Dean, Ebenezer	1		1		
Fling, Daniel	1				

WASHINGTON COUNTY.

BUCKS HARBOR NECK TOWN.

NAME OF HEAD OF FAMILY.	Free white males of 16 years and upward, including heads of families.	Free white males under 16 years.	Free white females, including heads of families.	All other free persons.	Slaves.
Newcomb, John	1	4	3		
Elliot, Simon	1				
Pettegrow, Benjamin	1	3	4		
Larrabee, Abner	1				
Larrabee, David	1	1	1		
Larrabee, Isaac	3		2		
Mayhew, Priscilla		1	3		
Fogg, Stephen	1	2	4		
Libbee, Nathan	1		2		
Libbee, Josiah	1	3	3		
Coolbroth, Peter	2	3	4		
Howard, John	1	1	3		

MACHIAS TOWN.

NAME OF HEAD OF FAMILY.	Free white males of 16 years and upward, including heads of families.	Free white males under 16 years.	Free white females, including heads of families.	All other free persons.	Slaves.
Avery, James	2	3	2		
Albee, William	1	4	2		
Aylwood, Partrick	1	2	3		
Averill, Joseph	1	4	3		
Andrews, Israel	1	3	2		
Ackly, Benajah	1	7	2		
Berry, Jonathan	2		6		
Berry, John	3	2	7		
Berry, Benjamin	1	1	3		
Burnum, Job	2	2	8		
Burnum, Samuel	1				
Bryant, Barthow	1		4		
Boynton, Amos	1	2	6		
Bowles, Ralph H	1	1	2		
Belighter, Jno	1	2	1		
Belfountain, Rana	1				
Brown, Philbrook	1	1	1		
Bryant, William	1				
Bryant, Joseph	1				
Bryant, John	1				
Barns, Ashble	1		3		
Cary, Edward	1				
Crocker, Benjamin	1				
Clark, Parker	4		2		
Chaloner, William	1	5	2		
Crocker, John	2		3		
Crocker, James	1	1	2		
Clark, Edward	1				
Conners, Partrick	1	1	3		
Chace, Ephraim	2	2	6		
Chace, William	1		1		
Cates, Samuel	1	2	4		
Crosman, Jacob	1				
Clefford, Joseph	1	4	4		

MACHIAS TOWN—con.

NAME OF HEAD OF FAMILY.	Free white males of 16 years and upward, including heads of families.	Free white males under 16 years.	Free white females, including heads of families.	All other free persons.	Slaves.
Drew, Consider	3	2	1		
Dunn, David	1				
Dowdele, Michal	1	1	3		
Dowe, Stephen	1				
Darby, John	1				
Davis, William	1				
Damons, Gamiel	1	3	1		
Dearing, Joseph	1				
Day, John	1				
Eden, Samuel	1		3		
Emmerson, William	1	1	4		
Elsmore, Moses	1	2	2		
Eustis, Mrs			1		
Foster, Benjamin	3	1	3	1	
Foster, Wooden	4	1	3		
Foster, John W	1	3	6		
Foster, John	1	1	4		
Foster, Levi	1		3		
Foster, Abijah	1				
Foster, Benjamin, Junr	1	2	4		
Foster, Moses	1		3		
Fenlason, Wallis	1	7	3		
Foss, Benjamin	1	2	3		
Foss, Joseph	1				
Foss, Benjamin, junr	1				
Flinn, James	2	1	2		
Hawes, Elizabeth			3		
Griffiths, Henry	1		1	1	
Getchell, Joseph	1		1		
Getchell, Joseph, Junr	1	4	3		
Gardner, Ebenr	1	5	3		
Gillmore, Arthur	1				
Gooch, Benjamin	1	1	7		
Gooch, James	2	2	5		
Gooch, William	1		2		
Gooch, Ebenezer	1		2		
Gardner, David	1		2		
Gardner, David, junr	2	3	4		
Harris, Josiah	1				
Howe, Tilly	1	3	3		
Hill, Sarah		2	4		
Hill, Hannah	1	1	4		
Hill, Samuel	1				
Hollway, Ladwick	1	2	3		
Holmes, James	1	3	2		
Hadley, Ephraim	1				
Hoit, Daniel	2	4	6		
Harmon, Benjamin	1	4	2		
Hanscom, Aron	3	4	4		

MACHIAS TOWN—con.

NAME OF HEAD OF FAMILY.	Free white males of 16 years and upward, including heads of families.	Free white males under 16 years.	Free white females, including heads of families.	All other free persons.	Slaves.
Hanscom, Aron, junr	1				
Hanscom, Nathan	1				
Hathaway, Eleazer	1	3	2		
Huntley, Jabez	1		1		
Hill, Joseph	1	1	1		
Harvey, Seth	1				
Howe, William	1				
Hitchings, Josiah	1				
Holmes, Samuel	3	2	2		
Innes, Partrick	1				
Jones, Stephen	3	1	4		
Johnson, Stephen	2	2	2		
Kelly, John	1	3	2		
Munson, Joseph	2		1	2	
Munson, Joseph, junr	1	2	1		
Munson, Stephen	1	4	1		
Munson, John	2	1	3		
Meservey, Daniel	3	1	3		
Mitchel, Noah	1		2		
Moore, Samuel	1				
Miller, Francis	1	1	2		
McGreger, Alexander	1				
Lord, Benjamin	1				
Libbee, Obed	1	1	2		
Libbee, Daniel	1		1		
Libbee, David	1	2	3		
Longfellow, Nathan	3	2	4		
Longfellow, Nathan, junr	2	2	5		
Longfellow, Jacob	1	1	1		
Longfellow, Olive			3		
Libbee, Joseph	2	2	2		
Lewis, Amasa	1	1	2		
Lowry, James	1				
Lyon, Revd James	2	1	4		
Obrien, Jerimiah	1	3	3	1	
Obrien, Gideon	1	3	7		
Obrien, Morris	1		4		
Elliot, Robert	1				
Brown, Andrew	1				
Phinny, Nathan	2	2	3		
Phinny, Nathanl, junr	1				
Phinny, Jonathan	1		2		
Pinco, Jonathan	4	4	3		
Palmer, Jacob	3	2	3		
Prescott, David	1	2	3		
Pepper, Anthony	1				
Penniman, Jacob	1				
Parker, Stephen	1		2		

WASHINGTON COUNTY—Continued.

NAME OF HEAD OF FAMILY.	Free white males of 16 years and upward, including heads of families.	Free white males under 16 years.	Free white females, including heads of families.	All other free persons.	Slaves.
MACHIAS TOWN—continued.					
Richardson, Peter	3	2	6		
Rich, Samuel	1	6	2		
Smith, Stephen	3	1	5		
Smith, Stephen, junr	1	2	2		
Smith, Ellis	1				
Stillman, George	2	2	4		
Sanborn, Ennoch	2		1		
Sanborn, John	1	1	2		
Sanborn, Richard	1	1	2		
Smith, Charles	1	2	1		
Smith, Ebenezer	1		2		
Sevey, George	2	1	8		
Sevey, Joseph	1		2		
Sevey, Sylvanus	1	3	2		
Sevey, Aron	1				
Sevey, John	1	1	2		
Singly, Frederick	1	1	1		
Scott, Samuel	2		3		
Scott, George	1	3	5		
Scott, John	1	3	5		
Scott, Jess	1	1	2		
Scott, Samuel, junr	1	4	3		
Scott, Daniel	1	1	1		
Scott, Mark	1	1	2		
Stone, Solomon & Son	2	2	6		
Smith, James	1	1	2		
Sinkler, Nathl	1				
Talbot, Peter	1	4	4		
Thompson, George	1	1	5		
Thaxter, Marshal	1	2	1		
Toby, Matthias	2				
Thompson, Abraham	1				
Thorp, Thomas	1	1	3		
Woodruff, Jonathan	1	1	1		
Watts, John	2		1	2	
Waterhouse, Enoch	2	1	8		
Wescoat, Benja	1				
Webb, William	1				
Dillaway, James	2		1		
Ingly, Moses	1				
Ingly, Eben	1				
Cooper, John	1				
Bruce, Phineas	1				
Jones, Asa	1				
Packard, Cyrus	1				
Western, Job	1				
PLANTATIONS EAST OF MACHIAS.					
No. 1.					
Lincoln, Moses	1		2		
Lincoln, Jacob	1		1		
Loring, Peter	1		1		
Frost, John	1	3	2		
Frost, Samuel	1				
Patterson, Alexr	1		4		
Hodges, Alexr	1	2	2		
Morrison, William	2	2	4		
Sweat, Daniel	1	1	2		
Tuttle, Samuel	2	4	3		
Wood, James	2	1	1		
Stoddard, Nathl	1	1	4		
Kilbey, William	1	1	1		
Damons, Abiah	1	1	3		
Chubbuck, James	1		2		
No. 2.					
Henderson, Thos	1				
Lincoln, Theodore	3	1	1		
Preston, Nathan	1	2	3		
Cushing, Solomon	1				
Cushing, Laban	1				
Lincoln, Zenas	1				
Willson, Joshua	1		3		
Ash, Robert	2	1	2		
Lea, Daniel	1	2	2		
Bridges, Josha Y Abra	3	3	1		
Blackwood, James	1	2	2		
Gardiner, Daniel	1		4		
Smith, Richard	1	1	4		
Harper, Richard	2		1		
Mahaw, Edmund	1	3	4		
Laton, Hatewell	2	2	8		
Huckings, Clement	1		1		
Willson, William	1	1	2		
Sprague, Samuel	1	4	1		
Wilder, Theophilus	1	1	4		
Wilder, Theos, junr	1		2		
Palmer, John	1		1		
Henry, Isaiah	3	1	5		
Hatch, Chris	1	2	3	1	

NAME OF HEAD OF FAMILY.	Free white males of 16 years and upward, including heads of families.	Free white males under 16 years.	Free white females, including heads of families.	All other free persons.	Slaves.
PLANTATIONS EAST OF MACHIAS—con.					
No. 2—Continued.					
Lincoln, Joshua	1				
Clark (Widow)	1		3		
Dalton, Sipio					5
Bender, Christopher	1		2		
Bridges, John	1		2		
Morain, Andrew	1				
Stoddard, Baley C	1	2	1		
Gardner, Warren	1				
Hersey, Zadock	1	2	5		
No. 4.					
Porter, Joseph	5		1		
Boyden, Jacob	1				
Johnson, John	1	1	1		
Bugby, William	1	3	2		
Jones, Samuel	1	2	4		
McDonald, Donald	2	2	5		
Somes, Daniel	1	1	2		
Brewer, John	2		3		
Johnson, Job	1	1	1		
Leshure, Samuel	1	2	3		
Fausett (Widow)			1	3	
No. 5.					
Sprague, James	1	5	3		
Sprague, Abiel	1	2	3		
Petigrow, Thomas	4	2	5		
Dyer, Jones	3	2	3		
Dyer, James	1	1	2		
Hill, Daniel	3	1	3		
Berry, John	1	1	3		
Lane, James	1	3	1		
Jackson, William	1	2	1		
Ryen, John	2				
Bohannon, John	2	3	3		
Noble, John	1	2	2		
Bayley, Nathl & Son	2	2	3		
Sprague, Eli	1		2		
No. 8.					
Allan, John	3	4	4		
Delesdernier, LewisFred	1	2	3		
Bowman, Andrew	1	2	4		
Foster, John	4		1		
Flagg (Widow)	1	4	2		
Rumney, Dominicus	1				
Kent, John	1	2	1		
Johnson, James	1				
Simpson, John	1				
Delesdernier, Gideon	1		1		
Ramsdell, William	2	2	4		
Reynolds, Benja	2	2	3		
Ramsdell, James	1		1		
Ramsdell, Isaac	1				
Ramsdell, Ebenezer	1	1	3		
Rumney, William	1	1	4		
Clerk, William	3	1	4		
Jinkins, Thos	3		1		
Gooe, Jacob	1		1		
Denbow, Nathaniel	3	1	6		
Huckings, Samuel	1	2	1		
Kelly, James	1	1	2		
Burr, Perez	1				
Bell, William	1	1	2		
Simpson, William	1	1	2		
Cockram, James	1	3	5		
Bower, Henry	2	2	2		
Hale, Richard	1	1	2		
Shackford, John	1	4	1		
Boynton, Caleb	2		4		
Clark, William	3	3	4		
Goddard, Nathanl	2	1			
McGuyer, John	1		3		
Clark, Joseph	2	1	5		
Dexter, Thomas	1	2	2		
Hacket, Alexander	1		1		
Clark, Nathanl	2	1	1		
Goudy, William	1	1	2		
Beaman, Thomas	2	1	1		
Ricker, William	1	1	3		
Maybe, Elias	1				
Fountain, Stephen	1		5		
Hammon, William	2		3		
Johnson, Paul	1	2	3		
Boynton, Caleb, junr	1	1	2		
Dummer, John	1				
Carlo, John	1	4	1		
Owen, Morgan	1	1	1		
Carter, James	1		1		
Clark, Henry	1		2		
Maybee, Solomon	1		2		

NAME OF HEAD OF FAMILY.	Free white males of 16 years and upward, including heads of families.	Free white males under 16 years.	Free white females, including heads of families.	All other free persons.	Slaves.
PLANTATIONS EAST OF MACHIAS—con.					
No. 8—Continued.					
Kent, Jonathan	1				
Sangmeid, Henry	1	2	3		
Coombs, Edward	1	1	3		
No. 9.					
Cook, John	1		2		
Reynolds, Samuel	2	2	2		
Edwards, Doctor	1	1	1		
Layton, Samuel	1	4	3		
Crew, John	1		2		
Holland, William	2		1		
Jourdan, Richard	1		2		
No. 10.					
Hale, James	1		2		
Ash, Samuel	1		2		
Hurley, William	1		3		
Smith, Daniel	2	1	3		
Shaw, Benjamin	2	1	3		
Ayer, Elijah	1		2		
Ayer, Elijah, junr	1	1	5		
Hobert, Nathl	2				
Shaw, James	1				
Oliver (Widow)	1	2	3		
Hatch, Hawes	1				
No. 11.					
Cates, Robert	1	4	3		
Davis, John	1	1	2		
Makem, John	1	2	3		
Andrews, Jerimiah	1	1	1		
Andrews, Timothy	1	1	4		
Niles, Jonathan	1		4		
Andrews, Nathan	2	1	2		
No. 12.					
Crane, John	3	1	4		
Trescutt, Lemuel	1		2		
Peck, George	1	1	4		
Harvey, Thomas	1	1	1		
Bryant, Davis	2	1	1		
Dowling, John	1	2	4		
Huntly, Jabez, junr	1	2	2		
Nickerson, Izachar	1	1	3		
Huntly, Frederick	2	6	2		
Howe, Sarah			3		
No. 13.					
Brown, James	1	5	1		
PLANTATIONS WEST OF MACHIAS.					
No. 4.					
Small, Joseph	1	1	2		
Robertson, David	1	1	2		
Archibald, Thomas	1		1		
Gross, Reuben	1	1	1		
Campbell, Alexr	4	1	4		
Foster, Robert	4		4		
Todd, John	1				
Todd, James	1				
Bracey, Joseph	3	2	5		
Joy, Francis	1		2		
Patten (Widow)	2	3	4		
Stout, Jeremiah	3	2	1		
Leighton, Thomas	4	2	3		
Leighton, Joseph	1	1	2		
Clark, James	1		1		
Leighton, Thomas, 3d	1	1	1		
West, Thomas	1				
Parker, William	1	3	4		
Pinkim, Tristram	1	4	5		
Pinkim, Richard	1	2	3		
Yeaton, John	4	2	5		
Dyer, Henry	4	4	6		
Sawyer, Joseph	4	1	3		
Leighton, Thomas, Junr	3	5	3		
Godfrey, Ichabod	1	1	3		
Stevens, Jonathan	2	1	6		
Townsley, Jacob	1	2	3		
Kinsley, Samuel	2	4	3		
Tracey, Wheeler	1		2		
Oakes, Atherton	1		2		
Guptell, William	1	3	3		
Moore, Robert	2	1	3		
Moore, Josiah	1				
Downs, Ebenezer	4	1	1		

WASHINGTON COUNTY—Continued.

PLANTATIONS WEST OF MACHIAS—con.

No. 4—Continued.

NAME OF HEAD OF FAMILY.	Free white males of 16 years and upward, including heads of families.	Free white males under 16 years.	Free white females, including heads of families.	All other free persons.	Slaves.
Downs, Ebenezer, Jr...	1	1	1		
Wakefield, Samuel...	3	2	5		
Townsley, Gad...	1				
Baker, Lemuel...	1	2	4		
Parrott, Thomas...	2	4	3		
Godfrey, Daniel...	1				

No. 5.

NAME OF HEAD OF FAMILY.					
Nash, Reuben...	1	1	2		
Cates, Edward...	1	2	4		
Small, Daniel...	1	2	3		
Libbee, Joseph...	1	1	4		
Nash (Widow)...		1	2		
Cole, Ebenezer...	2	3	4		
Cole, Ebenezer, Jr...	1				
Nash, Reuben, 2...	1				
Campbell, James...	1	2	1		
Grace, James...	2	4	4		
Dorman, Jabez...	2	2	6		
Jourdain, Ebenr...	3		3		
Stout, Joseph...	2	5	4		
Denbow, John...	2	5	3		
Fichet, Zebulon...	1	2	2		
Nickles, Alexr...	1	1	4		
Collins, Richard...	1	1			
Stout, Benjamin...	2		3		
Jones, Joseph...	1	1	4		
Brown, David...	1	5	2		
Sawyer, Josiah...	1	1	1		
Lovett, Isaac...	1	1	5		
Stout, Thomas...	3		6		
Wallis, Joseph, Junr...	1	1	2		
Rea, William...	1	4	1		
Brown, Jess...	2	2	3		
Wallis, Joseph...	2	1			
Cummings, John...	1				
Wallis, Benjamin...	2	1	3		
Ward, John...	1				
Wallis, James...	1				
Small, John, 3d...	1				
McCormick, Alexr...	1				

No. 6.

NAME OF HEAD OF FAMILY.					
Bickford, William...	1	3	2		
Batson, William...	1	3	2		
Dunbar, Josiah...	1				
Coffin, Richard...	3		3		
Coffin, Samuel...	1		1		
Coffin, Barnabas...	1		1		
Cornthwait, Thomas...	1				
Drisko, John...	2		4		
Drisko, Joseph...	2	3	4		
Hall, John...	2	4	6		
Jourdan, James...	1	1	2		
Knowles, Francis...	1	1	5		
Look, Daniel...	1	1	7		
Look, George...	1	3	2		
Look, Moses...	1				
Merrit, Daniel...	1	1			
Merritt, Wm...	1	1	4		
Merrit, Joseph...	1				
Masten, Samuel...	1	1	3		
Moore, Josiah...	1		2		
Miller, Robert...	1		2		

PLANTATIONS WEST OF MACHIAS—con.

No. 6—Continued.

NAME OF HEAD OF FAMILY.	Free white males of 16 years and upward, including heads of families.	Free white males under 16 years.	Free white females, including heads of families.	All other free persons.	Slaves.
Nash, Samuel...	1		1		
Nash, Isaiah...	2	5	2		
Norton, Seth...	2	1	3		
Nash, Samuel, junr...	1				
Nash, Isaac...	1	2	3		
Nash, Joseph...	1	3	2		
Norton, Elias...	1		1		
Norton, Abraham...	1				
Nash, Isaac, 2d...	1				
Plummer, Moses...	3	1	5		
Plummer, Moses, junr...	1				
Reynolds, Eliphalet...	1	2	3		
Ramsdell, Nathl...	1				
Stevens (Widow)...		2	4		
Steele, Reuben...	1	2	2		
Steele (Widow)...	1		4		
Tibbets, Joseph...	2	1	2		
Tibbets, William...	1				
Wass, Wilmot...	1				
Wass, Wilmot, junr...	2	5	3		
Wass, Willmot, 3d...	1				
Wass, Christor...	1				
White, Tilly...	1	3	4		
Whitney, Matthias...	1	5	4		
Yates, Francis...	1	1	5		

No. 11.

NAME OF HEAD OF FAMILY.					
Leighton, Theodore...	1		7		
Jordain, John...	1		3		
Willey, Ichabod...	3	2	4		
Roff, Moses...	2	1	2		
Laurence, John...	1		1		
Laurence, John, Junr...	1	3	3		
Willson, Gawing...	1	4	5		
Anderson, John...	1	1	4		
Corson, Samuel...	1	4	2		
Tucker, Josiah...	4	2	3		
Small, John...	1				
Small, Elisha...	1	1	3		
Corson, Samuel, Jr...	1	2	4		
Corson, John...	1		2		
Small, John, Junr...	1	3	3		
Small, Ebenezer...	1	1	3		

No. 12.

NAME OF HEAD OF FAMILY.					
Leighton, Samuel...	2	1	2		
Leighton, Isaac...	1		1		
Leighton, Parratt...	1				

No. 13.

NAME OF HEAD OF FAMILY.					
Allan, Obediah...	3	2	4		
Allan, Gideon...	1	2	4		
Archer, John...	1	6	4		
Buckman, John...	1	6	3	2	
Black, Sherbone...					4
Cox, Nathl...	2	2	7		
Coffin, Matthew...	1	3	2		
Coffin, Elisha...	1	1	2		
Calaghan, Wm...	1	1	2		
Cox, Edward...	1				
Crocker, William...	1	1	1		
Drisko, Samuel...	1	2	5		
Dunbar, Obed...	1	3	4		

PLANTATIONS WEST OF MACHIAS—con.

No. 13—Continued.

NAME OF HEAD OF FAMILY.	Free white males of 16 years and upward, including heads of families.	Free white males under 16 years.	Free white females, including heads of families.	All other free persons.	Slaves.
Dow, Jonathan...	2		3		
Hale, Stephen...	1	1	5		
Ingersole, William...	1	4	3		
Ingersole, Benja...	1		1		
Ingersol, Benja, Junr...	1				
Kelly, Elijah...	1	1	3		
Nash, Ebenr...	1				
McKinsey, Owen...	2	3	4		
Merritt, Daniel...	1	2	2		
Merritt, Richard...	1		2		
Mansfield, Thomas...	1	1	1		
McKasiegen, John...	1	3	4		
Nash, John...	1		5		
Nash, Isaac...	1	2	3		
Nash, Abraham...	1		2		
Reynolds, David...	1		2		
Tinny, George...	1	2	4		
Tucker, Samuel...	1	1	3		
Tibbets, Joseph...	1	3	2		
Tinny, John...	1				
Tinny, David...	1				
Tinny, George, junr...	1				
Tinny, Samuel...	1				
Whitney, Nathn...	2	4	4		
Willson, Joseph...	2		3		
Willson, Joseph, Jr...	1	1	2		
Willson, Gowen...	1				
Worseter, Moses...	3	2	7		
Wass, David M...	1	1	3		
Waymouth, James...	1				

No. 22.

NAME OF HEAD OF FAMILY.					
Peirpoint, Joseph...	3	3	1		
Whitney, Joel...	3	5	3		
Noyce, Josiah...	1	2	3		
Farnsworth, Isaac...	2	3	3		
Whitney, Napthm...	1				
Dunnaven, John...	1		2		
Watts, David...	1	1	4		
Watts, Samuel...	1		2		
Coolidge, Caleb...	1		4		
Tupper, William...	2	1	1		
Tupper, Joseph...	1		3		
Libbee, Reuben...	1	4	4		
Bean, Abner...	1	1	3		
Randall, Charles...	1	1	2		
Knight, Jonathan...	2	4	5		
Knight, Paul...	1	1	3		
Shappa, Athony...	1	3	1		
Kellon, Benj...	2	1	2		
Wessen, Josiah...	1	1	7		
Roberts, Thomas...				1	
Merret, Samuel...	1		1		
Kelly, Thomas...	2	3	5		
Sawyer, John...	1	2	7		
Sawyer, Nehemiah...	1		3		
Cumming, Francis...	1	2	7		
McDonald, Agnes...	2	2	2		
Buffet, John...	1		2		
Horton, Elihu...	2	2	2		
Beal, Jerimiah...	1		2	1	
Beal, Manwarren...	3	2	4		
Menett, David...	1				

YORK COUNTY.

ARUNDEL TOWN.

NAME OF HEAD OF FAMILY.	Free white males of 16 years and upward, including heads of families.	Free white males under 16 years.	Free white females, including heads of families.	All other free persons.	Slaves.
Staples, Willm...	1	4	2		
Bickford, Eliakim...	3	2	3		
Tarbox, Lemuel...	1	4	3		
Smith, Jona, Jr...	1	1	2		
Emery, Jeremiah...	1	1	6		
Blaisdel, John...	1				
Perkins, George...	3	1	4		
Towns, Danl...	2	2	5		
Hutchins, Josiah, Jr...	1	1	5		
Hutchins, Saml, jr...	1	1	1		
Abbot, Silas...	1	2	4		
Huff, Danl...	2	4	4		
Hancom, Timo...	3		3		
Dorman, Jesse...	4		3		
Dorman, Israel...	1	1	4		
Patten, John...	1	1	7		
Lewis, Saml...	3	1	2		
Mitchel, Danl...	2	2	4		
Mitchel, Dummer...	2	4	3		

ARUNDEL TOWN—con.

NAME OF HEAD OF FAMILY.					
Burbank, Asa...	2	2	2		
Thompson, Benja...	2	2	3		
Watson, Saml...	1		3		
Burnham, Jane...		1	1		
Lasdel, Bartholomew...	2	1	2		
Lord, Tobias...	1		1		
Lord, Thos...	2	1	2		
Burnham, Seth...	2	4	3		
Burnham, Grace...	1		2		
Burnham, Jacob...	2	1	5		
Dorman, Jabez...	2		3		
Stone, John...	1	2	2		
Dorman, John...	1	2	6		
Miller, John...	2	2	2		
Downing, Nicholas...	1	1	1		
Miller, Andw...	1		5		
Fairfield, Saml...	1	1	3		
Huff, Thos...	2	1	4		
Benson, Henry...	2	4	3		

ARUNDEL TOWN—con.

NAME OF HEAD OF FAMILY.					
Clough Joel...	1	1	4		
Clough, Joseph...	2	3	4		
Clough, Noah...	1	1	4		
Dearing (Widow)...			2		
Dearing, James...	2	4	3		
Hodgdon, Israel...	2	1	3		
Durrel, Thos...	1	1	5		
Burnham, Isaac...	2	1	3		
Burnham, Forrest...	1	2	4		6
Thompson, Stephen...	1	1	2		
Thompson, James...	1	1			
Dennico, John...	1		4		
Hutchens, Ezra...	1	1			
Ayers, George...	1		1		
Boston, Shipway...	1		2		
Butler, Stephen...	1	2	2		
Thompson, Benja...	1	3	3		
Towns, Josiah...	1	3	2		
Mitchel, John...	1		2	1	

ARUNDEL TOWN—con.

NAME OF HEAD OF FAMILY.	Free white males of 16 years and upward, including heads of families.	Free white males under 16 years.	Free white females, including heads of families.	All other free persons.	Slaves.
Stone, Jonᵃ	1	3	1		
Currier, Nathˡ	1		1		
Smith, John	1	3	1		
Cleaves, Eaton	2	4	2		
Hilton, Abraham	2		3		
Cleaves, Stephen	3	2	3		
Cleaves, John	2		2		
Cleaves, John, Jʳ	1	1	1		
Smith, Danˡ	1		6		
Smith, David	1	2	3		
Smith, Jonᵃ	1	2	3		
Burbank, John	1		2		
Lord, Danˡ	1	3	2		
Day, Samˡ	1		4		
Hovey, James	2		5		
Huff, Ebenezer	1	2	2		
Davin, Danˡ	1	3	3		
Stone (Widow)	1	1	2		
Brown, Andʷ	1	2	2		
Hutchens, Joseph	3	1	8		
Brown, Andʷ, Jʳ	1	1	2		
Mattocks, Pel. Graves	1	1	2		
Wilder, Benjᵃ	1	1	3		
Washbourn, Joseph	3	1	1		
Jeffery, John	3		3		
Jeffery, Benjᵃ	4	2	5		
Hide, Joseph	1	1	3		
Avery, Joseph	3	1	2		
Avery, Shadrack	1	4	2		
Hutchins, David	3		3		
Green, Andʷ	1		2		
Lasdel, Mary	1	2	2		
Perkins, Thoˢ	1	2	3		
Wiles, Israel	1		4		
Weeks, Nicholas	1		2		
Stone, Robert	2	3	6		
Stone, Dix	3		1		
Weeks, John	1	2	2		
Perkins, Thoˢ	2	1	3		
Chatman, Abraᵐ	1		1		
Perkins, Joseph	1	1	2		
Lasdel, Jere	1		1		
Wiles, Jacob	5		2		
Wiles, Ruth			2		
Wiles, Ephraim	1	2	4		
Emmons, John	2		2		
Emmons, John, Jʳ	1	7	2		
Emmons, Ebenᶻ	1				
Emmons, Eliakim	1	2	2		
Fletcher, John	1		1		
Fletcher, Stephen	3	1	1		
Fletcher, Pendleton	1	1	4		
Fletcher, Jonᵃ	1	1	1		
Goodrigde, Willᵐ	1		3		
Goodrige, Jere	1		3		
Fletcher, Joseph	1	4	5		
Ferren, Jonᵃ	1		6		
Stone, Benjᵃ	1	1	2		
Wiles, Benjᵃ	1	1	2		
Perkins, Thoˢ, 3ᵈ	1	2	3		
Downing, Benjᵃ	1	1	1		
Downing, John	1	2	3		
Perkins, Danˡ	1	2	3		
Robinson, John	2		4		
Robinson, Samˡ	2		3		
White, Danˡ	1		3		
Smith, Willᵐ	1	4	1		
Smith, Charles	1		1		
Smith, Samuel	1	2	4		
Hutchens, Josiah	2	2	4		
White, Robert	1		2		
Moody, Silas	1	5	4		
Walker, Samˡ	1	4	2		
Walker, John	3	1	8		
Whidden, Joseph	1	3	3		
McCloud, —	1		1		
Huff, Charles	1	1	2		
Barter, Mark	1	1	6		
Towns, Robert	1	1	3		
Walker, Andʷ	1	1	3		
Hutchens, David	1	3	3		
Hutchens, Levi	2		4		
Murphy, Joshua	1	4	3		
March, Saul	1	4	7		
Ridout, Abraham	1		6		
Leach, Nathˡ	1	1	1		
Huff, John	1	3	2		
Seavey, Nicholas	1		1		
Dempsey (Widow)			2		
Adams, John	1	1	2		
Adams, James	1	3	4		
Adams, Benjᵃ	1		2		
Adams, James, Jʳ	1	1	1		
Stone, Dudley	1		3		
Stone, Jonᵃ	2		1		

ARUNDEL TOWN—con.

NAME OF HEAD OF FAMILY.	Free white males of 16 years and upward, including heads of families.	Free white males under 16 years.	Free white females, including heads of families.	All other free persons.	Slaves.
Littlefield, Elijah	1	1	3		
Littlefield, Benjᵃ	1	1	1	3	
Curtes, Joseph	1	2	1		
Shepherd, Robert	1	1	2		
Chatman, Wilbon	1	1	2		
Miller, Jerᵉ	2	1	4		
Fairfield, John, Jʳ	1	2	2		
Walker, Jonᵃ	1		2		
Towns, Amos	2	3	8		
Smith, Willᵐ	2				
Miller (Widow)		1	2		
Downing, John	1		3		
Miller, Lemˡ	1	2	3		
Downing, Harrison	1	2	2		
Rhodes, Miles	3	2	4		
Perkins, Abner	3	2	3		
Murphy, John	2	3	4		
Perkins, Thoˢ	1		1		
Perkins, Thoˢ	1	1	5		
Perkins, James	5	2	3		
Perkins, Ephraim	3	2	5		
Wissel, Thoˢ	2	1	2		
Morse, Nathan	1	1	2		
Walker, John	1	1	3		
Walker, Danˡ	3	1	5		
Perkins, John	1	1	2		
Perkins, Joseph	1	2	3		
Gould, James	3	3	3		
Gould, John	1	1	1		
Fairfield, Willᵐ	1	2	3		
Stone, Benjᵃ	1		4		
Smith, Jere	1	1	1		
Ward, Nathˡ	1		3		
Cleaves, James	1	1	3		
Stone, Nehemiah	1		1		
Walker, Nathˡ	1	1	2		
Huff, Samˡ	3	4	4		
Huff, Israel	1		2		
Huff, Abner	1		1		
Seavey, Stephen	1	2	5		
Huff, James	1	6	3		
Mattuck, Thoˢ	1		1		
Barker, —	1	4	1		
Jackson, Joshua	1	3	3		
Wiles, Samˡ	2	3	2	2	
Bukford (Widow)	2		2		
Huff, Charles	2		3		
McCarr, Caleb	1		1		
Dishon, Peter	3	4	2		
Perkins, George	1	3	4		
Lewis, John	2		1		
Lewis, Johnᵃ	1	4	2		
Andrews, John	3	1	2		
Hovey, Susanna			1		
Davis, Eliphalet	1	2	1		
Merril, Abel	1	4	3		
Merrill, Gideon	1	1	2		
Merrill, Jacob	1		2		
Emery, Joseph	1	1	1		
Whidden, Israel	3	1	5		
McCullock, Adam	2	1	4		
Merril, Obed	3	2	5		
Downing, Jonᵃ	2	2	2		
Downing, Benjᵃ	1	3	2		
Curtes (Widow)		4	2		
Perkins, Abner	1		4		
Perkins, Jotham	2		4		
Durrel, Benjᵃ	2	3	5		
Durrel, Jacob	1	3	3		
Cows, Benjᵃ	1	1	3		
Durrell, Asa	3	1	4		
Thompson, Ephraim	3	3	1		
Ham, Joˢ	1	2	1		
Green, Benjᵃ	2	5	3		
Lock, Simeon	1	4	4		
Rhodes, Jacob	3		5		
Thompson, John	1	1	1		
Smith (Widow)	1	2	4		
Grant, Willᵐ	1	2	4		
Springer, John	2	2	4		
Miller, Benjᵃ	1	1	2		
Hutchens, Simeon	1	2	3		
Hutchins, David	1	1	1		
Wakefield, Nathˡ	1	3	2		
M'Cuen, John	1		1		
Crudiford, Abner	3	1	2		
Merrill, Nathˡ	2	2	3		
Davis, Nathˡ	2	1	2		
Goodwin, Benjᵃ	1	1	1		
Lord, Benjᵃ	1		1		
Lord, Abraᵐ	1	1	2		
Lord, Joseph	1	6	3		
Nason, Edward	1	4	3		
Nason, Moses	1	2	1		
Nason Joshua, Jʳ	1	1	2		

ARUNDEL TOWN—con.

NAME OF HEAD OF FAMILY.	Free white males of 16 years and upward, including heads of families.	Free white males under 16 years.	Free white females, including heads of families.	All other free persons.	Slaves.
Patten, Robert	1	2	5		
Goodwin (Widow)			2		
Goodwin, John	1	5	2		
Thompson, Jonᵃ	1	1	2		
Lord, John	2	1	7		
Nason, Joshua	1	1	4		
Patten, James			2		
Seavey, Nicholas	1		4		
Wiles, Samˡ, Jʳ	1	2	1		
Stone, Jonᵃ, Jʳ	1		1		
Whitten, Samˡ	2	2	4		
Cleaves, Benjᵃ	1	1	1		

BERWICK TOWN.

NAME OF HEAD OF FAMILY.	Free white males of 16 years and upward, including heads of families.	Free white males under 16 years.	Free white females, including heads of families.	All other free persons.	Slaves.
Chadbourne, Hon. Benjᵃ	2		2		
Goodwin, Hon. Ichabod	3	2	8		
Tucker, John	2	1	8		
Wood, Danˡ	3	1	2		
Roberts, Joseph	2	2			
Roberts, Joshua	1		1		
Haggens, John	4	4	7	1	
Grant, Moses	1	1	2		
Jenkins, Jedediah	2				
Low, Nathˡ	3		2		
Kirker, Henery	1	1	2		
Junkins, Robert	2	2	3	1	
Grant, John	2	2	6		
Butler, Samˡ	2	2	4		
Butler, Samˡ, Junʳ	1	2	3		
Butler, Ichabod	1	2	3	1	
Libbey, Nathan	1	1	4		
Morris, Wᵐ	1		2		
Haggens, Edmund	2		4	2	
Hamilton, Jonᵃ	1	1	1		
Hamilton, Millet	1	1	2		
Chadwick, Wᵐ	2	1	5		
Jordin, John	1		3		
Smith, Wᵐ	1				
Cutts, Ricᵈ Foxᵉ	1	2	4		
Abbot, Benjᵃ	2	4	2		
Lord, Paul	1	1	2		
Pike, Samˡ	2		3		
Lord, Mark	5	2	5	1	
Gerrish, Clark	2	1	6		
MᶜGeoch, Allexʳ	2	6	3		
Nason, Nathˡ	1		4		
Abbot, Thomas	1		3		
Abbot, Thomas	1		3		
Nason, John	1	1	5		
Lord, Nathan	2		3		
Lord, John	3	3	3	1	
Marshall, Nahum	2		2		
Hovey, Ivory	5	1	6	1	
Furness, Robert	2	1	4		
Lee, Martha	1	1	3		
Chadbourne, Mary			2		
Chadbourne, Jonᵃ C.	2	3	5		
Chadbourne, Benjᵃ	1		1		
Chadbourne, Humpʸ	1	1	2	5	
Emery, Moses	1	2	4		
Sullivan, Ebenezer	2	1	4		
Goodwin, Daniel	1		3	3	
Plaisted, James	1	1	1		
Gerrish, Allexʳ	3	3	2	3	
Hill, John	1	2	3	2	
Frost, James	1	1	3	1	
Plaisted, John	1	3	5		
Gᵉrrish, Benjᵃ	3	1	3		
Hill, Ichabod	1	3	2		
Goodwin, Dominicus	2	2	4		
Thompson, Rev. John	2	3	5		
Lord, Caleb	2	1	4		
Chadbourne, Thomas	3	1	3		
Brock, Simeon	2	1	4		
Ham, Wᵐ	1		2		
Verney, Davis	1		2		
Lord, Jeremiah	1		2		
Boyce, Jotham	1		2		
Lord, Joseph	4		1		
Lord, Richard	1	1	2		
Jones, Vaughn	1	3	3		
Stone, John	1	1	2		
Young, Stephen	1	1	3		
Stapole, Lenord	1	1	1		
Hearl, Joseph	1	1	1		
Hubbard, Timothy	1		2		
Nason, Danˡ	1		3		
Lord, Mary			1		
Cushing, John	3	4	4	2	
Hamilton, Jonᵃ	3	5	6	1	
Chase, Enoch	1	4	6		
Nason, Wᵐ	3		2		
Nason, Joshua	1	1	7		
Abbot, Theopholus	1		3		
Whitehouse, Abigail			3		

YORK COUNTY—Continued.

BERWICK TOWN—con.

NAME OF HEAD OF FAMILY.	Free white males of 16 years and upward, including heads of families.	Free white males under 16 years.	Free white females, including heads of families.	All other free persons.	Slaves.
Abbot, Jona	2		3		
Abbot, Ricd	1	1	1		
Coopper, John	2	2	4		
Warren, Wm	2		2		
Warren, John	1	1	1		
Warren, Wm	1	1	3		
Abbot, Patience		1	4		
Goodwin, Moses	1		2		
Goodwin, Wm	1	2	3		
Hubbard, Thomas	1		1		
Abbot, John	1	2	7		
Abbot, John, Junr	1	2	2		
Grant, Margret			1		
Grant, Nathaniel	1	4	5		
Grant, Peter	1		1		
Grant, Elijah	1	4	5		
Abbot, Samuel	1	1	1		
Abbot, Isaac	1		1		
Lord, Simeon	3	1	2		
Goodwin, Ebenezer	2	4	4		
Lord, Mercy		1	1		
Lord, Jedediah	1	1	4		
Emery, Simon	1	1	3		
Hubbard, Phillip	2		2		
Hubbard, John	1	1	3		
Hupper, John	1	1	2		
Hubbard, Joseph	1		2		
Hubbard, Saml	1		2		
Abbot, Joshua	1		3		
Abbot, Danl	1	2	3		
Abbot, Anney			3		
Hodsdon, Hannah	1	2	3		
Lord, Ichabod	1				
Abbot, Amos	1	1	4		
Hodsdon, Wm	1	3	2		
Hodsdon, Samuel	1	1	1		
Warren, Chadbourne	1	2	4		
Nason, Aaron	1	2	6		
Sharkley, Ricd	1	1	3		
Sharkley, Ricd	2	2	4		
Hodsdon, Ricd	1		1		
Hodsdon, Danl	1	1	5		
Hodsdon, Thos	1				
Hodsdon, Jeremiah	2	1	4		
Hodsdon, Benja	1	4	2	1	
Hodsdon, Stephen	2	2	3		
Emery, Wm	2	6	3		
Emery, Job	2	1	3		
Lord, David	4	1	4		
Lord, Jeremiah	2	1	4		
Grant, James	4	1	2		
Shorey, Joseph	2	2	5		
Smith, Thomas	1	1	3		
Hearl, Elisha	1	2	3		
Hearl, Wm	1	4	3		
Spencer, Wm	1	1	5		
Spencer, Wm, Junr	1		3		
Chadbourne, Sarah			2		
Young, John	1	1	3		
Nason, Meriam			1		
Marss, Ichabod	1	1	1		
Lord, Jabes	2	1	2		
Nason, Mary			1		
Nason, Amos	1	1	1		
Spencer, Thomas	1		1		
Wadley, Moses	1		3		
Goodwin, Jedediah	2	4	3		
Wadley, John	2	1	5		
Wadley, Hannah			1		
Goodwin, Silas	1	1	2		
Whitrow, James	1		1		
Bennet, John	1		1		
Whidden, Ricd	2	3	2		
Marrs, Surplus	3	1	2		
Marrs, Wm	1	1	1		
Cooper, Allexr	2	3	6		
Goodwin, James	2	1	2		
Bennet, Moses	2	2	2		
Abbot, Reuben	1		2		
Coopper, Danl	2	2	2		
Spencer, Joseph	2	1	3		
Hearl, John	1	1	6		
Hearl, Gilbert	1	1	5		
Wilkison, James	2		2		
Wilkison, George	1	2	3		
Wilkison, Samuel	1		2		
Wilkison, Wm	1		1		
Clark, John	2	2	5		
Hearl, Wm	1	1	4		
Jelison, Margret	1		4		
Goodwin, Amos	1	2	2		
Huntrus, Darling	3		1		
Huntrus, Wm	1	1	1		
Lord, Jacob	2	2	7		
Huntrus, George	2		3		
Marrs, Thomas	1	1	1		
Hearl, Lucia		1	2		
Warren, Gilbert	3	2	4		
Nason, Noah	1	1	3		
Warren, James	2		3		
Thompson, John	1	2	4		
Emery, James	2	2	4		
Emery, Joshua	1	1	2		
Emery, Joshua, Junr	1		2		
Emery, John (of York)	3	1	4		
Burdean, Timothy	1		3		
Stevens, Danl	1	3	3		
Goodwin, Jeremiah	2		2		
Standley, John	1		3		
Standley, Saml	1	2	1		
Standley, James	1		2		
Gray, James	1	1	2		
Gray, James, Junr	2	3	4		
Cheek, Isaac	1		2		
Joy, Wm	2	2	6		
Gray, Jona	1	4	4		
Thurrel, Jacob	3	2	4		
Dennet, Ebenezer	3		2		
Thurrel, Jno	1	2	3		
Dennet, Ebenezer, Jr	1	1	1		
Dow, Moses	1	3	3		
Hunssom, Jerusha		1	4		
Thompson, Jesse	2		3		
Hearl, Mary			3		
Hearl, John	1	2	4		
Brawn, John	1	2	4		
Walker, Jona	1	6	3		
Thompson, Amos	2	1	4		
Brawn, George	1	2	4		
Brawn, George	1		1		
Verney, Ricd	1	3	4		
Boyce, James	2	2	4		
Furbush, Abrm	2	2	3		
Dickson, Ichabod	1	3	1		
Dickson, Mary	1	1	1		
Page, Enoch	2	1	4		
Thurel, Jona	1	1	5		
Thurrel, Jona	2	1	3		
Verney, Hezekiah	2		4		
Austin, Andrew	3	1	6		
Hamilton, John	2	1	7		
Stakepole, Aaron	1		1		
Hamilton, Simeon	1	1	6		
Hamilton, Reuben	1	1	1		
Hamilton, Silas	1		2		
Frost, Benja	1		1		
Brawn, John	2		2		
Thompson, Noah	1				
Goodwin, Wm	1	1	1		
Jallison, Lusia			2		
Walker, Nathel	1	2	3		
Knight, John	1		3		
Knight, Benja	1	2	5		
Welsh, Jona	2	1	7		
Roberts, Simon	2	1	3		
Meriam, Nathel	2	1	1		
Hodsdon, Nathan	1	3	4		
Hodsdon, James	2	1	3		
Grant, Landers	1	1	1		
Grant, John	2	2	3		
Chadbourne, Joseph	1		2		
Chadbourne, Seamon	1		2		
Hodsdon, Simon	1	1	1		
Goodwin, James	2	1	6	1	
Goodwin, James, Jr	1		2		
Tuttel, Job	2	1	7		
Pierce, Wm	1	3	2		
Spencer, Frithe	1	2	3		
Smith, Elisabeth			1		
Smith, Danl	1	4	3		
Keay, John	1	3	8		
Keay, Love	1	3	4		
Wintworth, Timothy	2	2	7		
Kenney, John	1	3	1		
Goodwin, Charles	2		3		
Clark, Charles	1	1	2		
Nute, Daniel	1	4	4		
Hodsdon, Moses	1	3	4		
Hodsdon, Ebenezer	1	1	2		
Heard, Ebenezer	3		2		
Hodsdon, Benja	1		3		
Hodsdon, Isreal	2		2		
Worster, Lemuel	2	2	4		
Worster, Lydia			3		
Worster, Samuel	1	2	5		
Lord, Nicholas	1		1		
Bigford, Aaron	1	1	3		
Foye, Elisabeth			1		
Foye, Moses	1	1	3		
Foye, John	1		2		
McCarral, James	3		4		
Downs, Joshua	3	2	3		
Noak, Thomas	2	2	3		
Calley, Samuel	1	1	2		
Hupper, Wm	2	1	1		
Hupper, John	3		5		
Roberts, Joshua	1	1	2		
Roberts, Joshua	1		1		
Lord, Ebenezer	1		4	1	
Lord, Samuel	1	3	3		
Whittier, Jacob	2		2		
Fall, Stephen	3	4	5		
Downs, Nathel	3	3	5		
Wallingford, John	1		1		
Smith, Jemima		1	1		
Worster, Phillip	1	3	3		
Grant, Edward	1	3	2		
Heard, Tristam	1		2		
Heard, Tristam, Jr	1	1	3		
Ricker, Moses	2	1	2		
Stanton, Benja	3	1	3		
Horsum, John	2		3		
Horsum, James	1	2	1		
Tibbets, Ephrim	1	2	2		
Tibbets, Ichabod	1		2		
Tibbets, Ichabod, Jr	1	3	4		
Rendal, Danl	1	1	2		
Hubbard, Joseph	2		5		
Tibbets, Jedediah	1	2	3		
Wintworth, Ricd	2	2	3		
Hanson, Ebenezer	3		1		
Jones, Eliphelet	1	2	4		
Nock, Zachariah	3		4		
Nock, Jona	1	1	5		
Sullivan, John	1	2	1		
Nock, Mary		1	2		
Nock, Joseph	1	1	1		
Ricker, Ephrim	1	1	2		
Clark, Eleazer	1	3	2		
Nock, Wm	1	3	4		
Libbey, Joseph	2	4	5		
Clark, Jona Denna	2	3	5		
Clark, John	1				
Clark, Stephen	1				
Clark, William	1	4	3		
Whitehouse, Danl	2	2	4		
Nock, Abigail			2		
Horsum, Wm	1		3		
Lord, Benja	1	2	3		
Butler, Nehemiah	1	2	1		
Lord, Mary	2	4	7		
Lord, Love			1		
Nock, Benja	1	1	2		
Nock, Moses	1	1	2		
Hamilton, Joseph	2		3		
Downs, Aaron	2	1	3		
Downs, Moses	1		1		
Ricker, Dolley	1		3		
Ricker, Abigail	1		2		
Abbot, John	1	1	5		
Downs, Daniel	2	1	3		
Hanson, Gersham	1	1	1		
Downs, Jedediah	2	1	3		
Wintworth, Ezekil	1	5	6		
Fall, Tristam	1	3	3		
Hanson, Elisabeth	1	1	2		
Yeaton, Jonathan	1	1	3		
Young, Abner	1		2		
Stanton, George	1	1	2		
Goodrige, Danl	3	2	4		
Hodsdon, Benja	1		2		
Gubtail, Benja	1	1	5		
Abbot, Joshua	2	2	2		
Gubtail, Moses	1	2	2		
Libbey, Paul	1		2		
Goodrige, John	2	2	2		
Norton, Wintworth	1		2		
Manning, Patrick	1		1		
Pray, Peter	1	3	4	3	
Gerrish, John	1	2	4	1	
Gerrish, Wm	1		1		
Wirthwill, John	1	1	4		
Hodsdon, Stephen	1	2	3		
Peters, Andrew	1	3	2		
Shorey, Unies			2		
Goodrige, Jedediah	2	1	2		
Norton, Nathel	1		5		
Goodrige, John	1	1	2		
Wintworth, Judah	1		1		
Wintworth, Samuel	2	4	4		
Gowel, John	3	2	6		
Welsh, Paul	2		4		

NAME OF HEAD OF FAMILY.	Free white males of 16 years and upward, including heads of families.	Free white males under 16 years.	Free white females, including heads of families.	All other free persons.	Slaves.
BERWICK TOWN—con.					
Nock, Disso	1	1	5		
Brown, Paul	2	4	8		
Goodwin, Elijah	1	2	1		
Pierce, Elisabeth			3		
Worster, George	4	4	2		
Ricker, Eliphelet	2	3	3		
Lord, Jeremiah	1	2	4		
Furbush, Saml	1	1	1		
Gubtail, James	1		2		
Abbot, Unis		1	2	1	
Clements, Samuel	3	3	5		
Spencer, Simeon	1	3	2		
Hodsdon, Thomas	3	3	5		
Appelby, Halley	3	3	4		
Butler, Moses	3	4	3		
Goodwin, Wm	3		3		
Goodwin, Elijah	2	2	2		
Lord, Humphrey	1	2	5		
Goodwin, Elisha	3	2	3		
Lord, William	1	2	3		
Seats, John	1		1		
Lord, Elisha	3	1	2		
Frost, James	1	2	2		
Frost, Stephen	2	1	4		
Spencer, Humpy	2	1	5		
Shorey, Wm	2	1	4		
Shorey, Miles	3	3	5		
Shorey, John	2		4		
Bracket, Samuel	2	2	2	1	
Bracket, James	2		2		
Stone, Paul	1		2		
Davis, John	1	1	4		
Nichols, Phebe	2	1	3		
Nichols, David	2	1	3		
Nichols, Samuel	1		1		
Frost, William	4	1	4		
Prime, Lydia	5	2	5		
Pray, Joseph	4	3	5	2	
Tibbetts, Ebenezer	3	1	4		
Stone, Paul	2	2	3		
Clements, Hannah			1	3	
Hutchins, Jeremiah	1	1	3		
Thompson, Allexr	1	3	5		
Brewster, Joseph	2		5		
Hamilton, Solomon	2	1	5		
Hamilton, Jonas	2	3	4		
Goodwin, Shipway	3	2	4		
Chadboun, Humpy, Esqr	2		2		
Cheek, Joseph	3		5		
Hobbs, Stephen	2	3	3		
Ricker, Mary			1	1	
Ricker, Tristam	3	3	6	1	
Stasey, Benja	1	1	6		
Ricker, Noah	3	2	3		
Roberts, Aaron	2	2	3		
Stone, John	1	4	6		
Rendal, Eliphelet	1	1	2		
Ricker, Richard	1	1	3		
Hussey, Ebenezer	2		3		
Hussey, George	1	3	2		
Hayes, Ichabod	2	1	6		
Hayes, Elijah	4	1	6		
Rendal, Jeremiah	1	2	3		
Ricker, Reuben	1	1	3		
Neal, Andrew	2	1	1		
Jenkins, Elijah	2	1	3		
Parington, Moses	3		3		
Warren, Gedion	2		3		
Chase, Thomas	1	4	2		
Buffum, Joshua	1		2		
Buffum, Saml	2	1	3		
Buffum, Joshua, Jr	2	7	4		
Rogers, Paul	3	2	3		
Hussey, Simeon	1	2	3		
Hussey, Elisabeth			3		
Neal, Johnson	1		3		
Neal, Wm	1	3	4		
Hussey, Bachelor	3	2	2		
Hussey, Joanna	1		2		
Verney, Jonathan	1	3	1		
Parker, Saml	1	3	4		
Waymoth, Francis	1	3	4		
Hubbard, Lydia	1		4		
Nowel, Jona	2	2	5		
Waymoth, Moses	1	2	2		
Chadbourne, Frances	1	4	3		
Goodwin, Thomas	2	1	1		
Adams, Benja	1	1	4		
Buffum, John	2		4		
Nowel, Mark	1	1	5		
Estees, Henery	3	1	3		
Waymoth, Benja	3		1		
Waymoth, Benja, Jr	1	3	2		
Rogers, Levi	3	3	5		

NAME OF HEAD OF FAMILY.	Free white males of 16 years and upward, including heads of families.	Free white males under 16 years.	Free white females, including heads of families.	All other free persons.	Slaves.
BERWICK TOWN—con.					
Dennet, John	3	1	4		
Jumkins, Jotham	1	3	5		
Talckut, Jona	3		3	1	
Parington, Benajah	2	1	2		
Massey, Woodbuary	1	1	1		
Morrel, Peter	1		1		
Morrel, Peter, Junr	3	1	9		
Morrel, Abraham	2	1	1		
Morrel, Josiah	1	1	2		
Neal, James	2	3	3		
Winchel, Job	1		3		
Morril, Peaster	1	4	4		
Hamilton, Abial	1				
Hamilton, Jona	1		2		
Tuttel, Ebenezer	2	4	3		
Johnson, Daniel	2	3	3		
Warren, Alden	3		4		
Cheek, John	1	2	3		
Wire, John	2		2		
Morrel, Isaac	2	1	3		
Goodwin, Saml	2		1		
Hubbard, Benja	1	5	4		
Gowen, Richard	1	2	1		
Hobbs, Thomas	5		5		
Hammet, Thomas	1	1	1		
Hammet, Thomas, Jr	1		3		
Abbot, Joseph	2	1	3		
Lord, Nicholas	3	2	5		
Morrel, Thomas	5	1	3		
Plummer, Patiance	1	1	3		
Morrel, David	2	4	6		
Morrel, Wintrop	2	4	6		
Billem, John	2	2			
Vicker, Ambros	1				
Whicher, Ricd	1		1		
Whicher, Foxwell	1	5	1		
Thurston, John	4	2	6		
staple, Joshua	2	1	2		
Buffum, Caleb	1	2	6		
Rendal, Joanna	2	3	5		
Hussey, Wm	3	3	4		
Twombley, Mercy	2	2	7		
Joy, James	1	3	4		
Chadbourne, Humpy	3	3	6		
Lord, Nathel	1	1	2		
Rendal, Stephen	1	3	3		
Verney, Timo	2	3	3		
Hussey, Stephen	1	2	4		
Hanson, Nicholas	1		3		
Hunsum, Reuben	1	1	2		
Hanson, James	1	2	3		
Staple, Stephen	1		1		
Hussey, Stephen, Jr	1	2	4		
Jebson, James	1	1	2		
Green, Sarah			1		
Hill, Joseph	2		3		
Hill, Amos	1		1		
Abbot, Thomas	2	1	2		
Abbot, Thos, Jr	2		2		
Ford, Robert	4	4	5		
Hill, Mark	1		4		
Libbey, Marthew	1	1	2		
Abbot, Wm	1	1	2		
Allen, Jacob	2	2			
Ford, John	4	1	6		
Estees, John	1	1	5		
Hunssom, Mark	1	4	1		
Grant, James	1		3		
Grant, Daniel	1		3		
Grant, Peter	1	3	3		
Grant, Thomas	1	1	2		
Gerrith, Isaac	1		2	1	
Whittom, Andrew	1	3	1		
Quint, Wm	1	3	3		
Quint, John	1		1		
Quint, John, Junr	1	1	4		
Quint, Joshua	1		1		
Quint, Joshua, Junr	1	1	4		
Quint, Daniel	1	2	5		
Bowen, Nathaniel	1		1		
Heard, John	1		1		
Appelby, Simeon	1	1	3		
Appelby, Levi	1		1		
Cheek, John	1	1	1		
Fall, John	1		1		
Neal, Stephen	1		1		
Staple, Peter	3	1	4		
Staple, Peter, Junr	1	2	1		
Frye, Rowlen	2	4	3		
Staple, Gedion	1	3	4		
Staple, John	2	2	1		
Wills, Benajah	1	1	1		
Mase, Andrew	2	1	3		
Cheek, Ricd	1	3	4		
Beel, Anna					

NAME OF HEAD OF FAMILY.	Free white males of 16 years and upward, including heads of families.	Free white males under 16 years.	Free white females, including heads of families.	All other free persons.	Slaves.
BERWICK TOWN—con.					
Robberts, John	2	6	4		
Brawn, George	1	4	3		
Brawn, Micael	1	2	2		
Staple, Ricd	1	4	2		
Frost, Wm	1	1			
Lord, Ichabod	1	3	3		
Lord, Elisha	1	5	1		
Estees, John	1	1	2		
Estees, Joseph	1	3	2		
Abbot, Stephen	3	3	4		
Hearl, Benja	1	2	2		
Hardison, Stephen	1	3	3		
Kean, Jona	1	3	1		
Goodwin, Adam	1		1		
Goodwin, Moses	1		1		
Furnald, Wm	1	1	3		
Clark, Thos	1	1	5		
Murry, Saml	2	5	3		
Hunssum, Saml	2		2		
Hunssum, Robt	1	2	1		
Libbey, Zebulon	1	2	5		
Clark, Wm	1		1		
Furnald, Hercelus	2	2	7		
Reed, Lydia	1	1	3		
Bracket, Miles	1	3	3		
Bracket, John	1		4		
Bracket, Moses	1		2		
Bracket, John, Junr	2	2	5		
Keay, John	1				
Tusker, Betty			3	1	
Heard, Thomas	2	3	4		
Hall, Wm	2	3	6		
Hall, Silas	1	2	4		
Heard, Silas	1	2	3		
Heard, Benja	1		1		
Stillens, Peter	1	2	6		
Stillens, Luke	1		1		
Stillens, Mary			2		
Remmick, Jacob	1	1	2		
Pray, Saml	1	2	1		
Pray, Saml, Junr	1	2	1		
Heard, Joseph	2	1	6		
Heard, Benja	1	2	7		
Staple, Josiah	2	3	5		
Rogers, George	2		2		
Furnald, Eleazer	3	1	3		
Estees, Danl	1		1		
Estees, Benja	1		1		
Chase, John	1	5	3		
Bracket, James	2	3	4		
Pray, Stephen	1	2	3		
Estees, Peter	1	3	3		
Pray, Eliphelet	2	2	5		
Hardison, Saml	1	4	3		
Hearl, John	1	1	4		
Hearl, Sarah			3		
Gubtail, Nathel	1		5		
Gubtail, Nat., Junr	2	3	5		
Starpole, Absalom	1	3	3		
Peirce, Stephen	1	1	4		
Libbey, John	2	3	4		
Smith, Sarah	1	2	4		
Furnald, Nathel	1	2	3		
Holmes, Joseph	1	3	5		
Goodwin, Adam	1	3	5		
Gubtail, Wm	1		5		
Stone, Jonathan	3	2	6		
Stillens, Samel	1	1	6		
Hodsdon, Joseph	1				
Goodrige, Joseph	2	2	6		
Grant, Joshua	2	7	5		
Manning, Sarah			1		
Dunnel, John	1				
Gubtail, Stephen	1	3	3		
Woodman, Mary	1	1			
Holmes, Wm	2		2		
Murry, Hannah	1		1		
Murry, Nathan	1		2		
Frost, John	2	4	3		
Hupper, Saml	4	1	2		
Cheek, Aaron	3	2	6		
Cheek, Thomas	3	3	6		
Cheek, Elizabeth			1		
Gubtail, Saml	2		1		
Gubtail, Saml, Junr	1		4		
Fogg, James	1	1	2		
Fogg, Mark	1	2	3		
Bracket, Mary		1	3		
Bracket, Samuel			1		
Andros, Olive	2	1	2		
Hardison, Thomas	2	1	1		
Gowen, John	2	1	3		
Pike, Jane	1		2		
Pike, Amos	1		2		
Libbey, Daniel	2		3		

YORK COUNTY—Continued.

BERWICK TOWN—con.

NAME OF HEAD OF FAMILY.	Free white males of 16 years and upward, including heads of families.	Free white males under 16 years.	Free white females, including heads of families.	All other free persons.	Slaves.
Andros, Elisha	1		3		
Andros, Joanna	1	1	2		
Merriam, Revd Marthew	1	2	4		
Marther, Wm	1		2		
Shorey, Jacob	2	1	2		
Shorey, John	1	2	2		
Yeaton, Phillip	2	1	3		
Woodsum, John	3		3		
Woodsum, Daniel	1		2		
Andros, John	1	1	1		
Fales, Joshua	1	1	2		
Fogg, Joseph	2	3	2		
Libbey, Nathaniel	3		3		
Morton, Bryant	3	2	5		
Edgerly, Richard	2	2	3		
Hearl, James	1		1		

BIDDEFORD TOWN.

NAME OF HEAD OF FAMILY.	Free white males of 16 years and upward, including heads of families.	Free white males under 16 years.	Free white females, including heads of families.	All other free persons.	Slaves.
Jordan, Rishworth, Jr	1	2	2		
Jordan, Saml	1	1	1		
Spring, Seth	2	3	5	1	
Stacey, George	1				
Hill, Jeremiah	4	1	8		
Thompson, Paul	2				
Porter, Aaron	2	2	6		
Caxey, Elizabeth			1		
Cummins, Donald	1	1	2		
Chadwick, John	2		2		
Hooper, Benja	4	1	3		
Hooper, Daniel	2	1	3		
Cobb, Matthew	3	2	3		
Foss, Lemuel	1	1	4		
Smith, Theos	2		1		
Storey, Abram	2	3	3		
Gray, Elisha	1	1	3		
Perkins, Stephen	1		2		
Long, Josiah	1		1		
Lee, John	2	1	3		
Dwinnel, Thos	1	3	3		
Gray, Aaron	3	2	3		
McGra, John	2	3	5		
Cole, Benja	2	2	6		
Haley, Willm	1	2	3		
Long, Josiah	3		3		
Dearborn, Jacob	1	1	1		
Perkins, Nathl	1	2	1		
Morrill, Reuben	2		2		
Townsend, Thos	2	4	5		
Thatcher, George	2	2	4		
Menton, Phinehas	2	3	5		
Tarbox, John	2	3	4		
Staples, Andw	3	3	5		
Tarbox, Joroa	1	1	1		
Bickford, Pierce	1	2	6		
Bickford, Doddiford	2	4	3		
Cole, Danl	1	1	2		
McIntire, Theodore	2	2	2		
Staples, James	1	1	2		
Gilpatrick, Robert	1		4		
Carlisle, James	2	1	3		
Currier, David	1		1		
Bragg, Robert	1	1	2		
Smith, Jere	1	2	2		
Hooper, Benja, Jr	3	4	3		
Cole, Elizabeth	2	2	4		
Staples, Benja	3	3	4		
Smith, Nicholas	4		3		
Hooper, Noah	2	1	6		
Simpson, Josiah	1	1	4		
Stimpson, Loammi	1	1	2		
Gilpatrick, Willm	2	1	4		
Emmery, Hannah		1	2		
Merrill, Joshua	1	1	5		
Rummery, Jona	2		2		
Rummery, Thos	2	2	2		
Clark, James	2	1	2		
Bradbury, Saml	1	2	1		
Bradbury, Moses	3		2		
Mason, Benja, Jr	1	1	3		
Moor (Widow)		3	3		
Gray (Widow)		1	1		
Smith, Theos, Junr	1		4		
Swett, John	1		2		
Bickford, Pierce, Jr	1	1	1		
Emery, Obed	2	1	3		
Emery, Ralph	1	1	2		
Rogers, Thos	1	1	2		
Dunham, Joseph	1	3	4		
Perkins, Joseph	1		4		
Morrill, Joseph	1	2	5		
Allen, Elisha	2		2		
Burton, Thos	1	1	3		
Nason, Benja	1	2	4		

BIDDEFORD TOWN—con.

NAME OF HEAD OF FAMILY.	Free white males of 16 years and upward, including heads of families.	Free white males under 16 years.	Free white females, including heads of families.	All other free persons.	Slaves.
Nason, Noah	1		1		
GilPatrick, Thos	4	1	5		
Gorden, Amos	4	5	3		
Smith, Ellison	6	2	1		
Harman, John	1	2	3		
Goodwin, Richard	2	4	1		
Smith, Joseph	1		2		
Mason, Benja	1		2		
Mason, Amos	1	1	1		
Morril, Tristram	1	1	2		
Dishon, Danl	1		2		
Richardson, George	1	1	3		
Wengate, Simon	1	1	3		
Emery, Ebenezer	1	2	3		
Patten, Robert	2	1	2		
Patten, Lydia			2		
Hill, Joseph	2	2	5		
Beeman, Saml	1	1	8		
Moore, Peletiah	1	2	5		
Roff, Saml	1	1	2		
Emery, Jona	2	3	2		
Proctor, Joseph	1	1	2		
Davis, Josiah	3		3		
Stacey, Ebenezer	4		6		
Hill, Benja	2	1	3		
Hill, Josiah	1	3	5		
Proctor, Benja	4	2	4		
Benson, John	2	1	3		
Benson, Henry	1		2		
Benson, Robert	1	2	2		
Trueworthy, John	1	2	5		
Webster, Revd Nathl	1	1	4		
GilPatrick, Christopher	1	3	7		
Stockpole, John	1		1		
Shepherd, Thos	1	1	1		
Tarbox, Elisabeth		1	1		
Haley, Abram	1		2		
GilPatrick, Dominicus	1	1	4		
Stevans, Joseph	1	1	1		
GilPatrick, Sarah			2		
Jones, Stephen	1		2		
Tarbox, Thos	2	4	3		
Tarbox, Abijah	1	2	4		
Jordan, Rishworth	1	1	3		
Jordan, Tristram	1	1	1		
Hill (Widow)	1	2	2		
Lasdel, Israel	1	1	2		
Joy, Stephen	1	4	2		
Harris, Saml	1	1	4		
Tarbox, Danl	2	4	2		
Davis, John	2	1	5		
Haley, Joseph	1		3		
Tongue, John	1	2	2		
Perkins, Nathl	1	2	4		
Burnham, Joseph	1	1	1		
Dier, Elizabeth	1		3		
Dier, John	2	1	7		
Smith, Jona	3	1	3		
Tarbox, Ezekiel	3	1	2		
Foy, John	1		1		
Haley, Silvester	2	2	2		5
Tarbox, Jona	1	2	3		
Fletcher, Pendleton	3	2	4		
Hussey, Paul	2		3		
Wetherby, Elisabeth	1	2	4		
Bettes, Jere	1		6		
Cole, Robert	2		2		
Cole, Ezra	2		4		
Stevenson, Willm	3	2	4		
Coffin, Elihu	1	1	1		
Bunker, Batcheldor	2	2	2		
Tarbox, Rufus	1	3	4		
Harman, Willm	1	1	4		
Curtis, Ephraim	4		5		
Thomas, David	5		2		
Davis, John	1	5	1		
Stockpole, Andw	2	4	1		
Tarbox, Benja	4	1	3		
Shepherd, Thos	1		4		
Haley, Joshua	1	1	8		
Davis, John G	2	1	5		
Smith, Andw	2	1	4		
McKessuk, Matthew	2	2	7		
McKessuk, Zebadiah	1	2	4		
Staples, John	1	2	4		
Hill, Joshua	3	2	5		
GilPatrick, Christopher	3		3		
Davis, Robert	1	1	2		
Davis, Saml	1		3		
Davis, Joseph	1	1	1		
Beel, Joseph	1	4	1		
Murch, Willm	3	1	6		
Smith, Roger	1	4	3		
Smith, Dominicus	1	1	4		

BROWNFIELD TOWNSHIP.

NAME OF HEAD OF FAMILY.	Free white males of 16 years and upward, including heads of families.	Free white males under 16 years.	Free white females, including heads of families.	All other free persons.	Slaves.
Brown, Henry Young	3	1	3	1	
Osgood, Joshua Bailey	2	2	3	1	
Ayer, Joseph	1	4	3		
Colby, Saml	1	3	1		
Choat, Ammi	1	2	3		
Walker, Supply	1	1	3		
Walker, Joseph	3	3	4		
Osgood, William	1		2		
Emery, Joseph	1		2		
Haley, John	1	1	1		
Long, Daniel	2	1	5		
Boswell, William	1	2	3		
Kimball, Francis	1	1	3		
Poor, Amos	1	2	3		
Stearns, Dudley	1	1	2		
Miller, John Bolt	1	1	3		
Spring, Josiah	1	1	2		
Howard, James	2	1	1		
Howard, Joseph	2	1	3		
Stickney, John	1	1	3		
Lane, John	3	1	3		
Watson, John	1	2	2		
Neazey, Thos	3	1	3		
Burbank, Benjn	2	1	1		
Burbank, Israel	1	2	4		
Osgood, Asa	1	1	2		

BROWNFIELD TOWNSHIP—IN THE GORE ADJOINING.

NAME OF HEAD OF FAMILY.	Free white males of 16 years and upward, including heads of families.	Free white males under 16 years.	Free white females, including heads of families.	All other free persons.	Slaves.
Warren, Ichabod	1	1	2		
Jellison, Thoms	1	3	2		
Porter, David	1	1	2		
Stiles, Ezra					

BUXTON TOWN.

NAME OF HEAD OF FAMILY.	Free white males of 16 years and upward, including heads of families.	Free white males under 16 years.	Free white females, including heads of families.	All other free persons.	Slaves.
Ayer, Peter	3	1	3		
Ayer, Timothy	2	3	6		
Woods, John	1	1	2		
Ayer, Ebenr	1	1	1		
Ayer, Benja	2	1	4		
Moor, Capt. Hugh	4	2	6		
Thompson, Thos	1	3	4		
Smith, John	2		3		
Smith, Saml	1	3	2		
Lamb, Richd	1	3	4		
Irish, Willm	1	1	2		
Whitney, Stephn	1	1	4		
Kimball, Danl	1	1	1		
Thomes, Thos	1		2		
Thomas, Danl	1		1		
Hopkinson, Caleb	2	1	3		
Sands, John	1	3	2		
Hopkins, Benja	1		3		
Sawyer, Barnabas	1		3		
Emery, John	1	3	3		
Watson, ——*	1	4	4		
White, John	2	1	6		
Atkinson, Joseph	1	1	4		
Harmon, Pelatiah	1	4	2		
Kimball, Nathan	1	1	1		
Elwell, Joseph	2	2	5		
Whitney, Sarah		1	3		
Edward, Stephn	2				
Bab, Peter	2		1		
Smith, John, Junr	2	4	3		
Harmon, Josiah	1	2	2		
Davis, Wm	1	3	2		
Smith, Wm	1	4	3		
Thompson, Jno	1	2	8		
Edgley, Jno	1	3	2		
Whitton, Jno	1	3	2		
Emery, Charles	1		2		
Whitton, Richd	1	1	2		
Robison, Jno	1	1	4		
Graffam, Uriah	1	1	4		
Berry, Isaac	1	1	4		
plaisted, Roger	1	2	5		
Berry, Jona	2		3		
Millican, Joel	1	1	3		
Tole, Phinehas	1	3	3		
Sawyer, Jno	2	3	6		
Pennell, Thos	2	4	6		
Hanson, Phineas	2	3	6		
Billings, Enoch	1		2		
Lane, Jno	1		2		
Beard, Saml	1	2	4		
Andrews, Wm	1	2	1		
Woodman, Joshua	1		1		
Cole, Jno	1	4	4		
Gould, Isaac	1	1	1		
Dennett, Cadmiel	2		1		
Atkinson, Thos	2	2	3		

* Illegible.

YORK COUNTY—Continued.

BUXTON TOWN—con.

NAME OF HEAD OF FAMILY.	Free white males of 16 years and upward, including heads of families.	Free white males under 16 years.	Free white females, including heads of families.	All other free persons.	Slaves.
Whitney, Jonª	1	3	2		
Thompson, Theodore	2	2	1		
Thompson, Samˡ	1	1	3		
Jordan, Clemᵗ	1	3	5	1	
Rounds, Joseph	1	3	4		
Rounds, Mark	1	3	2		
Lewis, Abijah	3	1	4		
Eldridge, Wintrop	1	1	1		
Cresey, John	2	3	6		
Adams, Stephⁿ	1	1	1		
McDonald, Jnº	1	2	5		
McDonald, Robᵗ	3	3	3		
Whitney, Isaac	2		3		
March, Danˡ	3		8		
Sands, Ephᵐ	1		2		
Sands, James	1	3	4		
Harding, Samˡ	1		2		
Adams, Willᵐ	2	3	2		
Emery, Danˡ	1	2	2		
Dunn, Nathˡ	1	2	3		
Libby, Francis	1	2	3		
Ward, Danˡ	1	2	1		
Emery, James	2	2	2		
Haines, Benjⁿ	2				
Jose, John	3	2	5		
Elwell, Wᵐ	1		1		
Rounds, Samˡ	3	3	3		
Murch, James	1	2	2		
Edwards, Samˡ	1	2	6		
Decker, Joshua	2	5	3		
Harmon, Dorⁿᵉˢ	1		2		
Davis, Thºˢ	1	2	2		
Harmon, Joel	1	3	2		
Clay, Danˡ	1	3	4		
Robinson, Jnº	1	3	2		
Emery, Benjª	2		3		
Libby, Elisha	1	2	4		
Berry, Jonª, Junʳ	1	3	3		
Coolbroth, Jnº	2	2	1		
Harmon, Nathˡ	1	2	4		
Millican, Isaac	1	2	3		
Graffam, Increase	2		3		
Rice, Nathˡ	2	2	2		
Ridley, Ebenʳ	1	2	5		
Sawyer, Jabez	4	3	5		
Hanson, Moses	3	5	4		
Elden, Jnº, Junʳ	1	2	5		
Billings, Gershom	2	1	4		
Woodman, Jamˢ	2	3	5		
Cole, Jnº, Junʳ	1	4	1		
Bradbury, Joshᵇ	1	4	3		
McKenny, Jonª	2		1		
Woodman, Jerᵇ	1		2		
Atkinson, Thºˢ, Jr	1		3		
Dennett, Jnº	1	1	3		
Prescott, Stepⁿ	1	1	4		
Atkinson, Jnº	2		2		
Palmer, Richᵈ	3	4	6		
Hopkinson, Jnº	4	4	1		
Leavitt, Samˡ	3	1	4		
Kimball, Joshua	2	1	9	1	
Woodman, Nathˡ	1	3	1		
Andrews, Abel	1		2		
Toworgy, John	2	1	2		
Roberts, Joseph	1	2	3		
Elden, Gibeon	1	3	3		
Merrill, Jnº	1		3		
Merrill, Samˡ, Junʳ	1	2	3		
Hobson, Joseph	1	2	1		
Boynton, Danˡ	2		1		
Garland, Jnº	1	1	5		
Lane, Danˡ	1	1	4		
Brooks, Samˡ	2	3	1		
Woodman, Stepⁿ	1		5		
Haines, Benjⁿ	1	2	4		
Eaton, Jnº	2	4	3		
Hunscomb, Wᵐ	1		8		
Rand, Michˡ	1	1	2		
Hunscomb, Jnº	1	3	3		
Steele, Jnº	1		4		
Woodman, Ephᵐ	1	2	1		
Cutts, Samˡ	1	4	5		
Sands, Ephᵐ, Junʳ	2	4	6		
Boynton, Jnº	2	3	3		
Bradbury, Elijah	1	3	5		
Goodwin, Joseph	1	3	2		
Woodsom, Michˡ	2		1		
Bradbury, Jacob, Esqʳ	3	2	3		
Kimball, Joshua, Jun	1	1	1		
Mason, Joseph	1	4	2		
Cole, Wᵐ	1	1	3		
Millican, Nathˡ	2	2	4		
Donnell, Benjⁿ	2		2		
Donnell, Benjⁿ, Jun	3	3	3		

BUXTON TOWN—con.

NAME OF HEAD OF FAMILY.	Free white males of 16 years and upward, including heads of families.	Free white males under 16 years.	Free white females, including heads of families.	All other free persons.	Slaves.
Appleton, Jnº	2		2		
Bradbury, Samˡ	1	1	1		
Woodman, Joshᵇ, 2nd	2	2	8	1	
Parker, Chase	2	3	3		
Bradbury, Benjⁿ	2	5	3		
Bradbury, Thºˢ	1	1	3		
Leavitt, Thºˢ	1	1	1		
Newcomb, Jnº	3	3	4		
Dunnell, Joseph	1	3	5		
Knight, Edmund	2		4		
Hill, Nathˡ	3	4	7		
Sands, Samˡ	2		7		
Norton, James	2	3	4		
Newcomb, Joshª	1	2	1		
Trundy, Jnº	1		1		
Woodman, Joshª, Junʳ	1	2	1		
Patten, Hannah			2		
Dearborn, Jacob	1	1	7		
Billings, Joshᵇ	1	1	2		
Martin, Robᵗ	1	2	3		
Whitney, Amos	1	5	2		
Hancock, Jnº	2	1	2		
Cole, Nathˡ	1				
Elwell, Benjⁿ	2		1		
Martin, Jonª	1				
Bean, Elizabᵗʰ			2		
Hopkinson, Joses	1	1	7		
Gray, Cadwallader	3	1	2		
Woodman, Jnº	2	1	6		
Phinney, Jnº	1		1		
Gutterige, Aaron	1		1		
Roberts, Job	2		4		
Elden, Jnº	1	1	3		
Merrill, Samˡ	1		2		
Seamman, James	1		1		
Hobson, Samˡ	1	1	2		
Atkinson, Joshᵇ, Junʳ	1		2		
Taylor, Joseph	1	1	1		
Knights, Samˡ	2	1	7		
Hancock, Wᵐ	1	1	4		
Hazelton, Timº	3		4		
Hovey, Samˡ	1		4		
Merrill, Humphy	1	5	5		
Elden, Nathan	2	2	5		
Ridley, David	1	1	2		
Holmes, Samˡ	1	2	3		
Steele, Peter	1	1	2		
Ridley, Sarah	1		3		
Coffin, Revᵈ Paul	3	2	7		
Andrews, Elizaᵗʰ		2	2		
Muchemore, Jnº	1	1	3		
Leavitt, Danˡ	3	1	8		
Palmer, Stepⁿ	4	1	3		
Woodsom, Abiath	2	4	3		
Brooks, Isaiah	3	2	3		
Emery, Thºˢ	2	1	4		
Kimball, Jnº	3	1	3		
Hill, Samˡ	1	1	1		
Lord, Nathˡ	2	2	7		
Brooks, Robᵗ	2		3		
Rankin, Joseph	1	2	5		
Appleton, Danˡ	1	3	1		
Bradbury, Jabez	2	1	4		
Bradbury, Wᵐ	2	1	7		
Lane, Jabez	2	4	4		
Boothby, Brice	2	2	5		
Wentworth, Ebenⁿ	2	4	3		
Merrill, Abel	2	2	3		
Flood, Henry	1	4	2		
Wingate, Snell	2	4	3		
Boynton, Wᵐ	4	2	4		
Leavitt, Joshᵇ	4	2	3		
Hill, Danˡ	1	3	4		
Rolf, Jnº	3	1	3		
Owen, Jnº	1	2	8		
Newcomb, Solᵐ	1	3	1		
Smith, Solᵐ	1		2		
Harmon, Thºˢ	1	2	3		
Rounds, Lemˡ	1	1	4		
Hutchins, Joshª	1	4	1		
Elwell, Benjⁿ, Jun	1		2		
Thomas, Joshᵇ	1	1	6		
Smith, Thºˢ	2	5	2		
Clay, Richᵈ	1		2		
Woodman, Benjⁿ	1	3	4		
Elwell, Benjⁿ	1	2	3		
Hood, Edmᵈ	1		1		

COXHALL TOWN.

NAME OF HEAD OF FAMILY.	Free white males of 16 years and upward, including heads of families.	Free white males under 16 years.	Free white females, including heads of families.	All other free persons.	Slaves.
Brock, William	1	3	3		
Clarke, thomas	1	2	3		
goodwin, Jonathan	2	3	4		
Clarke, John	1		2		

COXHALL TOWN—con.

NAME OF HEAD OF FAMILY.	Free white males of 16 years and upward, including heads of families.	Free white males under 16 years.	Free white females, including heads of families.	All other free persons.	Slaves.
goodwin, Aaron	1	3	1		
Dame, Isachar	1	1	2		
Bracket, Nathaniel	1	3	4		
Roberts, Jeremiah	3	4	4		
Clarke, John, junʳ	1	2	3		
Clarke, William	1	1	2		
Goodwin, Amaziah	1		3		
Chadburn, Paul	3	4	4		
Ricker, George	1	4	3		
Ricker, Mark	1	2	3		
Ricker, Phinehas	1	1	2		
Nocks, Sylvanus	1	1	2		
Nocks, Reuben	1		3		
Ford, Paul	2	2	7		
Chadburn, Simeon	1	2	4		
tibbets, Joseph	1	3	3		
Lord, Elias	1		1		
Gray, Nehemiah	2	2	5		
Robberts, Joseph	1	4	4		
Grant, Benjamin	1	2	1		
Roberts, Samuel	1	3	3		
Grant, Alexander	1		1		
Goodwin, Jeremiah	1	2	1		
Grant, Silas	1	4	2		
Swanson, Robert	1	2	1		
Straw, Daniel	1	2	6		
Gould, Samuel	1	1	2		
Gould, Ezra	2		1		
Sands, James	2	3	2		
Low, Nathaniel	1	2	1		
Low,* —w	1		1		
Allen, Joseph	1		1		
Yeaton, Richard	1	4	5		
Foster, John	1	1	3		
Downs, Jershon	1	3	3		
Lasdale, Caleb	1	2	2		
Allen, John	1	1	3		
Lasdale, Asa	1	2	3		
Gutridge, Josiah	2		1		
Low, thomas	1	3	3		
Rayment, Samuel	2		3		
Low, John, Esqʳ	2		4		
Sands, thomas	1	2	4		
Downs, John	1		2		
Gray, Andrew	1	1	1		
Rayment, James	1	2	3		
Glass, John	1	2	3		
Emery, Daniel	1	1	3		
Quint, William	1	2	5		
Gutridge, John	1	2	2		
Roberts, Joseph, junʳ	1	3	2		
Andrews, John	1	2	3		
Smith, Charles	1	3	2		
Barker, John	1	1	2		
Bartlet, Benoni	1	2	2		
Waymouth (Widw)		2	2		
Jellison, John	1	2	2		
Clarke, Daniel	1	3	3		
Gould, thomas	1	4	2		
Hambleton, Elijah	1	1	3		
Davis, Reuben	2	3	2		
larabee, Tempʳ (Widw)	2	1	3		
Wakefield, Israel	1	3	3		
Burnham, Benjamin	1	1	1		
Goodwi—*, Nathaniel	1	(*)	(*)		
And——*, Stephen	(*)	(*)			
Hill, Volantine	3	2	5		
Goodwin, Benjamin	2	3	3		
Goodwin, Mark	1	2	4		
Hill, John	1	3	1		
Day, Abraham	1	1	3		
Dallop, Jonathan	3	2	3		
Drew, Elisha	2				
Hoof, thomas	2		5		
bridges, Moses	1	2	1		
Kimball, Daniel	3		4		
Burbank, John	1		3		
Smith, James	1	4	3		
Kimball, Ezra	1	4	5		
Kimball, Heber	1	1	3		
thomson, Joseph	1	3	2		
Eldridge, Frances	1	4	1		
Littlefield, Aaron	1	2	1		
Boston, Jonathan	1	3	5		
White, Joseph	1		1		
Huent (Widw)	1	2	2		
White, Charles	1	2	4		
Shackley, Joseph			3		
Currier, Isaac	1	2	2		
Going, Samuel	1		2		
Shackford, Paul	1		2		
Harris, Samuel	1	2	5		
Stimpion, Stephen, junʳ	1	2	1		
Evani, Benjamin	2	3	4		

*Illegible.

YORK COUNTY—Continued.

COXHALL TOWN—con.

NAME OF HEAD OF FAMILY.	Free white males of 16 years and upward, including heads of families.	Free white males under 16 years.	Free white females, including heads of families.	All other free persons.	Slaves.
Kimball, Caleb	1		2		
taylor, Joseph	1	3	4		
Smith, Elisha	1		1		
Smith, Elisha, jun	1	2	4		
littlefield, Elisha	2	3	3		
Drown, ——*	3	2	4		
Emmons, ——*	1	2	5		
Emmons, Obediah	2	3	5		
Stimpson, Stephen	1	4	5		
Burk, Joanna (Widw)		1	2		
Burk, Joseph	1	2			
Emmons, John	2	1	4		
Emmons, Samuel	2	1	4		
Stephens, Benjamin	1	1	5		
Emmons, Samuel, jun	1	1	1		
Littlefield, Joel	1	1	2		
Straw, William	1	1	4		
Cousins, John	3	3	1		
Dennit, Ebenezer	1	1	3		
Roberts, Peter	1	2	3		
Murphy, thomas	1	3	3		
Cousins, Benjamin	1		1		
Hill, Charles	1	4	1		
Gillpatrick, Joseph	1	1	3		
Going, Jane (Widw)		1	1		
Waterhouse, John	1	2	5		
taylor, Jerimiah	1	1	3		
Dennet, Joseph	1	3	2		
Waterhouse, Jacob	1	1	3		
Hanscomb, Gideon	1	1	3		
Martin, Samuel	1	2	4		
Wakefield, Gibbins	1	2			
lord, Samuel	2		4		
Lord (Widw)		1	1		
Martin, William	1	3			
Martin, Lewis	1	1	2		
Cousins, Ebenezer	1	2	1		
Cousins, Benjamin	1	1	2		

FRANCISBOROUGH PLANTATION.

NAME OF HEAD OF FAMILY.	Free white males of 16 years and upward, including heads of families.	Free white males under 16 years.	Free white females, including heads of families.	All other free persons.	Slaves.
Clark, Mr. Benja	3	4	2		
Barker, Noah	1	3	3		
Barker, Ebenezer	2	2	5		
Chadbourn, Levi	2	3	2		
Chadbourn, Wm	1	1	2		
Perry, James	2	1	9		
Barker, Nathel	1	1	3		
Perry, Saml	1	1	2		
Hebbert, Joseph	1	3	3		
Estman, Ezekil	2	1	2		
Pendexter, Paul	1		1		
Eastman, Obediah	1		2		
Sargent, Chase	2	3	3		
Merril, Enoch	2	1	5		
Treadwel, Marsters	1	2	2		
Waymoth, James	1	1	3		
Holmes, James	2		2		
Durgan, John	1	2	5		
Pendextor, Henery	3	1	2		
Sherburn, Susannah			2		
Lang, John	2	2	2		
Smith, Theophelus	1		1		
Pike, Bennet	1	1	1		
Pike, John	1	1	2		
Cheek, Isaac	1	1	3		
Cole, Obediah	2	2	5		
Cole, Robt	1	3	3		
Hammons, Edmund	2	3	4		
Cole, Arzael	1	3	2		
Shurban, Saml	1				
Gilpatrick, John	1	2			
Grafton, Unite	1		2		
Shute, John	1	1	4		
Day, Wm	3	3	4		
Day, Stephen	1		2		
Davis, Josiah	1	2	4		
Trafton, Charles	1		4		
Tynan, Ricd	1		4		
Pendextor, Eliab	1	1	3		
Estes, Benja	1		5		
Estes, Jona	1		2		
Linscot, Isaac	4	4	6		
Barns, Abram	1	2	5		
Gray, George	1		2		
Parkins, Daniel	1		1		
McKissek, John	1	2	5		
McKisseck, Frances	1		1		
Morrison, Samuel	1	2	3		
Gubtail, Daniel	1	5	4		
Sawyer, Wm	2		4		
Cole, Henery	1	1	1		
Wormwood, James	1	1	4		

FRANCISBOROUGH PLANTATION—con.

NAME OF HEAD OF FAMILY.	Free white males of 16 years and upward, including heads of families.	Free white males under 16 years.	Free white females, including heads of families.	All other free persons.	Slaves.
Gray, John	1	2	6		
Norton, Benja	2	2	1		
Harmon, Samuel	1		7		
Jewel, David	1	1	3		
Jewel, John	1				
Barker, Ezra	1				
Johnson, Simon	1		3		
Chadbourn, John	1	3	5		
Chadbourn, Joshua	2		4		
Allen, Joseph	1	1	3		
Barns, Timothy	2	1	3		
Chadbourn, Wm	1	3	2		
Storer, Wm	1	2	2		
Storer, Benja	1	3	1		
Thompson, Joseph	2	2	4		
Thompson, Isaac	1		2		
Hart, Aaron	1	1	4		
Neal Andrew	1	3	2		
Shurban, Andrew	1				
Hubbard, Asa	1				
Hubbard, Heard	1				
Grant, Daniel	1	1	2		
Estes, Ricd	1				
Cussens, Joseph	1	2	2		

FRYEBURGH TOWN.

NAME OF HEAD OF FAMILY.	Free white males of 16 years and upward, including heads of families.	Free white males under 16 years.	Free white females, including heads of families.	All other free persons.	Slaves.
Osgood, James	2	4	5	1	
Page, Phillip	2	1	4		
Ames, Moses	2		4		
Allen, Wright	1	1	3		
Merrill, Nathl	3	4	7		
Buck, Asa	1	1	2		
Evans, David	3		2		
Bean, Joseph	1	1	1		
Swan, Caleb	1		3		
Swan, Joseph Frye	2	1	3		
Colby, Asa	1		2		
Gammage, John	1	1	4		
Fessenden, Ebenezer	1	3	5		
Hutchins, Jonathan	1		1		
Frye, Simon	2	3	4		
Fifield, John	1	1	1		
Fessenden, William	1	5	6		
Dresser, Jonathan, Jr	1		4		
Dresser, Jonathan	3		4		
Frye, Richd	1		3		
Frye, Saml	3	1	4		
Evans, John	2	1	1		
Bragdon, Thoms	1		2		
Abbot, Isaac	2		2		
Abbot, Isaac, Junr	1	2	2		
Abbot, Simeon	1		1		
Langdon, Paul	1		4		
Walker, Ezekiel	3	4	3		
Sterling, John	1		3		
Chandler, Dan'l	2	1	2		
Kimball, William	2	2	2		
Farington, John	2	2	4		
Gordon, Henry	2		3		
Gordon, John	1	1	4		
Thoms, William	1	1	3		
Parker, James	1	2	3		
Bradley, Abraham	1	2	3		
Day, Moses	3	2	2		
Day, Ebenezer	1	4	5		
Knight, Stephen	2		1		
Farington, Daniel	1	1	3		
Farington, Putnum	2	3	5		
Frye, Nathl	1	2	2		
Wiley, Benjamin	2	5	2		
Wiley, William	2		3		
Eastman, Richard	3		2		
Eastman, Daniel	1	1	2		
Webster, John	2	2	5		
Carter, Hubbard	2		2		
Carter, Ezra	1	3	6		
Shirley, Edward	2	5	3		
Hardy, David	1	2	3		
Carlton, Edward	1	3	5		
Carlton, Woodman	1	3	4		
Hutchins, Nathaniel	3	1	1		
Winslow, Phebe		2	1		
Farington, Stephen	1		1		
Walker, Isaac	3		1		
Kelley, Edmund	1		1		
Walker, Samuel	3	2	5		
Howard, William	1	1	3		
Wyman, Jonas	1	2	3		
Stevens, John	3		3		
Stevens, John, Junr	1	1	2		
Gordon, Hugh	1	2	4		
Charles, John	2	5	5		
Walker, Nathl	1	2	4		

FRYEBURGH TOWN—con.

NAME OF HEAD OF FAMILY.	Free white males of 16 years and upward, including heads of families.	Free white males under 16 years.	Free white females, including heads of families.	All other free persons.	Slaves.
Richardson, Zebulon	2	3	4		
Charles, Abner	3	1	3		
Walker, Joseph	1	1	3		
Ames, John	1		2		
Charles, Saml	2	2	6		
Chandler, Joseph	1	2	2		
Kilgore, Trueworthy	1	3	3		
Kilgore, Benjn	1	4	1		
Walker, John	3	1	3		
Whiting, John	1		2		
Pattee, Moses	2	2	4		
Barker, John	4	2	5		
McIntyre, John	2	3	3		
Wilham, Morris	1	2	7		
Lord, James	2	2	3		
Bemus, Thaddeus	1	1	3		
McKean, James	3	3	3		
Hasetine, Barnes	1	3	3		
Evans, William	1	1	1		
Bean, Thomas	1		1		
Eatton, Sarah	1	1	2		

HIRAM TOWN.

NAME OF HEAD OF FAMILY.	Free white males of 16 years and upward, including heads of families.	Free white males under 16 years.	Free white females, including heads of families.	All other free persons.	Slaves.
Burbank, Benjn	1	1	2		
Bucknell, John	1		1		
Bucknell, Simeon	1	2	3		
Ayer, John	2	3	5		
Barker, Thomas	2		2		
Bucknell, John, Jn	1	1	5		
*——oston, Daniel	1	4	2		
Ryan, Curtis	1	3	2		
Dyer, Bickford	1	1	1		
Goald, Aaron	1	2	4		
Haywood, Lemuel	1				
McLucus, John	1	3	3		
Clements, John	1	1	1		
Midget, David	2	3	3		
*——sman, Solomon	1	3	1		
Libby, Jonathan	1		2		
Libby, Stephen	1	2	2		
Libby, John	2		2		

KITTERY TOWN.

NAME OF HEAD OF FAMILY.	Free white males of 16 years and upward, including heads of families.	Free white males under 16 years.	Free white females, including heads of families.	All other free persons.	Slaves.
Petegrow, William	2		3		
Spotzeswell, Dorothy			4		
Parsons, John	1		4		
Hayley, Joel	2	2	6		
Cole, Eli	1	3	4		
Johnston, James	2		3		
Johnston, James, Jur	1	2	2		
Lewis, Simon	1	2	6		
Lewis, Thos H	2	3	3	1	
Witham, Tobias	1	2	5		
Baker, Joseph	1		1		
Lewis, Mary	1	1	3	1	
Booker, Jacob	2	1	3		
Muggaridge, Thoms	1	2	3		
Curtis, Joseph	1		4		
Curtis, Phildelph	1		2		
Pope, David	1		2		
Rogers, William	2		2		
Pope, Dorcas			2		
Briez, Robert	1	4	3		
Pickenail, James	2	1	2		
Frost, Simon	1	1	2		
Furnald, Capn Denes	1	2	4		
Neal, Samuel	1	2	4	1	
Furnald, Coln Andw P	2	2	4		
Libby, Reuben	2	1	4		
Paul, Capn Saml	1	1	2		
Hunscum, Moses	1	1	2		
Tetherly, John	1	1	2		
Hunscum, Nathn	1	1	2		
Dame, Joseph	1	2	1		
Goodwin, Benjn	1		3		
Cato, Colten	1		3		
Staple, Nathan	1	1	4		
Forguson, Eliza			1		
Black, Henry	2		2		
Black, James	1		2		
Black, Henry, Jun	1	2	3		
Witham, James	1	1	3		
Furnald, Mary	2		2	2	
Black, Margery			3		
Laton, Major Saml	4	1	4		
Frost, John, Esqr	2	3	4		
Frost, Joseph	1	1	2		
Sherbourn, Henry	2	1	2	1	
Roberts, Jack					5
Patch, John	1		2		
Marsh, Amy			1		
Black, Cathrine			2		

*Illegible.

NAME OF HEAD OF FAMILY.	Free white males of 16 years and upward, including heads of families.	Free white males under 16 years.	Free white females, including heads of families.	All other free persons.	Slaves.
KITTERY TOWN—con.					
Moral, Patience	1	1	4		
Jordan, Nathn	1		1		
Muggarage, William	1	1	4		
Hutchins, Joseph	1		1		
Wason, Nathn	1	1	4		
Gullison, John	1		1		
Hutchens, John	1		3		
Leavitt, John	1	1	4		
Norton, Temperence	1	1			
Perry, Willm	1		1		
Brier, Nichos	1	1	3		
Norton, Saml	1	1	4		
Ingerson, Richd	1		7		
Moore, Saml	1	1	1		
Gullison, Deacn Jos	1	1	2		
Gullison, Saml	1		1		
Brier, Moses	1	1	3		
Gullison, Wm	1	3	2		
Weeks, Abrahm	1	1	1		
Moore, Edwd	1	1	2		
Perrey, Eunice	1		2		
Chisom, Hannah		1	2		
Brier, Saml	1		2		
Fenix, Abigail	3		2		
Trott, John	2		3		
Weeks, John	2	2	5		
Muggarige, John	1	1	6		
Stevens, John	2	2	3		
Fletcher, Saml	2		3		
Billings, Ephm	2	2	3		
Bellamy, John	2		2		
Westcoat, Isaac	1		2		
Billings, Benjn	1	1	2		
Billings, Saml	1	1	1		
Mitchel, Mary	1	1	7		
Mitchel, John	2	2	4		
Mitchel, Lucy		1	2		
Mitchel, Sarah		1	5		
Ryley, Mary	1		1		
Perkins, Magery	1	1	3		
Dearing, Clemt	2		2		
Mitchel, Saml	2	2	4		
Mitchel, James	1		3		
Williams, Amos	1	2	2		
Williams, Johan			3		
Garish, Wm	1		1		
Billings, Jas., Jur	1	1	6		
Billings, Joseph	2		3		
Cox, Clement	1	1	3		
Page, Edwd	1	1	4		
Furnald, Thos	1		2		
Fowler, Susanh	1	1	3		
Grace, Benjn	1	2	1		
Todd, Wm	2		3		
Davis, Elemuel	2	3	2		
Chancy, Charles, Esqr	3	1	4		
Chatman, Mary	1		2		
Welch, David	1	1	3		
Weeks, Lucy		1	1		
Fenix, John	1		4		
Hayley, Ebenz	1		2		
Perkins, Thos	1	2	2		
Hutchens, Lydia			2		
Hayley, Joseph	1	2	2		
Hayley, John	1		2		
Hayley, Robt	1	3	3		
Lewis, Dimond	1	4	3		
Lewis, Peter	2		6		
Wilson, Joseph	1	2	3		
Wilson, Thos	1	1	3		
Hutchins, Hannah	2		2		
Weeks, Nicks	3		6		
Frunald, Joel	2	4	6		
Cutt, Edwd, Esqr	2	3	4		
Cutt, Deacn Thos	1		1		
Cutt, Robt	4	3	4		
Cutt, Capn Thos	3		3		
Leach, Ebenz	3		2		
Leach, Nathn	1	1	3		
Harvy, William	1		3		
Weeks, Capn Saml	2		2		
Weeks, John	2	1	3		
Ellis, Laurance	2		3		
Grover, Martha	1		3		
Litchfield, Revd Joseph	1	2	4		
Hammond, Edmond	1	1	7		
Chase, Thos	2	1	3		
Leach, Benj	1	2	5		
Lewis, Enoch	1		3		
Cutt, Thos	1	2	3		
Oats, Sarah			2		
Cutt, Noah	1		4		
Pickernail, Wm	1	2	3		
KITTERY TOWN—con.					
Furnald, Wm	1	1	6		
Hammond, Deacn Saml	2	1	3		
Rogers, John, Junr	1	1	3		
Nutter, Jacob	1	2	6		
Goodwin, Danl	2	6	8		
Kingburg, Joseph	2	1	4		
Emory, Isaac	1	1	1		
Odehorn, Danl	3	2	5	1	
Jordan, John	1	1	3		
Rate, Miriam	2		1		
Johnson, Rebeck			3		
Johnston, Noah	1	4	5		
Rate, Cap. Wm	1	4	3	1	
Frost, Simon, Senr	1	1	4		
Frost, Abigl	1	1	3		
Johnston, Joseph	1	4	3		
Nason, Elizh			6	2	
Noulton, John	1	1	1		
Neal, James	3	1	1		
Frizzle, Mary			(*)		
Weeks, Joseph	1	1	2		
Weeks, Pellenak	1		3		
Henney, Sarah		1	2		
Smart, Hannah			3		
Pratt, John	1	1	1		
Clinton, ——*	1		2		
Dearing, Roger	2	1	2		
Landfar, Sam	1	1	2		
Mitchel, Elizh			1		
Mitchel, Roger	1	2	5		
Dearing, Capn Wm	1		1		
Odehorn, Saml	1		4		
Toby, Joseph	1	1	3		
Webber, Edwd	2	1	2		
Todd, John	1		2		
Stephens, John	1		1		
Hubbard, Phillip	1	3	2		
Moore, Capn Wm	3		2		
Moore, Capn Jno	1	1	4		
Shackford, Capn Jon	1	3	2		
Stephens, Moses	1	3	2		
Todd, Elizh		1	3		
Underwood, Capn Job	1		2		
Stephens, Jno	2	1	3		
Perkins, Sarah		1	2		
Furnald, Josha	3	2	3		
Welch, David	1	2	3		
Hayley, Saml	2	1	3		
Parsons, Richd	1	2	4		
Follet, Mercy			1		
Moore, Joshua	1		3		
Moore, Elizh	1	1	2		
Hutchans, Pelth	1	2	2		
Lampher, Johana			2		
Dayly, Sarah		1	2		
Wallingford, Abigl		4			
Stocker, John	1		2		
Chambers, James	1	1	4		
Sambo (Black)				4	
Smallcorn, Capn Saml	2	1	4		
Weeks, Elihu	3		3		
Brier, Josiah	2		3		
Furnald, John	1	4	5		
Stephens, Revd Benjn	2		1		
Parhook, Ebzah	1		3	1/2	
Sessoro (Black)				1/2	
Mendham, Wm	1	2	2		
Cutt, Richd, Esqr	3	1	5		
Norton, Saml	1		5		
Garish, Joseph	3	1	8		
Sowards, Richd	2	1	4		
Todd, Willm	1		2		
Billins, Dan	1	2	(*)		
Cutt, Capn Jos	2		(*)		
Lollar, John	1		3		
Garish, Johanna	1	1	3		
Garish, John	2		2		
Frost, Ellot	2	1	2		
Bartlet, John H	1	1	1	1	
Bartlet, Danl	2	2	3		
Bartlet, Jeremh	1	5	4		
Tetherly, Willm	1	3	3		
Sympson, Zebediah	1	5	2		
Emory, Saml	2	1	3		
Emory, Danl, Junr	1	2	1		
Emory, Nathn	2	4	4		
Emory, Steven	2		2		
Emory, Saml	1		2		
Emory, Saml, Junr	1		4		
Emory, Simon, Junr	1	1	4		
Nason, Jonathan	1		1		
Davis, Suanna		1	5		
Adams, Danl	1	1	3		
KITTERY TOWN—con.					
Smith, Wm	1	3	3		
Smith, Hozia			2		
Emory, Israel	1				
Patch, George	2	2	1		
Furnald, Dennis, Junr	1	2	3		
Furnald, Deacn James	1	2	4		
Seavey, Josiah	1		3		
Remick, Joseph	2		4		
Hunskum, Danl	2		3		
Varney, Peter	3	2	2		
Stephens, Johann			2		
Hunscum, Jack				3	
Roberts, James			2		
Hammond, Deacn Jonathn	1	1	3		
Hammond, Jonathn, Jur	2		5		
Toby, John	1		4		
Hunscum, Joathn	1		3		
Libby, Seth	2	2	3		
Hammonds, George	1	1	4		
Hammonds, Ebenz	1	1	5		
Hanscum, Tobias	1	3	2		
Cutt, John	1	1	2		
Furnald, Benjn	1	1	2		
Spinny, John	1	3	3		
Spinny, Samson	2	1	4		
Furnald, Wm	2		2		
Furnald, Nathn	1		2		
Wilson, Edmund	3	3	8		
Wilson, Danl	2	3	5		
Jones, Dorithy	1	2	2		
Parker, Capn Benjn	2	4	2	1	
Webber, Benjn	1	2	2		
Wilson, Saml	1	2	2		
Parker, Molly			2		
Parker, Danl	1		3		
Hayley, Noal	2		2		
Wilson, Elihu	3		1		
Wilson, Aaron	1	3	3		
Wilson, Elizh	1		3		
Hutchins, Edmund	1	5	4		
Presby, Darias	1		2		
Toby, Betty	3	1	2		
Amy, Saml	1	1	2		
Mitchel, Wm	2	2	3		
Foy, Steph	1		4		
Phillips, Andw	2	2	2		
Phillips (Widow)			2		
Furnald, Margt		1	3		
Furnald, Arculs	1		1		
Treferton, Henry	3	1	1		
Treferten, Danl	1	1	1		
Jenkins, Rowland	1		2		
Jenkins, Stephen	3	1	3		
Levey, Capn Stephn	2		1		
Furnald, Tobias	1	5	1		
Furnald, Benjn	3		2		
Phips (Widdow)		2	3		
Pray, Joshua	3	1	1		
Cane, John	1		1		
Pray, Saml	1	1	2		
Hooper, Nathn	3	1	1		
Winkley, John	2		5		
Winkley, Emerson	1		2		
Furnald, Sarah	1	1	2		
Brown, Thos	2	1	3		
Brown, Capn Thos	1	1	1		
Place, John	1	3	5		
Gullison, Benjn	1	1	7		
Furnald, Ebnezr	2		3		
Brown, Capn James	1	2	4		
Nahaney, Sarah		1	4		
Leach, Saml			2		
Furnald, David	1		1		
Furnald, Dorthy			2		
Furnald, Elihu	1	1	2		
Furnald, Benjn	2	5	7		
Furnald, Joseph	1		2		
Tripe, Elizh			2		
Witham, Magdalan			2		
Miles, Mary				5	
Peirce, Doct Danl	2	3	3		
Hayley, Majr Wm	2		3		
Ingram, Edwd	1	1	3		
Shapleigh, Isabel			3		
Pickenail, Nelson	1	2	4		
Pickenail, Esther			3		
Manson, John	1		2		
Fitts, Sarah			4		
Manson, Saml	2		3		
Manson, Benjn	1		1		
Rogers, Jno	1	1	4	1	
Rogers, Elizh			9	2	

* Illegible.

YORK COUNTY—Continued.

NAME OF HEAD OF FAMILY.	Free white males of 16 years and upward, including heads of families.	Free white males under 16 years.	Free white females, including heads of families.	All other free persons.	Slaves.
KITTERY TOWN—con.					
Furnal, John, 3d	1	2	3		
Furnald, Willm W	2		2		
Toby, Nathn	2		5		
Johnes, Alixandr	1		1		
Manson, Joseph	2	2	2		
Pettegrow, Joseph	4	1	3		
Monson, Thomas	3	5	1		
Rogers, Thos	1		3		
Monson, Saml	1	1	5		
Kane, Isaac	1		2		
Kane, Jane	2	1	2		
Shepherd, Mark	1		1		
Keen, Semeon	3	4	2		
Shepherd, Mark, Jur	2	1	3		
Jenkins, Lemuel	1	1	2		
Place, Elizh			2		
Keen, Wm	1	2	2		
Banks, Sarah		1	2		
Jenkins, Thos	1	3	2		
Jenkins, Margery		1	2		
Godsoe, —*		4	1		
Grover, —*			1		
Grover, Simon	1		3		
Rogers, —*	1	2	6		
Furnald, David	1		1		
Dame, Abigl			1		
Dame, Horsvil	1	3	2		
Stephens, Nance		1	2		
Dame, Nathan	1		3		
Chanlor, Thos	2		1		
Furnald, Josh W	1	1	2		
Monson, Josh	2	2	3		
Dame, Jonathn	1	1	6		
Tripe, Sarah			2		
Witham, Aaron	1	1	2		
Mendam, Wm	2		2		
Stoutley, Keturah	1		2		
Kinward, Wm	1		4		
Allen, John	1	2	4		
Pray, Wm	1	3	2		
Ore, Elle	1		1		
Adams, Mary	1	1	2		
Parker, Sarah			1		
Rice, Unice		2	2		
Rice, Alixr	3	1	4		
Rice, Saml	1		3	2	
Mendam, Joshua	2	5	7		
Spinny, Nicholas	2	2	3		
James, Mary		3	2		
Adams, Mark	4		4		
Carter, Sarah	3		1		
Lydston, Roby	1		3		
Lydston, Gedion	1	1	5		
Remick, Sarah	1		2		
Remick, Nathan	1		1		
Remick, Wm	2		1		
—*, Wm	1		4		
Staples, Wm	1	2	3		
Floyd, James	1	2	1		
Furnald, Wm	2		4		
Rogers, James	2		1		
Rogers, John	1		1		
Hammond, Joseph	1		4		
Furnald, Wm, Jur	1		3		
Green, Mary			1		
Dixon, Hannah			2		
Hanscum, Steven	1	2	1		
Libby, Joel	1	1	1		
Libby, Isreal	1		4		
Libby, Mary			2		
Libby, Sam	1	1	3		
Toby, Saml	3	2	4		
Toby, Stephn	2		3		
Hanscum, Jno	1	2	2		
Hanscum, Nathan	1	3	3		
Hanscum, James	1		3		
Hanscum, Jothan	1		3		
Hanscum, Jonathan	2	1	4		
Bartlett, Thos	1	2	4		
Libby, David	1	1	1		
Staples, Peter	1		2		
Hardge, Wm	1		1		
Libby, Nathan	2	3	4		
Remick, Mark	1		1		
Staples, Noah	2	1	3		
Fogg, John	2	3	4		
Fogg, Hannah			1		
Hill, Saml	1		2		
Hill, Sarah	1		1		
Hammond, Christn	1	2	7		
Hammond, Thos	2		2		
Johns, Wm	2	2	3		
Marriner, Esthr	1	1	4		
Frost, Caleb	1	2	3		
KITTERY TOWN—con.					
Stanley, Mark	1	2	2		
Kinnard, Dimond	2	4	4		
Kendal, Edwd	1	1	3		
Spring, Revd Alpheus	1		5	2	
Starcy, John	1		6		
Laton, Wm, Junr	1	1	5		
Kinnard, Michl	1		1		
Kinnard, Timoy	1	4	1		
Nason, James	2	3	3		
Garland, Jacob	2	1	2		
Garland, Wm	1		3		
Scammond, Umphy	2	2	6		
Layton, Deacn Wm	1		3		
Remick, Benjn	1	5	2		
Spinney, Ebenezr	1		3		
Sowards, Elizh			2		
Remick, John	1	1	7		
Coal, John	1	1	2		
Coal, Dorithy	1		3		
Dennet, Jno	1		1		
Dennet, Wm	4	3	2		
Dennet, Jno, Junr	3		4		
Furnald, Jno	3		3		
Dennet, Sally			3		
Furnald, Mark	1	2	5		
Spinny, John	1	2	4		
Remick, Steven	2	2	5		
Paul, James	2	2	5		
Remick, Samuel	2		5		
Dickson, Saml	1	2	4		
Paul, Joseph, Junr	1		4		
Foster, Parker	1	2	3		
Foster, Simon	1		2		
Field, Capn Joseph	1	3	3		
Paul, Joseph	1		2		
Brooks, Saml, Jur	1	1	1		
Brooks, Saml	2	5	3		
Staples, Soloman	3	2	3		
Spinney, Willm	3	2	2		
Paul, Timy	1		2		
Welch, John	1	2	4		
Brooks, Josiah	1		2		
Knight, George	1	1	6		
Brooks, Wm	1	2	4		
Lyssen, Wm	1	2	2		
Paul, Saml	1	1	3		
Knight, Danl	1	3	2		
Cole, Icabod	2	3	5		
Cole, Angnas			1		
Knight, Nathann	1	3	2		
Dixon, Peter	2	3	11		
Featherly, Anna	1		2		
Welch, Saml	1	1	4		
Paul, Amos	1	3	4		
Dixon, Steven	1		1		
Petegrow, Steven	2	3	4		
Cottle, Wm	3		2		
Layton, John	1		2		
Rendal, Willm	1	1	3		
Scammond, Humphy, Jun		1	3		
Scammond, Ephehm	1	1	1		
Hanscum, Paltiah	1	3	3		
Shapley, Saml	1	4	2		
Gould, —*	(*)	(*)	(*)		
Witham, Abner	2	4	3		
Woodman, Benjn	1	3	4		
Staycy, Wm, Junr	2	1	3		
Stacy, Ellis	1	1	2		
John, Capn Saml	1	2	3		
Hanscum, Ebenz	2	3	3		
Remick, Elemuel	2		4		
Staples, Enoch	1	2	1		
Remick, Jacob	1	1	2		
Richardson, Thimoy, Jur	1	1	4		
Kinnard, James	1	3	3		
Richardson, Timothy	1		2		
Foster, Abigl	1	1	2		
Tucker, Stephen	1		2		
Rogers, Nathanl	2		5		
Tucker, Saml	1		2		
Hill, Andrew	1	3	7		
Hill, John	3		4		
Morrell, Joel	1	3	6		
Fry, Tobias	1	1	4		
Forrel, Anna			1		
Jenkins, Renneldes	2	2	3		
Hill, Isaac	1	4	3		
Greno, Peltiah	1	3	4		
Shapleigh, Capn Elisha	2	3	4		
Shapleigh, James	2	3	7		
Shapleigh, Capn Dependc	2	3	6		
Fry, Ebenezr, Junr	1		5		
KITTERY TOWN—con.					
Bartlett, Sarah			3		
Bartlett, James	1	2	4		
Tucker, Jane			2	1	
Clark, Nathanl	3	1	3		
Ferguson, Stephen	1	4	2		
Ferguson, Reuben	1	2	5		
Ferguson, Timothy	1	3	3		
Paul, Moses	2	2	5		
Clark, Nathanl, Junr	1	2	3		
Frost, Nathanl	1	2	5		
Frost, Capn Charles	1	2	2		
Davis, John	1	4	3		
Hubard, Josha, Esqr	1	1	2	1	
Furbush, Danl	2		2		
Emory, Japhet	2	1	3		
Gould, Daniel	2	1	5		
Lord, Danl	1	2	5		
Lord, Mary			3		
Gowing, Lemuel	1	2	2		
Gowing, John	4		4		
Hodgsdon, Sarah	(*)	(*)	(*)	(*)	
Shapleigh, John	(*)	(*)	(*)	(*)	
Emory, James	1	3	3		
Gould, James	1		1		
Gould, Elixandr	1	4	3		
Spinney, Edmund	1	2	1		
Tedderly, Wm	4		1		
Tedderly, Saml	1	2	5		
Peck, Wm	2		2		
Spinney, John	2	2	2		
Spinney, John, Jur	1	1	4		
Spinney, Saml	1	2	2		
Spinney, Geo	1	2	1		
Petegrow, Saml	3	1	2		
Petegrow, Mary		2	1		
Remick, Isaac	1		1		
Remick, Isaac, Jur	1	1	4		
Welch, Wm	1	1	5		
Furnald, Moses	1	1	1		
Scrigens, John	1	2	4		
Scrigens, John, Jur	1	1	1		
Scrigens, Winthrop	1	1	1		
Scrigens, Thos	1		3		
Rogers, Nathanl	2	3	2		
Spinney, Timoy	3		1		
Remick, Josiah	2		2		
Dixon, Capn Thos	1	2	4		
Dixon, Thos	1		3		
Staples, Edwd	1	2	4		
Staples, Ruth			2		
Dixon, Abrhm	1	2	2		
Staples, Mary	3		2		
Remick, Mary		1	2		
Staples, David	1	2	2		
Garish, Timoy	1	1	1		
Petegrow, Saml, Jur	1	2	1		
Paul, Mary	2	1	4		
Remick, Dorcas			1		
Wherren, Wm		2	2		
Brooks, Joseph	1	2	2		
Paul, Stephen	2		2		
Staples, Isaac	1	2	4		
Lydston, Waymouth, Jr	2		1		
Lydston, Waymouth	1	1	1		
Emory, Hannah			2		
Emory, Anna	1		3		
Emory, Noah	1	3	4		
Paul, Ebenezr	2		4		
Gould, Danl, Junr	1	1	2		
—*, John	2	3	5		
Emory, Caleb	3	2	2		
Ferguson, Wm	1	2	6		
Furbush, Joseph, Jr	4	1	5		
Furbush, Joseph	2		2		
Shorey, Jacob	2	1	4		
Furbush, David	1		6		
Ferguson, Denis	1	4	4		
Gould, Joseph	3		2		
Gould, John	1	1	4		
Stacy, Ecabod	3	2	5		
Smith, James	1		2		
Smith, Wm	1		2		
Witham, Moses	1	3	2		
Witham, Kezia	1	1	1		
Hodgsdon, Benjn	2	1	3		
Kennington, Hugh	1	2	3		
Bartlet, Nathan	1		1		
Brewer, Jacob	1		2		
Chick, Amos	1	3	3		
Allen, Ephraim	2	2	2		
Allen, Elizh			2		
Allen, Zekiel	1	1	2		
Fry, Susanna	1		2		
Fry, Silas	1	3	3		

*Illegible.

NAME OF HEAD OF FAMILY.	Free white males of 16 years and upward, including heads of families.	Free white males under 16 years.	Free white females, including heads of families.	All other free persons.	Slaves.
KITTERY TOWN—con.					
Fry, Ebenezr	2	2	2		
Heath, Mary			2		
Davis, Anna			2		
Lewis, Paul	1		1		
LEBANON TOWN.					
Farnham, Joseph, Esqr	4	1	3		
Hasey, Revd Isaac	4		5		
Hardison, Joseph	3	2	5		
Kenney, John	1	2	3		
Pray, Joseph	1	3	3		
Gowen, Patrick	3	3	5		
Libby, James	1	1	3		
Woodsum, David	1	2	2		
Ross, Hugh	1	5	5		
Libby, Benja	1	4	2		
Brock, Frances	1	1	6		
Clark, Jona	2		1		
Hunssom, Isaac	1	4	2		
Wintworth, Amaziah	1	1	1		
Ricker, Ezekil	1	3	4		
Horsom, Benja	1	1	3		
Pray, Thomas	1	1	2		
Jones, James	1	2	4		
Ricker, Ebenezer	1		1		
Horsom, David	1		4		
Jones, Ebenezer	1		2		
Butler, Thomas	1		2		
Goodwin, Ruben	1		4		
Horsom, John	2	3	3		
Hart, Robt	1	3	1		
Downs, Ichabod	1	2	2		
Keay, Peter	3		5		
Pray, Moses	3	2	3		
Lord, Ebenezer	2	3	2		
Lord, Simon	2	1	3		
Frost, Mark	2	3	2		
Murry, Thomas	1	1	2		
Wallingford, Jno	2	1	1		
Wallingford, Tobias	1		2		
Wallingford, Moses	1	1	1		
Hanson, Moses	1	1	4		
Smith, John	1	1	2		
Roberts, Daniel	3	3	4		
Holmes, Thomas	1	1	3		
Peirce, Ebenr	1		2		
Peirce, Ebenr, Jr	1	2	5		
Horn, Ricd	1		1		
Jones, Ebenr	3	1	3		
Jones, Jno	1	2	1		
Keay, Jno	1	1	4		
Ricker, Simeon	1	2	4		
Teal, Robert	2	2	4		
Nock, Stase D	1	2	2		
Wintworth, Silas	1	4	2		
Lord, Wm	1	2	1		
Libby, Saml	1	1	5		
Goodwin, Reuben	1	1	3		
Goodwin, Elisha	1	1	1		
Fall, Stephen	1	2	2		
Fogg, James	1		1		
Horsom, Saml	1	1	3		
Keay, Oles	1		4		
Keay, Danl	1	2	1		
Smith, Ichabod	1	2	4		
Clements, Aaron	1	2	2		
Nock, Daniel	3	3	4		
Gowel, Benja	1	3	5		
Downs, Benja	1	1	5		
Austen, Nat	2	2	5		
Ricker, Meturen	1	3	2		
Ricker, Enoch	2	2	3		
Horsom, Jona	1	2	2		
Ricker, Joseph	1	1	4		
Horn, Benja	1	1	3		
Lord, Solomon	2	2	7		
Rines, Henery	1		2		
Farnham, David	1	2	2		
Downs, Daniel	1	2	2		
Horn, Ephrim	1		3		
Farnham, Benja	3	3	4		
Moody, John	1		4		
Austen, Moses	2	5	2		
Austen, Cathrine			1		
Pray, John	1	1	1		
Lord, Nicholas	1	2	2		
Blasdel, Enoch	1	2	2		
Hanson, Isaac	2	1	4		
Hanson, Jona	1	1	2		
Jones, Samuel	2	4	5		
Peirce, Benja	4	4	4		
Lord, William W	1		2		
Peirce, Moses	1		2		

NAME OF HEAD OF FAMILY.	Free white males of 16 years and upward, including heads of families.	Free white males under 16 years.	Free white females, including heads of families.	All other free persons.	Slaves.
LEBANON TOWN—con.					
Roberts, Samuel	1	2	3		
Nock, Zackh	1	2	4		
Yeaton, John	2	1	1		
Fall, Ebenezer	2	4	4		
Clark, Josiah	1	1	7		
Lord, Nathan	1	2	2		
Sullivan, Benja	1	1	4		
Pray, Abram	2	1	4		
Pray, Joshua	3	1	5		
Wheelrite, Snell	1		2		
Pray, Experince			2		
Pray, Nat	3	3	6		
Brock, John	3	4	4		
Libby, Charles	1	4	3		
Mills, John	1	1	2		
Richardson, Brady	1	2	2		
Young, Eliphelet	1	1	2		
Furbush, Benja	1		2		
Furbush, Benja, Junr	1	8	2		
Rankins, Jona	2	1	1		
Ricker, Ephrim	1	1	2		
Stvens, Jona	1	2	3		
Door, John	1	1	2		
Door, John, Junr	1	1	2		
Hussey, Ruben	1		3		
Hussey, Zackh	1	1	1		
Whitehouse, Nat	1		2		
Stvens, Thomas	1	1	7		
Hussey, Patience			1		
Stvens, Abijah	1		2		
Stevens, Wm	1	2	4		
Door, Jonathan	2		2		
Wintworth, Benja	1	1	3		
Wintworth, Stimson	1		1		
McCreelus, John	3		4		
Garlen, Dodifer	1		1		
Verney, Humpy	2	1	2		
Tibbets, Stephen	1	2	3		
Tibbets, Ephrim	1	2	3		
Tuttle, Benja	1	1	2		
Cook, Daniel	1	1	1		
Cook, Abram	1	2	4		
Cook, Daniel	1	1	4		
Blasdel, Thomas	1	1	2		
Blasdel, Elijah	1	1	1		
Ricker, Moses	3		6		
Ricker, Henery	1	1	1		
Harford, Solomon	1	2	5		
Libby, Jeremiah	1		3		
Shorey, Stephen	1		2		
Stillens, Isaac	1		2		
Furbush, Ricd	5	2	6		
Wintworth, Thomas M.	1	1	2		
Burrows, Edward	2		1		
Burows, Edward	1	2	1		
Foss, Daniel	3	1	3		
Norris, Jona	2		4		
Weitherill, James	1	3	2		
Chamberlin, Wm	1	2	2		
Chamberlin, Amos	1	1	2		
Blasdel, Eliphelet	1	2	1		
Chamberlin, Nat	1	2	2		
Critchet, John	1	1	2		
Corson, Levi	2	2	2		
Corson, Daniel	1	1	2		
Mills, James	1		2		
Corson, Mary			1		
Blasdel, Ephrim	3	5	3		
Goodwin, Samuel	1	2	4		
Copps, Samuel	4	3	3		
Copps, Ruben H.	1		4		
Cottel, John	1		1		
White, Silas	1	2	8		
Hayes, John	3	3	4		
Hayes, Elihue	1		2		
Wintworth, Jedediah	1	4	5		
Wintworth, Caleb	2	2	4		
Hanson, Mary			4		
Lord, Noah	2		3		
Hodson, Samson		1	2		
Hodson, Joshua	1	2	1		
Cowel, Edmund	2	2	1		
Warren, George	1	1	2		
Lord, Joseph	1	3	4		
Gerrish, John	1	3	1		
Kenney, Joshua	2	3	6		
Door, Henery	2	3	3		
Grant, Wm	1	2	3		
Goodwin, Thomas	1	4	3		
Furbush, Samuel	2	2	3		
Gerrish, George	3	2	5		
Hodson, Thos	2	1	8		
Nock, John	3	2	2		
Worster John	2	1	3		

NAME OF HEAD OF FAMILY.	Free white males of 16 years and upward, including heads of families.	Free white males under 16 years.	Free white females, including heads of families.	All other free persons.	Slaves.
LEBANON TOWN—con.					
Corson, Aaron	4		3		
Goodwin, John	1	2	3		
Jones, Wm	1	2	2		
Jones, Nat	1	1	2		
Perkins, Mark	1		2		
Hanson, Daniel	1	3	4		
Weitherill, Thos	1		1		
Burrows, Jona	1	3	4		
Stevens, Samuel	2	3	1		
Wingate, Saml	1	1	2		
Burrows, Joseph	1	3	5		
Farnham, David	1	4	2		
Legro, Thomas	1	1	2		
Legro, John	2	1			
Hill, Jeremiah	1		3		
Clark, James	1	1	3		
Bickford, Joseph	1	3	3		
Davis, John	1	2	1		
Appelbe, Thomas	1	1	1		
Legro, Samuel	2		3		
Legro, David	2		2		
Goodwin, Mary			2		
Blasdel, John	1	1	5		
Lord, Elisha	1	2	2		
Garling, Samuel	1	2	2		
Legro, John	1	3	2		
Fall, George	1	2	3		
Wallingford, Joshua	1	1	3		
Legro, John	1	1	2		
Cowel, Samuel	1		2		
Cowel, Ichabod	1		1		
Cowel, John	2	2	2		
Pray, Joseph	1	2	4		
Pollock, Thomas	1	3	3		
Woodman, John	2	2	7		
Fox, Daniel	1	6	1		
Bracket, Jacob	1				
Woodman, David	1	3	4		
Loud, Solomon	2	2	1		
Wintworth, Gersham	1		2		
Merrow, James	1	1	1		
Robinson, Samuel	2		1		
Kimball, Caleb	1		1		
Mason, Nat	1		1		
LIMERICK TOWN.					
Gilpatrick, Joseph, Esqr	2	2	4		
Bradbury, Jacob	3		4		
Felsh, Abijah	5	1	7		
Furnald, Joshua	1	2	4		
Libby, Azariah	3	1	4		
Stone, John	1		2		
Adams, John	1	8	4		
Morrel, John	1	1	4		
Wingat, John	2	3	6		
Gilpatrick, Thomas	2	2	6		
Libby, Nathel	1		3		
Perkins, Joseph	3	1	3		
Parks, Joseph	1	3	3		
Durgan, Wm	1	4	1		
Boothby, Wm	1		5		
Kneely, Danl	1		1		
Ricker, Aaron	1		2		
Hayes, John	1		1		
Favor, Jno	4		3		
Clark, David	1	3	1		
Hodsdon, Joseph	2	1	3		
Derban, Ricd	1	3	3		
Ricker, Rufus	1		1		
Ricker, Ebenezer	1		1		
Clark, Penewal	2	1	1		
Ford, George	2	2	2		
Johnson, Benja	3	4	3		
Hill, Joshua	1		2		
Barker, Danl	1	3	2		
Hill, Ruben	1	1	2		
Kean, Benja	1		1		
Beetel, Abial	2	3	3		
Mills, James	1	3	4		
Seve, John	2	3	3		
Lord, Thomas	1	2	2	1	
Mills, John	1	2	5		
Mills, Jacob	2	2	1		
Lord, Ammi R	2	1	5		
Durgan, Benja	2	2	4		
Hodsdon, John	1		2		
Hodsdon, Jonathan	1	1	2		
Hodsdon, Wm	1	2	2		
Fulsom, John	2	1	2		
Perry, Jesse	2	1	3		
Perry, James	1	1	2		
Perry, George	1	1	2		
Perry, John	1	2	3		

YORK COUNTY—Continued.

NAME OF HEAD OF FAMILY.	Free white males of 16 years and upward, including heads of families.	Free white males under 16 years.	Free white females, including heads of families.	All other free persons.	Slaves.
LIMERICK TOWN—con.					
Frye, Ebenezer	1		2		
Pane, James	1		2		
Bradbury, John	2		1		
Harper, Samuel	1	3	7		
Durnel, David	1	3	5		
Foster, Daniel	1	2	3		
Stimson, Jeremiah	1	1	2		
Gilpatrick, Sarah		3	3		
Howard, Amos	1	2	3		
Brown, Amos	1	2	3		
Bradbury, Daniel	1	2	2		
Bradbury, Jabez	1	1	2		
Sanbourn, Benja	1	2	2		
Durgan, Hannah			3		
Durgan, Ephrim	1	2	3		
Stimson, Joseph	1	4	5		
Staple, Carrel	1	3	3		
Furlong, Patrick	1	3	3		
Foster, Isiah	2	1	4		
Peirce, John	1	2	5		
Ricker, Moses	1				
Fitzgearld, Daniel	1	1	1		
LITTLE FALLS TOWN.					
Gorden, John	1		1		
Gorden, Zebulen	2	6	2		
Gorden, Andw	2	1	4		
Dow, Jeremiah	2		2		
Dow, Ebenezer, Jr	1		2		
Young, Danl	1	3	1		
Dow, Saml	1		2		
Dow, Jere, Jr	1	1	2		
Dow, Ebenz	2	2	6		
Gorden, John, Jr	1	2	2		
Emery, Benja	1	1	2		
Young, David	1	1	1		
Young, Hezekiah	1	1	3		
Young, Thos	1		1		
Young, Danl, Jr	1	1	1		
Townsend, Danl	1	2	4		
Dier, Joseph	3	5	2		
Downs, Phinehas	1		4		
Patterson, Joseph	1		6		
Leland, Joseph	2		3		
Chadborn, Joseph	2	2	5		
Dier, Humphry	1	3	3		
Haley, Willm	2		1		
Hill, Elisha	2	2	1		
Haley, Robert	1	1	3		
Cleaves, Ebenezer	1	1	1		
Haley, Joseph	1		2		
Smith, Dominicus	1	1	1		
Lock, Caleb	3	2	3		
Poke, Mary	1		5		
Smith, Anna	2		5		
Smith, Nathl	1	2	2		
Haley, Benja	3	3	2		
Bean, Jona	2		3		
Bean, Jona, Junr	1	1	2		
Gould, James	1	1	2		
Worth, Saml	1		2		
Parker, Enoch	1	3	6		
Wadley, Moses, jr	2	1	4		
Foss, Obadiah	1		1		
Hill, John	1	3	3		
Smith, Jedadiah	3		7		
Merry, Willm	1	2	2		
Smith, Edward	2		4		
Smith, Danl, Jr	1	1	2		
Russel, Nathl	2	2	5		
Cleaves, Israel	1	1	4		
Whittier, Nathl	1				
Jellitson, John	1	3	3		
Wadley, Willm	2	3	7		
Wadley, John	1		2		
Wadley, Moses	1		1		
Smith, Danl	3	3	6		
Smith, Benja	1	1	1		
Drew, Zebulon	2		1		
Drew, Hezekiah	1	1	2		
Haley, Joseph	1	3	1		
Townsend, Abram, Jr	1	3	3		
Townsend, Nathan	1	1	2		
Townsend, Abram	1		2		
Townsend, Isaac	1	1	5		
Ridley, Matthias	1	1	2		
Ridley, John	1	2	1		
Field, Danl	1	2	4		
Ridley, Thos	1	1	6		
Ridley, Abram	1	2	1		
Ridley, James	1	3	3		
Bryant, John	2	3	3		
Kimbal, Rufus	1		3		
Cousins, Ichabod	1	1	3		
Rummery, Moses	1		2		
Rummery, Jona	1		4		

NAME OF HEAD OF FAMILY.	Free white males of 16 years and upward, including heads of families.	Free white males under 16 years.	Free white females, including heads of families.	All other free persons.	Slaves.
LITTLE FALLS TOWN—continued.					
Nason, Joseph	1	2	3		
Young, John	1	1	4		
Berry, James	2	2	3		
Nason, John	4	1	2		
Nason, Robert	1		2		
Davis, James	1	2	3		
Davis, John	2	1	3		
Murphy, Pierce	1	1	1		
Hardy, Abel	3	1	3		
Robinson, Isaac	4	2	2		
Smith, Elisha	3	3	3		
Smith, Noah	1		3		
Tarbox, Carol	1	1	3		
Tarbox, Benja	1		1		
Barnes, Joseph	1		2		
Linscutt, Joseph	1	1	4		
Staples Joseph	1	1	3		
Simpson, Willm	1		1		
Haley, Saml	1	3	2		
Gookins, Joseph	1		2		
Smith, John	1	1	2		
Banks, Joseph	1	1	2		
Carl, Joshua	2	2	5		
Roff, Saml	1				
Cole, John	1	4	1		
Jordan, Joseph	1		2		
Woodman, Joseph	1	3	3		
Lane, Isaac	2		1		
Linscutt, Saml	1		1		
Warren, Joshua	2		1		
Warren, Joshua, Jr	1	3	1		
GilPatrick, Christopher	1	1	2		
Warren, Danl	1		3		
Simpson, Webster	2	2	2		
Hooper, Jacob	1	3	3		
Hooper, Joseph	1	2	2		
Lord, ——	1	1	2		
Goodwin, Danl	1	1	1		
Hooper, Tristram	1	4	2		
Clough, Thos	1	2	4		
Hooper, John	3		3		
Hooper, George	1	2	2		
Linscutt, Saml, Jr	1	1	1		
LITTLE OSSIPEE TOWN.					
Berry, James	1	3	4		
Staples, Robert	2	3	4		
Hasty, Robert	1	1	1		
Boody, Ezra	1	1	1		
Meservey, Nathl	1	2	3		
Cobb, Andw	1	2	2		
Grindley, ——	1	1	1		
Small, Danl	1	3	3		
Small, Henry	1	3	4		
Morton, Ebenz	1	1	1		
Irish, Ebenz	1	1	3		
Irish, Obadiah	1		1		
Morton, Joseph	1		2		
Small, Willm	1		6		
Libbee, Philemon	3	2	3		
Chick, Nathan	1	3	4		
Richardson, Thaddeus	1	4	2		
Small, Benja	2	2	4		
Duglass, John	1	1	3		
Wentworth, Willm	1	3	1		
Stone, George	2	1	1		
McKenny, Humphry	1		1		
Stone, John	1	2	2		
Fogg, Charles	1		2		
Fogg, George	1	1	2		
Bragdon, Willm	1	1	4		
Higgans, Walter	1		3		
Libbee, Robert	1	1	2		
Fogg, Danl	1		2		
Boothby, David	1	3	2		
Sawyer, Ebenz	1	3	2		
Sawyer, Saml	1	2	3		
Andrews, John	2	1	2		
Sutten, ——	1	2	2		
Small, James	2	3	1		
Meservey, Joseph	1	1	2		
Mars, Isaac	1	1	1		
Clark, Ebenz	1	1	2		
Latherby, Saml	1	1	5		
Small, Reuben	1	4	1		
Milliken, Phinehas	1	1	2		
Latherby, Isaac	1	2	3		
Boothby (Widow)	1	2	1		
Wiman, John	1	4	5		
Libbee, Aaron	1	1	4		
Tyler, Abraham	1		1		
Humprys, John	1		2		
Frost, Wingate	1		1		
Richardson, Elisha	1	1	2		
Stout, Saml	1	2	1		
Stout, Simon	1	2	3		

NAME OF HEAD OF FAMILY.	Free white males of 16 years and upward, including heads of families.	Free white males under 16 years.	Free white females, including heads of families.	All other free persons.	Slaves.
LITTLE OSSIPEE TOWN—continued.					
Clark, Ephraim	1	3	1		
Chick, Ephraim	1	1	1		
Brachet, Joshua	1	1	3		
Brachet, Abraham	1	1	4		
Cobb, Nicholas	1		4		
Foss, Job T.	1	1	1		
Richardson, David	1	4	1		
Rackley (Widow)	1	1	3		
Frost, Moses	1		1		
Stout, John	2	1	3		
Round, James	1	1	4		
Munson, Wm	2	4	3		
Foss, Peletiah	1	2	2		
Stout, Prince	1	2	4		
Hasty, Robert	1		1	1	
Hasty, David	1	2	2		
Boody, Robert	3	5	4		
Jackson, Robert	1	3	7		
Brachet, Saml	1	3	1		
Rendal, James	1	2	4		
Millar, Thomas	1	2	1		
Frost, Isaac	1	2	5		
Molloy, Dennis	1	7	2		
Gilkey, James	1	3	2		
Ridley, Daniel	1	2	4		
Edgcomb, Nicholas	3		2		
Libbee, Joseph	1	2	5		
Rummery, Thos	1	1	4		
Brachet, Reuben	1		1		
Mars, Pelatiah	1	1	2		
McCarty, John	1	3	6		
Clay, Benja	1	1	3		
Dier, Danl	1	3	4		
Richardson, David	1	3	1		
Davis, Ezra	1	4	6		
Johnson, Willm	3	2	4		
Small, Francis	1		1		
Young, David	1	2	2		
Berry, Saml	1				
Morton, Willm	1		3		
Davis, Nicholas	1	4	3		
Small, Isaac	1	2	3		
Boothby, Jona	1	2	4		
Libbee, Jesse	3	2	3		
Black, Josiah	1	3	3		
Edgcomb, Nicholas, Jr	1		2		
Tyler, Joseph	1	2	3		
Edmonds, Asa	1	1	1		
Whitman, Willm	1	2	5		
Chase, Amos	1	3	3		
Sawyer, Joshua	1		5		
Sawyer, Nathl	1	4	2		
Small, Jacob	2	2	2		
Small, Danl	2	3	4		
Jackson, Bartholomew	1	1	9		
McKenny, Dominicus	1		1		
Sparrow, Joseph	1				
Biter, Peter	1	1	4		
Stout, Richard	1	3	4		
Nason, Jona	3	2	5		
Nason, John	1	1	4		
Strout, Isaac	3	3	3		
Strout, Gilbart	1		2		
Strout, Willm	1		2		
Strout, Enoch	1	3	4		
Wing, Nathan	1		1		
Small, Joshua	2	1	2		
Small, Joshua, Jr	1	1	3		
Hunscum, Danl	1		2		
NEW PENACOOK TOWN.					
Kimball, Moses	1	3	3		
Putman, Stephen	1	1	1		
Mores, Aaron	1		3		
Dotloff, Richard	1		2		
Farnum, David	1		2		
Farnum, Benjamn	1		2		
Manuel, James	1		2		
Stone, Moses	1		2		
Elliot, Benja	1	1	5		
Capon, Thomas	1	2	2		
Keyes, Francis	1		3		
Lufkin, Benja	1	2	2		
Harper, Daniel	3		1		
Seger, Josiah	1		3		
Abbot, Phillip	2		1		
Merrill, Ezekiel	3	2	6		
Howard, Phinehas	1		2		
Howard, Samuel	1	1	2		
PARSONSFIELD TOWN.					
Kinsman, Jona, Esqr	2	3	4		
Parsons, Thomas, Esqr	1	2	7		
Sanborn, John	1		1		
Marsten, Daniel	1		1		

YORK COUNTY—Continued.

PARSONSFIELD TOWN—continued.

NAME OF HEAD OF FAMILY.	Free white males of 16 years and upward, including heads of families.	Free white males under 16 years.	Free white females, including heads of families.	All other free persons.	Slaves.
Hobbs, Samuel	1		5		
Doe, John	3		6		
Morss, Benjᵃ	1	1	5		
Sanbourn, Benjᵃ	1				
Doe, Levi	2		1		
Doe, Samuel	1		1		
Marsten, David	1	1	4		
Marsten, Caleb	1	2	1		
Cobbet, Nat	1	1	3		
Ames, John	3	2	3		
Page, Samˡ	1	2	3		
Brown, Robᵗ	1		1		
Holland, Elisabeth			2		
Brown, Benjᵃ	2		1		
Marsten, James	1	2	2		
Kent, Josiah	1	1	3		
Avery, Jeremiah	1	1	2		
Avery, Walter	1				
Doe, Gedion	3	2	4		
Doe, Jonᵃ	1	2	6		
Pees, Asa	1				
Peas, Josiah	1		1		
Ames, Nathᵃˡᵉ	2	1	6		
Bacheler, Benjᵃ	1		1		
Sanborn, Wᵐ	1		2		
Sanborn, Wᵐ	1	1	2		
Tole, Levi	2		2		
Tole, Stephen D	1		1		
Wiggen, Nathan	1	2	2		
Fulsom, John	1	3	2		
Wedgwood, Noah	1	2	1		
Moulton, Samuel	1	3	4		
Wedgwood, Jesse	1		4		
Hilton, Dudley	2		3		
Sargent, Robᵗ	1	2	1		
Peas, Zebulon	1	2	2		
Bickford, George	2	5	4		
Benson, James	1	2	3		
Quint, Joseph	1	2	1		
Quint, John	1				
Quint, Martha		1		1	
Piper, Elisha	3	3	5		
Morrison, James	1	3	3		
Pees, Joseph	1	3	6		
Norris, Joseph	1		1		
Norris, Jeremiah	1	3	4		
Chase, Lydia		1	1		
Mighill, Moses	1	1	1		
Mighill, Joseph	1		2		
Pees, Samuel	1		1		
Pees, Samuel	1	1	4		
Moore, Ebenezer	1	4	4		
Moore, John	2	3	2		
Furbacks, Joshua	3	4	3		
Wiggen, Nathˡ	1		1		
Burnham, Paul	1	2	3		
Hutchins, Enoch	2	1	2		
Bickford, John	1	3	2		
Pearl, Joseph	1	1	3		
Dockum, James	1	2	1		
Wintworth, Wᵐ	1	2	1		
Morrel, Stephen	1	2	4		
Moulton, Cuting	2	3	3		
Page, Taylor	1	3	3		
Brown, Robert	1	1	2		
Brown, John	3	1	5		
Parsons, Abigail		1	1		
Bickford, Wᵐ	1				
Palmer, Wᵐ	2	2	2		
Neal, Walter	1		4		
Neal, Enoch	1		2		
Parsons, Joseph	2		4		
Hobbs, David	1	1	4		
Hobbs, James	1	1	2		
Granvill, Josiah	2	2	5		
Cluff, John	1	1	1		
Colkut, Josiah	2	1	4		
Kennison, John	2	4	4		
Champen, James	1	4	2		
Chase, Edmund	3	2	3		
Gilman, Abijah	1	2	2		
Gilman, Samuel	1				
Hart, James	1	2	3		
Kennison, Abrᵐ	1		1		
Dalton, Samuel	2	1	2		
Ranckens, James	1		2		
Mugget, John	2		2		
Muget, Jeremiah	1	2	2		
Muget, Joseph	1		4		
Colkut, Job	1	2	4		
Chase, Moses	2	3	3		
Tole, Jonathan	1	1	2		
Blaso, Amos	2	3	1		
Peirce, Frances	1	1	4		
Pain, Phillip	3	4	6		

PARSONSFIELD TOWN—continued.

NAME OF HEAD OF FAMILY.	Free white males of 16 years and upward, including heads of families.	Free white males under 16 years.	Free white females, including heads of families.	All other free persons.	Slaves.
Divorux, Ricᵈ	1		3		
Floyd, Michael	2	1	3		
Pain, Wᵐ	1				
Libby, Enoch	1	2	6		
Blaso, Joseph	1				
Wedgwood, Lot	1	5	2		
Smith, Benjᵃ	1	1	3		
Mighill, Josiah	1	2	3		
Gilman, James	1	1	2		
Schegel, Jacob	1	3	2		
Schegel, George	2				
Wiggen, Bradstreet	1		3		
Fox, Edward	1	1	2		
Fox, John	3	1	2		
Remmick, James	1		2		
Lowge, John	1	3	1		
Stacy, Benjᵃ	1				
Lowge, Joanna		1	3		
Miles, Wᵐ	1	5	1		
Berry, James	1	1	2		
Lowge, Samul	2	1	2		
Kezer, George	3		3		
Kezer, George	1				
Kezer, Josiah	1		1		
Abbot, David	1		3		
Parsons, Stephen	1	1	2		
Blaso, John	1				
Blaso, Joseph	1		1		
Weeks, Samuel	5	4	3		
Mason, Jane	1	1	1		
Ellot, Wᵐ	1		2		
Fox, Elijah	2				
Muget, James	1	1	1		

PEPPERELLBOROUGH TOWN.

NAME OF HEAD OF FAMILY.	Free white males of 16 years and upward, including heads of families.	Free white males under 16 years.	Free white females, including heads of families.	All other free persons.	Slaves.
Abbot, Samuel	1	1	2		
Ellis, John	1	1	3		
Abbot, Moses	1	1	5		
Ayers, Moses	1	1	3		
Bradᵇʸ, Joseph	3	1	6		
Bryant, Stephen	1	2	4		
Bryant, Jerathwell	2	2	4		
Bryant, Ephraim	2	3	3		
Bryant, Stephen, Jur	2	2	6		
Bryant, David	1	1	4		
Bryant, Ephraim, Jur	1		3		
Berry, Richard	3	1	5		
Berry, Nicholas	2	5	7		
Bradᵇʸ, Edward	1	1	2		
Bachelor, David	1	1	1		
Bachelor, Jonathan	1		1		
Barker, David	1	1	2		
Bailey, Thoˢ	1	1	2		
Bryant, Daniel	1	2	2		
Banks, John	1	2	3		
Banks, Pheby	2	1	6		
Banks, Joseph	1	2	2		
Boothby, Samˡ	1	3	2		
Boothby, Josiah	3	2	2		
Boothby, John	2	2	3		
Bond, Robert	1	2	5		
Bond, Robert, Junᵃ	1	1	2		
Barry, Samˡ	1	3	5		
Bangs, John	2	1	3		
Branan, Thoˢ	1	2	1		
Barry, Richard, Junᵣ	1	1	1		
Brown, Jonathan	1	4	3		
Chase, Dr. Amos	3		3		
Cutts, Thoˢ, Esqʳ	11	2	5		
Chase, Samˡ	3	1	4		
Coffin, James	3	2	6		
Cole, Willᵐ	2	1	4		
Chandler, John	1	2	3		
Carll, Benjamin	2		2		
Carll, Robert	1		1		
Carll, John	1	2	2		
Carll, Wᵐ	1		3		
Carll, Elias	1		3		
Chamberlain, Thomas	1	3	4		
Chamberlain, Wᵐ	1		1		
Chamberlain, John	1	3	4		
Cutts, Foxˡ	1	1	2		
Chase, Amos, Jur	1	1	2		
Chase, Daniel	1		1		
Cleaves, Jonathan	2	2	1		
Coit, Hannah		1	3		
Cleaves, John	2	1	3		
Cleaves, Robert	1	2	2		
Chase, John	1	1	2		
Dennet, Samˡ	2	1	3		
Dennett, Nicholas	2	5	5		
Dennet, Samˡ, Jur	3	4	3		
Dennet, Ebenezer	3	2	3		

PEPPERELLBOROUGH TOWN—con.

NAME OF HEAD OF FAMILY.	Free white males of 16 years and upward, including heads of families.	Free white males under 16 years.	Free white females, including heads of families.	All other free persons.	Slaves.
Dearben, Thomas	2	2	4		
Dearben, Jacob	1	1	1		
Dearben, Ebenezer	1	2	4		
Deshon, Chase	1	2	4		
Durill, Benjᵃ	3		2		
Dorman, Charles	1		2		
Drinkworter, Thoˢ	2	1	7		
Dearing, John	1		1		
Dearing, Thoˢ	2	2	7		
Dearing, Joseph	2	3	3		
Dearing, John, Jurᵣ	1	4	1		
Dearing, James	1		1		
Davis, John	1	5	4		
Edgcomb, Samˡ	2	1	5		
Edgcomb, James	1	2	2		
Edgcomb, Thoˢ	1	3	3		
Edgcomb, Samˡ, Jur	1	1	1		
Emery, Job	1	2	4		
Elwell, James	1	1	1		
Elwell, Mehitable			2		
Fairfield, Revᵈ John	2	1	4		
Foss, James	2	3	5		
Foss, John	2	1	7		
Foss, Benjamin	1	5	3		
Foss, Wᵐ	2	3	3		
Foss, Daniel	1	2	2		
Foss, James, Jur	2	3	6		
Foss, James, 3ᵈ	1	1	1		
Foss, Walter	2	1	2		
Foss, Walter, Jurᵣ	1		4		
Foss, Walter, 3ᵈ	1		1		
Fernald, Nathˡ	1	2	1		
Fendarson, John	1	3	6		
Flood, Nathan	1	1	3		
Fairfield, Josiah	1	1	1		
Fowler, Ebenezer	1	1	2		
Foss, Joseph	3	5	5		
Gray, James	4	1	4		
Googins, John	3		2		
Googins, Wᵐ	3		3		
Gould, Samuel	3	3	4		
Gogens, David	1		2		
Gould, Joseph	2	2	4		
Googins, Joseph	2	2	4		
Guttridge, Benjamin	3		2		
Guttridge, Benjᵃ, Jurᵣ	1		4		
Gilford, Joseph	1	2	3		
Goulthrite, Philip	1	2	2		
Guttridge, Hannah		3	1		
Honycomb, Benaiah	2		1		
Hase, Zephemiah	1	3	2		
Harmon, Pettcah	1	2	2		
Hopkins, Solomon	1		3		
Heins, Samuel	1	2	3		
Hill, Benjamin	1	2	1		
Jordan, Tristram, Esqʳ	3	2	3		
Jordan, Samˡ, Esqʳ	2		2		
Jordan, Tristram, Jurᵣ	1		1		
Junkins, Sarah	3	1	6		
Jameson, Wᵐ	3	1	1		
Jameson, Robert	1		2		
Jewett, George	2				
Johnson, James	2	5	5		
Keindrick, John	2		4		
Keindrick, Joseph	1	1	3		
Keelly, Phinehas	3	2	2		
King, Josiah	1	2	1		
Libbey, Joseph	3		3		
Lumbard, Solomon	1	5	2		
Libbey, Thomas	2		2		
Libbey, Solomon	2	2	4		
Libbey, Philip	1		2		
Libbey, John	1	1	2		
Libbey, Elijah	1	3	1		
Lowel, John	1	2	3		
Loyns, Willᵐ	1	1	1		
Moody, Elizabeth	2	4	4		
Means, Thomas	1	4	4		
Means, George	1	3	2		
Mᶜkinney, John	1	2	3		
Mᶜkinney, Jeremiah	1	2	2		
Moody, George	1				
Hason, Benjᵃ, Jur	2	1	3		
Merrill, Joseph	1	4	4		
Newbegin, George	1	1	2		
Pike, Humphrey	4	1	4		
Pike, Israel	3	3	2		
Patterson, Robert	1	1	3		
Patterson, Robert, Jur	1	4	3		
Patterson, Samuel	1	2	5		
Patterson, Andrew	1	4	1		
Patterson, Benjᵃ	1		1		
Patterson, David	1	1			
Patterson, Elisha	1		2		
Patterson, John	4		6		

YORK COUNTY—Continued.

PEPPERELLBOROUGH TOWN—con.

NAME OF HEAD OF FAMILY.	Free white males of 16 years and upward, including heads of families.	Free white males under 16 years.	Free white females, including heads of families.	All other free persons.	Slaves.
Patterson, Abraham	1	1	4		
Patterson, Daniel	1	3	3		
Pritham, John	1	3	3		
Paul, Willm	1	2	2		
Phillips, John	1	3	2		
Phillips, Wm	1		1		
Phillips, John, Jur	1	1	1		
Page, Dan	2	2	5		
Page, Peter	2		1		
Parcher, George	1	1	2		
Parcher, Elias	2	2	5		
Rollings, James	1		2		
Richards, Nathl	1	4	4		
Ridlin, Mathias	1	2	3		
Rose, Solomon	1		1		
Rose, Solomon, Jur	2	1	3		
Ridlen, Daniel	2	2	1		
Ridlen, Ephraim	1	2	3		
Runnels, John	1		1		
Ridlen, Lewis	1	1	1		
Ridlen, Jeremiah	3	2	4		
Rumary, Edward	1	1	2		
Rumery, John	1		2		
Rumery, Edward, Jur	1	1	1		
Sawyer, David	1		1		
Sawyer, David, Jur	2	1	2		
Sawyer, David, 3d	1		1		
Sawyer, Joel	2	1	6		
Sawyer, John	1	1	3		
Sawyer, Abner	2	3	4		
Sawyer, Willm	1	4	5		
Staples, Elisha	1	3	6		
Sinnot, Thos	1	5	2		
Sillea, Nathan	1	1	1		
Sillea, John	1	1	1		
Scamman, Elizabeth	1	2	1		
Scamman, Samuel	2	1	5		
Scamman, Dominicus	2	2	7		
Scamman, James	2		1		
Scamman, Nathaniel	3	4	3		
Scamman, Isaac	3	5	2		
Scamman, Freman	1	3	5		
Scamman, John	1	4	4		
Scamman, Benjamin	1	2	3		
Scamman, Daniel	2		2		
Scamman, Nathl, Jur	1	2	1		
Storer, Seth	2	3	7		
Simpson, Benjamin	1	2	1		
Tucker, John	1	1	2		
Tucker, Catharine			2		
Tucker, Francis	1	1	1		
Tapley, Job	2	1	4		
Tapley, John	1		1		
Tappen, Wiglesworth	3	3	3		
Tiler, James	1	1	6		
Tiler, Humphrey	1	2	2		
Tarbox, Loring	1		2		
Thomas, John	1	2	2		
Tibbets, Stephen	2		1		
Tibbets, Saml	2	3	3		
Tibbets, Timothy	1		1		
Tibbets, Obidiah	1	1	3		
Warren, Samuel	1		3		
Warren, David	1		5		
Webster, Joseph	1	2	2		
Woodsom, Samuel	1	2	2		
Woodsom, John	1	2	3		
Whitney, Jesse	1		4		
Woodsom, Benja	1	3	1		
Withain, Robert	1		3		
Patterson, Loin	1		1		
Underwood, John	1	2	3		
Underhand, —	1	2	2		
Witham, Mary		2	1		
Swain, Elizabeth			3		
Pierce, Abigail		3	1		

PORTERFIELD TOWN.

NAME OF HEAD OF FAMILY.	Free white males of 16 years and upward, including heads of families.	Free white males under 16 years.	Free white females, including heads of families.	All other free persons.	Slaves.
Libby, Meshech	2		4		
Rankines, Moses	2		2		
Elenwood, Benjamin	2	3	4		
Lamson, Samuel	1		1		
Allod, David	2	2	2		
Clark, Joseph	1	1	3		
Bickford, Benjamin Jun	1		1		
Bickford, Benjamin	2		3		
Bickford, Samuel	1	2	1		
Briges, Paul	1	1	1		
Rankins, Moses, junr	2	1	1		
Clemons, Jonathan	2	1	2		
Haywood, Lemuel	1	1	3		
Dyer, Bickford	1	1	1		
Goald, Aaron	1	1	5		
Towl, Josiah	1				

SANFORD TOWN.

NAME OF HEAD OF FAMILY.	Free white males of 16 years and upward, including heads of families.	Free white males under 16 years.	Free white females, including heads of families.	All other free persons.	Slaves.
tripe, Samuel	2		5		
parsons, Olive (Wid.)	1	3	5		
Bragdon, Aaron	1	3	3		
taylor, Noah	1	1	2		
Stanyan, John	1	1	1		
Bragdon, Amous	1	1	1		
Tompson, John	2		2		
Thompson, Ruben	1	2	3		
Emeary, Caleb, Esq	3	1	2		
Emeary, William	1	2	3		
Young, Daniel	2	3	3		
Johnson, Samuel	1	2	3		
Standley, Edward	2		4		
Standley, John	1		2		
Johnson, Jonthan	4		3		
tibbls, Moses	1		1		
huzey, Daniel	1		2		
Lord, mary (Wid.)		1	1		
Gray, James	3		5		
Bennet, Nathinel	1	5	1		
Bennet, William	3		2		
Bennet, David		1	5		
powers, John	1	2	2		
Molton, Joel	1	2	4		
hanelton, heneary	1	3	3		
Swet, Moses	1	1	3		
paul, Josieah	2	3	5		
hale, Enoch	1	1	1		
thompson, phiness	1	3	3		
Johnson, Jonathan, Jur	1	1	1		
tripe, Robt	1	1	1		
Crain, John	1	1	5		
Jacobs, John	1	3	1		
Bostone, Thomas	2		5		
peary, Stephen	1	1	2		
morel, Samuel	3	1	4		
morel, Stephen	1				
Low, Ephraim	2		1		
Low, Obdiah	1	2	3		
more, William	1				
tibbits, Jonathan	3	5	3		
Nason, Samuel, Esq	7	2	8		
Withum, Ganzbury	1		1		
Withum, John	1	1	2		
Withum, Edmond	1	1	4		
Adams, John	1	1	2		
Adams, Jonathan	1		2		
Frost, William	2	1	3		
Adams, Jonathan, Sen	1		2		
Welch, Joseph	1	2	5		
Kicker, Dodford	1	1	3		
Morroson, David	3	4	2		
Cheaney, Elifalet	1	3	4		
Jelleson, Joseph	1	1	1		
morroson, Ebenezer	1	2	3		
Morroson, Daniel	1		1		
Welch, David	2	5	2		
Welch, Edmand	1		1		
morroson, Abraham	1		3		
morroson, Bradbury	1	1	3		
Chaney, Joseph	1	1	3		
Gatchel, Ephraim	1	1	2		
Beatle, John	1	1	2		
heartwell, James	1		1		
Bandwell, Nathaniel	1	2			
hatch, Jacob	1		2		
Firbush, William	1		2		
Chatman, Isaac	1	2	1		
Spener, Ichabod	1	2	3		
Jenkins, Jabis	1				
Coleords, Jesse	2		2		
More, John	2	1	3		
pugeley, Franes	2	2	7		
Dearing, Gideon	1		2		
Morefield, hipsebath (Wid.)	2	1	5		
Dennet, Samuel	2	3	6		
Kicker, William	1	3	5		
Kicker, Simeon	1		4		
Woster, William	1		2		
Woster, Thomas	1		3		
Kicker, Samuel	1	3	5		
hobbos, Stephen	2		3		
Dearing, John	2	1	2		
Carl, Joseph	1	1	3		
hall, Nellson	1	1	5		
Quint, John	1	1	5		
Quint, Joseph	2	3	3		
Quint, David	1	2	2		
hatch, Nathan	1		3		
Garey, Frost	1		2		
paul, Josiah	1		2		
ChadBourn, James	1	3	3		
husey, Ruben	1	3	3		
Bean, Daniel	1	3	3		

SANFORD TOWN—con.

NAME OF HEAD OF FAMILY.	Free white males of 16 years and upward, including heads of families.	Free white males under 16 years.	Free white females, including heads of families.	All other free persons.	Slaves.
Bean, Joshua	1	1	3		
hanson, Caleb	1	3	4		
Low, Jonathan	1	4	3		
Beal, Zebilon	1	3	1		
hanson, Joshua	3	2	3		
Withum, Jonathan	1	2	4		
ChadBourn, Ebenezer	1	4	2		
Withum, Mouses	1	1	1		
Withum, Jacob	1	1	1		
gouen, Ezekel	2	5	2		
Wodley, Daniel	1	3	3		
Batchellor, Joshua	1	4	3		
Webber, Daniel	1		3		
Gouen, Stephen	1	4	4		
Gouen (Widow)			2		
Low, Ephraim, Junr	2	1	5		
Low, David	1		3		
Bostone, Timothy	1	2	3		
Shaw, Samuel	1	1	2		
Withum, Jeremiah	1		3		
tripe, William	1	2	5		
thompson, Ezra	1	1	2		
powers, William	2	1	4		
powers, Nathan	1		3		
harmon, Napthalum, Jua	1	1	1		
harmon, Napthalum	2	1	1		
thompson, Ebenezer	2	1	3		
thompson, Solomon	1		5		
Gray, James, the 3	2	1	2		
true, Obdiah	1		5		
peare, James	1	1	2		
Norton, Josiah	1	1	4		
haskel, thomas	2	2	4		
Wilkeson, Joseph	1	3	1		
Beane, David, Senr	2	1	3		
Beane, David	1		2		
Beane, Joseph	1		3		
penney, Stephen	1		2		
penney, Thomas	1		2		
morroson, Francis	1	1			
Welch, Edmend, Jur	1	2	3		
annies, Nehemiah	1		2		
annies, Charles	1	1	1		
Welch, Solomon	1	2	3		
Staple, William	1		2		
meldrom, John	1	1	2		
Gray, Diminaus	1		3		
more, Ebenezer	1	2	1		
Estes, Benjamin	3	1	4		
parkins, David	2	4	4		
Cram, Joseph	1	1	2		
Warmwood, Amous	2	1	3		
more, William	2		1		
Noble, John	1	1	2		
Nutter (Widow)		3	2		
Gatchel, Seith	1	4	1		
hastey, James	2		1		
annies, John	1	1	4		
Litchfield, Joseph	3	4	5		
Spears, Isrul	1	1	2		
Spears, Ebenezer	3	4	2		
Hill, Joseph	1	3	2		
Butlor, Nathaniel	1		1		
Butlor, Thomas	2	1	8		
penney, Settathel	1	1	2		
Grant, Ephrain	2	4	3		
plumar, Moses	1	5	2		
Frost, Elht	1	4	3		
hatch, Samuel	2		4		
Wise, Jeremiah	1	6	2		
heard, James	3	1	4		
farbush, Isaac	2	3	4		
Cole, James	3	2	2		
Allen, Solomon	3	2	2		
Allen, Jerediah	1	1	2		
frost, Moses	1	1	1		
Brooks, Joshua	2		1		
Allen, Franes	2	3	5		
Cole, Tobias	1	3	5		
tripe, Jonthan	1	1	2		
pirkins, Josiah	1	1	3		
Davies, James	1	3	3		
Galahel, Daniel	1	2	7		
perkins, John	1	5	2		
haston, John, Jurer	1		1		
huston, John	2	2	3		
Willard, anna (Widow)	1	2	3		
Willard, Samuel	2	2	3		
Willard, John	2	2	1		
hatch, David	1		1		
hatch, Stephen	1		1		
Littlefield, Ithamor, Jua	2	3	6		
Withum, Zeblion	1	3	3		
Day, Aaron	1	3	4		

YORK COUNTY—Continued.

NAME OF HEAD OF FAMILY.	Free white males of 16 years and upward, including heads of families.	Free white males under 16 years.	Free white females, including heads of families.	All other free persons.	Slaves.
SANFORD TOWN—con.					
Day, hilkem	1		2		
Day, Dependence	1	1	2		
Littelfeield, Ithamor	1	1	1		
Bridges, Thomas	1	4	4		
Littelfield, Stephen	1	1	1		
Wakefield, hazakiah	3		2		
Wormwood, John	2	1	3		
Gatchel, Joshua	2	2	2		
Russall, John	1	3	1		
Linskit, Nathaniel	1	1	3		
Day, hiltten	1	1	2		
Goodwin, Joshua	2	2	7		
Jonnes, Bartholimu	1	2	7		
Jonnes, Elisha	2	2	2		
Shakford, John	1	2	3		
knight, Joseph	1	2	4		
martin, John	1		2		
Linskiet, John	1		4		
Linskiet, Jacob	1	2	1		
horn, Joseph	1	1	3		
Day, heneary	2	2	2		
horn, Samuel	1		1		
Norton, Nathaniel	1	2	1		
Jellison, Samuel	2	3	4		
taylor, Joshua	2	1	2		
Gray, William	1	2	5		
Gray, Daniel	1	3	4		
pugsley, John	1		1		
taylor, Elifilate	1	1	2		
pugsely, Benjemin	1		3		
Coule, Samuel	1		2		
Gouen, John, Junor	1		3		
Cleark, David	1	1	1		
Going, John	1	2	4		
Jellison, Jeddoh	2		2		
powers, Jonathan	1	3	1		
White, John	2		2		
White, John, Junor	1	3	1		
Kicker, Solomon	3	2	2		
White, Charles	1		1		
White, Samuel	1	2	1		
avery, Joseph	1		1		
friend, John	2	1	1		
Swett, Moses, Junr	3	3	3		
Cozont, Nathaniel	5	1	2		
Whitten, Umpery	3	6	3		
killam, John	1	3	3		
Whitten, Samuel	1	2	2		
Whitten, James	1	1	2		
Vitterin, Benjemin	2	1	5		
Webber, Paul	1		1		
Cluff, Samuel	2	3	4		
Willson, Jonathan	1	1	4		
hutchings, Levy	1	1	2		
hutchings, Edmand	1	1			
plumer, John	1	2	2		
tripe, Benjemin	4	3	4		
kimbull, Thomas	2	2	5		
Alley, Olais	1	1	1		
parsins, William	2	5	4		
——*, John	(*)	(*)	(*)	(*)	(*)
Emson, Joseph	2	3	3		
Luies, Saray (Wid.)	2	1	4		
Gray, Joseph	3	1	2		
Gray, James, the 3	1	1	5		
Linsent, Joseph	1		1		
Linsent, William	1	3	4		
haley, Richard	3	2	5		
manentier, Ebenezer	2	5	1		
williams, Simien	1	2	1		
trafen, Jeremiah	1	2	1		
trafen, Benjamin	1	1	1		
Linscot, theodah	1	2	2		
Lord, Ambrose	2	2	3		
Newell, Jonathan	2	2	7		
harden, Joshua	1	1	1		
Alley, Samuel	1	1	2		
Sayards, John	2	4	4		
Conant, Joshua	1	1	2		
allen, Told	4	2	3		
Sayards, Ebenezer	1		2		
Nble, abbigale (Wid.)	1	2	3		
Williams, Thomas	1	3	3		
Emeary, Stephen	1	3	3		
Luies, Jeremiah	1	1	4		
Whiton, Aaron	1	1	10		
Stevens, David	2	3	5		
Stevens, hubbard	2	1	3		
Stevens, Aaron	3		4		
Smith, heneary	2	2	4		
freeman, Nathan	2	2	6		
Writne, Josiah	1	3	3		
Brown, Samuel	3		4		
Godard, Samuel	1		1		

NAME OF HEAD OF FAMILY.	Free white males of 16 years and upward, including heads of families.	Free white males under 16 years.	Free white females, including heads of families.	All other free persons.	Slaves.
SANFORD TOWN—con.					
Rich, Barnbus	1	1	2		
hatch, Ezekel	1		2		
Emeary, Joshua	2	1	1		
Barnes, Benjmin	1	1	5		
Barnes, David	1		6		
Cotten, Elizebeth (Wid.)			3		
Walley, John	1	1	4		
fillpact, James	2				
Stone, Joseph	3				
Kicker, Samuel	1		1		
hall, Ebenezer	1	2	2		
hill, James, Junr	1	2	5		
——,—*	2	1	2		
Withum, Ichabod	2		2		
Kobards, Samuel	2	2	6		
Kobards, Ebenezer	2	1	3		
Juett, Benjmin	1	1	1		
Gastrige, Joshua	4	2	3		
moodey, Samuel	1	1	2		
yourk, Nathan	2	1	4		
tweed, Samuel	1	1	1		
Davies, Daniel	1		2		
Davies, David	1		4		
Stanton, paul	1	1	4		
Bean, mary (Wid.)		2	2		
Stanton, Benjmin	1		3		
Bean, Jeremiah	1	3	5		
Bean, John	1		4		
Stone, Gidon	1	2	5		
marshall, William	2	3	5		
Scribner, John	1		2		
Leavil, William	1	1	1		
Gile, Daniel	3	1	2		
Guile, Stephen	1	3	1		
Coffen, Eliphalet	1	3			
SHAPLEIGH TOWN.					
Rogers, Wm, Esqr	5	3	5		
Gilman, Jeremiah	2				
Ricker, Gersham	1	2	2		
Gilman, Jona	1	3	2		
Cook, Daniel	1	1	3		
Gilman, Benja	1				
Hussey, Benja	1	5	6		
Door, Phillip	1	2	2		
Wintworth, Paul	1	1	2		
Farnham, Ralf	1	2	2		
Stvens, Henery	1	2	3		
Farnham, Paul	1		2		
Farnham, Dummer	1		1		
Prescot, Jona	1	2	2		
Roberts, Love	2	3	4		
Hilton, Ricd	2	2	4		
Downs, Paul	1	3	4		
Drew, Benja	1	4	4		
Hussey, Robt	1	3	3		
Hussey, John	1	2	3		
Door, Ricd	1		1		
Bodwell, Jne	1	1	2		
Cook, Jno	1	2	2		
Heard, Abigail	1	1	1		
Hanson, Abram	1		5		
Door, Peter	1	1	3		
Door, Silas	1	2	2		
Kennikum, Aurther	2		1		
Blasdel, Ralf	2	2	1		
Thompson, Miles	1	2	5		
Door, Ricd	2		2		
Shorey, Benja	2	5	3		
Felsh, Jona	1	2	3		
Felsh, Hannah			1		
Tibbets, Ichabod	1	2	2		
Goodwin, Ephrim	1	1	2		
Shorey, Samuel	1	2	4		
Shorey, Saml, Junr	1	2	2		
Clark, Hanson	1	2	3		
Libby, Stephen	2	3	4		
Libby, Stephen, Junr	1		1		
Hersom, Jacob	5	1	3		
Grant, James	2	1	5		
Wintworth, Ruben	2	1	6		
Bracket, Joshua	4	1	3		
Grant, Joshua	1	2			
Nock, Eleazer	1		2		
Bracket, Nathan	1	4	3		
Heard, Jethro	3	2	6		
James, Jno	1		1		
James, Elisha	2	2	5		
Dudley, Trueworth	1	2	2		
Hubbard, Aaron	2	1	5		
Hubbard, Ricd	2				
Nock, Zackh	1	2	3		
Nock, Nicholas	1	3	4		

NAME OF HEAD OF FAMILY.	Free white males of 16 years and upward, including heads of families.	Free white males under 16 years.	Free white females, including heads of families.	All other free persons.	Slaves.
SHAPLEIGH TOWN—con.					
Grant, Charles	2	2	4		
Willey, Saml	3		8		
Gilman, Zebulon	2	2	2		
Gilman, Dudley	1		1		
Marsh, Isaah	1		2		
Marsh, Stephen	1		2		
Merrow, Joseph	3	1	3		
Corson, Moses	1	7	3		
Gubtail, Benja	1		1		
Corson, Lemuel	1	3	5		
Nason, Moses	2	3	3		
Bean, Willm	1	2	3		
Corson, Isaac	1	1	1		
Bracket, Danl	1	1	1		
Magoon, Edward	1	1	3		
Remmick, Joseph	1	1	2		
Row, John	3	1	2		
Merril, Levi	2	4	2		
Row, John	1	2	2		
Hussey, Ruben	1	1	1		
Door, James	2	4	4		
Tibbets, Ebenezer	1		3		
Wintworth, Grant	1		2		
Bracket, Benja	1				
Downs, Gersham	1				
Tibbets, Danl	1	2	2		
Merrow, Samuel	1	4	5		
Merrow, Edmund	1		2		
Bracket, Joshua	1		3		
Copps, Jona	1		1		
Copps, Peter	1		2		
Tibbets, Wm	1	4	1		
James, John	1	4	5		
Quemby, John	1	1	2		
Door, Joseph	2	2	5		
Fox, Joseph	1				
Runnels, Saml	1	2	4		
Farnham, Paul	1	1	2		
Horne, Benja	3	1	3		
Goodhue, Josiah	2		3		
Dodge, Benja	1	1	5		
Rogers, David	1	2	1		
Horne, Danl	1	2	1		
Levet, Joseph	1	1	5		7
Allen, Jude	3	1	2		
Thing, Wintrop	1	2	3		
Wilson, Humpy	2	1	3		
Bragdon, Saml	1				
Remmick, Timothy	1	1	1		
Hammon, Elisha	2	1	4		
Sanborn, Saml	1	2	4		
Sanborn, Joseph	1	3	2		
Gilman, Danl	1				
Quembe, Jona	2	1	2		
Lord, Josher	3	4	4		
Tibbets, Phillip	1	3	4		
Magoon, Benja	1	4	3		
Steel, Clement	2		4		
Kimmens, Benja	2	1	1		
York, Nicholas	2	4	6		
Merrow, David	2	4	4		
York, Edward	1				
Waldron, Ebenezer	1	4	2		
Magoon, Josiah	1	4	1		
Marsten, James	1		2		
Nason, Jacob	1	3	4		
Abbot, Jona	1	5	3		
Weeds, Jona	1	4	6		
Goodwin, Joseph	1	1	3		
Hubbard, Danl	1	3	2		
Goodwin, Nathan	2	4	4		
Hubbard, James	1	1	2		
Bragdon, Aurther	1	1	3		
Trafton, Josiah	1	3	3		
Patch, Jona	2	2	3		
Patch, Paul	1	1	3		
Patch, Jno	2		1		
Patch, Saml	1	3	4		
Saward, James	2	1	4		
Coffen, Nat	2	1	4		
Bartlet, John	3	1	1		
Coffen, Nathan	1	3	4		
Grant, Peter	3	1	2		
Huntrus, Ichabod	1	1	2		
Huntrus, Darling	3	2			
Hastyes, Saml	2		2		
Tynan, Joseph	2		4		
Tynan, Ricd	2		4		
Davis, James	1	2	3		
Morrel, David	1	1	2		
Abbot, Moses	2		1		
Abbot, Moses, Junr	2	1	4		
Trafton, Lemuel	1	3	1		
Trafton, Joshua	1	3	3		

* Illegible.

YORK COUNTY—Continued.

NAME OF HEAD OF FAMILY.	Free white males of 16 years and upward, including heads of families.	Free white males under 16 years.	Free white females, including heads of families.	All other free persons.	Slaves.
SHAPLEIGH TOWN—con.					
Tynan, Mary		1	1		
Low, Bazalial	1	3	2		
Low, Sam¹	1		1		
Moody, Joseph	1	2	2		
Davis, John	1	2	2		
Thing, Nathaniel	2		3		
Philpot, Moses	1	3	1		
Giles, Dan¹	1	2	3		
Giles, Joseph	1	1	3		
Giles, Sam¹	1	2	2		
Giles, John	1		1		
Kent, Nathᵉˡ	1	3	4		
Wood, Stephen	1	4	5		
Poland, Nat	1	1	2		
Pray, Joseph	1	1	2		
Wodley, John	1	1	3		
Warren. Aaron	1	1	4		
Warren, Gilbert	1	2	3		
Thompson, Wᵐ	5	2	5		
Welsh, Jonᵃ	1	1	2		
Haysles, Jnᵒ	1		5		
Neal, Edmund	2	2	5		
Hodsdon, Solomon	1		1		
Goodwin, Dan¹	1		3		
Goodwin, Thoˢ	1	3	3		
Davis, Nehemiah	1	3	4		
Stone, Wᵐ	3	4	3		
Stone, Judah			1		
Pilsbury, Stephen	2	4	4		
Crocket, Benjᵃ	1	1	3		
Ham, George	2		2		
Trafton, Zachariah	1	1	2		
Wilson, Dan¹	2	2	3		
Cheek, Abrᵐ	1	3	4		
Ross, Jonᵃ	1	5	3		
Perkins, Nat	1	1	3		
Goodwin, Benjᵃ	1	1	7		
Shackley, Thomas	1	3	7		
Standley, Wᵐ	2	5	3		
Emery, Charles	2		3		
Lord, Ichabod	1	2	3		
Ham, Sam¹	2	3	3		
Morrison, Edward	1				
Ham, George	6	1	6		
Webber, Benjᵃ	1		7		
Ricker, Simon	1	3	6		
Low, Jeddiah	2	2	3		
Patch, Andrew	1		1		
Standley, John	1		1		
Goodwin, John	1		2		
Standly, Mary			2		
Jallison, Joseph	2	3	4		
Abbot, Samuel	1	2	3		
Horn, Jonᵃ	1		5		
Pugsley, Abram	1		1		
Pugsley, Abrᵐ	1	3	3		
Murry, Wᵐ	1		4		
Murry, John	2	3	3		
Gowen, David	1	2	2		
Thompson, John	1	1	2		
Pugsley, Andrew	1		2		
Nason, Ham	1	1	6		
Emery, Jeremiah	1	4	2	1	
Fulsom, Moses	1	3	4		
Grant, Elisha	1	1	4		
Nason, Caleb	1	2	2		
Hearl, Moses	1		1		
Welsh, John	1	1	5		
Goodwin, David	1	3	3		
Emery, Simon	2	1	1		
Emery, Jotham	1				
Hupper, John	1		1		
Kent, Sarah			1		
Jones, Isreal	1	2	1		
Evely, Sarah		3	3	1	
Poland, Asa	1		4		
Bickford, Abner	1	2	4		
SUDBURY-CANADA TOWN.					
Duston, Jesse	2	2	4		
Swan, James	1		1		
Swan, Joseph G.	4	3	4		
Russel, Abraham	2	1	7		
Russel, Benjamin	2	1	2		
Russell, Theodore	1		2		
Bean, Jonathan	1		1		
Bean, Daniel	1	3	3		
Kilgore, John, Junᵣ	1	1	1		
Russel, Jacob	1	1	3		
Kilgore, Joseph	1	1	2		
Hastings, Amos	1	3	4		
Bartlett, Enoch	4		4		
Easters, Stephen	1		1		

NAME OF HEAD OF FAMILY.	Free white males of 16 years and upward, including heads of families.	Free white males under 16 years.	Free white females, including heads of families.	All other free persons.	Slaves.
SUDBURY-CANADA TOWN—con.					
Frost, Matthias	1	2	1		
Kilgore, John	1	1	3		
Russel, Benjᵃ, Junᵣ	1	2	2		
Holt, Zela	2		3		
Swan, James, Junᵣ	1	2	1		
Holt, John	1	1	1		
York, Isaac	1	1	3		
York, John	2	1	4		
Bean, Josiah	1	5	3		
Ingalls, Sam¹	1	4	3		
Bartlett, Thaddeus	2		6		
Bartlett, Jonathan	3	1	3		
Powers, Amos	2	2	3		
Goss, Sam¹	1		5		
Andrews, Jeremiah	1	3	2		
Seger, Nath¹	2	1	2		
Seger, Josiah	1		2		
Powers, Gideon	1	3	4		
Powers, Silas	1	1	1		
Bartlett, Stephen	1	2	1		
Bartlett, Moses	2	1	2		
Abbott, John	1		1		
Abbott, John, Junᵣ	1	2	2		
Bean, Jonathan, Junᵣ	1	2	3		
Harvey, William	1	2	2		
Smith, Thial	1	5	2		
Smith, Thial, Junᵣ	1				
Frost, Thomas	1				
Twitchel, Eli	1	1	2		
Twitchel, Ezra	1	4	3		
Stearns, Thomas	1				
Twitchel, Eleazar	2	4	4		
Chatman, Eliphaz	2	4	4		
Grover, Jedidiah	1		3		
Grover, John	1	2	4		
Mason, Walter	1				
Abbot, Jonathan	2	2	3		
Mason, John	1	1	1		
Mills, Deborah		2	3		
Asten, Peter	2	4	5		
Grover, James	2		3		
Gage, Amos	1	2	1		
Gage, Daniel	1		2		
Fannon, Oliver	1	2	3		
Clark, Benjᵃ	1	2	3		
Clark, Jonathan	2	1	5		
SUDBURY-CANADA TOWN, SETTLEMENTS ADJOINING.					
Foster, Asa	1	1	1		
Foster, Abner	2	2	3		
Littleale, John	3		2		
Spafford, Nath¹	1				
Jackson, Joseph	1	3	3		
Barker, Jonathan	1	1	1		
Barker, Jesse	1		3		
Swan, Elijah	1		2		
Barker, Benjamin	2	2	1		
Larey, Joseph	2	2	3		
Blake, David	1	2	1		
Messer, John	1		1		
SUNCOOK TOWN.					
Stearns, John	3	1	1		
Dresser, Levi	1	1	2		
Dresser, Stephen	1	2	4		
Kilgore, Joseph	2		4		
Kilgore, James	1		5		
Butters, Abel	1	2	2		
Andrews, Abraham	2	2	4		
Patch, Timothy	1	5	2		
Whiting, Oliver	1	2	2		
MᶜAllaster, Dan¹	1	1	1		
MᶜAllaster, Ananias	2	3	2		
MᶜAllaster, Joseph	1	2	2		
Hale, Josiah	1	3	4		
Whiting, Joshua	1		1		
Stearns, Benjᵃ	2				
MᶜKean, James	1	1	2		
WASHINGTON PLANTATION.					
Adams, Revᵈ John	4	2	4		
Nelson, Joseph	1	3	5		
MᶜClannen, James	1	1	2		
Smith, Jethro	1	3	2		
Ayers, Elisha	2	2	6		
Piper, Stephen	1	2	3		
Chelles, Wᵐ	1	1	1		
Chelles, Mary	1		3		
Symes, Ebenezer	1		4		

NAME OF HEAD OF FAMILY.	Free white males of 16 years and upward, including heads of families.	Free white males under 16 years.	Free white females, including heads of families.	All other free persons.	Slaves.
WASHINGTON PLANTATION—continued.					
Campernel, John	1		1		
Dunnel, John	1				
Symes, Wᵐ	1	1	2		
Adams, John	1				
Berry, Samuel	1		3		
Drew, Elisabeth	2	1	1		
Staple, David	2	1	1		
Doe, Brodstreet	3	1	4		
Davis, Thomas	1	3	3		
Balch, Nat	1	1	6		
Balch, Nat	1		1		
Turner, Stabert	1	1	4		
Cromwel, James	1		2		
Doe, Eliphelet	1		2		
Day, Thomas	1	2	2		
Nelson, Daniel	1		2		
Nelson, Leder	1		2		
Waymoth, Joshua	1		2		
Doe, Nathᵉˡ	1		2		
Campernel, Wᵐ	1		2		
Campernel, Wᵐ	1		1		
Dam, Joseph	1	2	2		
Doe, Henery	1		3		
Doe, Simon	1		3		
Doe, John	1				
Hayes, Peter	1	2	2		
Berry, James	1				
Berry, James	2	1	4		
Thompson, George	1	3	4		
Boothby, Ebenezer	1		3		
Hobbs, Josiah	1	1	2		
Atterd, Daniel	1		2		
Moulton, Simeon	1		2		
Moulton, Levi	1	1	1		
Moulton, Ephrim	1		1		
Moulton, Stephen	1		2		
Moulton, David	1	1	2		
Libby, Wᵐ	1	3	3		
Staple, Benjᵃ	1		3		
Stone, Levi	1		2		
Libby, Zebulon	3	1	5		
MᶜDannels, Paul	2				
Whitten, Thomas	1	3	3		
Thompson, Robᵗ	1	3	1		
Clark, James	1	1	2		
Kennison, Nicholas	1		2		
Smith, Thoˢ	1	1	3		
Durgan, David	2	2	3		
Richardson, Resolved	1		1		
WATERBOROUGH TOWN.					
Russull, Joseph	1		2		
Russull, Joseph, Junᵣ	1	4	3		
Wotson (Widʷ)	1		2		
Lord, Nason	1	4	2		
heselton, Jonathan	1		3		
Leuet, Daniel	3	2	6		
Giles, John	1	2	2		
Pits, John	2	4	5		
Scribner, Daniel	2	2	4		
Scribner, Samuel	3	1	5		
burley, Andrew	1		5		
Scribner, Edword	1	2	1		
thing, Coffin	1	1	1		
Scribner, Joseph	1	2	1		
taylor, Daniel	1		4		
harvey, James	2	1	2		
Dame, Samuel	2	2	3		
Kimball, David	4	4	4		
Colcord, Phineas	1	1	1		
Smith, John	3		2		
Smith, thomas, Junᵣ	1		1		
Smith, Jacob	2		1		
kinsman, Ebenezer	1	1	2		
Smith, Jonathan	1	3	2		
Coffin, Benjamin	1		2		
Coffin, Napthalim	1		2		
Coffin, Daniel	2	1	4		
Coffin, Daniel, junᵣ	1	2	2		
haines, Simeon	1	1	4		
Haines, Nathaniel	1	2	4		
bean, Richard	3	2	4		
Robbirson, James	1				
Robbirson, Daniel	1	1	2		
Bean, William	1		1		
Bean, William, junᵣ	4	2	2		
thing, Catharine (Widʷ)	1	3	2		
Pike, Joseph	1	2	4		
Smith, John	1	2	3		
Moody, Clament	2	2	4		
Smith, Israil	1	1	2		
Scribner, Edward, junᵣ	1		1		
barners, James	1	3	1		
Smith, Israil, junᵣ	1	4	3		

YORK COUNTY—Continued.

WATERBOROUGH TOWN—continued.

NAME OF HEAD OF FAMILY.	Free white males of 16 years and upward, including heads of families.	Free white males under 16 years.	Free white females, including heads of families.	All other free persons.	Slaves.
kimball, Joseph	1	3	1		
Smith, Nehemiah	1		5		
Pearey, Joseph	2		3		
Dudley, Peter	1		4		
pike, Joseph	1	1	1		
kimball, Levy	1	4	4		
Ricker, Noah	1	1	4		
Hill, David	1	4	2		
Jones, Stephen	1	2	2		
Bouden, Michal	1	1	1		
Mirick, John	1	2	3		
Penny, Frances	2	2	4		
folsom, Peter	1	2	5		
Hibbord, Israil	1	4	3		
henderson, Samuel	1	2	6		
Sambourn, Joseph	1	1	1		
Sanbon, Joseph, junr	1	1	2		
Sanbon, Paul	1	1	3		
Coak, John	2	1	6		
Shores, Joseph	1		2		
Night, Jonathan	1		2		
Ricker, timothy	1	1	4		
Emery, Jacob	1	1	5		
Hobbs, Moril	1	2	4		
Hobbs, Henery	1		1		
Hobbs, Goarge	1	1	2		
Androse, Samuel	1	1	3		
Parcher, timothy	2	1	3		
Farl (Widw)		3	2		
emery, Zachariah	1	3	2		
Bagley, John	1	4	4		
Stuart, Josiah	1	1	3		
Buzell, Ebenezer	1	1	1		
Hill, Joseph	1	1	2		
Scribner, Samuel, junr	1	6	1		
Foy, James	1	1	5		
Scribner, John	2		1		
Smith, John, junr	1	2	2		
Smith, thomas	7	3	1		
Hill, John	1	3	1		
Henderson, Joseph	1	2	1		
Henderson, John	2		1		
Webster, Joshua	1	1	1		
Perry, Benjamin	3	1	1		
Carpinder, Nocholas	1		1		
Carpinder, Nathaniel	1		1		
Carpinder, John	1	1	3		
Carpinder, thomas	1	2	3		
Gerlin, Nathaneal	1		1		
dudley, Truworthy	1	2	4		
Sinkler, Benjamin	1	1	2		
Cammat, Samuel	1	1	3		
Gelpatrick, William	2	1	3		
Webster, Waldren	1	1	3		
dudley, Stephen	1	2	2		
Tinglen, Paletiah	1	1	4		
Mills, Eligood	2	3	3		
Deshaun, Moses, junr	1	2	4		
Deshaun, James	1		1		
Hutchings, thomas	2	1	2		
Cortle, Stephen	1	1	1		
Carlile, James	1		2		
Smith, John	1	1	2		
Straw, Valintine	2	3	4		
Smith, Aaron	1	2	3		
laton, tobias	1	2	4		
Butler, John	2		1		
Leuer, William	1	3	2		
Brown, Jeremiah	4		4		
Brown, Jacob	1		3		
Night, Zebulon	1	2	3		
Page, Benjamin	1	2	4		
Carle, John	1	4	3		
Carle, Elizabeth (Widw)			2		
Carle, Anna (Widw)		1	1		
Gabtale, thomas	2	2	2		
Gubtale, Stephen	2	2	3		
ford, Mils	1		2		
hanson, William	1	3	4		
Gubtale, thomas, Jun	1	1	3		
tibits, William	1	1	1		
tibits, Mary (Widw)		2	2		
tibits, James	1		4		
Bilford, thomas	2		3		
Dearing, William	1	2	3		
Hodgdan, timothy	2	3	2		
Mattoks, Henory	1	2	1		
Harford, John	1	2	2		
tibits, Simeon	1	1	4		
tibits, Joshua	2		3		
Roods, Jacob	1		2		
Jeleson, George	1	5	2		
Jeleson, David	1	1	2		
fillpot, William	4	1	5		
Vrine, James	1		1		

WATERBOROUGH TOWN—continued.

NAME OF HEAD OF FAMILY.	Free white males of 16 years and upward, including heads of families.	Free white males under 16 years.	Free white females, including heads of families.	All other free persons.	Slaves.
Ricker, Levy	2	5	3		
Woodword, William	2	1	2		
Welch, thomas	1	5	5		
Gutterage, Anna(Widw)			2		
Goodwin, Amaziah	2	3	3		
Wodword, Sarah(Widw)			2		
Bogse, Elisha	1		2		
Sagiley, Daniel	1	2	1		
Moulton, William	1		2		
Sedgley, John	1	5	2		
Gray, Samuel	1	3	1		
Haeley, John	1	1	2		
Junkins, William	1	1	1		
luis, Joseph	1	4	3		
Rankins, Andrew	1	1	5		
Gous, Moses	1	2	2		
Jahnson, James	1	1	1		
Bridges, Samuel	1	2	3		
Bridges, Josiah	1	2	3		
Beedeen, Robert	2	4	2		
Goue, John	1		1		
harmon, Edward	2	1	6		
Night, John	1	3	4		
Worrim, Benjamin	3	4	5		
Bicker, Joseph	2	2	4		
Downs, Umphry	1	3	4		
Downs, Richard	2		1		
knock, Ebenezer	2	2	5		
Roberch, Ichabod	1	3	5		
Bunker, Elijah	1		1		
Walker, Gedeon	1	1	3		
Hamelton, Abel	1	3	3		
Hamelton, James	1	3	4		
Hamelton, Richard	1	1	4		
Hamelton, John	1	2	1		
Hamelton, Benjamin	1	2	6		

WATERFORD TOWN.

NAME OF HEAD OF FAMILY.	Free white males of 16 years and upward, including heads of families.	Free white males under 16 years.	Free white females, including heads of families.	All other free persons.	Slaves.
Sanderson, Stephen	1	2	3		
Barker, Joseph	1	2			
Holton, Jonathan	2	2	2		
Jewel, John	1	2	1		
Brown, Asaph	1	1	4		
Bryant, Richard	1	1	2		
Robbins, Jonathan	1	1	1		
Jewet, Stephen	4	1	5		
Green, Thoms	3	1	5		
Gates, William	1	1			
Johnson, Asa	1		3		
Hor, Phillip	4		2		
Sampson, Phinehas	1		3		
Langley, Eli	2	1	3		
Brown, Silas	1	1	2		
Brown, Thaddeus	1	2	2		
Chamberlain, Ephraim	1	1	2		
Nurse, John	1		3		
Homan, James	3	2	1		
McWane, David	1		1		
Langley, Jonathan	1	2	2		
Atherington, John	1		1		
Hamlin, Africa	1	1	3		
Hamlin, America	1	2	3		
Jewel, Ezra	2	2	3		
Hale, Oliver	1	1	2		
Hale, Israel	1		4		
Hapgood, Oliver	1	3	2		
Whitney, Joshua	1	3	3		
Whitney, Phinehas	1	2	3		
Chamberlain, Nathl	2		1		

WELLS TOWN.

NAME OF HEAD OF FAMILY.	Free white males of 16 years and upward, including heads of families.	Free white males under 16 years.	Free white females, including heads of families.	All other free persons.	Slaves.
Wakefield, Ezekiel	1	1	4		
Colburn, Ebenezer	2	1	3		
Littlefield, Jotham	1	2	3		
Littlefield, Reuben	1	3	1		
Cousens, Saml	1	1	4		
Thompson, Richd, Jr	1	1	1		
Thompson, Caleb	1	4	2		
Bussel, Jonathan	1	2			
Treadwell, Saml	1		4		
Bussel, Isaac	2	1	2		
Thompson, David	1	2	2		
Gil Patrick, John	5	1	4		
Littlefield, Lydia	1	1	3		
Noble, Stephen	1	1	3		
Littlefield, Jacob	1	1	3		
Shackley, Richd	1	4	2		
Cousins, Joseph	3		4		
Gil Patrick, Joseph	1	1	2		
Jones, Thos	1		5		
Treadwell, Nathl	1	4			
Day, Ebenezer	2	3	3		
Titcomb, Benjs	1	3	4		

WELLS TOWN—con.

NAME OF HEAD OF FAMILY.	Free white males of 16 years and upward, including heads of families.	Free white males under 16 years.	Free white females, including heads of families.	All other free persons.	Slaves.
Ross, John	1	2	4		
Hubbard, Moses	1	1	4		
Hubbard, James	1	1	3		
Taylor, John	2	2	2		
Lord, Benja	1	2	3		
Burnham, Abram	1	1	2		
Burnham, Saml	3		4		
Walker, Elephalet	3	5	4		
Kimbal, Saml	2	2	6		
Kimbal, Isaac	1	4	4		
Waterhouse, Saml	2		2		
Waterhouse, Saml, Jr	1	2	4		
Day, Benja	1		3		
Day, Benja, Jr	1	1	2		
Smith, James	4	1	2		
Littlefield, Moses	2		3		
Latherby, Stephen	2	1	3		
Taylor, John	5	2	3		
Thompson, Richd	2		2		
Maddix, John	1	2	2		
Maddix, John	1	3	3		
Littlefield, Anthony	1	1	2		
Littlefield, Edmond	1	2	2		
Littlefield, Abram	1	4	3		
Ross, Adam	1		1		
Hatch, Leml	2		1		
Storer, Isaac	2	3	1		
Kimbal, Baruch	1	3	3		
Hatch, Elisha	1	3	3		
Clark, Aaron	1	1	3		
Wells, Robert	2	4	3		
Storer, Jere	3	1	4		
Storer, Nathl	1		2		
Storer, Willm	2		3		
Borton, Willm	1		2		
Hatch, David	1	3	2		
Hilton, Joshua	1	2	3		
Williams, Saml	1	4	5		
Little, Revd Danl	1		2		
Storer, Jere, Jr	1		1		
Hatch, Gideon, Jr	1	1	4		
Sawyer, Willm	1	2	1		
Littlefield, Anthony	1	1	2		
Littlefield, Pelatiah	1	2	1		
Winn, Nathan	3	2	2		
Whittam, John	1				
Clark, John	2		3		
Going, Nicholas	2	1	4		
Wormwood, Ebena	1	1	4		
Wormwood, Joseph	1		1		
Cole, Remick	1	1	4		
Annis, Abram	3	3	6		
Annis, Stephen	2	3	5		
Hill, Jona	4	2	3		
Littlefield, Joseph	1	4	4		
Hatch, Benja	1	1	1		
Storer, Isaac	2	3	2		
Hatch, Noah	1		2		
Hatch, Ebenz	1		1		
Hatch, Leml	2	1	1		
Hill, Saml	1		2		
Littlefield, Nehemiah	2	2	5		
Moffat, John	2	2	4		
Hatch, Jere	2	1	2		
Hatch, Jesse	3		3		
Eaton, Joshua	2	3	3		
Annis, Nehemiah	1	1	6		
Hatch, Benja, Jr	2	1	2		
Pease, Richd	1		2		
Eaton, Joseph	1	1	5		
Chadbourn, Saml	1	3	4		
Hatch, Elias	1	1	1		
Littlefield, David	1	2	4		
Penny, George	1	2	2		
Littlefield, Stephen	1	1	1		
Penny, Danl	1	2	2		
Penny, John	2		1		
Storer, Amos	4		3		
Hatch, Jona, Jr	1	4	3		
Hatch, Elijah	1		1		
Gitchel, George	1	4	3		
Williams, Joseph	2	4	3		
Penny, Benja	2	1	4		
Staples, John	2	1	7	4	
Littlefield, Jona	4		3		
Littlefield, Willm	1	3	5		
Emery, Saml	1	1	2		
Bicknal, Tabitha			4		
Whitehouse, Saml	1		4		
Littlefield, Noah	5		3		
Aldrige, Amos	1	2	6		
Wheelright, Aaron	1	5	4		
Treadwell, James	2	3	3		
Stephens, Jere	2		1		
Winn, Saml	1	1	3		

YORK COUNTY—Continued.

WELLS TOWN—con.

NAME OF HEAD OF FAMILY.	Free white males of 16 years and upward, including heads of families.	Free white males under 16 years.	Free white females, including heads of families.	All other free persons.	Slaves.
Davis, James	4	2	2		
Furbush, Catharine	1	3	2		
Hubbard, John H	2		2		
Wheelright, Joseph	1	1	1		
Wheelright, Benj^a	1	1	2		
Winn, Josiah	1		6	2	
Hubbard, Joseph	1	4	3		
Jones, John	3	4	1		
Patten, Hance	1	2	3		
Bourne, Isaac	1	2	6		
Bourne, Joseph	2	3	3		
Cousins, Enoch	2		2		
Ross, Danl	2		2		
Smith, Stephen	1		2		
Hatch, Reuben	1	1	2		
Gil Patrick, Saml	3		4		
Kimbal, Israel	2	3	5		
Kimbal (Widow)			2		
Eaton, Joshua	1		2		
Hatch, Eliab	1	3	4		
Davis, Sarah	1	1	3		
Kimbal, Rich^d	2		2		
Ross (Widow)		2	1		
Shackley, John, Jr	2	4	2		
Shackley, John	1	1	3		
Latherby, Joel	2	3	5		
Kimbal, Nathl	2	2	3		
Wormwood, Abner	1		1		
Kimbal, James	4	3	3		
Taylor, Willm	2	3	2		
Currier, Abram	1	2	2		
Wakefield, James	1	1	2		
Nason, Benj^a	1	1	1		
Barnard, Joseph	3	4	3		
Hill, Saml	1	1	6		
Storer, Joseph	4	1	2		
Osborn, James	1	2	2		
Lord, Tobias	2	2	6	4	
Littlefield, Moses	2	1	1		
Condy, Thos H	1	1	2		
Howard, Pomper N	3				
Brown, Benj^a	1	1	3		
Silby, Benj^a	2	2	3		
Jewett, Joseph	1				
Tucker, Stephen	1				
Clark, Jonas L	1		3		
Fisher, Jacob	1	1	2		
Wakefield, John	2		3		
Wakefield, John, Jr	1		4		
Trickey, Willm	1	1	1		
Hubbard, Diamond	1		3		
Wise, Danl	1	1	3		
Little, David	3	1	1		
Little, Nathl	1		1		
Keating, Oliver	3	1	4		
Jellitson, Willm	1	3	3		
Littlefield, Elijah	1	3	3		
Goddard, Thatcher	1	1	4		
Bowen, John	2	2	2		
Hill, Abram	2	4	4		
Webster, Nathl	2	4	3		
Elwel, ——	1				
Murphy, Mich^l	1	1	3		
Emery, Jabez	1	1	5		
Bicknal, William	1	1	6		
Penny, Joseph	1	3	4		
Hatch, John	1	3	5		
Littlefield, Saml	3	5	5		
Hatch, Willm	1		6		
Maxwell, John	2				
Varney, Jon^a	3		2		
Robertson, Danl	2		4		
Merryfield, Simeon	2	2	2		
Kinard, John	2	2	7		
Maxwell, John, Jr	2	2	4		
Grant, Ebenezer	1	3	4		
Sargeant, Willm	1	3	3		
Littlefield, Dependance	2	1	2		
Bragdon, Thos	1		2		
Littlefield, Joshua	2		1		
Perkins, Elisha	3		2		
Brooks, Joshua	1	2	3		
Perkins, Josiah	2	1	3		
Perkins, Nusman	2		3		
Lord, John	1	1	5		
Perkins, Willm	2		6		
Perkins, Jon^a	1	1			
Littlefield, Susanna	3		2		
Perkins, Jacob	1	1	2		
Littlefield, Francis	1	1	3		
Bennet, Joel	2	1	3		
Goodale, Nehemiah	1		4		
Bennett, George	4	3	4		
Hatch, Eliakim	1	2	2		
Maxwell, Saml	1	4	2		
Winn, John	2	1	5		
Littlefield, Danl	2		5		
Littlefield, Joseph	4		2		
West, Nicholas, Jr	1		2		
West, James	1	1	2		
Stuart, Reuben	1		2		
Littlefield, Isaac	2	3	6		
Littlefield, Jesse	1	3	4		
Littlefield, James	2	4	2		
Gitchel, Joseph	2		1		
West, Nicholas	1	1	2	1	
Gitchel, Jonathan	1	5	2		
Gitchel, Joshua	4	1	1		
Morrison, Josiah	1	1	3		
Morrison, Willm	1	3	2		
Morrison, Benj^a	1	4	2		
Cain, Joshua	1		5		
Piercey, James	2		3		
Wadley, Thos	2		1		
Cruddiford, Willm	3	1	3		
Cruddiford, John	1	2	2		
Hatch, Saml	1	1	2		
Hatch, Jon^a	4		2		
Hubbard, Warwick	3		1		
Herd, Danl	4	2	3		
Lowe, Job	1	3	3		
Lowe, Asa	1	5	2		
Littlefield, Abram	3		3		
Chauncey, Reuben	3	1	5		
Curtes, Saml	1	5	2		
Wheelright, Joseph, Jr	1	4	3		
Furbush, Saml	2	1	3		
Wheelright, Joseph	1	1	1		
Wheelwright, Benj^a	1	1	2		
Merrifield, John	2	3	6		
Goodale, John	3	1	6		
Winn, Stephen	1		9		
Aldrige (Widow)	1		2		
Kimball, Joseph	1		2		
Kimball, Joshua	1	3	2		
Morse, Joseph	1	3	6		
Mitchel, John	1	1	3		
Dwinnel, Joseph	3	1	4		
Tibbets, John	1	4	4		
Winn, John	1		1		
Winn, Danl	1	4	5		
Winn, Joseph	1		1		
Winn, Benj^a	1	1	2		
Maxwel, Gershorn	1	3	6		
Littlefield, Timothy	1	1	3		
Littlefield, Jotham	1	3	5		
Maxwell, Alexander	1	1	6		
Maxwell, Baruch	6	4	4		
Maxwell, David	1		4		
Maxwell, Gershorn	1		1		
Perkins, Jacob	2	3	3		
Jacobs, Elias	2	2	6		
Titcomb, Stephen	1		2		
Fisk, Mark	1		1		
Fisk, John	1	1	4		
Towns, Jacob	1	2	2		
Mitchel, Jotham	1	2	5		
Emery, Isaac	1	1	4		
Emery, Job	1	3	2		
Towns, Saml	2		1		
Webber, Stephen	1	2	4		
Kimbal, Benj^a	4		2		
Mitchel, John	2	1			
Brown, Saml	2		3		
English, Edward	1	1	1		
Harden (Widow)		2	1		
Wells, Edward	1		1		
Varney, Francis	1	1	3		
Gouch, Saml	1	2	5		
Boothby, Thos	1	3	4		
Webber, George	1	2	3		
Spinney, Nathl	1	4	4		
Oaks, Jacob	2	1	3		
Meeder, Danl	1		3		
Drown, Moses	2	1	2		
Gouch, Jedediah	1	1	3		
Gouch, Joseph	1	1	3		
Bucknal, John	2	2	3		
Bucknal, Rebecca		1	2		
Wormwood, Benj^a	1	3	3		
Drown, Stephen	1	2	2		
Latherby, Jessa	3	2	5		
Latherby, Stephen	1		1		
Wakefield, Josiah	1	3	2		
Emmons, Saml	1	1	1		
Bragdon, John	1	2	3		
Howard, Saml	1	1	3		
Wormwood, Willm	2	2	4		
English (Widow)			2		
Gil Patrick, Rich^d	4	1	3		
Jeffreys, Willm	5	4	4		
Lord, Dominicus	1		3		
Wilson, Benj^a	2	1	3		
Blasdel, Moses	1	2	6		
Wells, Willm	2	1	4		
Hart, Henry	4	1	2		
Blaisdel, Jacob	1	3	5		
Cousins, Nathl, Jr	3	1	7		
Wormwood, Thos	2	2	2		
Chauncey, Joseph	3	1	3		
Boston, Gershom	1		4		
Curtes, Charles	1	5	5		
Goodwin, Danl	1	1	1		
Webber, Edmond	2	1	4		
Webber, Edmond, Jr	1		2		
Webber, Saml	1		2		
Webber, John	3	3	3		
Allen, Elijah	2	2	2		
Allen, James	3	1	4		
Allen, Jotham	1	2	1		
Boston, James	1	4	2		
Allen, James, Jr	1	1	5		
Chadborn, James	1	1	3		
Brooks, Joshua	1		1		
Hasty, James	2	1	4		
Brawn, Robert	1	2	3		
Littlefield, Jacob	2	1	3		
Jones, Lazarus	2	4	1		
Gitchel, Zachariah	1	1	7		
Hilton, Joseph	1	4	2		
Hilton, Willm	1		1		
Hilton, Ebene^s	1	1	3		
Boston, Shubal	1		2		
Wilton, Edmond	1	2	2		
Boston, John	1	1	1		
Boston, Elijah	3	2	2		
Boston, Elijah, Jr	1	1	3		
Boston, Willm	1	1	4		
Boston, Abraham	2	2	4		
Littlefield, Josiah	2	2	1		
Stevens, Solomon	1	1	4		
Littlefield, Merriam		4	2		
Littlefield, Anna		3	3		
Merrifield, John	3	3	4		
Allen, Elijah	1		1	1	
Stuart, Elijah	1	1	6		
Kimbal, Benj^a	1	2	2		
Stuart, Elijah, 3^d	1	1	5		
Stuart, Danl	1	4	2		
Brock, Joshua	1	1			
Goodale, Zachariah	3		4		
Stuart, David	1	1	3		
Stuart, Saml	3	2	5		
Elwell, Joseph	1	2	2		
Gray, Joshua	2	2	3		
Stuart, Elijah, Jr	1	3	2		
Brozzel, Ezekiel	1	3	7		
Littlefield, Saml	1		1		
Parsons, Alice			3		
Hatch, Seth	1	1	1		
Boston, Shubal	3		2		
Hatch, Francis	3		3		
Goodale, Zachariah, Jr	1	2	3		
Littlefield, James	1	1	3		
Hubbart, Moses	1		2		
Laban, Rich^d			4		
Banks (Widow)			2		
Rines, John	1	1	3		
Peasley, Enoch	1	1	2		
Gipson, Willm	1		2		
Gipson, Willm, Jr	1	3	2		
Gipson, Zedediah	1	1	4		
Jacobs, George	1	3	3		
Jacobs, Jon^a	1	1	2		
Jacobs, Josiah	1	2	3		
Littlefield, Johnson	1	2	3		
Littlefield, Levi	2	4	2		
Littlefield, Abram	1	1	1		
Littlefield, David	2	1	3		
Littlefield, Eliab	5		3		
Littlefield, Jer^e	3		3		
Littlefield, Danl	2	4	3		
Stevens, Jon^a	2	2	4		
Dutten, Rich^d	1	1	2		
Taylor, Jon^a	4	1	2		
Hatch (Widow)	1	1	3		
Littlefield, Moses	1	5	3		
Mitchel, Saml	4	2	3		
Stevens, Benj^a	3	2	2		
Day, John	1	4	2		
Littlefield, Nathan	2	1	6		
Dennick, John	2	1	2		
Day, Benj^a	2	2	6		
Stevens, Saml	4	3	2		

YORK COUNTY—Continued.

WELLS TOWN—con.

NAME OF HEAD OF FAMILY.	Free white males of 16 years and upward, including heads of families.	Free white males under 16 years.	Free white females, including heads of families.	All other free persons.	Slaves.
Cousens, John	3	1	3		
Stevans, Moses	3	3	5		
Stevans, Joel	1	4	4		
Hatch, Danl	1	2	7		
Hatch, Obadiah	1	1	4		
Littlefield, Seth	1	2	3		
Littlefield, Roger	1	3	3		
Littlefield, Ebenz	2	1	3		
Goodwin, Joshua	1	1	2		
Littlefield, Ebenez, Jr	1	1	1		
Littlefield, Danl	1	1	2		
Chick, Thos	1	1	2		
Chick, Joshua	2	1	6		
Hatch, Solomon	1		2		
Hobbs, Willm	1	1	3		
Hobbs, Joseph	1		4		
Edes, Willm	2	1	4		
Clark, Solomon	2	1	4		
Wakefield, Benja	1		3		
Cousins, Saml	2	5	3		
Clark (Widow)	2		4		
Meldrom, Saml	1	2	2		
Clark, Eleazer	4		1		
Littlefield, Noah	1	2	1		
Day, Joseph	1	1	6		
Day, Moses	1	1	2		
Littlefield, Elisha	2	1	1		
Hubbard, Jere	1	3	3		
Sherman (Widow)	2		3		
Hobbs, Joseph	1	1	2	1	
Goodwin, Joseph	3	2	5		
Storer, John	2	1	4		
Hobbs, Thos	1		2		
Day, Robert	1		5		
Hatch, Gideon	1		1		
Chick, Moses	2	3	7		
Lord, Richd	3		4		
Clark, Nathan	1		3		
Storer, John	2		6		
Wheelright, John	5	1	3	1	
Bourn, Saml	2		4		
Wheelright, Ralph	2		3		
Gouch, Saml	3	2	4		
Kean, John	1	3	1		
Bourn (Widow)	1		3		
Norman, John	2	2	2		
Bouden (Widow)		1	1		
Harvey, John	1	1	1		
Clark, Knowles	1	1	1		
Clark, Sarah	2		1		
Wells, John N	1	3	3		
Wells, Nathl	5	1	5		
Clark, Ebenez	1	1	1		
Cole, John	1	5	4		
Clark, Lydia	1	1	2		
Boothby, Henry	1		1		
Bankins, James	1	5	7		
Snow, James	1	1	4		
Eaton, Joseph	2	1	3		
Boothby, Benja	2	1	5		
Wells, Danl	4	2	3		
Wells, Dependence	2	3	3		
Clark, Adam	4		4		
Wells, Nathan	1	2	5		
Gould, Nathl	2	1	2		
Goodwin John	3	1	4		
Wells (Widow)	2	1	3		
Goodwin, Thos	3	1	5		
Jeffreys, Simon	3		6		
Fisk, Abner	1	2	3		
GilPatrick, James	1	1	2		
Storer, Abram	3		1		
Goodwin, Paul	1		7		
Wells, Josha	1	1	2		
Goodwin, Caleb	1	2	4		
Goodwin, John Jr	1		1		
Ricker, Stephen	1	2	2		
Taylor, Nathl	2	2	4		
Jeffers, Saml	1	2	4		
Eaton, Jere M	2	2	1		
Gates, John	2		4		
Bartlet, Saml	4		3		
Hemmingway, Revd Moses	3	1	4		
Hill, Benja	2	3	4		
Littlefield, David	2		5		
Littlefield, Seth	1	4	3		
Morrill, Nahum	2		3		
Bragdon, Joshua	3	1	3		
Patten (Widow)	1		1		
Hatch, Amos	1		1		
Sawyer, Danl	3	3	3		
Pope, Isaac	3	4	6		
Hill, Mary	2		1	1	
Young, Solomon	1	1	1		

WELLS TOWN—con.

NAME OF HEAD OF FAMILY.	Free white males of 16 years and upward, including heads of families.	Free white males under 16 years.	Free white females, including heads of families.	All other free persons.	Slaves.
Hatch, Joshua	3	1	4		
Jacobs, Saml	1		2		
Bucknal, Jessa	1	1	3		
Buzzel, Isaac	3		2		
Eaton, Willm	1	2	2		
Bucknal, Francis	1		5		
Hatch, Simeon	3	1	3		
Littlefield, Benja	3	1	6		

YORK TOWN.

NAME OF HEAD OF FAMILY.	Free white males of 16 years and upward, including heads of families.	Free white males under 16 years.	Free white females, including heads of families.	All other free persons.	Slaves.
Wilson, Miles	1		1		
Moody, Ebenz	1	2	3		
Kimbal, Joshua	1	2	3		
Kimbal, Joseph	1		2		
Winn, Stephen	1		9		
Winn, Joseph	1	2	2		
Winn, Jona	1	2	1		
Kimbal, Nathan	1	2	3		
Kean, David	1	1	1		
Kean, John	1	1	3		
Boston, John	1	1	1		
Norton, Joseph	2	3	5		
Dixon, Saml	1	1	1		
Littlefield, Elisha	1	3	3		
Sloman, John	3		3		
Staples, Willm	1	1	1		
Staples, Francis	1		3		
Perkins, John	1		1		
Perkins, Joseph	1	2	2		
Perkins, Jere	1	3	2		
Hutchens, Jere	1	2	1		
Hutchens, Enoch, Jr	1		6		
Hutchens, Enoch	3	1	3		
Parsons, Elihu	1		1		
Parsons, Joseph	3	4	4		
Philips, Henry	3		3		
Philips, Norton	1	2	4		
Littlefield, Jere	3	2	5		
Avery, Saml	2	3	5		
Perkins, Pelatiah	1	3	3		
Weare, Jere	3	1	5	3	
Weare, Jere, Jr	1	3	4	1	
Seavey, Eliakim	1	3	1		
Seavey, Thos	1	2	4		
Webber, Nathl	4	1	3		
Webber, Theodore	1		2		
Storer, Willm	1	1	2		
Bradbury, Danl	1	2	1		
Clark, Anna			2	3	
Clark, Jere	1		2		
Weare, John	2	1	3		
Adams, Ezekiel	1	2	4		
Webber, Matthias	2		2		
Weare, Joseph, Jr	2	1	3		
Weare, Joseph	1				
Weare, Danl	2	4	3	2	
Averall, Job	1	3	5		
Littlefield, Ephraim	1	2	3		
Madden, James	1	1	3		
Freeman, John	3	2	5		
Wilson, Jona	1	2	2		
Welch, Willm	1	2	6		
Welch, Joseph	1				
Ramsdale, Danl, Jr	2		3		
Ramsdale, Timo	1		1		
Wilson, Noah	1		3		
Wilson, Joseph	1	2	3		
Wilson, Michael	1		1		
Woodbridge, Norton	1		2		
Trafton, Abiah	2	1	3		
Card, Joseph	1	2	3		
Cole, James	1	1	2		
Littlefield, Peter	3	2	5		
Molton, Nathl	2	2	4		
Swett, Nathl	1	4	4		
Beel, Richd	3		3		
Trafton, Thaddeus	2		1		
Ramsdale, Nathl	2		5		
Ramsdale, Danl	3	1	2		
Chase, Josiah	4	3	6		
Carlisle, Danl	1	1	3		
Preble, Edward	1	1	2		
Preble, Joseph	4		2		
Beetle, Ithumer	3		4		
Pearsons, Nathl	1	2	3		
Sedgley, Joseph	1	2	3		
Sedgley, John	1		4		
Preble, Saml	2	1	4		
Simpson, Thos	2		3		
Bradbury, John	2	1	4		
Simpson, Joseph	1	1	2		
Sewall, Henry	2		2		
Bridges, Joshua	1	3	2		
Tolpy, Henry	3	4	7		

YORK TOWN—con.

NAME OF HEAD OF FAMILY.	Free white males of 16 years and upward, including heads of families.	Free white males under 16 years.	Free white females, including heads of families.	All other free persons.	Slaves.
Welch, Tabitha	1	1	2		
Simpson, George	4	1	2		
Hutchens, Job	1	1	4		
Clark, Danl	1	1	4		
Tolpy, Thos	1	3	4		
Leach, John	1		2		
Bowden, David	1	1	2		
Lord, Jere	1	1	3		
Stover, Saml	3		4		
Stover, George	1	5	2		
Norton, John	3	1	4		
Robinson, Sarah		2	3		
Gunnison, Willm	2	1	4		
Bouden, Danl	3		1		
Stover, Huldah	1	2	4	3	
Sewall, Moses	1	1	4		
Stover, Mary	1		2		
Mathews, Elijah	2		2		
Beal, Elisabeth		1	2		
Avery, Hannah		1	2		
Kinsley, James	1	1	1		
Bridges, Mary	1	1	4		
McCauley, Susanna			4	4	
Moody, Joseph	4	2	3		
Tinney, John	2	3	7		
King, Richd	1		2		
Whittam, Bartholomew	1		2		
Whittem, Elisabeth	1		2		
Dwinnels, Saml	1		1		
Dwinnels, Saml, Jr	1	2	3		
Freeman, Nathl	1	4	4		
Avery, David	1	2	4		
Verrill (Widow)	1		2		
Dwinnel, Jotham	1	2	4		
Stone, Josiah	2		2		
Stone, Saml	1		1		
Bradbury, James	1	2	4		
Banks, Peletiah	1	1	5		
Rose, Robert	2		2		
Preble, Abigail	1	3	5		
Grove, Olive	1		4		
Grove, Dorcas		1	4		
Dwinnel, Timothy	1	1	3		
Emerson, Edward	4	1	7		
Sewall, David	1	2	2		
Sargeant, Nathl	1	2	3		
Low, Thos	2	2	7		
Emerson, Edward, Jr	1	2	4		
Woodbridge, Paul D	1	3	3		
Young, John, Jr	1	2	2		
Young, John	1	3	3		
Young, Rowland	2	3	3		
Sewall, John	1				
Low, Edward	1	2	6		
Emerson, Eunice			1		
Safford, Moses	1	2	3		
Grove, Willm, Jr	2	2	3		
Kimbal, Abigail			5		
Sewall, Danl	1		2		
Horn, Joseph	1		2		
Sawyer, Abram	1	1	2		
Nowel, Paul	2		5		
Trivet, Saml	1	3	3	1	
Andrews, Solomon	2		1		
Andrews, Henry	2		1		
Sewal, Nicholas	3		3	1	
Black, ——	1		2		
Fletcher, John	1	2	2		
Soward, Willm	1	4	3		
Scott, Giles				6	
Dwinnel (Widow)	3	1	1		
Matman (Widow)			2		
Verril, Solomon	1	1	4		
Holman, John	4	2	6		
Philbrick (Widow)	2	1	6		
Dwinnel, Nathl	3		3		
Lewis, Hannah		1	1		
Verrill (Widow)		2	2		
Goodale, Timo	1	3	3		
Milbory, Saml	4	2	3		
Norward (Widow)	4	5	7		
Avery, David	1	1	2		
Bridge, Arthur	1	1	3		
Sayward, Jona	2		5	1	
Trevitt, Richd	1		2		
Bowdy, Edward	1	4	2		
Sayward (Widow)			4		
Keaton (Widow)		1	2		
Farn, John	2		1		
Derby, Saml	3		2		
Stover, John	3	1	6		
Stover, John, Jr	1	1	3		
Grove, Willm	2		1		
Tricet, John	1	3	3		

YORK COUNTY—Continued.

YORK TOWN—con.

NAME OF HEAD OF FAMILY.	Free white males of 16 years and upward, including heads of families.	Free white males under 16 years.	Free white females, including heads of families.	All other free persons.	Slaves.
Harris (Widow)			1		
Dwinnel, Obadiah	1	2	3		
Harman, Zebadiah	2		2		
Harman, Thos	2	1	7		
Rendal (Widow)		2	3		
Moor, Willm	1	1	1		
Bennett, John	1		3		
Cheswell, Peletiah	2	1	4		
Perkins (Widow)			2		
Stimpson, Joseph	1	1	2		
Crocher (Widow)	2	1	2		
Currier (Widow)		1	1		
Bragdon, Danl	2		1		
Bouden, Isaac	1	2	6		
Beal, Joseph	1	1	3		
Derby, Jere	1		2		
Harman, John	2		2		
Harman, John, Jr	1	1	1		
Jacobs, Joseph	1	1	5		
Liman, Job	4	1	8		
Simpson, Joshua	2		2		
Sellars, Willm	1	2	3		
Stacey, Willm	1	2	3		
Tucker, Susanna			2		
Sheaf, Saml	1				
Wheeler, John	1	2	6		
Woodbridge, John	1	1	2		
Tucker, Joseph	2		4		
Lindsey (Widow)	2	1	2		
Downs, Robert	1	1	1		
Adams, Nathl	1		1		
Adams, Betsey		3	4		
Currier, Joseph	1		1		
Lowe, Edward	1	2	5		
Nowel, Paul	2		6		
Simpson, Joseph	3	3	3		
Hatch, Saml	1	1	2		
Sayward, Willm	1	4	3		
Allenwood, Theodore	1	2	3		
Down, Solomon			3		
Keswell, Amos	1	2	5		
Keswell, Willm	1		1		
Perkins, Edward	2	1	1		
Moore, John	2	2	3		
Moore, Thos	1		2		
Hilton, Eliakim	1	1	6		
Shaw, Merriam			1		
Goodwin, Danl	1		2		
Young, Matthias	1		2		
Cawd, Joseph	1	3	2		
Cawd, John	1	2	6		
Babb, Saml	1		1		
Babb, Willm	1		4		
Haines, Thos	2		2		
Bradbury, Cotten	3		3		
Carlisle, Alexander	2		3		
Molton, Joseph	2	2	3		
Teel, Thos	1	1	2		
Soward, Joseph	1	2	3		
Lyman, Revd Isaac	2		6		
Preble, Caleb	2	1	2		
Preble, Esaias	1	3	10		
Preble, John	1	2	4		
Frost, Willm	1	2	6		
Bean, Mary	1		1		
Hunt, Willm	1		2		
Sewall, Saml	2		6		
Sewall, Story	1		3		
Banks (Widow)			1		
Moulton, Willm	1	3	2		
Preble, David	1		4		
Todd, Joseph	1	3	1		
Abbot, Thos	1	3	6		
Molton, Theodore	1	2	4		
Lunt, Danl	1	2	4		
Savage, John	3	5	3		
Simpson, Joseph	1	1	4		
Sewall, Henry	1	1	2		
Bridges, Joshua	1	3	2		
Bradbury, John	2	1	4		
Simpson, Thos	2		3		
Holman, John	3	3	2		
Harman, Nathl	1	2	4		
Varnum, Jona	1	2	2		
Parsons, Isaac	2		1		
Simpson, Danl	1		4		
Simpson, Nathl	1	1	2		
Miller (Widow)			2		
Bragdon, Lydia	1		2		
Currier, Anna		2	2		
Simpson, Joseph	3	1	2		
Simpson, Pelatiah	2	2	4		
Simpson, Timothy	1		2		
Bean, Nehemiah	1	1	2		
Bean, Lewis	1	1	1		
Swett, Sarah			6	1	
Bean, Mary	1		3		
Simpson, Tabitha	1		3		
Molton, Johnson	2		3		
Going, Hannah			2		
Grant, Jasper	1	1	3		
Carlisle, John	1		1		
Bean, James	1	4	1		
Preble, Benja	2	1	3		
Woodward, Leml	3		3		
Bank, Richd	2	3	2		
Nason, Sarah	2		2		
Austins, Woodward	1	3	2		
Grant, Joseph	2	2	3		
Bragdon, Warren	1		2		
Perkins, Isaac	1	1	2		
Young, Jona	3	1	3		
Whittem, Reuben	3	2	4		
Whittem, John S.	1		1		
FitsGerald, Patrick	1	1	4		
FitsGerald, James	2	3	3		
FitsGerald, David	1	1	4		
Lewis, Willm	2	1	4		
Welch, Paul	1	1	4		
Welch, Benja	2		4		
Welch, David	2	1	2		
Young, Joseph	1	2	2		
Moulton, Thos	3	3	1		
Austins, Benja	1	1	2		
Grant, Nathl	1	1	2		
Lunt, Saml	2	1	4		
Lunt, Henry	1		3		
Moulton, Abel	1	1	3		
Grant, David	3	2	5		
Grant (Widow)	1		2		
Grant, Joshua	1	3	4		
Grant, Stephen	1	2	1		
Plaisted, John	5		2		
Molton, John	1	4	3		
Molton, Danl	1	4	3		
Molton, Saml	1	1	1		
Molton, Ebenz	1		5		
Young, Marstinson	3		3		
Young, Joel	1	2	4		
Young, Saml	4	4	4		
Grant, Dorothy	2		5		
Frether, Saml	1	1	5		
Nowel, John	1	5	5		
Bragdon, Thos	4	3	2		
Bragdon, Danl	2	1	4		
Barnard, Jona	1	1	7		
Laneton, Revd Saml	1		4		
Junkins, Eunice	1	2	4		
Junkins, Alexander	2	2	6		
Moody, Thomas	2	2	2		
McIntire Saml	4		3		
Grant, Sarah	2	1	3		
Junkins, Hepsibath	2		3		
Haley, John		2	3		
Nowel, Joseph	3	3	3		
Nowel, Thos	1	1	4		
Nowel, Saml	2	1	3		
Shaw, John	3		4		
Shaw, Joseph	1		3		
Junkins, James	2	3	4		
Junkins, Joseph	1		1		
Junkins, Danl	1		2		
Junkins, Danl, Jr	2	1	6		
Junkins, Jona	1	1	2		
Junkins, Eliphalet	1	1	6		
Jellitson, Ichabod	1		1		
Jellitson, Joel	1	1	2		
Shaw, Saml	1		2		
Shaw, Abram	1	2	4		
Shaw, Willm	1	1	3		
Gary, John	1		3		
Gary, Danl	1	2	1		
Gary, Abel	1	3	1		
Nowel, Danl	1	4	4		
Nowel, Shadrach	2		6		
Nowel, Sarah	2		3		
Emery, Simon	1	2	1		
Furrel, Nicholas	1	2	2		
Smith, Danl	1	3	2		
Leavitt, Jere	2	1	6		
Thompson, Danl	4	1	4		
Bragdon, Solomon	1	2	4		
Smith, Ebenezer	1		5		
Smith, John	1		3		
Thompson, Ebenezer	2	2	4		
Preble, Joseph	1	2	6		
Preble, David	1		3		
Thompson, Joseph	2	1	3	1	
Linscutt, Jere	4		1		
Linscutt, Danl	3	2	5		
Linscutt, Saml	1		5		
Simpson, Ebenz	2		4	1	
Kingsbury, John	2		2		
Emery, Danl	1	2	5		
Kean, Arthur	3	3	4		
McIntire, Ebez	3	1	3		
Paul, Saml	2	2	4		
Rogers, Benja	1	1	3		
Rogers, Joseph	2		2		
Harvey, Willm	1	1	2		
Kingsbury, Saml	1		5		
Thompson, Jona	1	3	4		
Thompson, Dodiford C.	2		1		
Bridges, Edmond	2		3		
Linscutt, Isaiah	1	1	1		
Kingsbury, John	1	2	1		
Kingsbury, Benja	1		2		
McIntire, Joseph	3	4	4		
McIntire, Joseph, Jr	1	2	3		
McIntire, Saml	2	4	3		
Grover, Danl	2	1	4		
Grover, Simon	1	2	3		
Sargeant, Daniel	1		4		
McIntire, Micum	3	2	2		
Lewis, Nathl	5		3		
Blaisdel, Ebenz	3		3		
Thompson, Benja	1				
Sargeant, Jona	1	2	2		
Berry, Joseph	1		4		
Sargeant, Danl	1		4		
Blaisdel, David	1	2	2		
Welch, Moses	3		2		
Welch, Sarah			2		
Barrell, Nathl	2	1	7		
Trafton, Jotham	2	3	3		
Crosby (Widow)	2		2		
Allen, Eleanor			2		
Trafton (Widow)		1	1		
Trafton, James	1		2		
Gorden, Nathl	1	2	4		
Crawley, Hannah	1		2		
Trafton, Saml	1		2		
Maines, Elias	1	1	2		
Main, John	2		3	2	
Moulton, Danl	3		7		
Bragdon, Matthias	1	1	4		
Varnham, Jona	2	1	2		
Blaisdel, Elijah	2	3	5		
Baker, Issacar	1		2		
Baker, Joseph	1	1	3		
Smith, Edward	3	1	2		
Bragdon, Joseph	2	2	5		
Bragdon, Mary	1		3		
Bragdon (Widow)			1		
Bragdon, Saml	2	1	3		
Baker, Saml	1	3	4		
Baker, Thos	1		2		
Hill, Theodore	1	1	2		
Allen, Bassum	3	1	5		
Pell, John	2		4		
Sewall, Danl	2		4		
Parsons, Saml	2	3	7		
McIntire, Danl	1	2	4		
McIntire, Jedediah	1	2	2		
Bragdon, Hepsibah			2		
Young, Joshua	1	1	4		
Sewall, John	2	1	3		
Crawley, Rachael			3		
Holt, Ebenz	3	1	5		
Baker, John	1	3	4		
Beel, Josiah	4	1	4		
Booker, Aaron	1	3	3		
Hanes, John	1	3	4		
Harriss, Timothy	1	1	1		
Harriss, Saml	2	1	5		
Molton, Danl	3	2	6		
Moore, Joshua	4	2	3		
Perkins, Jona	2	3	4		
Johnston, Danl	3		2		
Narman, John	2		3		
Norman, Thos	1	1	1		
Harrison (Widow)			3		
Swett, Saml	1	2	3		
Swett, John	2		3		
Bridge, Benja	1		2		
Booker, Jacob	1		3		
Reins, Nathl	3	3	4		
Reins, Robert, Jr	2	1	4		
Reins, Francis	1		1		
Reins, Danl	2	2	2		
Reins, Nathl, Jr	2	2	4		
Paine (Widow)			6		

YORK COUNTY—Continued.

NAME OF HEAD OF FAMILY.	Free white males of 16 years and upward, including heads of families.	Free white males under 16 years.	Free white females, including heads of families.	All other free persons.	Slaves.	NAME OF HEAD OF FAMILY.	Free white males of 16 years and upward, including heads of families.	Free white males under 16 years.	Free white females, including heads of families.	All other free persons.	Slaves.	NAME OF HEAD OF FAMILY.	Free white males of 16 years and upward, including heads of families.	Free white males under 16 years.	Free white females, including heads of families.	All other free persons.	Slaves.
YORK TOWN—con.						YORK TOWN—con.						YORK TOWN—con.					
Reins, Robert	2		4			Oliver, Jotham	1		1			Warren, Moses	3	2	5		
Welch (Widow)			1			Oliver (Widow)	1		4			Joy, Saml	2	2	5		
Moore, Joshua, Jr	1	1	2			Bracey, James	2	1	2			Blaisdel, Elijah	1	2	1		
Moore, Saml	2	1	3			Bracey, Danl	1	2	3			Gray, Jona	1	3	4		
Moore, George	2	1	4			Adams, Willm	1	1	2			Abbott, Aaron	2	1	5		
Moore, Willm	1		4			Beal, John	2	2	3			Abbot, Aaron, Jr	1	3	1		
Reins (Widow)	3		4			Allen, Saml	1	1	2			Blaisdel, Danl	2	1	5		
Thompson, Alexander	1	2	3			Blaisdel, Zedediah	1	1	4	1		Emery, John	3	1	3		
Sargeant, Charles	1	1	4			Bussel, James	1	1	5			Joy, Ephraim	1	1	2		
Varnham, Jona	3		4			Bragdon, James	1	3	1			Allen, Bassam	1	1	4		
Bragdon, Benja	3	4	7			Beetle, Eleazer	1	1	1			Stevans, John	2	1	4		
Bragdon, Jethro	1		7			Allen, Saml	1	1	2			Walker, Edward	1	1	3		
Bragdon, Zachariah	1		2			Beetle, Henry	1	1	3			Stevans, John	1	1	1		
Cook, Danl	2	2	5			Stephens, Pelatiah	1	1	1			Stevans, Jona	1	1	1		
Oliver, James	1		4			Jellitson, James	1	3	2								

INDEX.[1]

Abbot, Aaron, 51.
Abbot, Aaron, Jr, 73.
Abbot, Amos, 56.
Abbot, Anney, 56.
Abbot, Benjᵃ, 55.
Abbot, Danˡ, 56.
Abbot, David, 65.
Abbot, George, 15.
Abbot, Henry, 34.
Abbot, Isaac, 56.
Abbot, Isaac, 60.
Abbot, Isaac, Junʳ, 60.
Abbot, James, 13.
Abbot, John, 34.
Abbot, John, 56.
Abbot, John, 56.
Abbot, John, Junʳ, 56.
Abbot, Jonᵃ, 56.
Abbot, Jonᵃ, 67.
Abbot, Jonathan, 68.
Abbot, Joseph, 57.
Abbot, Joshua, 56.
Abbot, Joshua, 56.
Abbot, Moses, 65.
Abbot, Moses, 67.
Abbot, Moses, Junʳ, 67.
Abbot, Nathaniel, 14.
Abbot, Patience, 56.
Abbot, Phillip, 64.
Abbot, Reuben, 56.
Abbot, Ricᵈ, 56.
Abbot, Samuel, 56.
Abbot, Samuel, 65.
Abbot, Samuel, 68.
Abbot, Silas, 54.
Abbot, Simeon, 60.
Abbot, Stephen, 57.
Abbot, Theopholus, 55.
Abbot, Thomas, 55.
Abbot, Thomas, 55.
Abbot, Thomas, 57.
Abbot, Thoˢ, 72.
Abbot, Thoˢ, Jʳ, 57.
Abbot, Unis, 57.
Abbot, Wᵐ, 57.
Abbott, Aaron, 73.
Abbott, James, 30.
Abbott, James, 31.
Abbott, John, 68.
Abbott, John, Junʳ, 68.
Abbott, Moses, 31.
Abbott, Reuben, 31.
Abbott, Reuben, junʳ, 31.
abraham, Susman, 41.
Abram, Paddy, 31.
Ackly, Benajah, 52.
Acorn, Jacob, 43.
Adam, John, 28.
Adam, John, junʳ, 28.
Adams, Abraham, 42.
Adams, Amos, 42.
Adams, Amos, Ju., 42.
Adams, Andʷ, 13.
Adams, Benjᵃ, 16.
Adams, Benjᵃ, 55.
Adams, Benjᵃ, 57.
Adams, Betsey, 72.
Adams, Danˡ, 61.
Adams, David, 27.
Adams, Ezekiel, 71.
Adams, Francis, 30.
Adams, Isaac, 32.
Adams, Jacob, 14.
Adams, James, 42.
Adams, James, 55.
Adams, James, Jʳ, 55.
Adams, Jerᵉ, 35.
Adams, Joel, 47.
Adams, John, 35.
Adams, John, 35.
Adams, John, 43.
Adams, John, 55.
Adams, John, 63.
Adams, John, 66.
Adams, John, 68.
Adams, Revᵈ John, 68.
Adams, Jonathan, 15.
Adams, Jonathan, 66.
Adams, Jonathan, Sen., 66.
Adams, Joshua, 16.
Adams, Joshua, 28.

Adams, Joshua, Jr., 16.
Adams, Mark, 62.
Adams, Mary, 62.
Adams, Moses, 15.
Adams, Moses, 44.
Adams, Nathan, 35.
Adams, Nathˡ, 72.
Adams, Richard, 36.
Adams, Samˡ, 34.
Adams, Samuel, 35.
Adams, Samˡ, Junʳ, 34.
Adams, Solomon, 44.
Adams, Stephⁿ, 59.
Adams, Thomas, 29.
Adams, Willᵐ, 59.
Adams, Willᵐ, 73.
Addams, John, 44.
addition, thomas, 40.
Adkins, Nathaniel, 41.
Adkins, Williams, 40.
Adle, Cornelius, 44.
Adridge, Nathˡ, 16.
Agrey (Widow), 43.
Agry, Thomas, 43.
Airs, Moses, 46.
Akers, John, 16.
Akers, Moses, 16.
Albee, William, 52.
Alby, Isaac, 45.
Alby, Jonathan, 45.
Alby, Obadah, 34.
Alby, Samuel, 45.
Alden, Abiather, 16.
Alden, Austin, 16.
Alden, Elisabeth, 13.
Alden, Josiah, 16.
Alden, Nathˡ, 16.
Aldrige, Amos, 69.
Aldrige (Widow), 70.
Alexander, David, 20.
Alexander, James, 34.
Alexander, James, 34.
Alexander, John, 26.
Alexander, John, 34.
Alexander, Robert, 46.
Alexander, Samˡ, 20.
Alexander, Willᵐ, 20.
Alexander, William, 34.
Alexander, William, 34.
Alford, Lore, 49.
All, James, 34.
Allan, Gideon, 54.
Allan, John, 38.
Allan, John, 53.
Allan, Nathaniel, 49.
Allan, Obediah, 54.
Allen, Abel, 11.
Allen, Abraham, 27.
Allen, Amos, 43.
Allen, Bassam, 73.
Allen, Bassum, 72.
Allen, Benjᵃ, 51.
Allen, Caleb, 37.
Allen, Daniel, 34.
Allen, Daniel, 49.
Allen, David, 13.
Allen, Ebenezer, 21.
Allen, Ebenezer, 37.
Allen, Ebenezer, Jʳ, 37.
Allen, Edman, 49.
Allen, Elanor, 72.
Allen, Elijah, 20.
Allen, Elijah, 20.
Allen, Elijah, 70.
Allen, Elijah, 70.
Allen, Elisabeth, 20.
Allen, Elisha, 20.
Allen, Elisha, 58.
Allen, Elizʰ, 62.
Allen, Ephraim, 20.
Allen, Ephraim, 62.
Allen, Francis, 50.
Allen, Franes, 66.
Allen, Gideon, 36.
Allen, Hannah, 15.
Allen, Isaac, 11.
Allen, Isaac, 14.
Allen, Isaac, 15.
Allen, Isaac, 20.
Allen, Jacob, 21.
Allen, Jacob, 57.

Allen, James, 20.
Allen, James, 70.
Allen, James, Jʳ, 70.
Allen, Jerediah, 66.
Allen, Joanna, 31.
Allen, Job, 22.
Allen, John, 11.
Allen, John, 44.
Allen, John, 59.
Allen, Jchn, 62.
Allen, Jonathan, 32.
Allen, Joseph, 20.
Allen, Joseph, 25.
Allen, Joseph, 49.
Allen, Joseph, 59.
Allen, Joseph, 60.
Allen, Joshua, 11.
Allen, Jotham, 70.
Allen, Jude, 67.
Allen, Nathaniel, 29.
Allen, Nathaniel C., 20.
Allen, Nehemiah, 20.
Allen, Nehemiah, 21.
Allen, Nehemiah, 31.
Allen, Pelatiah, 26.
Allen, Pelatiah, 46.
Allen, Peter, 30.
Allen, Peter, 43.
Allen, Philip, 51.
Allen, Phinehas, 39.
Allen, Pirkins, 45.
Allen, Rachael, 37.
Allen, Samˡ, 46.
Allen, Samˡ, 73.
Allen, Samˡ, 73.
Allen, Seth, 13.
Allen, Solomon, 66.
Allen, Thoˢ, 12.
Allen, Tobias, 29.
allen, Told, 67.
Allen, Wilᵐ, 11.
Allen, William, 44.
Allen, William, 49.
Allen, Woodard, 49.
Allen, Wright, 60.
Allen, Zacheus, 15.
Allen, Zekiel, 62.
Allenwood, Theodore, 72.
Alles, Micah, 50.
Allexander, Hugh, 20.
Allexander, Jane, 20.
Allexander, John, 34.
Allexander, Robart, 34.
Alley, Ephrom, 36.
Alley, John, 34.
Alley, John, Jnʳ, 34.
Alley, Joshua, 34.
Alley, Olais, 67.
Alley, Samˡ, 34.
Alley, Samuel, 67.
Alline, Benjᵃ, 29.
Allis, Benjamin, 52.
Allod, David, 66.
Amerson, Asa, 50.
Amerson, Calvin, 42.
Amerson, Daniel, 50.
Amerson, Daniel, 50.
Amerson, Ezekiel, 42.
Ames, Jabez, 29.
Ames, Jacob, 26.
Ames, Jacob, 26.
Ames, Jacob, 38.
Ames, James, 40.
Ames, John, 28.
Ames, John, 60.
Ames, John, 65.
Ames, Jonathan, 33.
Ames, Jonathan, 52.
Ames, Josiah, 29.
Ames, Justus, 32.
Ames, Margaret, 32.
Ames, Mark, 32.
Ames, Moses, 60.
Ames, Nathᵃˡᵉ, 65.
Ames, Samˡ, 24.
Ames, Samuel, 44.
Ames, Thomas, 29.
Ames, Winslow, 40.
Amory, George, 36.
Amory, George, 46.

Amory, John, 13.
Amy, Samˡ, 61.
And——, Stephen, 59.
Anderson, Abraham, 25.
Anderson, Ann, 25.
Anderson, Archibald, 49.
Anderson, Daniel, 20.
Anderson, Edward, 25.
Anderson, Jacob, 12.
Anderson, Jacob, 16.
Anderson, James, 16.
Anderson, James, 16.
Anderson, James, 49.
Anderson, Job, 31.
Anderson, John, 15.
Anderson, John, 16.
Anderson, John, 16.
Anderson, John, 16.
Anderson, John, 39.
Anderson, John, 54.
Anderson, Joseph, 16.
anderson, Joseph, 45.
Anderson, Nancy, 25.
Anderson, Robert, 16.
Anderson, Robert, 24.
Anderson, Robert, 40.
Anderson, Samuel, 49.
Andres, John, 49.
andres, Sthephen, 42.
andrew, michel, 42.
Andrews, Abel, 59.
Andrews, Abraham, 68.
Andrews, Amos, 16.
Andrews, Amos, 32.
Andrews, Asa, 43.
Andrews, David, 22.
Andrews, Elizaᵗʰ, 59.
Andrews, Ely, 42.
Andrews, George, 39.
Andrews, Henry, 71.
Andrews, Israel, 52.
Andrews, Jeremiah, 68.
Andrews, Jerimiah, 53.
Andrews, John, 12.
Andrews, John, 26.
Andrews, John, 33.
Andrews, John, 49.
Andrews, John, 55.
Andrews, John, 59.
Andrews, John, 64.
Andrews, Jonᵃ, 16.
Andrews, Jonᵃ, Jr., 16.
Andrews, Mark, 25.
Andrews, Nathan, 53.
Andrews, Perez, 11.
Andrews, Robert, 11.
Andrews, Samuel, 15.
Andrews, Saml., 25.
Andrews, Solomon, 71.
Andrews, Stephⁿ, 16.
Andrews, Timothy, 53.
Andrews, Wᵐ, 58.
andris, Ephram, 40.
Andros, Elisha, 58.
Andros, Joanna, 58.
Andros, John, 58.
Andros, Olive, 57.
Androse, Samuel, 69.
annies, Charles, 66.
annies, John, 66.
annies, Nehemiah, 66.
Annis, Abramᵐ, 69.
Annis, Benjamin, 32.
Annis, Nehemiah, 69.
Annis, Ralph, 31.
Annis, Samuel, 36.
Annis, Stephen, 69.
Anthbine, Nicholis, 25.
Appelbe, Thomas, 63.
Appelby, Halley, 57.
Appelby, Levi, 57.
Appelby, Simeon, 57.
Appleby, John, 32.
Appleton, Danˡ, 59.
Appleton, Francis, 29.
Appleton, John, 43.
Appleton, Jnᵒ, 59.
Archer, John, 54.
Archibald, Thomas, 53.
Arey, Ebenezer, 32.
Arey, Isaac, 32.

Armstrong, John, 13.
Armstrong, Jonathan, 15.
Armstrong, Richard, 32.
Arno, John, 49.
Arnold, Benjamin, 45.
Arnold, Bildad, 20.
arnold, thomas, 48.
Arnold, Willᵐ, 44.
Arvel, John, 43.
Ash, Benjamin, 29.
Ash, Robert, 29.
Ash, Robert, 53.
Ash, Samuel, 53.
Ash, Thomas, 31.
Ashley, Abner, 16.
Askins, Alexander, 43.
askins, alexᵈʳᵉ, 48.
Askins, Christopher, 44.
askins, david, 48.
Askins, George, 44.
askins, george, 48.
askins, John, 48.
askins, ninain, 48.
askins (widow), 48.
askins, william, 48.
Aspinwall, Caleb, 24.
Asten, Peter, 68.
Astery, Benoney, 49.
Astins, Jacob, 38.
Astons, Stephen, 38.
Athenton, Benjᵃ, 29.
Atherington, John, 69.
Atherton, Jona, 20.
Atkins, Cornelius, 27.
Atkins, David, 51.
Atkins, James, 44.
Atkins, Nathaniel, 23.
Atkins, Nathaniel, 30.
Atkinson, James, 51.
Atkinson, Jnᵒ, 59.
Atkinson, Joseph, 58.
Atkinson, Joshˡ, Junʳ, 59.
Atkinson, Moses, 16.
Atkinson, thomas, 51.
Atkinson, Thoˢ, 58.
Atkinson, Thoˢ, Jʳ, 59.
Atterd, Daniel, 68.
Atwood, Jesse, 30.
Atwood, Nathan, 32.
Atwood, Nathˡ, 37.
Atwood, Solomon, 20.
Atwood, Stephen, 13.
Ausburn, Ephrom, 50.
Ausburn, Isaac, 50.
Ausburn, Jonathan, 37.
Ausburn, Jonathan, 50.
Austen, Cathrine, 63.
Austen, Moses, 63.
Austen Nat., 63.
Austin, Andrew, 56.
Austin, Benjamin, 15.
Austin, George, 11.
Austin, Jonas, 25.
Austin, Ruth, 16.
Austin, Stephen, 19.
Austins, Benjᵃ, 72.
Austins, Woodward, 72.
Averal, Ezekiel, 41.
Averal, Israel, 44.
Averal, John, 44.
Averall, Job, 71.
Averel, Job, 43.
Averel, Mary, 43.
Averel, Samuel, 43.
Averel, Samuel, 43.
Averel, Willᵐ, 44.
Averill, Joseph, 52.
Avery, David, 71.
Avery, David, 71.
Avery, Hannah, 71.
Avery, James, 52.
Avery, Jane, 13.
Avery, Jeremiah, 65.
Avery, Joseph, 55.
avery, Joseph, 67.
Avery, Samˡ, 71.
Avery, Shadrack, 55.
Avery, Thatcher, 30.
Avery, Walter, 65.
Avrill, Samuel, 33.
awstin, Ichabod, 35.

INDEX.

Maxwell, William, 13.
Maxwell, William, 14.
Maxwell, Willm, 18.
Maybe, Elias, 53.
Maybee, Solomon, 53.
Mayberry, David, 22.
Mayberry, James, 25.
Mayberry, John, 25.
Mayberry. John, 25.
Mayberry, John, 25.
Mayberry, Richard, 24.
Mayberry, Richard, 25.
Mayberry, Thomas, 22.
Mayberry, William, 25.
Mayberry, William, 25.
Mayberry William, 26.
Mayew, Andrew, 30.
Mayew, Reuben, 30.
Mayew, Whitewood 13.
Mayhew, James, 12.
Mayhew, Priscilla, 52.
Mayhew, Samuel, 51.
Mayo, Ebenezer, 28.
Mayo, Israel, 28.
Mayo, James, 27.
Mayo, James, 28.
Mayo, Joseph, 29.
Mayo, Joshua, 29.
Mayo, Nathaniel, 27.
Mayo, Nathaniel, 28.
Mead, George, 11.
Means, George, 65.
Means, James, 14.
Means, Robert, 32.
Means, Thomas, 65.
Mecaheny, Michal, 39.
Meeder, Danl, 70.
Meeder, Tobias, 40.
Megraw John, 50.
Meirs, George, 44.
Melcher, Ammi, 21.
Melcher, Joseph, 12.
Melcher, Noah, 12.
Melcher, Saml, 12.
meldrom, John, 66.
Meldrom, Saml, 71.
Mellet, Willm, 46.
Melony, Walter, 36.
Meloon, Abraham, 35.
Meloon, Elizabeth, 36.
Melvil, Jno, 18.
Melzar, John, 36.
Mendal, John, 37.
Mendam, Joshua, 62.
Mendham, Wm, 61.
Mendom, Wm, 62.
Menett, David, 54.
Menton, Phinehas, 58.
Merchant, John, 47.
Meriam, Nathel, 56.
Merithue, Roger, 28.
Mero, Amariah, 47.
Merrel, Abel, 20.
Merrel, Edmund, 14.
Merrel, Edmund, 15.
Merrel, Enoch, 15.
Merrel, Humphrey, 15.
Merrel, Jacob, 15.
Merrel, James, 14.
Merrel, John, 19.
Merrel, John, 20.
Merrel, Joseph, 15.
Merrel, Joseph, 19.
Merrel, Moses, 15.
Merrel, Nathan, 19.
Merrel, Peeter, 21.
Merrel, Silas, 15.
Merrel, Stephen, 15.
Merrell, Adam, 14.
Merrell, Adam, 15.
Merrell, Amos, 15.
Merrell, Daniel, 15.
Merrell, Ebenezer, 25.
Merrell, Elias, 14.
Merrell, Elias, 21.
Merrell, Ezekiel, 21.
Merrell, Humphrey, 15.
Merrell, Jacob, 15.
Merrell, James, 14.
Merrell, James, 14.
Merrell, James, 14.
Merrell, John, 21.
Merrell, Joseph, 14.
Merrell, Joshua, 15.
Merrell, Joshua, 20.
Merrell, Moses, 21.
Merrell, Samuel, 21.
Merret, Samuel, 54.
Merriam, Revd Marthew, 58.
Merrifield, John, 70.
Merrifield, John, 70.
Merril, Abel, 55.
Merril, Bradley, 18.
Merril, Daniel, 18.
Merril, Danl, 18.
Merril, Danl, 18.
Merril, Emly, 40.
Merril, Enoch, 60.
Merril, Henry, 20.
Merril, John, 46.
Merril, Levi, 18.
Merril, Levi, 67.
Merril, Moses, 40.

Merril, Nathan, 21.
Merril, Obed, 55.
Merril, Roger, 14.
Merril, Samuel, 34.
Merril, Sarah, 21.
Merril, Stephen, 37.
Merril, Susanna, 16.
Merril, thomas, 35.
Merrill, Abel, 59.
Merrill, Caleb, 30.
Merrill, Danl, 25.
Merrill, Danl, 55.
Merrill, Edmund, 11.
Merrill, Ezekiel, 64.
Merrill, Gideon, 55.
Merrill, Giles, 11.
Merrill, Humphy, 59.
Merrill, Jabesh, 24.
Merrill, Jabesh, 25.
Merrill, Jacob, 16.
Merrill, Jacob, 55.
Merrill, James, 11.
Merrill, John, 16.
Merrill, Jno, 59.
Merrill, Joseph, 65.
Merrill, Joshua, 58.
Merrill, Levi, 25.
Merrill, Nathan, 11.
Merrill, Nathl, 22.
Merrill, Nathl, 60.
Merrill, Saml, 22.
Merrill, Saml, 59.
Merrill, Saml, Junr, 22.
Merrill, Saml, Junr, 59.
Merriman, Hugh, 20.
Merriman, James, 20.
Merriman, Michl, 20.
Merriman, Thomas, 12.
Merriman, Thomas, 20.
Merriman, Timo, 20.
Merriman, Walter, 20.
Merriman, Walter, 20.
Merriner, John, Jur., 12.
Merrit, Daniel, 54.
Merrit, Joseph, 54.
Merritt, Daniel, 54.
Merritt, Richard, 54.
Merritt, Wm, 54.
Merrow, David, 67.
Merrow, Edmund, 64.
Merrow, James, 63.
Merrow, Joseph, 37.
Merrow, Joseph, 67.
Merrow, Patrick, 43.
Merrow, Saml, 37.
Merrow, Samuel, 67.
Merry, Willm, 46.
Merryfield, Simeon, 70.
Meserve, Danl, Senr, 18.
Meserve, Elisha, 18.
Meserve, Elisha, Jr., 18.
Meserve, Eliza, 18.
Meserve, George, 18.
Meserve, Gideon, 18.
Meserve, John, 18.
Meserve, Solo, 18.
Meserve, Thos, 18.
Meserve, Wm, 18.
Meservey, Daniel, 52.
Meservey, Joseph, 64.
Meservey, Nathl, 64.
Meservy, Clement, 18.
Messer, John, 68.
Messerve, Benja, 26.
Messerve, Joseph, 26.
Metcalf, Joseph, 39.
Metcalf, Leonard, 26.
Metguin, John, 20.
Metguin, William, 20.
Michaels, George, 38.
Michaels, James, 12.
Michals, Josiah, 51.
michel, Danbr., 45.
Midcalf, John, 45.
midcufs, Joseph, 51.
Midget, David, 60.
Miers, Philip, 43.
Mighill, Joseph, 65.
Mighill, Josiah, 65.
Mighill, Moses, 65.
Milbory, Saml, 71.
Milekin, John, 22.
miler, peter, 41.
Miles, Mary, 61.
Miles, Nathan, 26.
Miles, Wm, 65.
Milikin, John, 33.
Millar, Thomas, 64.
Millbank, Phillip, 40.
Millens, Robert, 25.
Millens, Thomas, 25.
Miller, Andw, 54.
Miller, Benja, 55.
Miller, David, 13.
Miller, David, 27.
miller, francis, 41.
Miller, Francis, 52.
miller, frank, 41.
miller, frank, jun., 41.
miller, henry, 41.
Miller, Hugh, 13.
Miller, James, 13.
Miller, James, 26.

Miller, James, 31.
Miller, Jere, 55.
Miller, Jno, 18.
Miller, John, 32.
miller, John, 48.
Miller, John, 54.
Miller, John Bolt, 58.
Miller, Joshua, 13.
Miller, Leml, 55.
Miller, Margaret, 12.
Miller, Mary, 22.
miller, nickles, 48.
Miller, Noah, 27.
Miller, Robert, 32.
miller, Robert, 48.
Miller, Robert, 54.
miller, thomas, 48.
Miller (Widow), 55.
Miller (Widow), 72.
Miller, William, 40.
Millet, David, 11.
Millet, Elisha, 13.
Millet, John, 11.
Millet, John, 24.
Millet, Solomon, 40.
Millet, Thos, 16.
Millican, Isaac, 59.
Millican, Joel, 58.
Millican, Nathl, 59.
Millikan, Benjn, 18.
Millikan, Edwd, 18.
Millikan, Isaih, 18.
Millikan, John, 18.
Millikan, Jona, 18.
Millikan, Jos, 18.
Millikan, Joshua, 18.
Millikan, Leml, 18.
Millikan, M. John, 18.
Millikan, Polly, 18.
Millikan, Saml, 18.
Millikan, Thos, 18.
Millikan, Wm, 18.
Milliken, Phinehas, 64.
Millikin, Abner, 27.
Millikin, Benjamin, 15.
Millikin, Elias, 32.
Millikin, Robert, 31.
Millikin, Samuel, 29.
Mills, Alexander, 22.
Mills, Deborah, 68.
Mills, Eligood, 69.
Mills, Jacob, 63.
Mills, James, 63.
Mills, James, 63.
Mills, John, 50.
Mills, John, 63.
Mills, John, 63.
Mills, Josiah, 44.
Mills, Robart, 50.
Mink, John, 49.
mink, pacel, 42.
Mink, Peter, 49.
mink, philip, 41.
Mink, valantin, 42.
Minot, John, 12.
Minot, Thomas, 14.
Mirach, Josiah, 41.
Mirach, Willm, 22.
Mireck, Bazaliel, 24.
Mirick, John, 47.
Mirick, John, 69.
Miriek, Andrew, 35.
Mirrick, Nathaniel, 28.
mirrit, Jonathan, 49.
misherve, clemt., 45.
misherver, nath., 48.
Mitcalf, Hugh, 35.
Mitchal, Thomas, 40.
Mitchel, Abraham, 16.
Mitchel, Abram, 16.
Mitchel, Benja, 21.
Mitchel, Danl, 16.
Mitchel, Daniel, 21.
Mitchel, Danl, 54.
Mitchel, David, 21.
Mitchel, Dominicus, 24.
Mitchel, Dummer, 54.
Mitchel, Elizh, 61.
Mitchel, Horton, 21.
Mitchel, Jacob, Jr, 22.
Mitchel, James, 61.
Mitchel, James M., 33.
Mitchel, Jeremiah, 14.
Mitchel, Jereh, 18.
Mitchel, Job, 18.
Mitchel, John, 16.
Mitchel, John, 36.
Mitchel, John, 47.
Mitchel, John, 54.
Mitchel, John, 61.
Mitchel, John, 70.
Mitchel, John, 70.
Mitchel, Jonas, 51.
Mitchel, Jona, 21.
Mitchel, Jona, 21.
Mitchel, Jona, 33.
Mitchel, Jonathan, Jr, 22.
Mitchel, Joseph, 47.
Mitchel, Joseph, Junr, 16.
Mitchel, Joshua, 16.
Mitchel, Josiah, 40.
Mitchel, Jotham, 70.
Mitchel, Loring, 21.

Mitchel, Lucy, 61.
Mitchel, Mary, 61.
Mitchel, Mehitable, 21.
Mitchel, Noah, 52.
Mitchel, Richd, 14.
Mitchel, Roger, 61.
Mitchel, Saml, 21.
Mitchel, Saml, 61.
Mitchel, Saml, 70.
Mitchel, Sarah, 61.
Mitchel, Seth, 21.
Mitchel, Solomon, 21.
Mitchel, Thomas, 14.
Mitchel, Willm, 12.
Mitchel, Willm, 16.
Mitchel, Wm, 18.
Mitchel, Willm, 21.
Mitchel, Wm, 61.
Mitchell, Benjamin, 26.
Mitchell, John, 24.
Mitchell, Jonathan, 13.
Mitchell, Robert, 23.
Mitchell, Robert, 26.
Moffat, James, 43.
Moffat, John, 69.
mograge, Charly, 45.
mograge, Thomas, 45.
Molloy, Dennis, 64.
Molton, Danl, 72.
Molton, Danl, 72.
Molton, Ebenz, 72.
Molton, Elizabeth, 22.
molton, James, 48.
Molton, Joel, 66.
Molton, John, 72.
Molton, Johnson, 72.
Molton, Joseph, 72.
Molton, Nathl, 71.
Molton, Saml, 72.
Molton, Theodore, 72.
Molton, William, 23.
Monro, Stephen, 43.
Monson, Josh, 62.
Monson, Saml, 62.
Monson, Thomas, 62.
Montgomery, Lydia, 34.
Montgomery, Robert, 49.
Montgomery, Saml, 34.
Moodey, Gilman, 61.
moodey, Samuel, 67.
Moody, Benjamin, 15.
Moody, Benjamin, 23.
moody, Cernes, 35.
Moody, Clament, 68.
Moody, Daniel, 19.
Moody, Dorcas, 14.
Moody, Ebenz, 71.
Moody, Elizabeth, 65.
Moody, George, 65.
Moody, James, 24.
Moody, Jeremiah, 42.
moody, John, 35.
Moody, John, 63.
Moody, Joseph, 18.
Moody, Joseph, 68.
Moody, Joseph, 71.
Moody, Joshua, 24.
Moody, Josiah, 14.
Moody, Mary, 18.
Moody, Moses, 27.
Moody, Nathaniel, 23.
moody, Richard, 35.
Moody, Robt, 18.
Moody, Saml, 33.
Moody, Scribner, 42.
Moody, Silas, 55.
Moody, Thomas, 72.
Moody, William, 23.
Moody, William, 27.
Moody (Widow), 18.
Moon, Joseph, 31.
Moon, Thomas, 31.
Moor, Collins, 47.
Moor, Capt. Hugh, 58.
Moor, Levi, 47.
Moor (Widow), 58.
Moor, Willm, 72.
Moore, David, 43.
Moore, Ebenezer 37.
Moore, Ebenr, 47.
Moore, Ebenezer, 65.
Moore, Edmond, 22.
Moore, Edwd, 61.
Moore, Elizh, 61.
Moore, Elkins, 16.
Moore, George, 73.
Moore, Isaac, 37.
Moore, James, 37.
Moore, James, 39.
Moore, Joanna, 21.
Moore, John, 23.
Moore, John, 65.
Moore, John, 72.
Moore, Capn Jno, 61.
Moore, Joshua, 61.
Moore, Joshua, 72.
Moore, Joshua, Jr, 73.
Moore, Josiah, 53.
Moore, Josiah, 54.
Moore, Nathl, 37.
Moore, Peletiah, 58.
Moore, Reuben, 43.
Moore, Robert, 53.

Moore, Samuel, 52.
Moore, Saml, 61.
Moore, Saml, 73.
Moore, Thomas, 43.
Moore, Thos, 72.
Moore, Willm, 73.
Moore, Capn Wm, 61.
Moors, Timothy, 49.
Morain, Andrew, 53.
Moral, Patience, 61.
Morcan, John, 24.
More, Benja, 32.
More, Benjamin, 42.
More, David, 30.
more, Ebenezer, 66.
More, Edward, 32.
More, Goff, 42.
More, James, 30.
More, Jeremiah, 29.
More, Joel, 29.
More, John, 30.
More, John, 42.
More, John, 45.
More, John, 66.
More, John, junr, 30.
More, Joseph, 31.
More, Joseph, 42.
More, Miriham, 42.
More, Mordica, 39.
More, William, 28.
More, William, 30.
more, William, 66.
more, William, 66.
More, Wyat, 32.
Morefield, hipsebath (Wid.),66.
morel, Samuel, 66.
morel, Stephen, 66.
Mores, Aaron, 64.
Mores, Abraham, 45.
Mores, Jonathan, 22.
Mores, Joseph, 52.
Mores, Nathan, 40.
Mores, Thomas, 44.
Mores, William, 11.
Morey, Elias, 27.
Morey, Ezekiel, 27.
Morey, Ezekiel, 32.
Morey, Phillip, 34.
morfey, John (mescongus Island), 48.
morfey, peter (mescongus Island), 48.
Morgan, Benja, 32.
Morgan, John, 21.
Morgan, Joseph, 41.
Morgan, Luke, 21.
Morgan, Saml, 11.
morgin, James, 41.
Morgin, John, 45.
Morgrage, Peter, 30.
morphi (widow), 42.
Morrel, Abraham, 57.
Morrel, David, 57.
Morrel, David, 67.
Morrel, Isaac, 57.
Morrel, John, 63.
Morrel, Josiah, 57.
Morrel, Peter, 57.
Morrel, Peter, Junr, 57.
Morrel, Stephen, 57.
Morrel, Stephen, 65.
Morrel, Thomas, 57.
Morrel, William, 15.
Morrel, Wintrop, 57.
Morrell, Benjamin, 25.
Morrell, Benjamin, 26.
Morrell, Jedediah, 26.
Morrell, Joel, 62.
Morrell, John, 15.
Morrell, Peeter, 26.
Morril, Abraham, 49.
Morril, Jedediah, 40.
Morril, Peaster, 57.
Morril, Tristram, 58.
Morrill, Benja, 28.
Morrill, Joseph, 58.
Morrill, Levi, 51.
Morrill, Nahum, 71.
Morrill, Reuben, 58.
Morris, Chs, 18.
Morris, Charles, 18.
Morris, Dennis, 18.
Morris, Wm, 55.
Morrison, Benja, 70.
Morrison, Edward, 68.
Morrison, James, 65.
Morrison, Jona, 40.
Morrison, Joseph, 31.
Morrison, Josiah, 70.
Morrison, Moses, 38.
Morrison, Nathl L., 33.
Morrison, Robert, 15.
Morrison, Saml, 38.
Morrison, Samuel, 68.
Morrison, Thomas, 49.
Morrison, Wllm, 11.
Morrison, William, 53.
Morrison, Willm, 70.
morroson, Abraham, 66.
morroson, Bradbury, 66.
Morroson, Daniel, 66.
Morroson, David, 66.
morroson, Ebenezer, 66.

O